The Whisper of the Oak

LIVING THE CRUCIFORM LIFE THROUGH

CELTIC CHRISTIAN WISDOM

BOOK TWO

"I ARISE TODAY THROUGH A MIGHTY STRENGTH, THE INVOCATION OF THE TRINITY."

Stuart McGhie

ISBN (Paperback) 979-8-90148-423-4

Contents

Introduction: The Whisper of the Oak

Welcome back, fellow traveller. I am so deeply glad you have chosen to continue this journey with me.

In our first book together, The Ever-Flowing Stream, we embarked on a pilgrimage. It was a journey born from a deep ache in my own soul, a feeling of spiritual homelessness in a world that often felt loud, fractured, and disconnected from the sacred. Perhaps you felt it too. We walked a path that led us away from the rigidity of institutional religion and into the wild, vibrant, and deeply personal landscape of Celtic Christianity. We were not seeking a new religion, but a new way of being in relationship with the faith we thought we knew. We were seeking a homecoming.

Together, we learned to see the world through new eyes—or rather, through ancient eyes, the eyes of the Celtic saints. Our key, the map to this new territory, was the concept of the "thin place." We discovered these sacred thresholds where the veil between this world and the Otherworld feels almost transparent. We sought them first in the geography of the Celtic world, making pilgrimages in our hearts to the holy islands of Iona and Lindisfarne, places scoured by wind and sea, where the prayers of saints seem to hang in the very air. We walked the pilgrim paths to Glendalough, feeling the deep peace of St. Kevin's valley, and stood among the ruins of Clonmacnoise, sensing the presence of a great cloud of witnesses.

But the most important discovery of that journey was that thin places are not just geographical locations. We learned that a thin place can be a moment in time, a piece of music, a line of poetry. We found that the most powerful thin places are those we cultivate within our own hearts. Through the practice of contemplative prayer, through the discipline of the Céile Dé— the servants of God—we learned to create our own inner Iona, a sanctuary of peace we could carry with us into the chaos of our daily lives. We learned that the sacred is not "out there" but is always and everywhere available to us if we have the eyes to see and the heart to receive.

This led us to the core of Celtic spirituality: the profound, unshakable belief in God's immanence. We moved away from the image of a distant, clockmaker God, a remote monarch ruling from a far-off heaven, and we embraced the God who is the lifeblood of creation. We saw this in the theology of John Scotus Eriugena, who declared that "every visible and invisible creature is a theophany or appearance of God." We saw it in the simple, profound prayer of St. Patrick, who found Christ in the sun and the moon, in the flash of lightning and the rush of the wind. We began to understand that the world around us is not a fallen, profane place to be escaped, but a living, breathing sacrament, a revelation of divine beauty and goodness.

This healed a wound in me, a wound I had carried for years without even knowing its name. It was the wound of separation, the false dichotomy between the "sacred" and the "secular." In the Celtic vision, there is no such divide. All of life is sacred. Baking bread can be a prayer. The tending of a garden can be an act of co-creation with God. Welcoming a stranger can be an encounter with Christ himself, as St. Brigid taught us. This realisation did not just change my spiritual life; it changed my whole life. It infused the mundane with meaning and turned the ordinary into an ongoing occasion for grace.

We drank deeply from that ever-flowing stream. We found a spiritual language that spoke of blessing, of belonging, and of the fundamental goodness of creation. And for a long time, that was enough. It was more than enough. It was a wellspring of joy and peace.

And yet. And yet…

As the months turned into a year after finishing that first journey with you, a new feeling began to stir in my soul. It was not a doubt, not a crisis of faith. It was a quiet, persistent, and holy curiosity. It was a spiritual restlessness that felt less like an anxious searching and more like a gentle but insistent pull, a tug on a thread that I knew led somewhere important.

The stream is beautiful, I kept thinking, but what are its sources? What hidden springs, deep in the earth, feed this river of Celtic wisdom? The Christian story in Ireland began in the fifth century, but the soul of the Celtic people is far, far older. What nourished that soul for the thousands of years before the coming of the Cross? What was the spiritual landscape into which the seeds of the Gospel were sown?

This question became a constant companion. It led me to the edge of a new and, I must admit, frightening territory. It led me to the world of the Druids.

My spiritual struggle began here in earnest. Everything I had been taught, both in my secular education and in my religious upbringing, had conditioned me to see the word "Druid" as synonymous with "pagan." And "pagan," in that context, meant something to be overcome, something superseded, something that stood in opposition to the truth of the Gospel.

The stories of St. Patrick I had heard as a boy were all about his triumphant defeat of the Druids at Tara, the victory of light over darkness. To willingly turn my attention toward the Druids felt like a betrayal. It felt like turning my back on the saints who had become my dearest companions. It felt like leaving the clear, flowing stream of Christian faith to go wading in a murky, stagnant pond of superstition.

I resisted the pull for a long time. I told myself it was an academic distraction, an unhealthy fascination with the occult. I returned to the writings of the Celtic saints, hoping to silence the question. But it was no use. The question did not come from outside; it arose from within. It felt like trying to understand a beautiful, ancient tree by studying only its leaves and branches, while resolutely refusing to look at its trunk and roots. I began to realise that my fear was a product of the very worldview I had sought to heal—the worldview of conflict and division, of "us versus them," of "light versus dark." The Celtic Christianity I had come to love was a faith of integration and wholeness. Could it be that my fear of the Druids was a remnant of a less integrated, more fearful faith?

This internal battle came to a head on a quiet, grey afternoon in County Kildare. I had made a small pilgrimage to the town, a place whose very name, Cill-Dara, means "the Church of the Oak." It is the site of St. Brigid's great double monastery, one of the most important spiritual centres in early Christian Ireland. I had hoped that being in a place so deeply associated with one of my favourite saints would ground me, would silence the distracting whisper about the Druids. But Brigid, in her wisdom, had other plans for me.

After visiting the cathedral and the site of the ancient fire temple, I found myself wandering away from the town, drawn by an inexplicable pull toward a solitary field. And there it stood. A single, magnificent oak tree. It was not just a tree; it was a presence. It was immense, its gnarled, twisted branches reaching out in every direction like the arms of a great, multi-limbed elder. Its trunk was a fortress of deeply furrowed bark, a landscape in itself, covered in mosses and lichens. It was impossible to know its age, but it felt ancient beyond measure, a silent witness that had stood on this spot long before the town, long before the cathedral, long before Brigid herself. It was, I felt in my bones, a descendant of the very oak that had given the place its name.

I approached it with a sense of reverence I could not explain. I sat down at its base, my back pressing against the rough, solid trunk. The world seemed to fall away. The noise of the distant road faded. The grey sky, the damp air, my own anxious thoughts—all of it receded. There was only the tree. I closed my eyes and did what the Celtic saints had taught me: I listened. I listened with the ears of my heart.

I listened to the sound of the wind moving through its leaves, a sound that was not one voice, but a thousand whispering voices, a gentle, sibilant chorus. I listened to the subtle creak and groan of its great limbs, the sound of immense strength bearing its own weight with patience. I listened to the deep, profound silence that seemed to emanate from its very core, a silence not empty but full, pregnant with a deep, slow, patient wisdom.

And in that listening, something shifted. The boundary I had so carefully constructed between "me" and "the tree" began to dissolve. It was not a thought, but a feeling, a deep, somatic knowing. I could feel its life, a slow, powerful pulse that was utterly different from my own frantic human heartbeat. I felt the sap rising from the deep, dark earth, a steady, cool current of nourishment. I felt the miraculous alchemy happening in its leaves, sunlight and air being transformed into life. I felt its strength, its endurance, its absolute, unshakeable, rooted presence. It was not just a plant; it was a being. And it was radiating a quality of profound peace, a wisdom that did not need words.

In that moment, the whisper in my soul became a clear, undeniable voice. It did not speak English. It spoke in the language of pure knowing. It told me that the wisdom I felt in this tree was not, and could never be, separate from the wisdom I sought in my faith. It told me that the God who had breathed life into Adam was the same God who pulsed with life in this ancient oak. It told me that my fear was an illusion. To understand St. Brigid, I had to understand the sacred oak she had chosen as the heart of her community. To truly understand Celtic Christianity, I had to have the courage to look at the spiritual soil in which it had grown. I had to understand the Druidic reverence for the sacred grove.

The stream and the spring were one. The leaf and the root were one. My spiritual struggle was over, not because I had found an answer, but because the question itself had been transformed. The journey into the world of the Druids was not a departure from the Christian path; it was an essential part of it. It was the only way to make my understanding of it whole.

THE WORLD WE HAVE INHERITED: A CIVILISATION AT THE CROSSROADS

That experience beneath the oak tree opened a door, and once opened, it could not be closed. I began to read everything I could find about the Druids and the ancient Celtic world. As I did so, I began to see not just a historical curiosity but a mirror reflecting our own time. I began to understand that the journey into the grove was not just about the past; it was about finding a path forward.

We live in a time of profound crisis. You know this. I know this. We all feel it, even if we struggle to name it. It is not merely one crisis but a convergence of ecological, social, and spiritual crises. Our planet is heating. Species are vanishing at a rate not seen since the age of the dinosaurs. Our forests are burning. Our oceans are rising and being choked by plastic. Our political systems are fracturing. Our communities are fragmenting. Amid this external chaos, there is an internal crisis as well. Rates of anxiety, depression, and a deep sense of meaninglessness are at historic highs, particularly among the young. We are, as a civilisation, profoundly unwell.

At the root of all these crises, I believe, is a single, fundamental error in our worldview. It is the belief that the human is separate from, and superior to, the natural world. It is the belief that the earth is not a living community of which we are a part, but a storehouse of "resources" that exist for our use. It is the belief that matter is dead, that only humans have souls, and that the purpose of life is to transcend this "fallen" physical world and escape to a purely spiritual realm.

This worldview has many names and many sources—Cartesian dualism, the legacy of the Enlightenment, the distortions of certain strands of Christian theology—but its effect is the same. It has severed us from our roots. It has made us aliens in our own home.

This is not just an environmental problem; it is a spiritual crisis. When we view the Earth merely as a thing, we lose our sense of belonging. When we see trees as merely timber, we lose our sense of kinship. When we forget that we are part of the web of life, we become isolated, anxious, and deeply lonely. The wound in the earth and the wound in the human soul are the same.

And here is where the Druids, and the Celtic Christianity that grew from their soil, have something urgent and vital to teach us. The worldview of the ancient Celts was the exact opposite of the one that has brought us to this precipice. They did not see the world as dead matter. They saw it as alive, ensouled, and sacred. They did not see themselves as separate from nature. They saw themselves as part of a great, interconnected web of being.

The Druids were not primitive nature-worshippers; they were sophisticated philosophers who understood what modern science is only now beginning to rediscover: that everything is connected, that the health of the whole depends on the health of each part, and that to harm the earth is to harm ourselves.

This book, then, is not just a historical exploration. It is an act of recovery. It is an attempt to retrieve a way of seeing and being that our culture desperately needs. It is a quest to find the spiritual antidote to the poison of separation. And the remarkable, beautiful, and hopeful truth is that we do not have to invent this antidote from scratch. It already exists. It has been preserved, like a seed in the earth, in the stories of the saints, in the carvings on the high crosses, in the very names of the places on the map, and in the silent presence of the ancient trees themselves. Our task is not to create something new, but to remember something very, very old.

THE DRUIDS: KEEPERS OF A SACRED WORLDVIEW

To understand the medicine this tradition offers, we must first understand who the Druids truly were. The historical Druids were the intellectual and spiritual elite of the Celtic peoples who inhabited much of Europe—from Ireland and Britain in the west, through Gaul (modern France), and into parts of Spain, Germany, and even Asia Minor—during the Iron Age, roughly from 500 BCE to 500 CE. They were not a single, unified priesthood with a central authority, but rather a class of learned individuals who shared a common training, worldview, and role within their societies.

The Celts themselves were not an empire like Rome. They were a collection of tribes, each with its own king or queen, its own territory, and its own identity. But what united these diverse tribes was a shared language family, a shared artistic style, and, most importantly, a shared spiritual culture, presided over by the Druids. In a world without writing (at least for sacred purposes), without universities, and without a centralised church, the Druids were the living repositories of all knowledge.

They were the judges who settled disputes and interpreted the law. They were the historians who memorised the kings' genealogies and the deeds of their ancestors. They were the astronomers who charted the movements of the stars and created the calendar. They were the physicians who knew the healing properties of every plant. They were the poets whose words could make or break a king's reputation. And they were the priests who presided over the great seasonal festivals and maintained the relationship between the human community and the divine powers.

Becoming a Druid required training that could last up to twenty years, a period of intense study and spiritual discipline that rivalled anything in the ancient world. The Roman writer Julius Caesar, who encountered the Druids during his conquest of Gaul, noted with a mixture of admiration and suspicion that they committed vast amounts of knowledge to memory and refused to commit their sacred teachings to writing. This was not because they were illiterate—they knew the Greek alphabet and later developed their own script, the Ogham—but because they believed that the act of writing would weaken the faculty of memory and, more importantly, that sacred knowledge was too profound to be entrusted to the page. It had to be passed from heart to heart, from teacher to student, in an unbroken chain of transmission.

The core of their teaching was a worldview that saw the entire cosmos as alive and sacred. They believed in the immortality of the soul and taught a doctrine of transmigration, the idea that the soul journeys through many forms and many lives. They saw the divine not as a distant, transcendent being, but as an immanent presence woven into every part of creation. Every mountain had its spirit. Every river had its goddess. Every tree, especially the great oaks, was a dwelling place of the sacred. The forest was not a wilderness to be feared or conquered; it was a temple, the sacred grove or nemeton, the holiest place on earth.

This was not a primitive animism, a childish projection of human qualities onto inanimate objects. It was a sophisticated philosophy, a recognition of the fundamental interconnectedness and aliveness of all things. It was a worldview that understood what the poet Gerard Manley Hopkins would later call "the dearest freshness deep down things," the sense that the world is charged with the grandeur of God. It was a spirituality that did not need to escape the earth to find the divine, because it knew that the divine was already and always present in the earth.

This is the worldview that the early Christian missionaries encountered upon arriving in Ireland. And this is the worldview that, in the unique alchemy of Celtic Christianity, was not destroyed, but transformed and fulfilled.

WHAT YOU WILL ACHIEVE ON THIS JOURNEY

That experience was the seed of this book. It is an invitation to you to join me on this new pilgrimage, a journey into the Grove of Wisdom. It is a quest to uncover the profound, often overlooked connection between the nature-based spirituality of the ancient Druids and the Celtic Christianity that followed. This is the necessary next step in our journey. If The Ever-Flowing Stream was about finding our home in the heart of Celtic Christianity, The Grove of Wisdom is about digging the foundations of that home down to the living bedrock of the earth itself.

This book is not just a historical exploration; it is a practical and spiritual guide. My promise to you is that this will be a transformative journey. It is designed to provide not just new information but also a new way of being in the world.

By the time you turn the final page, you will have gained the tools and the understanding to:

1. Heal the Great Wound: The Split Between Spirit and Nature.

We live in a civilisation built upon a fundamental error, a deep and painful wound that affects us all. It is the belief that the spiritual is separate from the physical, that God is "up there" in heaven while the earth is "down here," a mere stage for the human drama, a collection of resources to be exploited. This single idea is the source of our ecological crisis and much of our personal spiritual alienation. This book is a direct antidote to that poison.

You will be guided into a worldview where the sacred and the material are one. You will learn to see the natural world as the primary revelation of the divine, a living scripture written in a language of beauty and wonder. We will explore how this was the foundational belief of the Druids and how it was not rejected, but affirmed and deepened by the Celtic saints. You will learn practices that will allow you to move beyond simply appreciating nature to entering into a genuine communion with it. This will change everything. A walk in the woods will become a pilgrimage. The tree outside your window will become a spiritual teacher. You will learn to find God not by escaping the world, but by falling more deeply in love with it.

2. Gain a Deep and Authentic Understanding of the Druids

To heal the wound, we must first understand its history. We will travel back in time, moving beyond the romantic fantasies of white-robed wizards and the religious propaganda of pagan antagonists, to meet the historical Druids. You will discover a sophisticated and powerful intellectual class that served as the spiritual and legal backbone of Celtic society for centuries. We will piece together evidence from Roman accounts, Irish myths recorded by Christian monks, and archaeology to build a picture of the Druid as a philosopher, a judge, a healer, a poet, and a priest. You will learn about their legendary twenty-year training in the forest universities, their mastery of a vast oral tradition, and their core philosophical tenets: the immortality of the soul, the transmigration of life, and the sacred, living nature of the cosmos. Understanding who the Druids truly were is key to why the early Celtic Christians did not simply dismiss them but engaged them in a profound and respectful dialogue.

3. Witness the Great Integration: How Christ Became the True Druid

You will discover the startling and beautiful truth that Celtic Christianity did not conquer Druidism; it absorbed, transformed, and fulfilled it. This is the central, radical claim of this book. We will explore the unique historical circumstances of Ireland, a land never conquered by Rome, which allowed for a peaceful and organic encounter between the old ways and the new. We will deconstruct the myth of St. Patrick as a vanquisher of paganism and see him instead as a master of spiritual integration. The theological heart of our journey will be to unpack the full meaning of St. Columba's breathtaking declaration: "Christ is my Druid." You will learn how Christ was seen as the ultimate fulfilment of the Druidic ideal—the perfect Wisdom-Keeper (the Logos), the ultimate Mediator between heaven and earth, and the divine Poet whose parables reveal the secrets of the kingdom. You will see how this principle of integration worked in practice, as the sacred wells of the goddesses became the holy wells of the saints, and the sacred groves of the Druids became the consecrated enclosures of the monasteries. This is not just a history lesson; it is a powerful model for our own lives, teaching us how to welcome new truths and experiences without betraying our roots.

4. Learn the Sacred Language of the Trees through the Ogham

Having understood the "why" of the integration, we will turn to the "how." You will be initiated into the secrets of the Ogham, the ancient Celtic alphabet, where each of the twenty letters is named for a tree. This is the whispering alphabet of the grove itself, a system of wisdom that encodes the spiritual properties of the forest. You will learn the history and structure of this fascinating system, from its origins in the 4th century to its use as a tool for divination and magic. We will then embark on a detailed journey through the entire Ogham, meeting each of the twenty trees. You will learn their names, their symbolism, and the specific spiritual lesson that each one offers. This section will serve as a comprehensive reference you can consult repeatedly. Moreover, it will serve as a practical introduction. You will be guided through an exercise to write your own name in the language of the trees, creating a deep, personal, and immediate connection to this ancient and living wisdom tradition.

5. Enter into Personal Communion with the Great Trees

Our journey will then take us even deeper, from the alphabet of the forest to the great elder trees themselves. We will move from the symbolic to the experiential. In a series of dedicated chapters, we will sit in council with the most sacred and powerful trees of the Celtic world. You will spend time in the presence of the mighty Oak, the tree of strength, endurance, and sovereignty. You will connect with the great Ash, the World Tree that links the realms. You will stand before the ancient Yew, the guardian of eternity, death, and rebirth. We will explore the protective power of the Rowan, the intuitive wisdom of the Hazel, the purifying energy of the Birch, and the otherworldly magic of the Hawthorn. For each of these great teachers, you will learn their mythology, folklore, their role in the saints' lives, and a unique meditative practice designed to help you connect with their specific energy and medicine. You will learn not just about the trees, but from them, directly.

6. Master the Art of Sacred Communion: A Practical Guide

This book is, above all, a practical manual for spiritual transformation. All the history, theology, and symbolism we explore serve one ultimate goal: to equip you to enter into your own direct, personal, and life-changing relationship with the living world. In the final section of the book, I will distil everything we have learned into a clear, step-by-step guide to the core practice of "tree communion." You will learn the practical arts of approaching a tree with reverence, quieting your mind and opening your heart, listening with your senses and your intuition, and engaging in a genuine, two-way exchange of energy and wisdom. This is a skill that, once learned, will stay with you for the rest of your life. It will transform every walk in the park, every hike in the woods, into a potential pilgrimage, an opportunity for a sacred encounter.

7. Develop a Powerful Ecological Spirituality for Our Time

Finally, you will learn how to weave this ancient wisdom into the fabric of your modern life and apply it to the urgent challenges of our time. A spirituality that sees the earth as sacred is not a retreat from the world; it is a call to action within it. We will examine how the Celtic and Druidic worldview provides a compelling ethical framework for environmental conservation, restoration, and climate action. You will discover that caring for the earth is not a political issue, but a fundamental spiritual practice, an act of devotion to the Creator. You will be guided in creating your own personal plan for ecological service, whether that means planting a tree, cleaning a local river, changing your consumption habits, or advocating for environmental justice. You will learn how to become a true partner in the healing of our beautiful, wounded planet.

This is the promise of The Grove of Wisdom. It is a journey that will take you from the historical past to the living present, from intellectual understanding to profound, heart-opening experience. It will give you not just new ideas, but new eyes with which to see the world and a new heart with which to love it. It is an invitation to come home to the earth, to find your true place in the great, living web of creation, and to discover the God who whispers in the rustling of the leaves.

Our path is laid out before us. It is a path that spirals inward, like the markings on a Neolithic stone or the growth pattern of an ivy vine. It begins by seeking the truth behind the myths, by stepping into the world of the ancient Druids with courage and respect. From there, it moves to the great revelation of the integration, to the foot of the Cross, understood as the new and everlasting Tree of Life. And finally, it leads us out of our heads and into our hearts, into the heart of the grove itself, to a direct, personal encounter with the sacred trees, patiently waiting to share their wisdom with us.

If you are ready to listen to the whisper of the ancient oaks, if you are ready to find a faith that is as strong as the yew and as resilient as the birch, if you are prepared to find God in the heart of the grove, then take my hand.

The journey begins now.

Let us walk on.

Stuart McGhie

Chapter 1:

In the Time of the Druids: Keepers of the Grove

Before we can truly step into the grove, before we can begin to hear the whispering of the ancient trees, we must first do something that requires a little courage. We must quiet our minds and gently, respectfully, set aside the images that the word "Druid" so often conjures.

For many of us, the name evokes a figure of pure fantasy, a character stepped from the pages of a storybook. We see a white-robed, long-bearded old man, perhaps standing within the great stone circle of Stonehenge at dawn, a golden sickle in his hand. We think of Merlin, the archetypal wizard, a master of shape-shifting and prophecy. We think of the magical antagonists in St. Patrick's legends, defeated by the superior power of a new faith. We think, perhaps, of modern-day groups who gather to celebrate the solstices, admirable in their intent but adding another layer to the myth.

These images, while romantic and powerful in their own right, are a veil. They are a mist of fantasy, folklore, and propaganda that has settled over the centuries, obscuring a reality that is far more profound, far more intellectually rigorous, and far more spiritually relevant to our modern lives. To understand the true spiritual heritage of the Celtic world, to find the deep spring that feeds the ever-flowing stream of Celtic Christianity, we must have the courage to look past the caricature and seek the wisdom-keeper who stands behind it.

This chapter is an invitation to do just that. It is a journey back in time, not with the wide-eyed credulity of a tourist seeking magic, but with the focused, respectful curiosity of a pilgrim seeking to understand a lost world. The historical Druids were not wizards or mystics in the modern, sensational sense.

They were the intellectual, spiritual, and legal backbone of Celtic society for a thousand years.

They were the philosophers and the scientists.

They were the judges and the lawmakers.

They were the healers and the poets.

They were the theologians and the priests of their people.

Their university was not built of stone, but of oak and ash and yew. Their library was not written in books, but was held in the sacred, disciplined vessel of the human heart and in the living language of the land itself.

To embark on this journey into the grove of wisdom, we must become archaeologists of the soul. We must be willing to sift through the fragments left to us by history, by myth, and by the very earth itself. We must piece them together, not to create a perfect, complete picture—for that is forever lost to us—but to catch a glimpse, a powerful and illuminating glimpse, of these true Keepers of the Grove. Let us begin.

THE CHALLENGE OF THE SOURCES: A MURKY WELL

Our quest begins with a profound and humbling challenge:

The Druids themselves wrote nothing down. This was not, as is sometimes assumed, because they were a primitive people who lacked the technology of writing. The Celtic tribes of Gaul were familiar with the Greek alphabet, and the Irish later developed their own distinctive script, Ogham, which we will explore in a later chapter. The Druids' commitment to an oral tradition was a deliberate, philosophical choice, a cornerstone of their entire worldview. Julius Caesar, the Roman general who provides one of our most detailed (if deeply biased) accounts, tells us that they refrained from writing for two primary reasons.

First, they believed that an overreliance on the written word would weaken the faculty of memory, which they held sacred and powerful. In a world without books, a trained memory was the most advanced information storage and retrieval system available. It was a living library, dynamic and responsive. To weaken it was to weaken the very foundation of their culture.

Second, and more importantly, they considered their sacred teachings—their theology, their philosophy, their laws—to be too profound, too alive, to be entrusted to the inanimate page. They understood that written words can be easily misunderstood, taken out of context, or fall into the hands of those who would misuse them. Their wisdom was a living thing, a sacred fire to be passed directly from the heart of a teacher to the heart of a student. It was a process of embodiment, not just information transfer.

The knowledge had to be lived, breathed, and spoken into being.

This profound commitment to oral tradition means that we have no primary, firsthand accounts from the Druids themselves. We have no Druidic gospel, no Druidic book of law, no Druidic philosophical treatise. We see them only through the eyes of others, and often, those others were their adversaries. Our sources are like three different kinds of light shining into a dark room from different angles; each reveals something, but each also casts its own shadows.

To be responsible historians of the spirit, we must understand the nature of each of these sources.

1. The Classical Accounts: The View from the Enemy's Camp

Our earliest and most detailed descriptions of the Druids come from Greek and Roman writers, a body of work known as the classical or ethnographic accounts. The most famous of these is Julius Caesar's Commentaries on the Gallic War, written in the 50s BCE. Others include the historian Tacitus, the geographer Strabo, and the naturalist Pliny the Elder. These accounts are invaluable. They provide specific details about the Druids' organisation, training, beliefs in reincarnation, and role in society. It is from them that we learn of the twenty-year training period, the exemption from military service, and the supreme authority they held as judges.

However, these accounts are also deeply problematic. They were written by outsiders, members of an imperial power that viewed the Celtic peoples as "barbarians" in need of Roman civilisation. Roman political agendas and cultural biases inevitably colour their descriptions. Caesar, for example, wrote a report to justify his brutal and costly conquest of Gaul to the Roman Senate. It was in his interest to portray the Gauls as both a formidable threat and a savage people. His lurid descriptions of large-scale human sacrifice, for which there is scant archaeological evidence, may well have been exaggerated for political effect. He also tended to describe Celtic society in Roman terms, comparing the Druids to Roman priests and equating their gods with the Roman pantheon, a process that obscures as much as it reveals.

Reading the classical accounts is like reading a colonial administrator's report on an indigenous people. There is useful information, but it is filtered through a lens of cultural superiority and political expediency. We must always ask: What was the author's agenda? Who was their audience? What did they have to gain by portraying the Druids in this way? These accounts provide a window, but it is a window frosted with prejudice.

2. Early Irish Literature: The Echo in the Monastery

This is perhaps our richest and most tantalising source of information. After the Christianization of Ireland in the fifth and sixth centuries, Irish monks embarked on one of the great intellectual projects of the early Middle Ages: they began to write everything down. In their monastic scriptoriums, they painstakingly recorded the ancient myths, the epic sagas, the genealogies, and the intricate legal system of their pre-Christian ancestors. This body of work, which includes masterpieces such as the Táin Bó Cúailnge (The Cattle Raid of Cooley) and the stories of the Mythological Cycle, is filled with figures identified as Druids (druí in Old Irish).

Here, we see the Druids from the inside, as it were. They are not foreign curiosities; they are integral figures in the cultural memory of the Irish people. We see them as powerful advisors to kings, as prophets who foretell the future, as sorcerers who conjure mists and storms, and as wise teachers of heroes like Cú Chulainn. The great irony, and our great good fortune, is that we owe our knowledge of the pre-Christian Druids to the Christian monks who made them characters in their manuscripts. They did not seek to erase their pagan past; they sought to record it and integrate it into their new Christian identity.

However, these sources also come with a significant caveat. These stories were written down centuries after the Druidic order had faded into an organised institution. They are not historical documents; they are myths, legends, and literary creations. They tell us what the early medieval Irish remembered and believed about the Druids, but this memory is filtered through the lens of a now-dominant Christian worldview. The Druids in these tales are often portrayed as powerful yet ultimately flawed figures who must yield to the Christian saints' superior power. Their "magic" is contrasted with the "miracles" of the new faith. While these stories provide invaluable insight into the Druid archetype in the Irish imagination, we must be cautious about treating them as literal history.

3. Archaeology: The Silent Stones

The third source of evidence is the most tangible, yet the most silent. Archaeology provides the physical traces of the world inhabited by the Druids. The excavation of high-status burials, such as the one in Deal, Kent, where a man was buried with a ceremonial crown and a bronze-coated shield, provides insight into the regalia of the Celtic elite.

The discovery of votive offerings in lakes, bogs, and wells—hoards of swords, shields, cauldrons, and even golden torcs—points to the practice of offering precious objects to the gods. The identification of sacred sites, including the nemetons, or sacred groves, mentioned by classical writers, confirms that their worship was centred in the natural world.

Archaeology can ground the literary sources in physical reality. It can confirm the locations of sacred activity, the types of objects considered valuable, and the timelines of cultural change. But its silence is profound. The stones cannot reveal the content of the prayers offered at the sacred well. The buried artefacts cannot tell us the philosophy that guided the ritual. Archaeology shows us the what and the where, but it can never fully tell us the why.

Piecing together these three disparate sources—the biased reports of enemies, the mythologised memories of descendants, and the silent testimony of the earth—is like trying to reassemble a shattered mirror. We will never see the full, perfect reflection of the Druids as they saw themselves. But if we hold the pieces carefully, if we are mindful of the distortions in each fragment, we can catch a powerful and illuminating glimpse of their world. It is a world not of fantasy, but of profound intellectual and spiritual depth.

The University of the Forest: The Making of a Druid

To become a Druid was not a matter of birthright or sudden, ecstatic inspiration. It was the culmination of one of the most rigorous and demanding educational programs in the ancient world. Caesar reports that the training could last up to twenty years, a period of intense memorisation, philosophical inquiry, and spiritual discipline. This was, in essence, the university system of pre-Roman Northern Europe, and its campus was the natural world.

The curriculum was encyclopedic. A student, or novice, would be expected to commit to memory a vast body of knowledge. This included thousands of poems, stories, and myths that collectively reflected the history and worldview of their people. It included the intricate genealogies of every family and the lineage of every king, a vital function in a society structured around kinship. It encompassed a vast and complex legal system, with its elaborate precedents and restorative justice.

The student would study astronomy, tracking the movements of the sun, moon, and stars to create the calendar that governed the agricultural and ritual cycles. They would learn the medicinal properties of hundreds of plants, becoming the healers of their community. They would study what we would now call physics, geography, and moral philosophy. This was a truly holistic education, in which science, art, law, and religion were not regarded as separate disciplines but as interwoven threads of a single, unified tapestry of wisdom.

The absolute insistence on oral transmission was the key to this system. In a world without a printing press or a library, the trained human memory was the most sacred and sophisticated technology available. The act of memorising was not a rote, mechanical process. It was an act of embodiment. The student did not just know the information; they became the information.

The laws and stories lived within them, ready to be recalled and recited with perfect accuracy. This created a culture where the spoken word held immense power. A solemn oath was an unbreakable bond. A poet's satire could destroy a person's reputation more effectively than a sword. A person's worth was measured not by their material wealth, but by the depth of their knowledge and the truth of their speech.

This long apprenticeship was also, and perhaps primarily, a period of profound spiritual formation. The student was not just learning facts; they were being shaped, body and soul, into a vessel worthy of holding this sacred knowledge. They would spend long periods in solitude, deep in the heart of the forest or on a remote, wind-swept mountaintop.

Here, they learned to listen. They learned to listen to the subtle language of the natural world—the flight of a bird, the shape of a cloud, the rustle of leaves, the sound of water flowing over stones. They learned to observe the patterns of the cosmos and to see their own reflections in those patterns. They learned to find the divine presence not in a man-made temple, but in the living, breathing world around them. This deep, experiential, and intimate connection to nature was the bedrock of their worldview. It was not a subject they studied; it was the medium in which they lived and moved and had their being.

THE THREEFOLD CALLING: POET, PROPHET, AND PRIEST

Within the broad class of the learned, which the Irish sources call the aes dána or "people of the arts," our evidence suggests a threefold hierarchy of function. While the lines could be blurry, and one person might embody multiple roles, these three callings—the Bard, the Ovate, and the Druid—represent the different facets of the wisdom-keeper's service to the community.

The Bard (Poet): The Keeper of Memory

The Bards were the masters of poetry, music, and story. They were the living libraries, the guardians of the tribe's collective memory. In a culture without writing, the Bards held the sacred trust of preserving the kings' genealogies, the heroes' great deeds, and the gods' myths. Their poems were not mere entertainment; they were the very glue that held the society's identity together. To forget the stories was to forget who you were.

The Bard's training was incredibly rigorous, involving the memorisation of hundreds of complex poetic meters and thousands of stories. Their power was immense. A poem of praise (moladh) from a master Bard could elevate a chieftain to legendary status, ensuring his fame for generations. Conversely, a satirical poem (áer), believed to have the power to raise boils on the victim's face, could destroy a person's reputation and honour, a fate considered worse than death in a society built on public esteem. The Bards understood that words create worlds, and they wielded this creative and destructive power with immense skill and responsibility.

The Ovate (Prophet/Seer): The Reader of Signs

The Ovates were the seers, the diviners, and the healers. They sought to understand the will of the gods and the unfolding patterns of fate. They were masters at observing the natural world, deriving wisdom from the flight of birds (augury), the shapes of clouds, the patterns of smoke from a fire, and the movements of animals. They were the healers who knew the secret properties of herbs and the power of incantations to restore balance to the body and spirit.

The Ovate's practice was rooted in the belief that the physical world is a mirror of the spiritual world and that there is an ongoing conversation between the visible and the invisible. They did not believe in a random, chaotic universe, but in a cosmos filled with meaning, purpose, and intelligence. Their art was the art of listening, of paying deep attention to the subtle language of the world around them to discern the divine patterns woven throughout it.

The Druid (Priest/Philosopher/Judge): The Arbiter of Truth

At the apex of this learned class stood the Druid. The title "Druid" itself is thought to mean "Oak-Knower" or perhaps "Knower of the Hidden," pointing to their deep connection with the sacred oak tree and their role as seekers of the most profound wisdom. The Druids held the ultimate spiritual and legal authority in Celtic society. They presided over the major seasonal festivals—Imbolc, Beltaine, Lughnasadh, and Samhain—serving as intermediaries between the human community and the divine powers. They were the supreme judges, and their authority was absolute.

Caesar notes that their rulings were binding on all, from the lowest commoner to the highest king. A king who defied the judgment of a Druid could be excommunicated, barred from the sacrifices, which was the greatest punishment imaginable. This effectively stripped him of his power and his place in the tribe. The Druids were the philosophers who contemplated the nature of the cosmos, the soul, and the gods. They taught the core doctrines of their tradition and guided the spiritual life of their people. So great was the respect they commanded that they were exempt from military service and taxation. They were the still point at the centre of the turning Celtic world, the guardians of its sacred order.

THE CORE PHILOSOPHY: THE SOUL'S GREAT JOURNEY

What did the Druids teach during their long years in the forest university? While the specifics of their liturgy and theology are lost to us, classical writers and Irish myths provide a clear, consistent picture of their core philosophical and spiritual beliefs. These beliefs are not only profound in their own right but also help us understand why the Celtic soul was uniquely prepared for the Christian message.

The Immortality of the Soul and Transmigration

Nearly every Roman commentator who wrote about the Druids noted with a sense of awe their absolute and unwavering conviction in the immortality of the soul. They did not believe that death was an end. As one writer put it, they saw death as merely a "middle point in a long life." They taught a doctrine of transmigration, or what we might loosely call reincarnation. The soul, upon the death of the body, would pass into another form. This belief, the Romans observed, made Celtic warriors utterly fearless in battle, as they did not fear the finality of death. They were known to lend money on the promise that it would be repaid in the next life.

It is essential to distinguish this from the karmic system of reincarnation found in Eastern traditions. There is little evidence that the Celts saw the next life as a direct reward or punishment for the actions of the previous one. Instead, it seems they viewed it as a continuous journey of experience, a great adventure of the soul through different forms and different worlds. The soul might be reborn as another human, or it might spend time in the Otherworld, the realm of the gods and spirits, before returning. This belief fostered a long-term perspective on life, a sense that one's existence was part of a vast, unfolding cosmic story.

The Living Cosmos: Animism and Immanence

Fundamental to the Druidic worldview was the belief that the entire universe is alive, conscious, and filled with spirit. This is often called animism, but the term can carry a misleading connotation of primitivism. This was a sophisticated, philosophical position. For the Druids, there was no such thing as "dead matter."

Every mountain had its spirit, every river its goddess, every tree its indwelling presence. The divine was not a distant, transcendent being who created the world and then left it to its own devices. The divine was immanent, present, and active in every part of creation. The wind was the breath of the gods. The sun was the eye of a great deity. The earth itself was a living, breathing mother.

This worldview had profound ethical implications. It meant that the natural world was not a resource to be exploited, but a community of beings to be respected and communed with. To cut down a sacred tree without cause was not just an act of vandalism; it was an act of sacrilege. To pollute a holy well was to offend the spirit that dwelt within it. This fostered a profound ecological consciousness, a sense of kinship with all of life that stands in stark and tragic contrast to the modern world's alienation from nature. It was a spirituality of belonging, a way of being at home in the universe.

THE SACRED GROVE: THE CATHEDRAL OF NATURE

If the cosmos were a living temple, the sacred grove (nemeton) would be its inner sanctum. The Druids did not build large stone temples like those of the Greeks and Romans. Their place of worship was the forest itself, often a clearing surrounded by ancient, venerated trees, particularly oaks. These groves were regarded as powerful sites, charged with spiritual energy, where the veil between this world and the Otherworld was naturally thin. The word nemeton is related to the Irish word *nemed*, which means "sacred" or "privileged." These were places set apart.

Within these groves, they would perform their rituals, make their offerings, and teach their students. Access was often restricted; these were not public parks, but holy ground, the domain of the gods and their priests. The grove's atmosphere was essential to their practice. The silence, broken only by the wind in the leaves; the dappled light filtering through the high canopy; the immense, silent presence of the ancient trees—this was the atmosphere in which they sought and found the divine. It was a spirituality that was literally and figuratively rooted in the earth.

The Oak and the Mistletoe

Our most vivid, if perhaps romanticised, image of a Druidic ritual comes from the Roman writer Pliny the Elder. He describes a ceremony that he says was of the utmost importance to the Druids. It involved the ritual harvesting of mistletoe from a sacred oak tree. According to Pliny, the Druids held the oak in the highest veneration and would not perform any ritual without its leaves.

The mistletoe, which grows as a parasite on the oak, was considered especially sacred. On the sixth day of the moon, a Druid priest, dressed in white, would climb the oak and cut the mistletoe with a golden sickle. It was caught in a white cloak, as touching the ground was considered a profanation. Two white bulls were then sacrificed, and a feast was held, with prayers offered to the god for a prosperous offering.

Whether this ritual was a common practice or a rare, specific event, its symbolism is potent and reveals the heart of the Druidic worldview. The Oak, the king of the forest, symbolises strength, endurance, and connection to the Earth and the Underworld. The Mistletoe, which remains green in the depths of winter when the oak appears dead, is a powerful symbol of life, eternity, and the undying spirit.

It grows between the earth and the sky, a bridge between worlds. The golden sickle suggests a connection to the sun and the heavens. The ritual is a beautiful and dramatic enactment of the union of heaven and earth, spirit and matter, a core principle of the Druidic philosophy.

THE PRACTICE: CONNECTING WITH THE WISDOM-KEEPER ARCHETYPE

As we close this first chapter of our journey, we have moved beyond the caricature of the Druid and begun to see the outlines of a profound, sophisticated wisdom-keeper. We have seen a figure dedicated to lifelong learning, a master of memory and poetry, a reader of the sacred signs of nature, and a philosopher who contemplated the soul's great journey. We have seen a spiritual leader whose temple was the living forest and whose core belief was the sacredness of all creation.

This figure is not merely a historical curiosity; it represents a timeless archetype—the wisdom-keeper who finds truth not in dogma or ancient books, but in deep, attentive listening to the world. This is an archetype that lives within each of us. The part of you that is drawn to the silence of the woods, that feels a sense of wonder when you look up at the stars, that longs for a deeper, more authentic connection to the earth—that is the whisper of your own inner Druid, your own inner wisdom-keeper.

Our first practice, then, is not a complex ritual, but a simple act of inner recognition. It is a guided meditation to help you connect with this archetype within your soul and acknowledge the part of you that already knows the truth of the living cosmos.

A Meditation on the Inner Druid

1. Find a Quiet Place: Find a place where you can be undisturbed for ten to fifteen minutes. If possible, sit outdoors, perhaps near a tree or even just a small plant. If you are indoors, you might hold a stone, a leaf, or a glass of water in your hand to create a tangible connection to the natural world.

2. Ground Yourself: Close your eyes. Take three slow, deep breaths. With each exhale, release the busyness of your day, the chatter of your mind. Feel your feet on the ground. Feel the support of the chair or the earth beneath you. Become aware of the physical sensations of your body—the air on your skin, the feeling of your clothes, the gentle rhythm of your own breathing.

3. Enter the Inner Grove: In your mind's eye, imagine yourself standing at the edge of a beautiful, ancient forest. The light is soft and green, filtering through a high canopy of leaves. The air is fresh and alive with the scent of damp earth and growing things. You feel a sense of peace and safety here. This is your own inner sacred grove, a place of deep knowing within you. You step across the threshold and begin to walk along a soft, mossy path.

4. Meet the Archetype: As you walk, you become aware of a figure standing in a sunlit clearing ahead. This is not a specific historical person, but the archetype of the Druid, the wisdom-keeper from within your own soul. They may appear as a man or a woman, old or young, dressed in white or in the colours of the forest. Trust the image that arises in your own heart. This figure radiates a sense of deep peace, profound strength, and ancient, patient wisdom. They are not here to judge you or to test you, but simply to welcome you.

5. Listen with the Heart: You approach this figure and stand before them in respectful silence. You need not ask a question or perform any ritual. Your only task is to be present and to listen with your heart. What do you feel in their presence? What quality do they embody that your soul is longing for in this moment? Is it peace? Is it wisdom? Is it a deeper connection to nature? Is it courage? Is it simply a sense of belonging? Allow yourself to receive this quality as a silent blessing, a transmission of grace.

6. Receive a Symbolic Gift: The wisdom-keeper reaches out and offers you a simple, symbolic gift. It might be a single, perfectly formed leaf. It might be a smooth, grey stone from a riverbed. It might be a feather from a hawk's wing, or a sip of cool, clear water from a wooden cup. Receive this gift in your hands. Feel its texture, its weight, its temperature. Recognise that it is a symbol of the quality you seek. It is a reminder that this quality—this peace, this wisdom, this courage—already exists within you. It is your birthright.

7. Give Thanks and Return: Bow your head in gratitude to the wisdom-keeper for their presence and their gift. Know that you can return to this inner grove whenever you wish, simply by closing your eyes and setting the intention. Now, slowly, gently, begin to bring your awareness back to your physical body. Feel your feet on the floor, your hands in your lap. Take another deep breath, and when you are ready, open your eyes.

8. Reflect and Integrate: Take a moment to journal about your experience. What did the wisdom-keeper look like? What quality did they represent for you? What was the gift, and what does it mean to you? How can you carry the energy of this encounter, the feeling of this gift, into the rest of your day?

This is how we begin to weave the grove's wisdom into the fabric of our lives.

This practice is a first step. It is an act of honouring the deep, ancient wisdom that lies at the root of the Celtic tradition and, more importantly, at the root of your own soul. In the chapters to come, we will explore how this Druidic wisdom was not lost, but was baptised and transformed into the beautiful, earth-honouring faith of the Celtic Christians. We will see how the sacred grove was not abandoned but rediscovered within the monastic enclosures, and how the whisper of the oak became one with the voice of the Holy Spirit.

The journey to the stream's source has begun. We have taken our first steps into the grove.

Let us walk on.

Chapter 2:

Christ, My Druid: The Great Integration

In our last chapter, we journeyed back in time, pushing past the veils of myth and fantasy to meet the true Druids, the wisdom-keepers of the ancient Celtic world. We found not wizards or mystics in the modern sense, but a sophisticated intellectual and spiritual class who served as the judges, poets, philosophers, and priests of their people. We discovered a worldview rooted in the conviction that the soul is immortal and that the entire cosmos is alive, a sacred, living temple.

Their university was the forest, their scripture the book of nature, and their holiest site the nemeton, the sacred grove. We ended by connecting with this timeless archetype of the wisdom-keeper that lies dormant within each of our souls.

We now arrive at the central turning point in our story, the pivotal moment of encounter. What happens when this ancient, earth-honouring spirituality, with its deep roots in the soil of Ireland, Scotland, and Wales, meets a new story arriving from the East? What happens when the wisdom of the Oak-Knowers meets the story of the Carpenter from Nazareth?

The conventional narrative of religious history, the one most of us have been taught, is a story of conflict and eradication. A new faith arrives, declares the old ways demonic or ignorant, and a battle for souls ensues, ending in the triumphant suppression of the old religion. The old gods are banished, the old temples are torn down, and the old wisdom is forgotten.

But this is not what happened in the Celtic world. The story of Christianity's coming to the Isles is not one of conquest but of a deep and mysterious conversation. It is a story of recognition, of translation, and of transformation. It is a story of integration. This process is captured in one of the most startling, beautiful, and theologically profound declarations in the history of Christianity, a line attributed to the great sixth-century Irish saint, Columba, also known as Colmcille: "Mo Chríost, mo druí.

Christ is my Druid.

Let those four words sink into your heart. Feel their weight, their strangeness, their power. This is not the statement of a man who has vanquished an enemy. This is the statement of a man who has found the ultimate fulfilment of his people's highest spiritual ideals. It is a declaration that the new story did not abolish the old, but completed it. It suggests that the role of the Druid—the wisdom-keeper, the mediator between heaven and earth, the one who reads the signs of the cosmos, the poet of the sacred— was not made obsolete by Christ, but was perfectly and eternally embodied in Him. This chapter explores that great integration. We will walk the path from the sacred grove to the monastic enclosure and discover that the journey was not as long, or as fraught with peril, as we might imagine.

A DIFFERENT KIND OF CONVERSION: THE IRISH EXCEPTION

To understand the unique nature of the Celtic conversion, we must first grasp a crucial fact of history that shaped the destiny of the Irish soul: Ireland was never conquered by the Roman Empire. While the legions of Rome subdued neighbouring Britain and spread their administrative, military, and cultural systems across Gaul, Ireland remained outside the imperial frontier. The Romans called it Hibernia, "the land of winter," and while they traded with it, they never brought it under their control.

This is a fact of immense spiritual significance. In most of the Roman Empire, Christianity spread along the network of Roman roads, within the framework of Roman cities, and, often enough, with the backing of Roman power. When Christianity became the empire's state religion in the fourth century, its relationship with the old paganisms became one of opposition and suppression. The old gods of the Roman state were now rivals to be defeated, their temples to be torn down or reconsecrated, their rituals to be forbidden. The conversion was often a top-down, politically driven process.

But Christianity arrived in Ireland in a completely different manner. It did not arrive on the back of an imperial warhorse. It did not involve legions, governors, or the imposition of a foreign legal and social system. It arrived, for the most part, peacefully. It trickled in through the quiet work of merchants trading across the Irish Sea, through the return of former slaves who had been converted abroad, and through the dedicated, often perilous, work of early missionaries. It spread not from a centralised imperial authority but from person to person and from tribe to tribe.

This meant that the encounter between native spirituality and the new faith was fundamentally different from that in the Romanised world. In Ireland, there was no imperial paganism to oppose. There was only the deeply ingrained, ancient, nature-based spirituality of the people, a worldview guided and articulated by the Druids. The missionaries who succeeded in Ireland were not those who came with fire and sword, but those who came with a listening ear and a respectful heart. They were masters of what modern theologians call "inculturation." They understood that to be heard, they first had to understand the soul's spiritual language. They had to find the points of resonance, the places where the story they carried could connect with the one already being lived.

And they found these points of resonance everywhere. The missionaries recognised in the Celtic spirit a natural kinship with the core of the Gospel message. The Druidic belief in the immortality of the soul and its journey after death provided fertile ground for the Christian teaching of the resurrection and eternal life. The Druidic sense of the immanence of the divine —the belief that the world was charged with the presence of spirit — was a natural precursor to the Christian doctrine of the Incarnation—the belief that God had become fully present in the world in the person of Jesus Christ. The missionaries did not have to teach the Celts that the world was sacred; they only had to introduce them to the one through whom, and for whom, that sacred world was created. They did not come to extinguish a light, but to reveal its source.

PATRICK AND THE DRUIDS: BEYOND THE BONFIRE

The figure who looms largest in this story is, of course, St. Patrick. Unfortunately, the popular image of Patrick is a caricature, a cartoon bishop in a pointy hat who, in a fit of righteous power, drove all the "snakes" out of Ireland. This story, which appears in writing only centuries after his death, is a powerful but misleading metaphor. Ireland, an island cut off from the mainland after the last Ice Age, never had any literal snakes. The "snakes" are widely understood by scholars to symbolise the Druids and their native, earth-based faith. The myth, therefore, portrays Patrick as a conqueror, a single-handed hero who eradicated paganism from the island.

The historical reality, which we can glimpse through Patrick's own writings—his deeply personal and moving Confessio and his fiery Letter to the Soldiers of Coroticus—is far more complex, more humble, and infinitely more interesting. These documents reveal a man very different from the legend. They show a man who was captured as a teenager from his home in Roman Britain, spent six years as a slave in Ireland herding sheep, and in that lonely, desperate time, found a deep and personal faith. Years after escaping, he felt a powerful, irresistible call to return to the land of his captivity, not as a conqueror, but out of a profound and aching love for the very people who had enslaved him.

Patrick speaks of travelling to the "remote parts" of the island, where no missionary had gone before, of baptising thousands, and of ordaining clergy. He did this not by force, but by engaging directly with the local chieftains and kings of the many small kingdoms (túatha) that made up Irish society. And who were the chief advisors, the prime ministers, the spiritual guides to these kings? The Druids. Patrick's success, his very survival, depended on his ability to navigate this complex social and spiritual landscape. He could not have succeeded without entering into a direct and often perilous dialogue with the very wisdom-keepers of the old tradition.

The most famous story of this encounter is the legend of the Paschal fire on the Hill of Slane. The story, as recorded in later hagiographies, is dramatic. Patrick arrives in Ireland at the time of the great festival of Beltaine, a major fire festival that marked the beginning of summer. The High King, Lóegaire, is at his royal seat on the Hill of Tara, and he has decreed that no fire may be lit anywhere in the land until the great ceremonial bonfire is kindled on Tara. This is a sacred prohibition, enforced by the king's Druids. In an act of audacious, holy defiance, Patrick lights the Easter bonfire on the nearby Hill of Slane, its light shining out across the plains in full view of the king at Tara.

Enraged, the king and his Druids go to confront this upstart missionary. The legend then portrays a series of magical contests, a kind of spiritual duel between the Druids' power and Patrick's God. The Druids conjure a deep darkness, and Patrick prays for the sun to shine. The Druids bring down a magical snow, and Patrick clears it. It is a dramatic tale of "my magic is better than your magic."

But if we look past the legendary embellishments, we can see a deeper, more profound truth.

This was not simply a display of supernatural power. It was a profound act of spiritual theatre, a masterclass in inculturation. Patrick was not just defying the king; he was making a powerful theological statement. He was claiming that the fire he lit—the fire symbolising the resurrection of Christ, the light of the world who overcomes the darkness of the tomb—was the true fire. It was the fulfilment of what the Beltaine fires had always pointed towards.

He was not extinguishing the light of the Druids; he was revealing its ultimate source. He was showing that the turning of the seasons, the return of the sun's warmth, the renewal of life in the fields, all of which the Druids celebrated at Beltaine, were held within the greater, cosmic story of Christ's victory over death.

He was not saying, "Your fire is false." He was saying, "Let me show you the One who is the source of all fire, all light, all life."

This is the very essence of integration. It is not about destroying the old symbols, but about filling them with new and deeper meaning. Patrick and the early missionaries did not say, "Your love of the sun is wrong." They said, "Let us tell you about the one who is the Sun of Righteousness." They did not say, "Your reverence for the sacred well is foolish." They said, "Let us introduce you to the one who is the Living Water." They did not say, "Your belief in the three realms is a fantasy." They said, "Let us tell you about the One who descended to the dead, walked the earth, and ascended to the heavens, uniting all three realms in his own person."

They built bridges, not walls.

BRIGID OF KILDARE: THE MARY OF THE GAEL

If Patrick represents the missionary impulse that brought the Christian story to Ireland, then St. Brigid represents the deep, fertile soil of the native tradition that received it and made it its own.

Brigid, after Patrick and Columba, is the third great patron saint of Ireland, and in many respects, she is the most beloved. She is known as *Muire na nGael*, the "Mary of the Gael," a title that speaks to her role as a nurturing, protective, and profoundly feminine presence in the Irish spiritual imagination. Her story is a perfect and beautiful example of the seamless integration of the pre-Christian and Christian worlds.

The historical Brigid was a real woman, an abbess who founded a great double monastery for both men and women at Cill-Dara, the "Church of the Oak," in the late fifth or early sixth century. Her monastery became a major centre of learning, artistry, and charity. But the stories that surround her, recorded in her hagiographies, are woven with threads far, far older than the historical abbess herself. They connect her directly to a powerful pre-Christian goddess of the same name.

The goddess Brigid was one of the Tuatha Dé Danann, the great pantheon of Irish deities.

She was a goddess of the triple flame: the flame of poetry and inspiration (imbas), the flame of the smith's forge (creativity and transformation), and the flame of healing. She was a goddess of the land, of fertility, of livestock, and of the sacred wells.

Her festival, *Imbolc*, celebrated on February 1st, marked the first stirrings of spring, the ewes' lactation, and the return of light after the darkness of winter.

The Christian stories about St. Brigid show remarkable continuity with the goddess's attributes. St. Brigid is the patron saint of poets, blacksmiths, and healers. Her legends are filled with agricultural miracles and the land's abundance. She is said to have miraculously multiplied food and beer for her guests, a sign of her divine hospitality. She is a protector of livestock.

Her connection to fire is central. At her monastery in Kildare, a sacred flame was kept perpetually burning for centuries, tended by a community of nuns. This practice is a direct continuation of the pre-Christian tradition of the sacred, eternal fire tended by priestesses.

Unlike Patrick's stories, which often involve confrontations with the Druids, Brigid's stories depict a deep, harmonious relationship with the natural world and its ancient rhythms. One of the most beautiful stories tells of how she came to acquire the land for her monastery. She approached the local king of Leinster and requested a parcel of land on which to establish her community. The king, a pagan, laughed at her and mockingly offered her as much land as her cloak could cover. Brigid took off her cloak, and she and her companions each took a corner. They began to walk, and as they walked, the cloak expanded, covering acre after acre of lush, green pastureland. The king, seeing this miracle, was converted and became a patron of her monastery.

This story is a perfect parable of integration. Brigid does not conquer the land with a sword. She does not demand it. She covers it, gently, with her cloak. The cloak is a symbol of her protective, nurturing, feminine power. It does not destroy what is underneath; it embraces it, it sanctifies it, it brings it under a new and holy mantle. This is the essence of the Celtic conversion. It was not an act of violent displacement, but of gentle, miraculous covering. The old ways were not eradicated; they were brought under the cloak of Christ, under the care of saints like Brigid, who understood both the old world and the new.

THE GREAT DECLARATION: "CHRIST, MY DRUID"

This process of integration, of finding the fulfilment of the old in the new, finds its most perfect and powerful expression in that phrase from St. Columba: "Mo Chríost, mo druí." Christ is my Druid.

Columba, or Colmcille ("Dove of the Church") as he is known in Irish, was a towering figure who lived a century after Patrick. He was an Irish prince of royal blood, a passionate and brilliant man, a gifted poet, and a dedicated monk. Following a dispute in Ireland, he entered self-imposed exile and founded the great monastery on the island of Iona, off the coast of modern-day Scotland, in 563 AD.

Iona would become a beacon of learning and artistry, a spiritual centre whose influence would spread across Scotland, Northern England, and back into Europe. Significantly, Iona itself was said to have been a sacred island for the Druids long before Columba arrived, another example of the Christian mission consecrating, rather than conquering, a place of ancient power.

Columba was a man who stood with one foot in the old world and one in the new. He was a devout Christian monk, but he was also a master of the Irish poetic tradition, a tradition once the domain of the Bards and Druids. The declaration, "Christ is my Druid," attributed to him, is a theological bombshell. It is the key that unlocks the entire Celtic Christian worldview.

Let us take the time to unpack the profound theology contained in this simple, four-word sentence.

First, Christ is the ultimate Wisdom-Keeper. As we explored in the last chapter, the word "Druid" likely means "Oak-Knower" or "Knower of the Hidden." The Druids were the philosophers of their people, the ones who contemplated the deep truths of the cosmos, the nature of the soul, and the will of the gods. They sought wisdom in the patterns of nature and in the depths of their own disciplined minds. In the Christian tradition, Christ is identified with the Logos, a Greek term meaning "Word," "Reason," or "Divine Mind."

The Gospel of John begins with one of the most profound philosophical statements ever written: "In the beginning was the Word, and the Word was with God, and the Word was God. He was in the beginning with God. All things were made through him, and without him was not anything made that was made." For Columba, a man steeped in both traditions, Christ is the ultimate Wisdom through whom the universe was created. The wisdom the Druids sought by studying the patterns of nature was a reflection, a glimmer, of the deeper, foundational wisdom that is Christ himself. To know Christ was to know the very mind of God, the source of all truth, the one who is the answer to every question the Druids ever asked.

Second, Christ is the ultimate Mediator. The Druids served as the essential intermediaries between the human world and the divine realm. They stood in the gap. They presided over the rituals and sacrifices that maintained the sacred balance between the people and the gods, that restored harmony when it was broken.

In Christian theology, this is Christ's unique and central role. He is the great High Priest, the one who is both fully human and fully divine, and who, through his life, death, and resurrection, bridges the chasm between humanity and God. The Druid offered a sacrifice to restore harmony; Christ is the sacrifice that restores harmony, once and for all. He is the perfect bridge, the ultimate pontifex (the Latin title for a priest, which literally means "bridge-builder").

Third, Christ is the ultimate Poet and Law-Giver. The Druids, particularly in their Bardic function, were the keepers of the sacred stories, the myths that shaped the identity of their people. They were also the supreme judges who upheld the law. Christ, in the Gospels, is the master storyteller, the one who speaks in parables to reveal the nature of the Kingdom of God.

He is also the one who fulfils and deepens the law, summarising all the commandments in the great injunction to love God and love our neighbour. The justice the Druids sought to uphold in the community was a shadow of the perfect justice and mercy found in the person of Christ. The stories the Bards told were echoes of the one great story that God was telling in and through him.

By calling Christ his Druid, Columba was making a radical and deeply contextual claim. He was saying that everything his ancestors had yearned for, everything they had sought in the sacred grove and in the stars, every function of the highest and most respected figures in his culture, had been made real, personal, and perfect in the person of Jesus.

Christ was not a foreign deity who had come to displace the old ways. He was the fulfilment of the deepest desires of the Celtic soul. This was the key that unlocked the people's hearts. It allowed them to embrace the new faith wholeheartedly, without feeling they had to betray their ancestors or their sacred connection to their land.

FROM SACRED GROVE TO MONASTIC ENCLOSURE: A CHANGE OF FORM, NOT OF HEART

A physical, social, and artistic transformation mirrored this spiritual integration. The roles, places, and art forms that had been central to the Druidic world were not destroyed but were baptised and given a new purpose and meaning within a Christian framework.

The Transformation of Roles: The Druid's role did not simply vanish; it was transformed into that of the Celtic monk and abbot. The great monastic settlements, like Columba's Iona, St. Brigid's Kildare, or St. Ciarán's Clonmacnoise, became the new spiritual and intellectual centres of the society, just as the Druidic schools had been. The monks and abbots assumed many of the functions the Druids had once performed.

• **Keepers of Knowledge:** The Druids had preserved the entire culture through their vast oral tradition. The monks became the great scribes and scholars of their age, known throughout Europe for their learning. They painstakingly wrote down not only the scriptures, the Church Fathers' commentaries, and the lives of the saints, but also the ancient pre-Christian myths, the epic sagas, and the complex Brehon laws of their people. The great irony is that we know what we know about the pre-Christian Celts precisely because Christian monks valued that knowledge enough to preserve it in manuscripts such as the Book of the Dun Cow and the Book of Leinster.

• **Poets and Artists:** The Bardic tradition of the Druids flowed directly into the monasteries. The monks became the new poets, composing exquisite verses in both Irish and Latin, often celebrating the beauty of nature as a sign of God's glory, just as their pagan ancestors had. The intricate, swirling, mind-bendingly complex knotwork that adorns the great High Crosses and the pages of illuminated manuscripts such as the Book of Kells is a direct continuation of the La Tène artistic style of the pre-Christian Celts. It is an art form that refuses to see space, that fills every corner with vibrant, interwoven life, a perfect visual representation of the Celtic belief in the interconnectedness of all things.

• **Spiritual Guides:** The Druid's role as a spiritual teacher was transformed into the uniquely Celtic practice of the Anam Cara, or "soul friend." This was not the formal, hierarchical confession of the later Roman church, but an intimate spiritual friendship in which two people would share their innermost selves, their struggles and joys, and guide each other on the path to God. The abbot or abbess of a monastery held immense spiritual authority, just as the chief Druid had, and served as the soul friend to the entire community.

The Transformation of Places: Just as the roles were transformed, so were the sacred places. The early Celtic Christians had a profound sense that holiness was not an abstract concept, but was present and potent in specific locations. They recognised that the places their ancestors had identified as sacred—the wells, the hills, the ancient trees, the stone circles—were indeed places of power, "thin places" where the veil between heaven and earth was especially transparent. Their strategy was not to desecrate these places, but to re-consecrate them, to claim them for Christ.

• **From Sacred Well to Holy Well:** A well that had been sacred to a local goddess, like Brigid, was rededicated to a Christian saint, often St. Brigid, who herself is a remarkable fusion of the pre-Christian goddess and a historical Christian abbess. The practice of leaving offerings (clooties, or strips of cloth), of circumambulating the well in a sun-wise direction, of praying for healing—all of this continued, but it was now done in the name of Christ and his saints.

• **From Sacred Grove to Monastic Enclosure:** The nemeton, the sacred grove of the Druids, found its Christian counterpart in the monastic enclosure. The early Celtic monasteries were not the grand stone fortresses of later medieval Europe. They were often simple collections of beehive-shaped huts made of wood and earth, surrounded by a circular wall or ditch. They were, in essence, consecrated groves, sacred spaces set apart from the ordinary world for seeking God. And very often, these monasteries were founded in or near places that had been sacred to the Druids, like St. Brigid's "Church of the Oak."

This practice of rededication was a profound statement of continuity. It was a way of saying that God had been present in this land and with these people long before the missionaries arrived. The new faith was not an erasure of the past, but a fulfilment of it. It was a grafting of a new branch onto an ancient and healthy rootstock.

THE PRACTICE: AN INTEGRATION OF YOUR OWN

We have seen how the early Celtic Christians masterfully wove together the old ways and the new. They lived in a world where it was possible to be deeply Christian while still honouring the wisdom of their ancestors and the sacredness of the natural world. They did not experience their faith as a set of conflicting beliefs that needed to be compartmentalised, but as a single, integrated, harmonious whole.

Many of us in the modern world lack this sense of integration. Our lives are often fragmented. We may have a spiritual life that feels separate from our work life, our family life, and our political life. We may hold beliefs that appear to be contradictory. We may feel a tension between the scientific worldview we have been taught and the spiritual experiences we have had. We may feel a pull toward the wisdom of ancient, earth-based traditions, but are unsure how to reconcile that with the faith we grew up with or with a rational, modern mindset. We live in a world of "either/or," while the Celtic soul lived in a world of "both/and."

This chapter's practice invites you to begin your own process of integration. It is a journaling exercise to help you identify the different streams of belief, value, and experience that flow through you, and to see where they might be brought into a more harmonious relationship. It is an exercise in becoming your own "Patrick," your own "Columba," finding the points of connection and building the bridges in your own soul.

A Journaling Exercise: Mapping Your Inner Landscape

1. Prepare Your Space: Find a quiet time and place where you will not be disturbed. Make yourself a cup of tea. Light a candle. Have your journal and a pen ready. Take a few deep breaths to centre yourself and to signal to your soul that you are creating a sacred space for reflection.

2. Identify the Streams: On a fresh page in your journal, draw two large, overlapping circles, like a Venn diagram. Label the left circle "Old Ways," "Deepest Intuitions, or "Earth Wisdom." Label the right circle "New Ways, "Current Beliefs, or "Learned Wisdom."

3. Explore the "Old Ways" Circle: In the part of the left circle that does not overlap, begin to list the beliefs, values, feelings, and experiences that feel ancient, intuitive, or foundational to you, even if they don't fit neatly into a formal religious or philosophical system. Don't censor yourself. Let the words flow. Consider these prompts:

• What did you believe about the world as a child? What felt magical, alive, or sacred to you before you were taught otherwise?

• What does nature teach you? What do you feel when you are in a forest, by the ocean, under a starry sky, or in a garden?

• What are the values your ancestors passed down to you, even if they were unspoken? (e.g., hospitality, courage, a love of storytelling, a connection to a particular place).

• What are the "pagan" or "earthy" parts of you? The parts that love ritual, cycles, seasons, the body, dance, song, and the senses?

4. Explore the "New Ways" Circle: In the part of the right circle that does not overlap, list the beliefs, values, and ideas that you have consciously adopted or been taught. This could be your current religious faith (Christian,

Buddhist, Jewish, etc.), your scientific or philosophical worldview, your political convictions, or your ethical code.

This is the framework you use to make sense of the world.

Consider these prompts:

• What is your current stated belief system? What are its core tenets?

• What are the key principles you consciously try to live by?

• What have you learned from your formal education, from science, and from reason?

• What new ideas, beliefs, or experiences have challenged or changed you in your adult life?

5. Find the Integration: The "Christ, My Druid" Space: Now, turn your attention to the overlapping space in the centre. This is the space of integration, the place where "Christ is my Druid." This is where the old and new ways meet, affirm, and deepen each other. Based on what you wrote in the outer circles, what belongs in this middle space? Where do you see connections? Where do you feel harmony? This is the most creative and important part of the exercise.

Consider these prompts:

• Is there a way that your love for nature (Old Way) deepens your understanding of God as Creator (New Way)? Can the forest be a cathedral?

• Does your intuition about the interconnectedness of all things (Old Way) resonate with a spiritual teaching about unity, compassion, or the Body of Christ (New Way)?

• Can a ritual you feel drawn to, like lighting a candle or celebrating the solstice (Old Way), be seen as a form of prayer or a way of honouring God's creation (New Way)?

• Where do you see a deeper truth that holds both sides together? For example, could the "magic" you felt as a child be seen as the "grace" you now pray for? Could the "spirit of the mountain" be an expression of the "Holy Spirit"?

6. Reflect on the Dialogue: Look at your completed map. It is a map of your own soul. There will be things that overlap beautifully. There may also be things that still feel separate or in conflict. That is okay. This is not about forcing everything to fit. It is about starting a conversation, an inner dialogue.

In your journal, reflect on what you see. What surprised you? Where is there unexpected harmony? Where is there still tension? Write a short intention or prayer for greater integration in your life, asking for the grace to build more bridges and tear down more walls within yourself.

This practice is the beginning of a lifelong journey. The Celtic saints show us that it is possible to build a faith that is both faithful to the Gospel and deeply rooted in the earth's wisdom. They show us that we do not have to choose between the head and the heart, between reason and intuition, between the sacred story and the sacred land. We can, like Columba, stand with one foot in the ancient grove and one foot in the community of Christ, and declare with joy and confidence that the God we meet in both places is the same.

In our next chapter, we will delve even deeper into this integrated vision by exploring one of the most potent symbols shared by the Druids and the Celtic Christians: the great, life-giving World Tree. We will see how the Crann Bethadh, the sacred tree at the centre of the Celtic world, was not cut down, but was transformed into the Cross of Christ, the ultimate bridge between heaven and earth.

Chapter 3:

The Tree of Life and the World Tree

To date, we have followed a path of integration and discovery.

We have sought the historical truth of the Druids, the wisdom-keepers of the old Celtic world, pushing past the veils of fantasy to find a sophisticated class of philosophers, poets, judges, and priests whose university was the forest itself.

We have witnessed the remarkable process by which their earth-honouring spirituality was not vanquished by Christianity, but was instead baptised and transformed.

We heard the echo of St. Columba's radical declaration, "Christ is my Druid," a testament to a faith that found its fulfilment, not its negation, in the person of Jesus.

We saw how St. Patrick engaged the Druids in dialogue rather than conquest, and how St. Brigid gently covered the old ways with the protective cloak of the new faith.

We now arrive at the core of this integrated vision. We encounter a symbol so powerful, so ancient, and so universal that it serves as the central pillar connecting the Celtic pagan and Celtic Christian worlds. We come to the Tree of Life, the Crann Bethadh, the World Tree that holds up the cosmos and connects all the realms of existence.

Long before the first Christian missionaries set foot on the shores of Ireland, the tree stood at the centre of the Celtic cosmos. It was not merely a plant, not merely timber or decoration. It was a map of the universe, a ladder between worlds, a source of wisdom, and the living, breathing soul of the community.

When the story of the Cross arrived, it was not seen as the story of a dead piece of wood used for execution. It was understood, immediately and intuitively, as the ultimate fulfilment of the story of the living tree. The Celtic soul, which had always venerated the tree that connected heaven and earth, immediately recognised its ultimate expression in the tree upon which God himself stretched out his arms to embrace all of creation.

This chapter is an exploration of the heart of that symbol.

We will explore the pre-Christian understanding of the World Tree, and then we will see how its every branch, its trunk, and its roots were grafted onto the life-giving cross of Christ.

We will discover that for the Celtic Christian, the cross was not a symbol of death, but the ultimate Tree of Life, flowering with redemption for all the world.

We will examine how this ancient symbol speaks with urgent relevance to our modern ecological and spiritual crisis, offering a way to heal the wound of separation that has brought our civilisation to the brink.

THE ROOTS OF OUR CRISIS: A WORLD WITHOUT THE TREE

Before we step into the sacred grove, we must first understand why the World Tree symbol matters so profoundly to us today. As we explored in the introduction, we live in a time of converging crises. Our planet is in peril. The climate is destabilising. Species are vanishing. Our forests, the lungs of the Earth, are being destroyed at an alarming rate. Alongside this ecological collapse, there is a parallel collapse of meaning, community, and mental health. We are, as a culture, profoundly disconnected.

At the root of all these crises is a fundamental error in our worldview, an error that the ancient Celts never made.

We have come to see the world as a collection of separate, isolated objects rather than as a living, interconnected whole.

We see ourselves as standing apart from nature, as observers and exploiters rather than as participants and kin.

We have forgotten that we are not the masters of the earth, but its children.

We have cut down the World Tree in our collective imagination, and in doing so, we have lost our sense of belonging, our sense of the sacred, and our understanding of our place in the cosmos.

The symbol of the World Tree is the antidote to this poison of separation. It is a map of interconnectedness. It shows that the heavens, the earth, and the underworld are not separate realms but are woven together into a single, living tapestry. It shows that we are not isolated individuals but part of a great web of being that includes the ancestors who came before us, the community we live in now, and the generations yet to come. It shows that the divine is not distant or abstract but is present and flowing through every root, branch, and leaf of the great tree of existence.

To recover the symbol of the World Tree is to recover a way of seeing that can heal us. It is important to remember that we are rooted in the earth, that we stand in the present moment with strength and purpose, and that we reach for the heavens with hope and aspiration. It is important to remember that to harm the tree is to harm ourselves, and to honour the tree is to honour the sacred interconnectedness of all life. This is not a retreat into primitivism or superstition. It is a recovery of a profound ecological and spiritual wisdom that our ancestors knew in their bones, and that we, in our peril, must learn again.

THE GREAT PILLAR: THE CRANN BETHADH

In the centre of every early Irish settlement, from the smallest cluster of huts to the royal seat of a High King, stood a great, venerated tree. This was the Crann Bethadh (pronounced roughly "krawn ba-ha"), which translates to "Tree of Life." It was also known as the bile (BILL-eh), a sacred, ancient tree imbued with immense spiritual power.

This was not a decorative feature, not a pleasant bit of greenery to soften the landscape. It was the spiritual and social axis of the tribe. It was their living connection to the three worlds: the heavens above, the earth on which they lived, and the world of the ancestors and spirits below.

The Crann Bethadh was the tribe's symbol of its own sovereignty, security, and vitality. As long as the tree stood, the tribe would prosper. Its health was the health of the people. Its roots were the tribe's connection to its past, to the deep wisdom of the ancestors buried in the earth. Its trunk was the tribe's present, its strength and stability in the world, the solid foundation on which the community stood. Its branches were the tribe's connection to the future, to the heavens, and to divine blessing. The tree was, in a very real sense, the soul of the tribe made visible.

The inauguration of a king often took place at the sacred tree, for he was regarded as the human embodiment of the tree's role: to connect his people to the land, to the gods, and to one another. In some traditions, the king was ritually "married" to the land itself, represented by the goddess of sovereignty, and this sacred marriage was solemnised at the Crann Bethadh.

The tree witnessed the most important moments of the tribe's life: births, marriages, treaties, and the settling of disputes. It was the still point around which the entire community revolved.

So central was this tree to the tribe's identity that the most devastating act of war one tribe could commit against another was to cut down their Crann Bethadh. To do so was not just an act of ecological vandalism or a tactical military strike. It was an act of profound spiritual violation, a kind of cosmic murder. It was to sever the enemy's connection to their past, their power, and their gods.

It was to declare that they were no longer a people, that they had no right to the land, that their sovereignty was broken. The Irish annals, the monastic records of the kingdom's history, are filled with accounts of this very act, recorded with a tone of horror and grief. The felling of the Crann Bethadh was the ultimate desecration.

This central tree was not just a local symbol; it was a living map of the cosmos. The Celtic imagination, like many ancient cultures worldwide—from the Norse Yggdrasil to the Mayan Ceiba—envisioned the universe as structured around a great World Tree. This cosmic tree was the pillar that held up the sky, its roots delving deep into the earth, its branches brushing against the stars. It was the axis mundi, the world's axle, the cosmic centre around which everything else revolved. To understand this map is to understand the Celtic worldview, and to understand the Celtic worldview is to know how they could so readily embrace the Cross as the ultimate fulfilment of their deepest spiritual intuitions.

THE THREE WORLDS OF THE TREE

The World Tree was a ladder, a bridge, a living pathway that connected three distinct, yet interwoven, realms of existence. These were not seen as entirely separate places, like different countries on a map, but as different dimensions of reality, all accessible to those who knew how to travel between them—the shamans, the poets, the seers, the Druids, and the heroes of myth. To be a whole and integrated person was to live in conscious relationship with all three of these worlds. Let us explore each in turn.

1. The Roots and the Underworld (An Domhan Íochtarach)

The roots of the World Tree plunged deep into the earth, into the Underworld. We must set aside the modern Christian image of the underworld as a fiery hell of punishment, a place of eternal torment for the wicked. That is a later theological development, heavily influenced by Greek and Roman ideas. For the Celts, the Underworld was not a place of punishment; it was the source of all life. It was the realm of the ancestors, the place where the tribe's collective memory was stored. It was a world of wisdom, of dreams, and of the deep, feminine powers of creation. It was the womb from which all life emerged and to which it returned in the great cycle of death and rebirth.

At the base of the World Tree, there was often said to be a sacred well, the Well of Wisdom. The most famous of these in Irish mythology is the Well of Segais, from which the great rivers of Ireland—the Boyne, the Shannon, the Liffey—are said to flow. In this well lived the Salmon of Wisdom, who gained its knowledge by eating the nine hazelnuts of poetic inspiration that fell into the water from the Hazel tree growing beside the well. To drink from this well or to eat the salmon was to gain profound insight, poetry (imbas), and prophetic ability. This is the story of Fionn mac Cumhaill, the great hero who accidentally tasted the salmon and gained the gift of second sight.

This Underworld was also the realm of the Sidhe (pronounced "shee"), the faerie folk or people of the hollow hills. In later folklore, they became diminutive, whimsical beings, the stuff of children's stories. But in the older tales, they are the powerful, ancient inhabitants of the land, the pre-human gods and goddesses who retreated into the earth when the Milesians (the ancestors of the Irish) arrived. They are the Tuatha Dé Danann, the "People of the Goddess Danu," the guardians of the land's deep magic and memory.

They are not gone; they are beneath, waiting, watching, and occasionally breaking through into our world at the thin places and the liminal times. The roots of the World Tree were the gateway to their realm, the pathway into the deep memory of the land itself.

To journey to the Underworld was to seek the wisdom of the ancestors, to face the shadow, to confront death, and to be reborn. It was a descent into the unconscious, into the deep well of the soul. It was a dangerous journey, but a necessary one for anyone who sought true wisdom.

2. The Trunk and the Middle World (An Saol)

The trunk of the tree represented the Middle World, the world of humanity. It is the physical, manifest world that we experience every day. It is the realm of action, of community, of the challenges and joys of mortal life. The trunk is the strong, stable pillar that connects the deep wisdom of the roots with the soaring inspiration of the branches. It is here, in this middle realm, that we have the opportunity to integrate the energies of the worlds above and below. We are the trunk, grounded in the earth of our bodies and our past, but reaching for the sky of our spiritual aspirations.

The Middle World is the world of the *túath*, the tribe, the small kingdom. It is the world of the farmer ploughing his field, the blacksmith at his forge, the mother nursing her child, the bard reciting the old stories by the fire. It is the world of the seasons, of planting and harvest, of birth and death. It is the world of relationship, of obligation, of honour, and of law. The Druids, as we saw in Chapter 1, were the arbiters of this world, the ones who maintained the balance and ensured that the community lived in right relationship with the land, with each other, and with the gods.

To live well in the Middle World was to live with one's feet firmly planted on the earth, to be fully present in the body, to honour the cycles of nature, and to contribute to the well-being of the community. It was not a realm to be escaped or transcended, but a realm to be fully inhabited and honoured.

3. The Branches and the Upper World (An Domhan Uachtarach)

The highest branches of the World Tree reached into the heavens, the Upper World. This was the realm of the great gods and goddesses, the celestial beings. It was the source of divine inspiration, of intellect, of light, and of cosmic order. It was the home of the sun, the moon, and the stars, whose cycles governed the rhythms of life in the Middle World below. The Druids, as we learned, were master astronomers, tracking the movements of the heavens to create the calendar that governed the agricultural and ritual year.

Often, a great eagle or hawk, a creature that could soar to incredible heights and see the world with a divine perspective, was said to perch on the topmost branch of the tree. This bird was a messenger between the gods and humanity, a symbol of the far-seeing vision that comes from connection to the Upper World. To access the Upper World was to gain clarity, vision, and a connection to the divine mind. It was to receive the gift of *Imbas*, the poetic inspiration that allowed the Bard to see the truth and speak it with power.

The Upper World was the realm of aspiration, of ideals, of the divine blueprint for creation. It was the realm of the Aes Dána, the "people of the arts," the poets and visionaries who could perceive the patterns of the cosmos and bring them down into the Middle World through their words and their art.

For the pre-Christian Celt, to be a whole and balanced person was to live in conscious relationship with all three of these worlds. It was to be rooted in the wisdom of the ancestors, to live strongly and honourably in the present moment, and to be open to the inspiration of the heavens. And the symbol that held all of this together, the map that made sense of the entire cosmos, was the living, breathing, magnificent tree.

THE CROSS: THE NEW AND EVERLASTING CRANN BETHADH

Now, imagine you are a fifth-century Irish farmer. This image of the World Tree has shaped your entire spiritual imagination. You know in your bones that the most sacred thing in the universe is the great tree that connects the worlds. You have stood beneath the Crann Bethadh of your tribe. You have felt its power. You have seen your king inaugurated at its base. You have prayed to the gods through its branches. And then, a missionary arrives.

He does not come with an army. He does not come with threats or condemnation. He comes with a story. It is the story of a man who is also God, a man who willingly allowed himself to be crucified. And on that tree, he stretched out his arms and reconciled all three worlds. He descended to the dead, he walked the earth, and he ascended to the heavens. He is the bridge, the ladder, the ultimate World Tree.

This story would not have sounded alien. It would not have sounded like a foreign religion trying to displace your own. It would have sounded like the fulfilment of the deepest truth you had ever known. The Cross was not a foreign symbol; it was the ultimate Crann Bethadh, the tree that your ancestors had been waiting for, the tree that would never be cut down, the tree that would stand forever at the centre of the cosmos.

Let us look at the Cross through these Celtic eyes. The Christian story, seen through this lens, becomes a profound mapping onto the ancient cosmology. This is not a forced or artificial connection; it is a recognition of a deep, archetypal truth that resonates across cultures and across time.

The Roots of the Cross and the Redemption of the Underworld

The base of the Cross stands firmly on the earth, its wood a conduit to the world below. In the Christian story, after his death, Christ "descended to the dead." This is the event known as the Harrowing of Hell, a doctrine central to Eastern Orthodox Christianity and depicted in countless icons. But again, we must see this not as a raid on a place of torment, but as a journey to the realm of the ancestors, to the Underworld.

Christ went into the Underworld to proclaim his victory over death and to liberate the righteous souls who had been waiting for him—Adam, Eve, the prophets, all those who had lived before his time. He went to the very roots of humanity and brought his healing light. He drank from the well of death and transformed it into a fountain of life. The Celtic mind, which already regarded the Underworld as the realm of the ancestors and the source of wisdom, would have regarded this not as a strange new doctrine but as the ultimate act of ancestral healing. Christ went to the roots of the World Tree and healed them, ensuring that the wisdom of the past would flow into the present and the future.

St. Brigid, with her gentle, nurturing spirit, would have understood this profoundly. She, who honoured the goddess of the same name, who tended the sacred flame, who built her monastery at the Church of the Oak, knew that the old ways were not to be destroyed but to be brought under the cloak of Christ. The descent to the Underworld was not a conquest; it was a covering, a blessing, a bringing of light to the deep places. The ancestors were not forgotten; they were honoured and redeemed.

The Trunk of the Cross and the Embrace of the Middle World

The horizontal beam of the Cross is stretched out across the Middle World, the world of humanity. Christ's arms are not pinned back in defeat; they are opened wide in a gesture of universal embrace. On the Cross, he gathers all of humanity to himself. He stands at the centre of human history, the still point of the turning world. His suffering is not a private agony, but the suffering of all people in all times. His love is not for a select few, but for every soul in the Middle World.

The trunk of the old Crann Bethadh provided stability for the tribe; the trunk of the Cross provides salvation for the entire world. St. Patrick, standing on the Hill of Slane, lighting the Paschal fire, was declaring that the Cross was the new centre, the new axis around which all of life revolves. But he was not destroying the old centre; he was revealing its ultimate meaning. The fire of Beltaine, which celebrated the return of the sun and the renewal of life, was fulfilled in the fire of Easter, which celebrated the resurrection of Christ, the true Sun of Righteousness.

The Middle World is the world of the body, of the earth, of the community. And the Cross, far from being a symbol of escape from this world, is a symbol of God's total commitment to it. The Incarnation—the belief that God became flesh—is the ultimate affirmation of the Middle World. God did not disdain the earth; he entered it. He accepted the body; he took one on. He did not stand apart from human suffering; he embraced it on the Cross. This is the message that the Celtic soul, which already honoured the earth as sacred, could receive with joy.

The Top of the Cross and the Union with the Upper World

The top of the Cross reaches towards the heavens. Christ's head, even when bowed in death, is the link to the Upper World. His final words are a prayer to his Father: "Into your hands I commit my spirit." He is the eagle on the topmost branch, the one who sees all things from a divine perspective. Through his perfect obedience, he reopens the path to the Upper World that had been closed by human sin. He is the ladder that Jacob dreamed of, on which the angels of God are ascending and descending. He is the bridge between heaven and earth, the one in whom the divine and the human are perfectly and eternally united.

For the Druids, who studied the stars and sought the divine mind, Christ is the ultimate revelation of that mind. He is the Logos, the divine reason through whom all things were made. To know him is to know the pattern of the cosmos, the blueprint of creation. St. Columba, the poet-monk, understood this when he declared, "Christ is my Druid." Christ is the ultimate wisdom-keeper, the one who knows the hidden things, the one who connects the Upper World of divine inspiration with the Middle World of human life.

THE HIGH CROSSES: THE TREE CARVED IN STONE

This understanding of the Cross as the Tree of Life is not just a poetic metaphor or a theological abstraction. It is written in stone all across the Celtic lands. The great High Crosses of Ireland and Scotland are perhaps the most magnificent artistic expression of this integrated theology. These are not the simple, stark crucifixes of later Catholic tradition, the emaciated figure on two bare beams. They are massive, intricate sculptures, standing sometimes fifteen feet tall or more, covered in swirling knotwork and biblical scenes. They are, in essence, a Christian Crann Bethadh, telling the entire story of salvation with the trunk, branches, and roots of the new World Tree.

A circle, a symbol of the sun, eternity, and the cosmos, often surrounds the cross. This is the Celtic Cross, and it is a perfect fusion of the old and the new. The circle is an ancient symbol of the sun, venerated by the Celts for millennia. But now, the sun is held within the Cross, showing that Christ is the true Sun, the light of the world. The cross itself seems not to be dead wood, but to be flowering, branching out with life. The intricate knotwork that covers the surface is not mere decoration; it is a visual representation of the interconnectedness of all things, the endless weaving of the divine through creation.

On the faces of the High Crosses, we see scenes from the Bible: the sacrifice of Isaac, the three young men in the fiery furnace, Daniel in the lion's den, the crucifixion, and the resurrection. But we also see scenes that are uniquely Celtic: spirals, interlaced animals, and patterns that echo the art of the pre-Christian La Tène culture. The crosses are a visual sermon, a stone book that tells the story of how the old and the new are woven together. They stand in the landscape, often at the sites of ancient monasteries, as enduring witnesses to the faith of the Celtic Christians, a faith that saw the Cross not as a symbol of death, but as the ultimate Tree of Life, flowering with redemption for all the world.

THE FLOWERING WOOD: SAINTS, TREES, AND THE LIVING CROSS

This reverence for the tree as a sacred symbol did not end with the acceptance of the Cross. It continued to flourish within Celtic Christianity, creating a faith that was uniquely attuned to the sacredness of the woods. The lives of the Celtic saints are filled with stories that reveal this deep, abiding love for trees. This love is not sentimental or merely aesthetic, but is rooted in a profound theological conviction that the natural world is a primary revelation of God's presence.

We have already met St. Brigid of Kildare, arguably the most beloved saint in Ireland after Patrick, a figure who perfectly embodies the fusion of the pagan and the Christian. The goddess Brigid was a daughter of the Dagda, one of the chief gods of the Tuatha Dé Danann, and was a patroness of poetry, healing, and smithcraft. The Christian St. Brigid founded a monastery at Cill Dara, meaning "the Church of the Oak." It was a double monastery for men and women, built in and around a sacred grove of oaks that was likely a Druidic centre long before her time.

Brigid did not cut down the sacred trees; she made them the heart of her Christian community.

She saw the strength and wisdom of the oak as a reflection of the strength and wisdom of Christ. Her monastery was a living embodiment of the principle that the old ways were not to be destroyed, but to be brought under the protective cloak of the new faith. The oak grove became a place of Christian prayer, but it never ceased to be a place of profound natural holiness.

St. Kevin of Glendalough, a sixth-century hermit, was so attuned to the natural world that the stories about him seem to blur the line between man and nature. One famous story recounts that he was praying with his arms outstretched in the shape of a cross when a blackbird landed in his open palm, built a nest, and laid her eggs. So committed was Kevin to not disturbing this act of creation that he remained in that position for weeks until the eggs hatched and the fledglings flew away. For Kevin, the tree of his own body became a source of life and shelter, a living embodiment of the life-giving Cross. He became the World Tree, his feet rooted in the earth, his body the trunk, his outstretched arms the branches that sheltered the creatures of God.

These stories, and countless others like them, reveal a Christianity that did not see nature as something to be subdued, exploited, or escaped, but as a primary revelation of God's presence. The forest was not a dangerous wilderness to be cleared; it was a cathedral, a place of prayer and encounter with the divine. The trees were not just timber, resources to be harvested; they were companions in prayer, fellow creatures in the great web of being. The rustling of the leaves was the whisper of the Holy Spirit.

This is the legacy of the Crann Bethadh, a legacy that sees the wood of the Cross not as a symbol of an ancient, brutal execution, but as a living, flowering branch of the great tree that is the cosmos itself, a tree whose sap is the very life of God.

THE PRACTICE: JOURNEYING ON THE WORLD TREE

We have explored the deep symbolism of the World Tree. We have seen how it formed the spiritual backbone of the ancient Celtic world and how it was transformed into the life-giving Cross of Christ. We have seen how it speaks to our modern crisis, offering us a map of interconnectedness to heal the wound of separation. Now, it is time to make this journey with our hearts. The World Tree is not just an ancient myth or a historical curiosity; it is an archetype, a living map of consciousness that exists within each of us. Your own body, your own soul, is a World Tree. You have roots that connect you to the earth and to your past. You have a trunk that stands in the present moment. And you have branches that reach for the heavens and for your highest potential.

This chapter's practice is a guided visualisation to help you travel along your own inner World Tree, to connect with the wisdom of the three worlds that live within you.

A Visualisation of Your Inner World Tree

1. Prepare Your Space: Find a quiet place where you will not be disturbed for at least twenty minutes. Sit comfortably, either in a chair with your feet flat on the floor or cross-legged on a cushion. Close your eyes. Take several deep, slow breaths, allowing your body to relax and your mind to settle.

2. Become the Tree: Imagine that you are a great, ancient tree. Feel your spine as the trunk, strong and stable. Feel your legs and your seat as the roots, extending down into the earth. Feel your arms and the crown of your head as the branches, reaching up towards the sky. You are not just visualising a tree; you are becoming the tree. You are the World Tree, the axis of your own cosmos.

3. Journey to the Roots (The Underworld): Begin to send your awareness down into your roots. Feel them extending deep, deep into the earth. As you descend, the world around you becomes darker, quieter, cooler. You are entering the Underworld, the realm of the ancestors and the deep unconscious. At the base of your roots, you find a well, the Well of Wisdom. The water is dark and still, but it is not frightening; it is peaceful, full of ancient knowing. Ask the well: "What wisdom from my past do I need to remember? What have I forgotten that I need to reclaim?" Listen. An image, a word, a feeling may arise. Receive it with gratitude. When you are ready, begin to draw the water of the well up through your roots, feeling it nourish and strengthen you.

4. Return to the Trunk (The Middle World): Bring your awareness back to your trunk, to your spine, to the present moment. Feel the strength and stability of your body. Feel your connection to the earth beneath you and the air around you. This is the Middle World, the world of action and relationship. Ask yourself: "What is mine to do in this world? How can I live with strength, integrity, and love in the present moment?" Listen. Feel the answer in your body, in your heart. You are here, now, fully present, fully alive.

5. Journey to the Branches (The Upper World): Now, send your awareness up through your trunk and into your branches. Feel them reaching up, up, up towards the sky. As you ascend, the world becomes brighter, lighter, more expansive. You are entering the Upper World, the realm of divine inspiration and vision. At the top of your highest branch, you see a great light, the light of the divine. Ask the light: "What is my highest calling?

What vision do I need to guide my life?" Listen. An image, a word, a feeling may arise. Receive it with gratitude. Feel the light pouring down through your branches, through your trunk, and into your roots, filling your entire being with divine energy.

6. Integration: Now, feel all three worlds within you at once. You are rooted in the wisdom of the past. You are standing strong in the present. You are reaching for the vision of the future. You are the World Tree. You are the bridge between heaven and earth. You are whole. Take a few deep breaths, feeling this integration. When you are ready, gently open your eyes.

7. Journaling: Take a few moments to write down what you experienced. What wisdom did the well offer you? What is yours to do in the Middle World? What vision did the light reveal? How can you live more fully as the World Tree in your daily life?

This practice is a gift from the ancient Celts, a way of remembering that we are not separate from the cosmos, but are an integral part of it. We are the tree. And the tree, ultimately, is the Cross, the place where all the worlds meet, where all is reconciled, and where the love of God flows freely to heal and to bless.

In our next chapter, we will move from the great World Tree to the individual trees of the forest. We will explore Ogham, the ancient Celtic tree alphabet, and examine how each tree was regarded as a teacher, a guide, and a bearer of specific wisdom for the soul's journey.

Chapter 4:

The Ogham: The Whispering Alphabet of the Trees

We have journeyed deep into the grove of wisdom, seeking the heart of the Celtic spiritual imagination.

We have met the Druids, the ancient Keepers of the Grove, and witnessed the great integration that allowed their earth-honouring wisdom to be baptised into a vibrant and unique form of Christianity.

We have stood in awe before the Crann Bethadh, the great World Tree, and seen its ultimate fulfilment in the life-giving Cross of Christ.

Throughout, we have heard a constant refrain: the natural world, and trees in particular, are not a silent backdrop to the human drama; they are primary characters, sacred teachers, and living revelations of the divine.

Now, we attune our ears to a more specific frequency. We move from the universal symbol of the World Tree, which holds the entire cosmos, to the particular, individual spirits of the trees that make up the forest. If the World Tree is the great cathedral of the Celtic soul, we are now leaving the main nave to visit the side chapels, each dedicated to a different saint, each with its own story, its own energy, its own medicine for the soul.

For the ancient Celts did not just see "the forest"; they saw the Oak, the Ash, the Hazel, and the Birch. They believed that each tree had its own personality, its own wisdom, its own song to sing in the great chorus of creation.

They developed a system for encoding this wisdom, a way to listen to the whispering of the leaves and translate it into a form that could be learned, contemplated, and passed down through generations. This system is the Ogham.

At first glance, Ogham (pronounced OH-am) is simply an alphabet, an ancient script used in Ireland and other Celtic lands. But to see it as only that is like seeing the Book of Kells as merely a collection of letters, or seeing a cathedral as just a pile of stones. The Ogham is far more. It is a calendar, a system of divination, a school of philosophy, and a spiritual path, all encoded in a series of simple lines carved into stone and wood. It is an alphabet in which each letter is named for a tree, and learning the alphabet is to learn the forest's sacred properties. It is the language of the Grove itself, the very bones of the trees made into a script.

In this chapter, we will be initiated into the secrets of this whispering alphabet. We will examine its history, structure, and meaning. We will meet each of the twenty primary trees of the Ogham, listen to their stories, and learn the wisdom they have to offer. This is not just an academic exercise. It is a practical path to deepening your own communion with the sacred life of the earth, a way to fulfil the promise we made in the introduction: to heal the wound of separation by learning to see the world not as a collection of objects, but as a communion of subjects. It is learning to read the book of nature in its own native tongue.

THE BONES OF THE TREES: HISTORY AND STRUCTURE OF THE OGHAM

The Ogham is the earliest form of writing found in Ireland. It consists of a series of straight lines and notches carved along a central stem line, much like the branches growing from a tree trunk. There are approximately 400 surviving examples of Ogham inscriptions, most carved vertically along the edges of large standing stones, primarily in southern Ireland but also in Wales, Scotland, and the Isle of Man. These inscriptions are typically memorials that record a person's name and lineage, for example, "Of Maqqi-Decceddas, son of the Torani." They date from roughly the 4th to the 6th centuries AD, a period that overlaps precisely with the arrival and spread of Christianity in Ireland—the very era of Patrick and Brigid.

This timing is not coincidental. The Ogham stands at the threshold, at the liminal moment when the old ways and the new faith meet, recognise each other, and begin their great dance of integration. It is a script that was likely created by the Druids or the learned class of the fili (poets) who succeeded them, but it was preserved and transmitted by Christian monks. It is, in its very existence, a testament to the Brigidine principle of covering rather than conquering, of honouring the wisdom of the ancestors while bringing it into the new dispensation.

The origin of the Ogham is a subject of scholarly debate. Was it an indigenous Irish invention, created by a genius who understood the principles of Latin grammar but wanted a script uniquely suited to the Irish language and the Irish soul? Was it a secret code, developed by the Druids to communicate in a way that the Romans could not understand, a way to preserve their wisdom in a time of threat? The legendary origin story, recorded in the 14th-century Book of Ballymote, attributes its invention to the Scythian king Fenius Farsaid, who supposedly created it after the fall of the Tower of Babel. But its true creator is lost to the mists of time, hidden in the deep memory of the land.

What is clear is that it was designed by someone with a deep and intimate knowledge of both language and the natural world, someone who saw the connection between the structure of speech and the structure of the forest, someone who understood that to name a thing is to know it, and to know the trees is to know the very alphabet of creation.

THE STRUCTURE: FOUR FAMILIES, TWENTY TREES

The script itself is beautifully logical and straightforward, a perfect marriage of form and function. It is based on a series of one to five lines, arranged in one of four ways relative to a central stem line. Imagine the edge of a stone or a wooden staff as the trunk of a tree, and the letters as branches growing from it. The script is divided into four groups, or families, of five letters each. These families are called aicmí (singular: aicme, pronounced ACK-meh).

The four aicmí are:

1. Aicme Beithe (the Birch Group): One to five straight lines extending to the right of the stem-line, like branches reaching toward the rising sun, the east, the direction of new beginnings.

2. Aicme hÚatha (the Hawthorn Group): One to five straight lines extending to the left of the stem-line, like branches reaching toward the west, the direction of the setting sun, the Otherworld, the realm of challenge and mystery.

3. Aicme Muine (the Vine/Bramble Group): One to five angled lines that cross the stem-line diagonally, like vines that weave and connect, that spiral and entangle.

4. Aicme Ailme (the Pine/Fir Group): One to five notches or short straight lines placed directly on the stem-line itself, like the marks of time, the rings of the tree, the vertical ascent toward the heavens.

This gives a total of twenty primary letters, twenty trees, and twenty teachers. Later, a fifth group, the Forfeda, or "extra letters," was added in the manuscript tradition to account for sounds from the Latin alphabet that had no equivalent in Irish. Still, the original, core system comprises these twenty characters, each a tree, each a world of meaning.

THE COSMOLOGICAL LINK: THE OGHAM AND THE THREE WORLDS

Here is where the Ogham reveals its most profound wisdom. The structure of the alphabet is not arbitrary; it reflects the cosmology we explored in the previous chapter. The Ogham is a map of the World Tree, and each aicme corresponds to a different dimension of existence.

The Aicme Beithe (Birch Group), with its branches reaching to the right, toward the dawn, represents the energies of the Upper World—new beginnings, purification, vision, and the light of divine inspiration. These are the trees that help us reach upward, that connect us to the heavens, that give us hope and clarity.

The Aicme hÚatha (Hawthorn Group), with its branches reaching to the left, toward the dusk, represents the energies of the Underworld—the Otherworld, the realm of the ancestors, the deep wisdom that comes from facing challenges, from crossing thresholds, from descending into the well of the soul. These are the trees that help us go deep, that connect us to the hidden realms, that give us strength and sovereignty.

The Aicme Muine (Vine Group), with its diagonal, crossing lines, represents the energies of the Middle World—the world of growth, connection, harvest, and sometimes entanglement. These are the trees that help us navigate the complexities of human life, that teach us about relationships, abundance, and the spiral dance of existence.

The Aicme Ailme (Pine Group), with its marks directly on the stem-line, represents the vertical axis itself, the spine of the World Tree, the ascent from earth to heaven, the qualities of endurance, perspective, and the long view. These are the trees that help us stand tall, that give us the strength to endure, that connect us to the eternal.

This is the Brigidine lens applied to the Ogham. Just as Brigid did not destroy the sacred oak grove but built her monastery within it, the Ogham accepts the old cosmology but encodes it, preserves it, and brings it into the new faith. The alphabet is a cloak, gently covering the ancient wisdom, keeping it safe, keeping it alive. To learn the Ogham is to learn the language of integration, to speak fluently in both the old tongue and the new.

THE LIVING SCRIPT: OGHAM AS DIVINATION AND SPIRITUAL PRACTICE

While the stone inscriptions are our primary archaeological evidence, the Irish manuscript tradition makes it clear that the Ogham was also carved on wood. The Auraicept na n-Éces ("The Scholars' Primer"), a medieval Irish text on grammar and poetry, describes how the letters were carved into wands of yew or other woods for divination and magical purposes. A set of Ogham staves would be cast, and the letters that appeared would be interpreted to answer a question or to provide guidance for a decision. This is the deeper, more spiritual use of the Ogham that we will now explore. We are not just learning an ancient alphabet; we are learning a system of spiritual direction, a way to ask the trees for their wisdom, a way to listen to the whisper of the grove. Each tree is a teacher, and each offers a specific lesson for the soul's journey.

In the sections that follow, we will meet the twenty trees of the four aicmí, one by one, and listen to the wisdom they whisper. As you read, I invite you to do more than just absorb the information. Try to feel the energy of each tree. Which ones resonate with you? Which ones challenge you? Which ones are calling to you right now, in this moment of your life? This is the beginning of your own conversation with the grove.

THE FOUR AICMÍ: A FOREST OF WISDOM

What follows is a journey through the twenty trees of the Ogham. For each tree, we will explore its name, its letter, its core symbolism, and the spiritual lesson it offers. As you read, I invite you to do more than absorb the information. Try to feel the energy of each tree. Which ones resonate with you? Which ones challenge you? This is the beginning of your own conversation with the grove.

AICME BEITHE: THE BIRCH GROUP (THE UPPER WORLD - NEW BEGINNINGS AND VISION)

This first group represents the foundational energies of life, the qualities needed to begin a journey, the light of the Upper World breaking through.

1. Beith (Birch) - B

Symbolism: New Beginnings, Purification, Hope, Youth

The Birch is the pioneer tree, the first to return after devastation. It is among the first trees to regrow in a forest cleared by fire or storm. Its white bark shines like a beacon of hope in the darkness of winter, like the first light of dawn breaking over the hills. It is the tree of new beginnings, of starting fresh, of washing away the old to make way for the new. In the Ogham, Beith is the very first letter, the alpha, the beginning of the journey. It represents the courage to take the first step, the promise of renewal, and the purity of a fresh start. The Birch teaches us that no matter how dark the night has been, the dawn will come. The spiritual lesson of the Birch is to let go of the past, to cleanse yourself of regret and negativity, and to step forward into the future with the hope and resilience of a young sapling reaching for the light.

2. Luis (Rowan) – L

Symbolism: Protection, Insight, Vision, Warding off Negativity

The Rowan, with its bright red berries like drops of blood or fire, has been a tree of protection in Celtic lands for millennia. Its branches were hung over doorways to ward off evil spirits and malevolent magic. Its wood was used to make divining rods and Druidic staffs. The Rowan is the tree of the seer, the one who can see beyond the veil, who can perceive the hidden dangers and the hidden blessings. It offers spiritual protection and enhances intuition. The lesson of the Rowan is to trust your inner sight, to pay attention to your dreams and intuitions, and to know that you are protected on your spiritual path. It teaches us to be vigilant, to guard our energy from those who would drain or harm us, and to seek the hidden wisdom that lies just beyond the surface of things. The Rowan stands at the threshold, a guardian, a watcher, a friend to those who walk the path between the worlds.

3. Fearn (Alder) – F

Symbolism: Foundation, Strength, Passion, The Oracle

The Alder loves water. It grows along riverbanks and in wetlands, its roots holding the soil together and providing a stable foundation even in the shifting, flowing world of the river. Its wood is remarkably water-resistant; much of Venice is built on Alder piles driven deep into the lagoon. This gives it symbolic significance as a symbol of strength, reliability, and the ability to stand firm amid change. When cut, the white wood of the Alder turns a fiery red, as if it is bleeding, linking it to passion, sacrifice, and the fire of life that flows through all living things. The head of the mythical giant Bran the Blessed, a great oracle and king, was said to be hidden in a place where Alders grew, still speaking prophecy even after death. The lesson of the Alder is to build your life on a strong foundation, to connect with your passions, and to trust the oracular voice of your own soul. It teaches that true strength comes not from rigidity, but from being grounded in the flow of life, from having roots that go deep into the watery realms of emotion and intuition.

4. Saille (Willow) – S

Symbolism: Flexibility, Emotion, The Moon, Imagination

Like the Alder, the Willow loves water, but its energy is very different. Where the Alder is about foundation and strength, the Willow is all about flexibility and surrender. Its branches can be bent and woven into almost any shape without breaking. It is deeply connected to the cycles of the moon, to the tides, and to the ebb and flow of human emotion. It is the tree of the poet and the dreamer, the one who can navigate the watery realms of the imagination, the one who can cry and grieve and then bend back toward the light. The lesson of the Willow is to learn the art of surrender, to bend without breaking in the face of life's storms. It teaches us to honour our emotions, to let the tears flow when necessary, to connect with our creative and intuitive gifts, and to find strength not in resistance but in flexibility. The Willow whispers, "You do not need to be hard to be strong. You can be soft, and supple, and still endure."

5. Nuin (Ash) – N

Symbolism: Connection, The World Tree, The Link Between Worlds, Justice

The Ash is one of the three great sacred trees of the Celts, along with the Oak and the Yew. It is often identified as the World Tree itself, the Crann Bethadh, the cosmic axis. Its roots go deep into the Underworld, its trunk stands firm in the Middle World, and its branches reach high into the Upper World. It connects all three realms. It is the tree of connection, of seeing the big picture, of understanding how everything is related—how your past informs your present, how your present shapes your future, how the earth and the heavens are woven together in a single tapestry. Its wood is both strong and pliable, used for the shafts of spears and the handles of tools, for the things that connect human intention to action. The lesson of the Ash is to see the connections in your own life, to understand how your past, present, and future are interwoven. It teaches us to act with a sense of justice and balance, to see ourselves not as isolated individuals, but as bridges between the earth and the heavens, between the ancestors and the descendants, between the human and the divine.

AICME HÚATHA: THE HAWTHORN GROUP (THE UNDERWORLD - CHALLENGE AND SOVEREIGNTY)

This second group represents challenges, obstacles, thresholds, and the powerful forces of the Otherworld. These are the trees that test us, that make us strong, that give us sovereignty over our own souls.

6. hÚath (Hawthorn) – H

Symbolism: The Faerie Tree, Thresholds, The Otherworld, Challenge

The Hawthorn is a tree of immense power and paradox. Its beautiful white blossoms, which appear in May, are a sign of fertility and the coming of summer, a celebration of life. But its sharp thorns are a warning, a defence, a reminder that the sacred is not always safe or comfortable. It is known as the Faerie Tree, a gateway to the Otherworld, and it is considered terrible luck—even dangerous—to cut one down. The Hawthorn stands at the threshold between this world and the next, between the tame and the wild, between the known and the unknown. It represents a challenge, a test, or a period of enforced waiting. The lesson of the Hawthorn is to respect boundaries, both your own and those of others. It teaches us to be patient, to prepare for a spiritual initiation, and to recognise that sometimes the most significant growth comes from confronting a thorny obstacle that forces us to pause, re-evaluate our path, and seek permission before proceeding. The Hawthorn guards the gate. You may not pass until you are ready.

7. Duir (Oak) – D

Symbolism: Strength, Endurance, Sovereignty, The King of the Forest

The Oak is the undisputed king of the forest, the most sacred tree of the Druids. The word "Druid" itself may derive from *dru-wid*, meaning "Oak-Knower" or "Oak-Seer." The Oak represents immense strength, stability, and endurance. It can live for a thousand years, its deep roots holding it firm against any storm, its massive trunk a pillar of the forest. It is the tree of the sovereign, the leader, the one who provides protection and security for others. It is a doorway to inner strength and courage. The Oak teaches us that true sovereignty is not about dominating others; it is about ruling yourself, about standing tall in your truth, about being so deeply rooted in your integrity that no storm can shake you. The lesson of the Oak is to find your own inner sovereignty, to claim your power, and to be a source of strength and shelter for your community. It teaches that true power comes not from force or aggression, but from deep-rooted integrity, from knowing who you are and standing firm in that knowledge.

8. Tinne (Holly) – T

Symbolism: The Holly King, Action, Protection, The Warrior Spirit

If the Oak is the king of the summer, the Holly is the king of the winter. It remains green and vibrant when all the other trees are bare, a defiant splash of life in the darkest time of the year. Its sharp, spiky leaves are a powerful symbol of protection and defence. Its red berries are a promise that life endures, even in the heart of winter. The Holly is the tree of the spiritual warrior, the one who knows when to fight and when to defend. It represents the energy of focused action, of courage in the face of a challenge, and of the will to fight for what is right. The lesson of the Holly is to take action, to be assertive, and to defend your principles and your boundaries. It teaches us to channel our anger and passion into constructive, honourable deeds, to stand up for the weak, and to know that sometimes love requires us to be fierce. The Holly does not seek conflict, but it does not shrink from it either.

9. Coll (Hazel) – C

Symbolism: Wisdom, Divination, Intuition, Poetry

The Hazel is the tree of wisdom and poetic inspiration, the tree of the imbas, the sacred fire of insight. As we saw in the last chapter, the nine nuts of poetic wisdom fell from the Hazel tree into the Well of Segais, feeding the Salmon of Wisdom. To know Hazel is to gain deep insight, creativity, and the gift of prophecy. Hazelwood is the traditional material for divining rods, for dowsing for water, for seeking what is hidden beneath the surface. The lesson of the Hazel is to seek wisdom within oneself, to trust one's intuition, and to open oneself to the flow of creative inspiration. It teaches that wisdom is not something you acquire through force or study alone; it is something you receive when you are quiet and receptive, when you sit by the well and wait for the nuts to fall. The Hazel whispers: "Be still. Listen. The answers you seek are already within you."

10. Quert (Apple) – Q

Symbolism: The Silver Bough, The Otherworld Journey, Love, Healing

The Apple tree, notably the wild Apple, is another gateway to the Otherworld, a tree of magic and mystery. In Celtic myth, a hero is often lured to the Otherworld by a beautiful faerie woman carrying a silver branch of an apple tree that bears blossoms and fruit at the same time, a symbol of a land where time does not flow as it does in our world, a land of eternal youth, beauty, and healing. The island of Avalon, the "Isle of Apples," is the place where King Arthur was taken to be healed of his wounds. The Apple is also a tree of love and relationships, of the heart's deepest desires. The lesson of Apple is to open your heart to love, to embark on the inner journey of healing and self-discovery, and to choose the path of beauty and wholeness. It teaches that the Otherworld is not a distant place; it is a dimension of reality that is always available to us if we are willing to follow the silver bough, to take the risk of love, to seek the healing that our souls long for.

AICME MUINE: THE VINE/BRAMBLE GROUP (THE MIDDLE WORLD - GROWTH AND CONNECTION)

This third group represents the energies of growth, connection, harvest, and, at times, entanglement. These are the trees of the Middle World, the world of human relationships and complexity.

11. Muin (Vine/Bramble) – M

Symbolism: The Harvest, Abundance, Entanglement, The Spiral

The original meaning of Muin is debated among scholars; it may refer to the grapevine (though grapes are not native to Ireland) or to the Bramble (Blackberry), which is abundant in the Irish landscape. Both carry a similar energy. They grow in a spiral, reaching and connecting, weaving through the forest. They produce a rich harvest—wine from the grape, sweet berries from the bramble—but they can also create a thorny, tangled thicket that is difficult to navigate. Muin represents the joy of the harvest, the abundance that comes from hard work and patience, but also the danger of getting entangled in the complexities of life, in relationships that bind rather than free, in addictions and compulsions. The lesson of Muin is to celebrate your successes, to enjoy the fruits of your labour, but also to be mindful of the situations and relationships that might be holding you back or trapping you. It teaches the importance of finding clarity amidst complexity, of knowing when to prune, when to harvest, and when to walk away from the thicket.

12. Gort (Ivy) – G

Symbolism: The Spiral Path, Persistence, Connection, The Labyrinth

The Ivy is a tree that is not a tree; it is a vine that climbs, that spirals, that connects. It can grow up the trunk of an oak and reach heights it could never achieve on its own. It is a symbol of persistence, of the spiral path of spiritual growth, of the labyrinth that leads to the centre. The Ivy teaches us that growth is not always a straight line; sometimes we must spiral, circle back, and revisit old lessons at a deeper level. It also teaches the importance of connection and support; we do not have to do everything alone. We can lean on others, we can climb together, we can reach heights we could never achieve in isolation. The lesson of the Ivy is to trust the spiral, to be persistent, and to honour the connections that support your growth.

13. nGéadal (Reed/Broom) – nG

Symbolism: Direction, Clarity, The Arrow, Purification

The Reed grows straight and tall in the wetlands, a perfect shaft for an arrow. It represents direction, clarity of purpose, and the ability to cut through confusion and reach your target. The Broom, another possible meaning, was used to sweep, to clear away the old and make space for the new. Both carry an energy of purification and focus. The lesson of the Reed is to find your direction, to clarify your purpose, and to move toward your goal with focus and determination. It teaches that sometimes we need to clear away the clutter, both external and internal, to see the path clearly. The Reed whispers, "Know where you are going. Aim true. Do not be distracted."

14. Straif (Blackthorn) – St

Symbolism: The Dark Half of the Year, Fate, Necessity, The Thorn of Awakening

The Blackthorn is the dark twin of the Hawthorn. Where the Hawthorn blooms white in May, the Blackthorn blooms white in the depths of winter, often while snow is still on the ground. Its thorns are even sharper and more dangerous. It is the tree of fate, of necessity, of the challenges that we cannot avoid, the dark night of the soul that forces us to confront our shadow. The Blackthorn represents the difficult lessons, the painful initiations, the losses that break us open. But it also represents the strength that comes from enduring those trials. The lesson of the Blackthorn is to accept what cannot be changed, to face your fate with courage, and to know that the thorn that pierces you is also the thorn that awakens you. It teaches that sometimes the greatest gifts come wrapped in the darkest packages.

15. Ruis (Elder) – R

Symbolism: The Crone, Endings, Transformation, The Threshold of Death and Rebirth

The Elder is the tree of the Crone, the wise woman, the one who stands at the threshold of death and rebirth. It is a tree of endings, but also of transformation. Its berries can be made into a healing wine, but its wood was traditionally never burned, for it was sacred to the faerie folk and to the goddess. The Elder teaches us that every ending is also a beginning, that death is not the opposite of life but a part of it, and that the wisdom of the Crone is the wisdom of letting go. The lesson of the Elder is to honour the cycles of life, to release what no longer serves you, and to trust the process of transformation. It teaches that the end of one chapter is the beginning of another, and that the most incredible wisdom comes from having lived through many seasons.

AICME AILME: THE PINE/FIR GROUP (THE VERTICAL AXIS - ENDURANCE AND PERSPECTIVE)

This fourth group represents the vertical axis of the World Tree, the qualities of endurance, perspective, and the long view. These are the trees that help us stand tall and see far.

16. Ailm (Pine/Fir) – A

Symbolism: Perspective, The Long View, Endurance, The Evergreen

The Pine and the Fir are evergreen trees that remain green and vital throughout the year, symbols of endurance and eternal life. They grow tall and straight, reaching for the sky, offering a perspective from above. The lesson of the Ailm is to take the long view, to see your life from a higher perspective, to understand that the challenges of this moment are part of a much larger pattern. It teaches endurance, patience, and the ability to remain green and hopeful even in the darkest times. The Pine whispers: "Stand tall. Breathe deep. You are stronger than you know."

17. Onn (Gorse/Furze) – O

Symbolism: Gathering, Community, The Hearth Fire, Warmth

The Gorse is a spiky, golden-flowered shrub that blooms almost year-round, even in winter. Its flowers smell like coconut and honey. It was traditionally gathered as fuel for the hearth, providing warmth and light to the home. The Gorse represents the gathering of resources, the warmth of community, and the light that sustains us through the dark times. The lesson of the Gorse is to gather what you need, to build your hearth fire, to create warmth and welcome for yourself and others. It teaches that even in the coldest season, there is light and warmth to be found if you know where to look.

18. Úr (Heather) – U

Symbolism: Passion, Romance, The Moorland, Solitude and Community

The Heather covers the moorlands in a carpet of purple, a symbol of wild beauty and passion. It is associated with romance, wild places, and the balance between solitude and community. Bees make their honey from Heather, a sweet gift from the wild. Heather's lesson is to honour your passions, to seek beauty in the wild places, and to find balance between time alone and time with others. It teaches that passion is not something to be tamed, but something to be honoured and expressed.

19. Eadhadh (Aspen/Poplar) – E

Symbolism: Endurance, Overcoming Fear, The Trembling Tree, Communication

The Aspen is known as the "trembling tree" because its leaves flutter and shake in the slightest breeze, creating a whispering sound. It is a tree of communication, of overcoming fear, and of endurance. The Aspen teaches us to speak our truth, even when our voice trembles, to communicate clearly, and to know that fear is natural but need not stop us. It teaches that endurance is not about being fearless; it is about acting despite the fear.

20. Iodhadh (Yew) – I

Symbolism: Death and Rebirth, Eternity, The Ancestors, Transformation

The Yew is the most sacred and mysterious tree of all. It can live for thousands of years, its trunk becoming hollow with age, but still producing new growth. It is the tree of death and rebirth, of eternity, of the ancestors. It was planted in graveyards, a guardian of the threshold between life and death. The Yew teaches us that death is not an ending but a transformation, that the ancestors are not gone but are present in the land, and that we are part of a continuity that stretches back to the beginning of time and forward to the end. The lesson of the Yew is to honour the ancestors, to face your own mortality with courage, and to know that you are part of something eternal.

THE PRACTICE: WRITING YOUR NAME IN OGHAM

We have journeyed through the twenty trees of the Ogham, listening to their wisdom, feeling their energy. Now it is time to make this knowledge personal, to bring it into your own life in a tangible way. This chapter's practice is simple but profound: you will write your own name in Ogham.

This is not just a creative exercise. In the Celtic tradition, knowing someone's true name conferred power and a deep connection to their essence. Your name is not just a label; it is a sound, a vibration, a key to your soul. To write your name in the alphabet of the trees is to claim your connection to the forest, to the ancestors, to the deep wisdom of the earth. It is to say: "I am part of this story. I belong to the grove."

HOW TO WRITE YOUR NAME IN OGHAM

Step 1: Transliterate Your Name

The Ogham alphabet corresponds to the sounds of the Irish language, but it can be adapted to write any name.

Here is a simple guide:

• B = Beith (Birch)

• L = Luis (Rowan)

• F or V = Fearn (Alder)

• S = Saille (Willow)

• N = Nuin (Ash)

- H = hÚath (Hawthorn)

- D = Duir (Oak)

- T = Tinne (Holly)

- C or K = Coll (Hazel)

- Q = Quert (Apple)

- M = Muin (Vine)

- G = Gort (Ivy)

- nG = nGéadal (Reed)

- St or Z = Straif (Blackthorn)

- R = Ruis (Elder)

- A = Ailm (Pine)

- O = Onn (Gorse)

- U = Úr (Heather)

- E = Eadhadh (Aspen)

- I or Y = Iodhadh (Yew)

For sounds not directly represented (like J, P, W, X), you can use the closest equivalent or use the Forfeda (extra letters) if you wish to research them further.

Step 2: Draw the Ogham Script

On a piece of paper, draw a vertical line down the centre. This is your stem-line, the trunk of your tree. Now, for each letter of your name, draw the corresponding Ogham character along the stem-line, starting at the bottom and working your way up (the traditional direction).

For example, if your name is "Sarah," you would write:

• S (Saille - Willow): Four lines to the right

• A (Ailm - Pine): One notch on the line

• R (Ruis - Elder): Five lines to the right

• A (Ailm - Pine): One notch on the line

• H (hÚath - Hawthorn): One line to the left

Step 3: Reflect on the Trees of Your Name

Look at the trees that make up your name. What wisdom do they offer you?

What energies do they bring?

For example, if your name contains the Oak (Duir), you are called to embody strength and sovereignty. If it includes the Willow (Saille), you are called to embrace flexibility and emotion. If it contains the Yew (Iodhadh), you are called to honour the ancestors and the cycles of death and rebirth.

Step 4: Create a Personal Ogham Talisman

If you feel called to go deeper, find a small branch or a smooth stone and carve or paint your name in Ogham on it. Keep it on your altar, carry it in your pocket, or place it somewhere in nature as an offering. This is your personal connection to the grove, a reminder that you are part of the great forest of being.

Step 5: Journal

Take a few moments to write about your experience. What did it feel like to write your name in the language of the trees? Which trees in your name spoke to you most strongly? How can you embody their wisdom in your daily life?

CONCLUSION: THE CLOAK OF THE OGHAM

We have journeyed through the whispering alphabet of the trees, from the bright Birch of new beginnings to the ancient Yew of eternity. We have met twenty teachers, each one offering a unique gift, a unique medicine for the soul. Before we close this chapter, let us step back and view the Ogham as a whole, as a complete system, and recognise what it truly represents.

The Ogham is not just an alphabet. It is a living testament to the Brigidine principle of integration, the gentle covering that we explored in Chapter 2. Just as St. Brigid did not destroy the sacred oak grove but built her monastery within it, the Ogham does not erase the old cosmology but encodes it, preserves it, and brings it into the new dispensation.

The Four Aicmí and the Brigidine Lens

Let us look again at the four families of the Ogham through the lens of Brigid's cloak:

The Aicme Beithe (Birch Group) represents the Upper World, the realm of divine inspiration, new beginnings, and the light that breaks through the darkness. This is the realm of the Holy Spirit, the breath of God that hovered over the waters at creation, the light that shines in the darkness and the darkness has not overcome it. Brigid, who tended the sacred flame, understood this light. She did not extinguish the old fires; she brought them under the mantle of Christ, the true Light of the World. The Birch Group teaches us to reach upward, to seek the light, and to trust that every new beginning is a gift from above.

The Aicme hÚatha (Hawthorn Group) represents the Underworld, the realm of the ancestors, the deep wisdom, the challenges that make us strong, and the sovereignty that comes from facing our shadow. This is the realm of the descent, the Harrowing of Hell, the journey to the roots to bring healing and redemption. Brigid, who was herself a bridge between the goddess and the saint, understood the power of the deep places. She honoured the old ways, the old gods, the old wisdom, and she brought them gently into the new faith. The Hawthorn Group teaches us to go deep, to honour the ancestors, and to claim our sovereignty.

The Aicme Muine (Vine Group) represents the Middle World, the realm of human life, of growth, connection, harvest, and the complexities of relationships. This is the realm of the Incarnation, of God becoming flesh and dwelling among us, of the divine entering into the messiness and beauty of human existence. Brigid, who founded a double monastery, welcomed both men and women, fed the poor, and healed the sick, understood the sacredness of the Middle World. She did not escape into the heavens or retreat into the Underworld; she lived fully in the present, in the community, in the work of love. The Vine Group teaches us to live fully, to connect deeply, and to harvest the fruits of our labour.

The Aicme Ailme (Pine Group) represents the vertical axis, the spine of the World Tree, the connection between earth and heaven, the endurance that comes from standing tall and seeing the long view. This is the realm of the Cross itself, the ultimate World Tree, the vertical beam that connects all the worlds. Brigid, who lived a long life of service, who endured hardship and remained faithful, who saw the big picture of God's work in the world, understood this vertical axis. She stood firm, she endured, she reached for the heavens while remaining rooted in the earth. The Pine Group teaches us to stand tall, to endure, and to trust the long arc of God's love.

THE CLOAK THAT COVERS ALL

The Ogham, then, is Brigid's cloak woven into an alphabet. It is a system that honours the old cosmology—the three worlds, the sacred trees, the wisdom of the Druids—while bringing it all under the protective covering of the Christian faith. It does not destroy; it transforms. It does not erase; it fulfils. It does not conquer; it integrates. This is the gift of the Ogham to us today. It shows that we need not choose between the wisdom of the earth and the wisdom of the heavens, between the old ways and the new faith, between our pagan ancestors and our Christian heritage. We can honour both. We can weave them together. We can stand in the grove and see the Cross rising from the centre, the ultimate Crann Bethadh, and know that we are home.

In the chapters that follow, we will go even deeper into the wisdom of individual trees. We will meet the Council of the Elders—the Oak, the Ash, and the Yew—and learn their deepest secrets. We will explore the trees of protection, the trees of wisdom, and the trees of healing. We will learn to walk in the forest not as strangers or tourists, but as kin, as children of the grove, as those who know the language of the leaves.

But for now, rest in this: you have learned the alphabet.

You have met the twenty teachers. You have written your name in the language of the trees. You are no longer an outsider to the grove. You are part of the story. You belong.

Chapter 5:

The Council of the Elders: Oak, Ash, and Yew

CONVENING THE COUNCIL

In our journey so far, we have learned the language of the Grove. We have taken the twenty letters of the Ogham alphabet, the whispering wisdom of the trees, and written our own names into the great story of the earth. We have moved from the universal, cosmic symbol of the World Tree to the particular, individual spirits of the twenty trees that form the foundation of the Celtic spiritual landscape. We have learned the alphabet; now it is time to begin the conversation.

But where do we begin? In any great council, one does not start with the lesser officials or the junior members. One goes to the elders, to the great ones who hold the most profound wisdom, who have seen the ages turn, and whose roots go down into the very bedrock of existence. In the sacred grove of the Celtic soul, this Council of the Elders is comprised of three great beings, three trees of such immense power and significance that they form the three pillars upon which the entire spiritual world rests. They are the Oak, the Ash, and the Yew.

These are not just three trees among many. They are archetypes, fundamental forces of the cosmos made manifest in wood and leaf.

They represent the three great principles of a fully integrated spiritual life:

• **The Oak (Duir),** the King of the Forest, represents Power, Strength, and Sovereignty. It teaches us how to stand firm in our truth, how to rule ourselves with integrity, and how to be a source of shelter and protection for others. It is the wisdom of the present moment, of living with courage and purpose in the world.

• **The Ash (Nuin),** the World Tree, represents Connection, Relationship, and the Cosmos. It teaches us how to see the intricate web of connections that binds all things—past, present, and future; heaven, earth, and the underworld. It is the wisdom of perspective, of understanding our place in the great, unfolding story of the universe.

• **The Yew (Iodhadh),** the Ancestor Tree, represents Eternity, Transformation, and the Great Cycle of Death and Rebirth. It teaches us how to face our mortality with courage, how to honour the ancestors who came before us, and how to trust in the promise of eternal life. It is the wisdom of the long view, of seeing our individual lives as part of a story that never ends.

In Chapter 4, we encountered these trees briefly as letters of the alphabet. Now, we will go deeper. We will move beyond the brief descriptions and engage in a substantive conversation with each of these great elders. We will explore their rich mythology and folklore, the ways their wisdom was integrated into the Christian faith, and the practical spiritual applications they offer for contemporary life. We are no longer just learning the language; we are using it to seek counsel from the masters.

So, take a deep breath. Quiet your mind. We are entering the heart of the sacred grove, the inner sanctum where the great ones dwell. We come with respect, with humility, and with an open heart, ready to listen. The Council of the Elders is now in session.

THE OAK (DUIR): THE KING OF THE FOREST AND THE DOORWAY TO STRENGTH

If you were to walk through an ancient Irish forest and ask the trees to elect a king, there would be no debate, no campaign, no contest. Every branch would point to the Oak. The Oak is the undisputed sovereign of the forest, not because it is the tallest or the oldest (though it can be both), but because it embodies the very essence of what it means to rule: strength, stability, endurance, and the capacity to shelter and protect.

The Oak can live for a thousand years. Its roots go down deep into the earth, anchoring it so firmly that no storm, no matter how fierce, can uproot it. Its trunk grows thick and strong, a pillar of the forest, a living monument to the power of slow, steady growth. Its branches spread widely, creating a canopy that shelters countless creatures—birds, insects, mammals, and fungi—making it not just a tree but an entire ecosystem, a commonwealth of life.

To stand beneath an ancient Oak is to feel the presence of something greater than yourself, something that has endured, something that will endure long after you are gone.

This is the Oak: The King of the Forest, the tree of sovereignty, the doorway to strength.

SOVEREIGNTY: THE POWER TO RULE YOURSELF

In the Celtic world, sovereignty was not simply about political power or military might. It was a sacred concept, deeply intertwined with the land itself. The king was not just a ruler; he was the living embodiment of the relationship between the people and the land. His health was the land's health. His integrity was the land's fertility. His strength was the people's prosperity. And the place where this sacred bond was forged was at the Crann Bethadh, the sacred tree of the tribe—and more often than not, that tree was an Oak.

The inauguration of a king in ancient Ireland was a ritual of profound spiritual significance. The king-to-be would stand at the base of the sacred Oak, often at the centre of the tribal territory, and would be ritually "married" to the land, represented by the goddess of sovereignty. This was not a metaphor; it was understood as a real, mystical union. The king promised to care for the land as a husband cares for his wife, to be faithful to her, to protect her, and to ensure her flourishing. In return, the land would grant him the authority to rule, the wisdom to lead, and the strength to endure.

But here is the crucial insight that the Oak teaches us: true sovereignty is not about ruling others. It is about ruling yourself. The king who cannot govern his own passions, his own fears, his own ego, cannot govern a kingdom. The Oak, with its deep roots and unshakable trunk, is a living parable of self-mastery. It does not bend to every wind. It does not uproot itself and move when the weather turns harsh. It stands firm. It endures. It knows who it is, and it does not apologise for taking up space in the world.

This is the first great lesson of the Oak: Find your roots. Know who you are. Stand firm in your truth. In a world that constantly tries to pull you in a thousand directions, that bombards you with messages about who you should be and what you should want, the Oak invites you to sink your roots deep into the bedrock of your own soul and to stand tall in your own integrity. This is sovereignty. This is true power.

THE DOORWAY: DUIR AND THE THRESHOLD OF COURAGE

The Irish word for Oak is Duir (pronounced roughly "DOO-ir"), and it is closely related to the word for "door" (doras). This is not a coincidence. The Oak is a doorway, a threshold, a gateway to another realm. But what realm does it open into?

In the physical world, Oak wood was prized for its strength and durability. It was used to build the doors of homes, the gates of fortresses, and the hulls of ships. An Oak door was a symbol of security, of protection, of the boundary between the safe interior and the dangerous exterior. But in the spiritual world, the Oak is the doorway to something far more profound: it is the gateway to courage, to inner strength, to the Otherworld itself.

To pass through the Oak is to pass through your fear. It is to step from the realm of hesitation and self-doubt into the realm of action and power. It is to cross the threshold from who you have been into who you are called to become. The Oak does not promise that the journey will be easy. It does not promise that there will be no storms. But it does promise that if you root yourself deeply enough, if you stand firm enough, you will endure. You will not break. You will become the shelter that others need.

THE RITUAL OF THE OAK AND THE MISTLETOE: A MARRIAGE OF SUN AND MOON

One of the most famous accounts of Druidic ritual comes from the Roman naturalist Pliny the Elder, writing in the first century AD. He describes a ceremony in which the Druids would climb a sacred Oak tree on the sixth night of the new moon, cut the Mistletoe growing on its branches with a golden sickle, and catch it in a white cloth before it touched the ground. Two white bulls would then be sacrificed, and prayers would be offered for the fertility of the land and the health of the people.

Modern readers often see this as a quaint or even barbaric pagan ritual, but to understand it properly, we must see it through Celtic eyes. This was not superstition; it was sophisticated theology, a ritual enactment of the cosmic marriage between the masculine and the feminine, between the sun and the moon, between strength and life.

The Oak, with its massive, solid trunk and its association with thunder and lightning (it is often struck by lightning due to its height and the moisture in its wood), was seen as a masculine tree, a tree of the sun, of fire, of power. The Mistletoe, on the other hand, is a parasitic plant that grows on the Oak's branches. It has no roots in the earth; it draws its life from the tree itself. Its white berries appear in the depths of winter, a symbol of life persisting even in the darkest time of the year. It was regarded as a feminine plant, a plant of the moon, of water, of fertility, and of healing.

The ritual of cutting the Mistletoe from the Oak was a symbolic act of balancing these two energies. The strength of the Oak alone is barren; it needs the life-giving spirit of the Mistletoe to be fruitful. The Mistletoe alone is rootless and fragile; it needs the strength of the Oak to survive. Together, they form a complete whole, a sacred marriage, a union of opposites that brings forth life.

This is the deeper wisdom of the Oak: Strength without compassion is tyranny. Power without love is violence. The Oak teaches us to be strong, yes, but it also teaches us to use that strength in the service of life, in the protection of the vulnerable, and in the creation of a space where others can flourish. True sovereignty is not about domination; it is about stewardship.

THE BRIGIDINE LENS: THE CHURCH OF THE OAK

When St. Brigid founded her monastery in the late fifth century, she did not choose a barren hilltop or a cleared field. She chose a sacred grove of Oak trees, a place that had likely been a centre of Druidic worship for centuries. The place was named Cill-Dara, meaning "the Church of the Oak." This was not an accident. This was a deliberate, profound theological statement.

Brigid understood the wisdom of the Oak. She understood that the strength and sovereignty it represented were not opposed to the Christian faith but were a perfect reflection of God's strength and sovereignty. The Oak was not a pagan idol to be destroyed; it was a natural sacrament, a living sermon, a teacher that had been preparing the Irish soul for the coming of Christ.

So, Brigid did not cut down the sacred Oaks. She built her church among them. She made the grove the heart of her Christian community. She said, in effect: "The strength you have always revered in the Oak is the strength of Christ. The sovereignty you have always sought at the base of this tree is the sovereignty of the Kingdom of God. The shelter you have always found under these branches is the shelter of the Cross."

This is the Brigidine model of integration at its finest. It is not conquest; it is covering. It is not destruction; it is fulfilment. The Oak remains the Oak, but now it is understood in its deepest truth: it is a sign pointing to the ultimate King, the ultimate source of strength, the ultimate shelter for all who are weary and heavy-laden.

In the Christian tradition, Christ is often called the "Lion of Judah," a symbol of royal power and courage. But in the Celtic tradition, he might just as easily be called the "Oak of Heaven," the tree whose roots go down into the very heart of God, whose trunk stands firm against every storm of history, and whose branches spread wide enough to shelter the entire world.

THE PRACTICE: A MEDITATION ON INNER SOVEREIGNTY

Now it is time to make this wisdom personal. Find a quiet place where you will not be disturbed. If possible, sit beneath an Oak tree, or at least bring an Oak leaf or a piece of Oak wood to hold in your hands. Close your eyes and take several deep, slow breaths.

Step 1: Find Your Roots

Imagine that you are an Oak tree. Feel your legs and your seat as roots extending deep, deep into the earth. With each breath, send those roots down further. Feel them pushing through the soil, through the rock, down into the bedrock of the earth. These roots are your connection to your ancestors, to your deepest values, to the core of your identity. Ask yourself: What are the non-negotiable truths that I stand on? What are the values that I will not compromise? Feel those truths as the bedrock beneath you, solid and unshakable.

Step 2: Stand Firm in Your Trunk
Now bring your awareness to your spine, your trunk. Feel it strong and straight, rising from the earth toward the sky. This is your integrity, your sense of self, your sovereignty. Ask yourself: Where in my life am I being asked to stand firm? Where am I being pushed or pulled by others' expectations, and where do I need to reclaim my power? Feel the strength of the Oak filling your spine, giving you the courage to stand tall in your truth.

Step 3: Spread Your Branches

Now feel your arms and the crown of your head as branches spreading wide. These branches represent your capacity to shelter and protect others and to be a source of strength for your community. Ask yourself: Who needs my strength right now? How can I use my power in the service of life, in the service of love? Feel your branches spreading wide, creating a canopy of safety and welcome for all who need it.

Step 4: Breathe and Integrate

Take a few deep breaths, feeling yourself as the Oak: rooted, strong, sheltering. When you are ready, gently open your eyes.

Journaling Prompts:

• Where in my life do I need to embody the strength of the Oak?

• What does it mean to be truly sovereign over my own life, my choices, and my energy?

• How can I use my strength to shelter and protect others?

THE ASH (NUIN): THE WORLD TREE AND THE AXIS OF CONNECTION

If the Oak is the king who rules with strength and sovereignty, the Ash is the sage who sees the entire pattern, the one who understands how all things are woven together in the great tapestry of existence. The Ash does not dominate the forest; it connects it. It does not stand apart; it stands at the centre, linking heaven and earth, past and future, the visible and the invisible. The Ash is the World Tree, the Crann Bethadh, the cosmic axis around which all of reality revolves.

In Chapter 3, we explored the archetype of the World Tree in general terms, seeing how it connected the three worlds of Celtic cosmology: the Underworld of the ancestors, the Middle World of humanity, and the Upper World of the gods. However, we must now be more specific. While many trees could symbolise this cosmic connection, the Ash was the prime candidate, the tree most often identified as the living embodiment of the axis mundi, the world's axle. And when we understand why, we begin to see not just a tree, but a profound theological vision that would find its ultimate fulfilment in the Christian doctrine of the Holy Trinity.

THE PHYSICAL ASH: A TREE BUILT FOR CONNECTION

The Ash is a tree of remarkable physical characteristics, each one a perfect metaphor for its spiritual role. Its roots go deep, deeper than almost any other tree, seeking water and nutrients far below the surface. Its trunk grows tall and straight, a perfect pillar, with wood that is both strong and flexible, used for everything from tool handles to spear shafts to building frames. Its branches reach high into the sky, creating a light, airy canopy that allows sunlight to filter through to the forest floor below.

In other words, the Ash is perfectly designed to connect. Its roots connect it to the deep waters of the Underworld. Its trunk connects it to the solid earth of the Middle World. Its branches connect it to the light and air of the Upper World. It is a living bridge, a ladder, a pathway between the realms. To stand beneath an Ash is to stand at the centre of the cosmos, at the point where all things meet.

THE FIVE SACRED TREES OF IRELAND: GUARDIANS OF THE LAND

The importance of the Ash in Irish spirituality is demonstrated most powerfully in the legend of the Five Sacred Trees of Ireland. According to the medieval text Dindsenchas ("The Lore of Places"), there were five great trees that stood as spiritual guardians over the five provinces of Ireland. These were not just any trees; they were cosmic pillars, each one a Crann Bethadh for its region, each one a living connection between the people and the land, between the earth and the heavens.

Of these five sacred trees, three were Ash trees. The most famous was the Tree of Uisnech, which stood at the Hill of Uisnech in the very centre of Ireland, the point where the five provinces met. This tree was understood as the axis mundi of the entire island, the cosmic centre, the navel of the world. When it fell (the annals record its destruction in 665 AD), it was regarded as a catastrophe, a sign that the old order was passing away.

The other two Ash trees were the Tree of Tortu in County Westmeath and the Branching Tree of Dathi in County Meath. The remaining two sacred trees were an Oak (the Oak of Mugna in County Kildare) and a Yew (the Yew of Ross in County Wexford). Together, these five trees formed a sacred geography, a map of the spiritual structure of Ireland itself. But the fact that three of the five were Ash trees tells us everything we need to know about the Ash's central role in the Celtic imagination.

The Ash was not just a World Tree; it was the World Tree, the ultimate symbol of connection, of relationship, of the intricate web that binds all things together.

THE ASH AND THE HOLY TRINITY: THREE-IN-ONE

Here, the Brigidine lens reveals something profound. When the Christian faith came to Ireland, it brought with it the doctrine of the Holy Trinity: the belief that God is one being in three persons—Father, Son, and Holy Spirit.

This was a difficult concept for many cultures to grasp. How can God be both one and three? How can unity and diversity coexist?

But for the Celtic soul, which had been contemplating the Ash for centuries, this was not a paradox; it was a confirmation. The Ash had always been teaching this truth. The Ash is one tree, but it exists in three distinct realms: its roots in the Underworld, its trunk in the Middle World, its branches in the Upper World. It is not three trees; it is one tree in three dimensions. And yet, each dimension is fully real, fully present, fully the Ash.

This is the mystery of the Trinity. God the Father is the root, the source, the deep ground of all being, the one from whom all life flows. God the Son is the trunk, the incarnation, the one who stands in the Middle World, who takes on flesh and dwells among us, who connects the divine to the human. God, the Holy Spirit, is the branches, the breath, the wind that moves through the Upper World, the one who inspires, who enlightens, who brings the life of God into every corner of creation.

Three persons, one God. Three dimensions, one tree. The Ash had been preaching the Trinity long before the missionaries arrived.

St. Brigid, who built her monastery among the Oaks, understood this. She understood that the natural world was not a rival to the Christian faith, but a preparation for it, a teacher that had been readying the Celtic soul to receive the fullness of revelation. The Ash was not a pagan symbol to be rejected; it was a natural sacrament, a living icon of the Triune God.

In the Celtic Christian tradition, the Trinity was not an abstract theological doctrine to be debated by scholars in distant monasteries. It was a lived reality, experienced in the rhythms of nature, in the structure of the cosmos, in the very trees that surrounded them.

To pray to the Trinity was to pray to the God who is as close as the roots beneath your feet, as present as the ground you stand on, and as high as the branches above your head. It was to pray to the God who connects all things, who weaves all things together, who is the very fabric of existence itself.

THE CROSS AS THE ULTIMATE ASH TREE: THE PATRICIAN FULFILMENT

If Brigid saw the Ash as a natural icon of the Trinity, St. Patrick saw it as a prophecy of the Cross. The Cross, in the Patrician vision, is the ultimate World Tree, the final and perfect Crann Bethadh that the Ash had always been pointing toward.

Consider the structure of the Cross. Its vertical beam extends into the earth (some traditions hold that the Cross was planted on the very spot where Adam was buried, linking it to the first human and to the roots of humanity). Its vertical beam also rises up toward heaven, connecting earth to the divine. Its horizontal beam extends across the Middle World, embracing all of humanity and gathering all people to the heart of God.

The Cross, like the Ash, connects the three worlds. But it does more than connect them; it reconciles them. On the Cross, Christ descended to the dead, bringing light to the Underworld. On the Cross, Christ stretched out his arms in the Middle World, embracing all of humanity in his suffering and his love. On the Cross, Christ opened the way to the Upper World, tearing the veil that separated heaven and earth.

The Ash had always been a symbol of connection. The Cross is the reality. The Ash had always been a bridge. The Cross is the bridge made flesh, made wood, made real. The Ash had always whispered of a God who holds all things together. The Cross is the place where God reveals himself fully, where the Trinity is made visible in the suffering and triumph of the Son.

This is the Patrician model of integration: the old symbols are not destroyed, but fulfilled. The Ash is accepted; it is honoured as the teacher who prepared the way. And now, standing at the centre of the grove, where the Ash once stood, there is the Cross, the ultimate World Tree, the final revelation of the God who connects all things in himself.

Justice, Balance, and Right Relationship

There is one more dimension of the Ash's wisdom that we must explore: its association with justice and right relationship. The wood of the Ash is both strong and flexible, making it ideal for tools and weapons that require precision and balance. It was used for the shafts of spears, which must fly straight and true. It was used for the handles of axes and hammers, which must connect human intention to action in the world. It was used for the frames of houses and the keels of boats, which must hold things together under stress.

All of these uses point to the same spiritual principle: the Ash is the tree of right relationship, of balance, of justice. It teaches us that we are not isolated individuals, but are part of a vast web of relationships—with other people, with the natural world, with the past and the future, with the divine. And to live well is to honour those relationships, to act with integrity, to ensure that our actions contribute to the balance and harmony of the whole.

In the Celtic legal tradition, the Druids were the judges, the arbiters of disputes, the keepers of the law. And the law they kept was not an arbitrary set of rules, but a reflection of the natural order, the dán or destiny of each person and each community. To break the law was not just to violate a social contract; it was to disrupt the cosmic order, to damage the web of relationships that held the world together. The Ash, as the World Tree, was the ultimate symbol of this interconnectedness and thus of justice.

In the Christian tradition, this understanding of justice is deepened and personalised. Justice is not just about maintaining the cosmic order; it is about restoring right relationships when they have been broken. This is the work of Christ on the Cross, the ultimate Ash Tree. He takes upon himself the brokenness of all our relationships—with God, with each other, with ourselves, with creation—and he heals them. He reconciles all things to himself, whether things on earth or things in heaven, making peace by the blood of his cross (Colossians 1:20).

The Ash teaches us to see the connections. The Cross teaches us that those connections, when broken, can be healed. The Ash teaches us to honour the web. The Cross teaches us that we are all part of that web, and that the God who wove it will never let it unravel.

THE PRACTICE: A MEDITATION ON INTERCONNECTEDNESS

Find a quiet place and sit comfortably. If possible, sit beneath an Ash tree, or hold a piece of Ash wood in your hands. Close your eyes and take several deep, slow breaths.

Step 1: Connect to the Roots (The Past)

Imagine that you are an Ash tree. Feel your roots extending deep into the earth, down into the Underworld, the realm of the ancestors. With each breath, feel your connection to all those who came before you—your parents, your grandparents, your great-grandparents, stretching back through the generations to the very beginning. You are not alone. You are part of a long line, a great continuity.

Ask yourself: What gifts have my ancestors given me? What wisdom do they have for me? Feel their strength flowing up through your roots, nourishing you.

Step 2: Stand in the Trunk (The Present)
Now bring your awareness to your trunk, your spine, standing firm in the Middle World, the world of the present moment. This is where you live, where you act, where you love. Ask yourself: How am I connected to the people around me? How am I connected to the natural world? What is my responsibility in this web of relationships? Feel the solidity of the present moment, the gift of being here, now, alive.

Step 3: Reach with the Branches (The Future)

Now feel your branches reaching up into the Upper World, the realm of the heavens, the realm of possibility and hope. These branches are your connection to the future, to your descendants, to the world you are helping to create. Ask yourself: What kind of world am I leaving behind? What is my highest calling? What vision is guiding my life? Feel the light of the Upper World pouring down through your branches, filling you with hope and purpose.

Step 4: Feel the Unity

Now, feel all three dimensions at once. You are rooted in the past, standing in the present, reaching for the future. You are connected to the ancestors, to your community, to the divine. You are not alone. You are part of the great web of being, the cosmic tree, the body of Christ. Take a few deep breaths, feeling this unity. When you are ready, gently open your eyes.

Journaling Prompts:

• How can I better see the connections in my own life?

• Where am I called to be a bridge between people, ideas, or worlds?

• What does it mean to live in right relationship with all things?

THE YEW (IODHADH): THE ANCESTOR TREE AND THE GUARDIAN OF ETERNITY

If the Oak teaches us how to live with strength in the present, and the Ash teaches us how to see the connections that bind all things together, the Yew teaches us the most challenging and most necessary lesson of all: how to face death, how to honour the ancestors, and how to trust in the promise of eternal life. The Yew is the tree of the threshold, the guardian of the final gate, the ancient witness who has seen empires rise and fall, who has watched generations come and go, and who stands, silent and enduring, as a living testament to the truth that life is stronger than death.

The Yew is, in many ways, the strangest and most mysterious of the three great trees. It does not grow as tall as the Ash or as broad as the Oak. It does not dominate the forest. But it outlives them all. A Yew can live for thousands of years—some of the ancient Yews in the British Isles are estimated to be over 2,000 years old, and a few may be as old as 5,000 years. These trees were already ancient when the Druids walked beneath them. They were already old when Christ was born. They are living bridges to a past so distant that it feels like a myth.

And yet, the Yew is not just a relic of the past. It is a living, growing, regenerating being. As it ages, its trunk becomes hollow, decaying from the inside out. But even as the centre dies, new roots descend from the branches into the hollow core, and new growth emerges. The Yew dies and is reborn, again and again, in an endless cycle. It is the ultimate symbol of transformation, of the great mystery of death and resurrection, of the eternal life that flows through all things.

THE YEW IN THE GRAVEYARD: GUARDIAN OF THE ANCESTORS

If you visit an old church in Ireland, Scotland, Wales, or England, you will almost certainly find a Yew tree in the churchyard, often standing near the entrance or beside the graves. This is not a Christian innovation; it is a continuation of a practice that goes back to the pre-Christian Celts. The Yew has always been the tree of the dead, the guardian of the threshold between this world and the next.

But we must be careful not to misunderstand this association. The Yew is not a symbol of death as an ending, as a final darkness, as a defeat. It is a symbol of death as a transformation, as a passage, as a doorway into another dimension of existence. The Celts did not fear death in the way that many modern people do. They believed in the immortality of the soul, in the transmigration of the soul from one life to another, and in the continuity of existence beyond the grave. Death was not the opposite of life; it was a part of life, a necessary transition, a return to the source before the next beginning.

The Yew, standing in the graveyard, is a living reminder of this truth. Its roots extend into the earth, where the ancestors are buried, drawing nourishment from their bodies and connecting the living to the dead. Its branches reach up toward the heavens, pointing to the realm where the ancestors now dwell. It is a bridge, a ladder, a guardian who ensures that the dead are not forgotten, that the ancestors are honoured, and that the living remain connected to the great chain of being that stretches back to the beginning of time.

In the Christian tradition, this understanding is deepened and fulfilled. The Yew in the churchyard is not just a reminder of the ancestors; it is a reminder of the resurrection. It is a living sermon, preached by the earth itself, that death is not the end, that the grave is not the final word, that life is stronger than death because Christ has conquered death and opened the way to eternal life.

THE OLDEST LIVING THINGS: WITNESSES TO ETERNITY

To stand before an ancient Yew is to stand before a living witness to the vastness of time. Consider the Fortingall Yew in Perthshire, Scotland, which is estimated to be between 2,000 and 5,000 years old. If the higher estimate is correct, this tree was already ancient when the Egyptian pyramids were built. It was already old when Moses led the Israelites out of Egypt. It was a mature tree when the Druids performed their rituals in the sacred groves. It was standing when St. Patrick arrived in Ireland. It was there when the Vikings raided the coasts. It was there when the Normans invaded. It was there through the Reformation, the Enlightenment, the Industrial Revolution, and the two World Wars. And it is still there, still growing, still green.

What does such a tree know? What has it seen? What wisdom does it hold in its ancient, hollow heart?

The Yew teaches us the long view. It teaches us that our individual lives, as precious and significant as they are, are part of a broader narrative. We are not isolated moments in time; we are part of an excellent continuity, a river of life that flows from the past into the future. The Yew teaches us to honour the ancestors, to learn from their wisdom, to carry their legacy forward. And it teaches us to live in such a way that we, too, will be honoured ancestors, that our lives will be a blessing to those who come after us.

THE YEW AND THE RESURRECTION: THE CHRISTOLOGICAL LENS

The Yew's ability to die and be reborn from its own centre is one of the most powerful natural parables of the resurrection. As the tree ages, its heartwood decays, leaving a hollow trunk. In any other tree, this would be the beginning of the end, a sign of death and collapse. But in the Yew, it is the beginning of a new life. New roots descend from the branches into the hollow core, drawing nourishment from the decaying wood. New shoots emerge from the trunk. The tree is reborn from within itself.

This is the mystery of the resurrection. Christ descended into the tomb, into the heart of death itself. But death could not hold him. On the third day, he rose again, not as a ghost or a spirit, but in a transformed, glorified body— still himself, still bearing the wounds of the crucifixion, but now radiant with the life of God, now imperishable, now eternal. He died and was reborn from the very centre of death, transforming it from an ending into a beginning, from a defeat into a victory.

The Yew in the churchyard is a living icon of this truth. It stands as a witness to the promise that Christ made: "I am the resurrection and the life. Whoever believes in me, though he die, yet shall he live" (John 11:25). The Yew does not argue this truth; it demonstrates it. It lives it. It is a sermon in wood and leaf, a promise carved into the very fabric of creation.

St. Brigid and St. Patrick, in their different ways, both understood this. They did not see the Yew as a pagan symbol to be uprooted. They saw it as a natural sacrament, a gift from God, a teacher that had been preparing the Celtic soul for the full revelation of the gospel. The Yew had always been teaching the resurrection; now, in Christ, that teaching was fulfilled.

THE YEW AND THE ANCESTORS: HONOURING THE CHAIN OF BEING

One of the most profound gifts that the Celtic tradition offers to the modern world is its deep reverence for the ancestors. In a culture that is obsessed with youth, that worships novelty, that constantly looks forward and rarely looks back, the Yew invites us to remember. It invites us to honour those who came before us, to learn from their wisdom, to carry their legacy forward.

The ancestors are not gone.

They are present in the land, in the stories, in the very cells of our bodies. We carry their DNA, their memories, their traumas, and their triumphs. We are not isolated individuals; we are the latest chapter in a story that began long before we were born and will continue long after we are gone. To honour the ancestors is to honour the chain of being, to acknowledge that we are part of something much larger than ourselves.

In the Christian tradition, this reverence for the ancestors is deepened and expanded. We are not merely connected to our biological ancestors; we are connected to the great "cloud of witnesses" (Hebrews 12:1), the saints, martyrs, and faithful who have gone before us in the faith. We are part of the communion of saints, the mystical body of Christ that transcends time and space, that includes the living and the dead, the Church on earth and the Church in heaven.

The Yew, standing in the churchyard, is a reminder of this communion. Its roots go down into the graves, connecting us to the ancestors. Its branches reach up into the heavens, connecting us to the saints. It is a bridge between the living and the dead, a reminder that we are all part of one family, one body, one great tree of life.

THE PRACTICE: A MEDITATION ON ANCESTRAL CONNECTION AND ETERNITY

Find a quiet place, ideally near a Yew tree or in a place where you feel close to the ancestors.

Sit comfortably and close your eyes. Take several deep, slow breaths, allowing your body to relax and your mind to settle.

Step 1: Call to Mind the Ancestors

Begin by calling to mind your ancestors—your parents, your grandparents, your great-grandparents, and all those who came before them, stretching back through the generations. You do not need to know their names or their stories. Feel their presence, the long line of life that has led to you. Say quietly, either aloud or in your heart: "I honour you. I thank you. I carry your legacy forward."

Step 2: Feel Your Place in the Chain

Now, bring your awareness to yourself, to your own life, to this present moment. You are not just the product of the past; you are also the seed of the future. The ancestors live on in you, and you will live on in those who come after you. Ask yourself: What kind of ancestor do I want to be? What legacy do I want to leave? How can I live in such a way that future generations will honour my memory?

Step 3: Open to the Promise of Eternity

Now, imagine the Yew tree, ancient and enduring, dying and being reborn again and again. Feel the truth that it teaches: life is stronger than death. You are not just a body that will one day decay. You are a soul, an eternal being, a child of God. Death is not an ending; it is a transformation, a passage into a fuller, deeper life. Say quietly: "I am part of something eternal. I am held in the love of God, now and forever."

Step 4: Rest in the Silence

Sit in silence for a few moments, feeling the presence of the ancestors, the promise of eternity, the peace that comes from knowing that you are part of a story that never ends. When you are ready, gently open your eyes.

Journaling Prompts:

•What wisdom do my ancestors have for me?

•How can I live in a way that honours their legacy?

•What does it mean to me to know that life is eternal?

CONCLUSION: THE THREE PILLARS OF THE GROVE

We have sat at the feet of the three great elders of the Celtic grove. We have listened to the Oak teach us about strength, sovereignty, and the courage to stand firm in our truth. We have listened to the Ash teach us about connection, relationship, and the intricate web that binds all things together.

We have listened to the Yew teach us about eternity, the ancestors, and the great mystery of death and resurrection. Now, as we prepare to leave this council and continue our journey deeper into the forest, let us step back and see these three trees not as separate teachers, but as three pillars of a single, unified wisdom.

THE COMPLETE HUMAN BEING: STRENGTH, CONNECTION, AND ETERNITY

The Oak, the Ash, and the Yew together form a comprehensive model of what it means to be a fully integrated human being, and to live a life of wholeness and holiness.

The Oak teaches us how to live with strength in the present moment. It teaches us to know who we are, to stand firm in our values, to be a source of shelter and protection for others. Without the Oak, we are weak, rootless, blown about by every wind of opinion and circumstance. We become victims, unable to take responsibility for our own lives, unable to serve others from a place of genuine power. The Oak grounds us. It gives us the courage to be ourselves, to take up space in the world, to say "yes" to our calling and "no" to what does not serve our highest good.

The Ash teaches us how to live with connection and awareness of the whole. It teaches us to see the relationships that bind us to the past, the present, and the future, to the earth and the heavens, to the human and the divine. Without the Ash, we are isolated, lonely, trapped in the prison of our own ego. We see ourselves as separate from others, from nature, from God. We lose the sense of meaning and purpose that comes from knowing that we are part of something larger than ourselves. The Ash opens our eyes. It shows us the web. It invites us to live in right relationship with all things.

The Yew teaches us how to live with wisdom in the face of mortality and eternity. It teaches us to honour the ancestors, to face our own death with courage, and to trust in the promise of eternal life. Without the Yew, we are trapped in the fear of death, clinging desperately to youth, to health, to the illusion of permanence. We live shallow lives, avoiding the deep questions, refusing to look at the shadow. The Yew frees us. It shows us that death is not the end, that we are part of a continuity that stretches back to the beginning and forward to the end, that we are held in the love of a God who is eternal.

Together, these three trees constitute the foundation of a well-lived life. We need the strength of the Oak to stand firm. We need the Ash's connection to see the whole. We need the wisdom of the Yew to face the ultimate questions. We need all three. We need to be rooted, connected, and eternal.

The Three Pillars and the Three Aspects of Brigid

Here, the Brigidine lens reveals something truly beautiful. St. Brigid, as we have seen, is not just a single figure, but a triple goddess, a three-in-one, a reflection of the Trinity itself. In the Irish tradition, she is honoured in three aspects: Brigid the Healer, Brigid the Smith, and Brigid the Poet. And these three aspects correspond perfectly to the three great trees of the grove.

Brigid the Healer is the Oak. She is the one who provides shelter, protection, and strength to the weak and the vulnerable. She is the one who stands firm in the face of suffering, who does not turn away from the broken and the wounded, who uses her power in the service of life. The Oak's strength is not the strength of domination; it is the strength of compassion, the strength that creates a safe space in which healing can occur. Brigid the Healer embodies the sovereignty of love, the power that serves rather than rules. She is the Oak that shelters the weary, the strong trunk that the broken can lean against.

Brigid the Smith is the Ash. She is the one who forges connections, who takes raw materials and shapes them into tools, who understands how things work together, how the parts relate to the whole. The smith is a mediator, a transformer, one who takes the ore from the Underworld, heats it with fire from the Upper World, and shapes it in the Middle World into something useful and beautiful. The Ash, as the World Tree, is the ultimate connector, the bridge between the realms. Brigid the Smith embodies the wisdom of right relationship, the understanding that we are all part of a great web, and that our work is to forge the connections that hold the world together. She is the Ash that links heaven and earth, that brings the divine into the material, that makes the invisible visible.

Brigid the Poet is the Yew. She is the one who remembers, who tells the old stories, who keeps the memory of the ancestors alive. The poet is the keeper of the long view, the one who sees beyond the present moment to the great arc of time, the one who understands that we are part of a story that began long before us and will continue long after us. The Yew, as the tree of eternity and the ancestors, is the ultimate poet, the living witness to the continuity of life. Brigid the Poet embodies the wisdom of the ages, the understanding that we are not alone, that we are part of a great communion of saints and ancestors, and that our lives have meaning because they are part of a story that never ends. She is the Yew that stands in the churchyard, that connects the living to the dead, that whispers the old songs and the ancient truths.

This is the genius of the Brigidine tradition: it does not separate the sacred from the practical, the spiritual from the material, the Christian from the Celtic. It weaves them together. It shows us that the strength of the Oak, the connection of the Ash, and the wisdom of the Yew are not just natural phenomena; they are reflections of the divine, manifestations of the three-in-one God who is Father, Son, and Holy Spirit, who is Healer, Smith, and Poet, who is the ground of all being, the web of all relationships, and the promise of eternal life.

LIVING AS THE GROVE: INTEGRATION IN PRACTICE

So, what does it mean to live as the grove? What does it mean to embody the wisdom of the Oak, the Ash, and the Yew in your daily life?

It means that when you are faced with a challenge, you call upon the strength of the Oak. You root yourself in your deepest values, you stand firm in your truth, and you do not allow yourself to be swayed by fear or by the opinions of others. You become a source of shelter and protection for those who need it.

It means that when you are making a decision, you call upon the wisdom of the Ash. You ask yourself: How does this decision affect my relationships? How does it affect the web of connections that I am part of? Am I acting in a way that honours the past, serves the present, and blesses the future? You see the whole, not just the part.

It means that when you are facing loss, grief, or your own mortality, you call upon the wisdom of the Yew. You remember the ancestors, you honour their legacy, and you trust in the promise of eternal life. You do not cling to the illusion of permanence, but you embrace the great cycle of death and rebirth, knowing that life is stronger than death.

This is the path of the grove. This is the way of integration, the Brigidine way, the Celtic Christian way. It is not about choosing between the old and the new, between the pagan and the Christian, between the natural and the supernatural. It is about seeing that they are all part of one great whole, one great tree, one great story. It is about standing in the grove and knowing that you are home.

BRIDGE TO THE NEXT CHAPTER

We have now consulted the Council of the Elders. We have learned the foundational wisdom of the Oak, the Ash, and the Yew. We have seen how these three trees form the pillars of a fully integrated spiritual life, and how they correspond to the three aspects of Brigid and the three persons of the Trinity.

But the grove is vast, and there are many more trees to meet, many more teachers to learn from. In the chapters that follow, we will explore the other trees of the Ogham in greater depth. We will meet the Guardians of the Grove—the trees of protection and power like the Rowan, the Holly, and the Hawthorn. We will meet the Trees of Wisdom—the Hazel, the Apple, and the Elder. We will meet the Trees of Healing and Transformation—the Birch, the Willow, and the Alder.

Each tree has its own unique gift, its own unique medicine for the soul. Each tree is a doorway into a different dimension of the sacred. And as we meet them, one by one, we will find that we are not just learning about trees; we are learning about ourselves, about the many facets of our own souls, about the many ways that the divine speaks to us through the natural world.

But for now, rest in this: you have sat at the feet of the great elders.

You have learned the three pillars of the grove.

You have been given the foundation.

You are ready to go deeper.

The Council of the Elders has spoken.

The journey continues.

Chapter 6:

The Guardians of the Grove: Trees of Protection and Power

WHY WE NEED GUARDIANS

We have sat in council with the great elders. The Oak has taught us to stand firm in our own sovereign strength. The Ash has taught us to see the intricate web of connection that binds all of creation together. The Yew has taught us to honour the ancestors and to face eternity with courage and trust. We have been given the three pillars of strength, connection, and eternity, and we have been taught the three strategies of seeing, acting, and waiting. We are rooted. We are guarded. We are ready.

But a foundation, no matter how strong, is not a home. A foundation is only the beginning. To create a true dwelling place for the soul, a space where we can be safe, where we can grow, where we can commune with the divine, we also need walls and a door. We need a sacred enclosure, a protected space, a boundary that separates the inner world from the outer, the sacred from the profane. We need guardians.

In our modern world, the need for spiritual protection has never been more urgent. We live in an age of unprecedented noise, distraction, and spiritual pollution. Our attention is constantly pulled in a thousand directions by social media, the 24-hour news cycle, and the relentless demands of a consumer culture that tells us we are not enough. Our energy is drained by toxic relationships, by demanding jobs, by the psychic weight of a world in crisis. We are, in many ways, spiritually defenceless, our souls left open and exposed to a constant barrage of negativity, manipulation, and despair.

This is not a sustainable way to live. To be a spiritual person in the modern world is not to be a passive receptacle for whatever the world throws at you. It is to be a wise steward of your own soul, a guardian of your own inner flame. It is to learn the ancient art of spiritual self-preservation, not as a fearful or paranoid act of walling yourself off from the world, but as a loving and necessary act of self-care that allows you to serve the world from a place of fullness rather than depletion.

This is where the Guardians of the Grove come in. The Celtic tradition, with its deep understanding of the seen and unseen worlds, has always known the importance of protection. It has always turned to the trees for assistance. In this chapter, we will meet the three great guardian trees of the Celtic world: the Rowan, the Holly, and the Hawthorn. These are not just three more trees on our Ogham list; they are a complete system of spiritual protection, a trinity of guardians, each offering a different strategy for keeping our souls safe and our spirits strong.

• **The Rowan (Luis)** is the Guardian of Insight. It protects us by helping us see clearly, discern the truth, trust our intuition, and recognise danger before it arrives. It is the seer's shield, the lantern in the dark.

• **The Holly (Tinne)** is the Guardian of Action. It protects us by teaching us to act decisively, to set firm boundaries, to defend what is sacred, and to channel our righteous anger into constructive, protective force. It is the warrior's shield, the fire in the heart.

• **The Hawthorn (hÚath)** is the Guardian of Patience. It protects us by teaching us to wait with respect, to honour sacred thresholds, to understand the wisdom of timing, and to approach the divine with humility and preparation. It is the gatekeeper's shield, the wisdom of the threshold.

Together, these three trees offer a complete education in the art of spiritual self-defence.

They teach us when to see, when to act, and when to wait. They demonstrate discernment, courage, and respect simultaneously. They invite us to build a sacred enclosure around our souls, not to hide from the world, but to create a space where we can heal, grow, and become strong enough to be a source of healing and strength for others.

We now turn to the guardians. Let us learn their secrets. Let us ask for their help. The world is noisy, but the grove is safe. The journey into the heart of protection begins now.

THE ROWAN (LUIS): THE TREE OF INSIGHT AND THE SEER'S SHIELD

If you walk through the Scottish Highlands or the hills of Ireland in late summer or early autumn, you will see them: small, elegant trees with delicate, feathery leaves and clusters of bright red berries that glow like embers against the green landscape. These are the Rowan trees, and they are unmistakable. Their berries are so vivid, so startlingly red, that they seem almost unnatural, as if they have been painted by an artist's hand. They are like lanterns hung in the forest, beacons of light in the gathering darkness of the year.

This is the first and most important thing to understand about the Rowan: it is a tree of seeing, of illumination, of clarity. Its primary function is not to fight or defend, as the Holly does. Its power is to reveal, to make visible what is hidden, to shine a light into the shadows so that you can see danger before it arrives and truth before it is obscured. The Rowan is the tree of the seer, the prophet, the one with clear intuition and unclouded vision.

In the Celtic tradition, the Rowan was considered one of the most potent protective trees, but its protective qualities worked in unique ways. It did not create a physical barrier or a wall. It created a spiritual awakening. To carry a piece of Rowan wood, to plant a Rowan tree by your door, to invoke the spirit of the Rowan in your prayers—these were not acts of magical thinking. They were acts of intentional consciousness, ways of reminding yourself to stay awake, to pay attention, to trust your inner knowing. The Rowan's protection is the protection of awareness.

THE FOOD OF THE GODS: ENLIGHTENMENT AND LONGEVITY

In Irish mythology, the Rowan is associated with the gods themselves. There is a beautiful story in the Táin Bó Cúailnge (The Cattle Raid of Cooley) and other tales of a magical Rowan tree that grew in the Otherworld, guarded by a fierce dragon. This tree bore berries that were said to be the "food of the gods," granting those who ate them not only physical nourishment but also spiritual enlightenment, longevity, and protection from harm. Each berry was said to have the nourishing power of nine meals, and to taste them was to taste the divine itself.

This myth encodes a profound spiritual truth: the Rowan offers a higher perspective, a glimpse into the divine reality beneath the surface of ordinary life. To eat the berries of the Rowan is to see with the eyes of the gods, to perceive the world not as a collection of separate, meaningless objects, but as a living, interconnected web of sacred relationships. It is to wake up from the trance of ordinary consciousness and to see things as they truly are.

In the Christian mystical tradition, this is called the "beatific vision," the direct perception of God that is promised to the saints in heaven. But the Rowan teaches us that we do not have to wait until we die to taste this vision. We can cultivate it here and now, in this life, by learning to see with spiritual eyes, by trusting our intuition, and by paying attention to the subtle signs and symbols that the divine continually offers us.

THE DRUID'S STAFF: DIVINATION AND HIDDEN KNOWLEDGE

The Rowan was also closely associated with the Druids, the ancient wisdom-keepers of the Celtic world. Rowan wood was prized for making staffs, divining rods, and wands—tools used to seek hidden knowledge, connect with the spirit world, and channel divine guidance. The staff of a Druid was not just a walking stick; it was a symbol of authority, a tool of power, and a conduit for spiritual insight.

To carry a staff of Rowan was to declare yourself a seeker of truth, a walker between the worlds, one who is not content with surface appearances but who digs deeper, who asks the hard questions, who listens for the whisper of the divine in the rustling of leaves and the flight of birds. The Rowan staff was a reminder that the world is full of signs, full of messages, full of guidance—if only we have the eyes to see and the ears to hear.

This is the Rowan's great gift: it awakens the seer within us. It teaches us to trust our intuition, that quiet inner voice that knows things before the rational mind can explain them. It teaches us to pay attention to our dreams, to the synchronicities that appear in our lives, to the subtle feelings of unease or attraction that guide us toward or away from certain people, places, and situations. The Rowan teaches us that we are not blind, that we are not helpless, that we have been given the gift of spiritual sight—if only we will use it.

CHRISTIAN INTEGRATION: THE GIFT OF DISCERNMENT

In the Christian tradition, this gift of spiritual sight is called the "discernment of spirits," and St. Paul lists it as one of the spiritual gifts given by the Holy Spirit (1 Corinthians 12:10). It is the ability to distinguish between the spirit of truth and the spirit of error, between the voice of God and the voice of the enemy, between what is life-giving and what is death-dealing. It is not a paranoid or suspicious gift; it is a loving, clear-eyed awareness that allows us to navigate the spiritual landscape with wisdom and grace.

The Rowan is a natural sacrament of this gift. It is a living reminder that God has not left us defenceless in a world full of deception and manipulation. He has given us the Holy Spirit, the Comforter, the one who "will guide you into all the truth" (John 16:13), and he has given us the natural world as a teacher and a constant source of wisdom and guidance. The Rowan, with its bright red berries shining like beacons in the forest, is a sign of this divine guidance, a promise that we will always be able to see the path if we are willing to look.

Jesus himself taught his disciples to be discerning and wise. He said, "Behold, I am sending you out as sheep in the midst of wolves, so be wise as serpents and innocent as doves" (Matthew 10:16). This is the Rowan's wisdom: to be clear-eyed and aware, to see the world as it truly is, but not to become cynical or hard-hearted. To see the danger without losing the capacity for love. To be discerning without being judgmental. To be awake without being anxious.

The Rowan teaches us that protection begins with seeing. If we can see clearly, trust our intuition, and recognise the subtle signs of danger or deception before they take root in our lives, then we can avoid so much unnecessary suffering. We can avoid toxic relationships. We can recognise manipulative people and situations. We can discern whether a spiritual teaching or practice leads us toward God or away from him. We can protect ourselves not by building walls, but by opening our eyes.

THE PRACTICE: A MEDITATION ON CLEAR SEEING

Now it is time to make this wisdom personal. Find a quiet place where you will not be disturbed. If possible, sit beneath a Rowan tree, or hold a piece of Rowan wood or a cluster of Rowan berries in your hands. Close your eyes and take several deep, slow breaths.

Step 1: Awaken the Inner Seer

Imagine that there is a third eye in the centre of your forehead, just above and between your physical eyes. This is your spiritual eye, your inner seer, the part of you that can perceive things that are hidden from ordinary sight. As you breathe, imagine this eye opening slowly, gently, like a flower opening to the sun. With each breath, it opens a little wider, and you begin to see with a new kind of vision.

Step 2: Scan Your Energy Field

Now, with your inner eye open, scan your own energy field, the invisible aura of light and life that surrounds your body. Notice where it feels bright and strong, and where it feels dim or depleted. Are there any places where your energy feels drained, where there seems to be a leak or a hole? Are there any dark spots, any areas of confusion or heaviness? Just notice, without judgment. The Rowan is helping you to see.

Step 3: Ask for Clarity on a Specific Situation

Consider a specific situation in your life in which you feel confused, uncertain, or drained. It might be a relationship, a job, a decision you need to make, or a spiritual question you are wrestling with. Hold this situation gently in your awareness, and ask the Rowan, ask the Holy Spirit, ask your own deepest intuition: "What is the truth here? What am I not seeing? What do I need to know?" Then, wait. Listen. Be open to whatever comes—a word, an image, a feeling, a knowing. Trust what you receive.

Step 4: Give Thanks and Close

When you feel complete, thank the Rowan for its guidance. Thank the Holy Spirit for the gift of discernment. Gently close your inner eye, knowing that you can open it again whenever you need to. Take a few deep breaths, and when you are ready, open your physical eyes.

Journaling Prompts:

• Where in my life do I feel confused, uncertain, or drained?

• What hidden dynamics might be at play in this situation?

• What does my deepest intuition, the Rowan within me, tell me about this?

• How can I cultivate the gift of discernment in my daily life?

THE HOLLY (TINNE): THE WARRIOR'S SHIELD AND THE FIRE OF ACTION

If the Rowan is the tree of seeing, the Holly is the tree of acting. If the Rowan teaches us to discern the truth, the Holly teaches us to defend the truth. If the Rowan is the lantern that illuminates the path, the Holly is the shield and sword that protect us as we walk it. The Holly is the tree of the spiritual warrior, the one who does not seek conflict but who does not shrink from it, the one who knows that love sometimes requires fierce action, that compassion sometimes demands a firm "no," and that the sacred must be defended.

The Holly is unmistakable in the winter landscape. While other trees have shed their leaves and stand bare against the cold, the Holly remains green, vibrant, alive. Its leaves are thick and waxy, edged with sharp spines that deter any creature from browsing on them. Its berries are a brilliant red, like drops of blood against the dark green foliage, a sign of life persisting in the heart of winter. The Holly does not hide. It does not retreat. It stands firm, beautiful and dangerous, a living testament to the power of endurance and the necessity of boundaries.

In the Celtic tradition, the Holly was revered as the king of the dark half of the year, the evergreen sovereign who rules from the autumn equinox to the spring equinox, the time when the sun is weak and the nights are long. It represents the light and life that endure even in the harshest times, the fire of the spirit that cannot be extinguished, the strength that does not depend on external conditions but burns from within.

THE SPIRITUAL WARRIOR: BOUNDARIES, DEFENCE, AND HOLY RESISTANCE

To speak of the Holly is to speak of the spiritual warrior, and we must be very clear about what this means. The spiritual warrior is not someone who is aggressive, domineering, or violent.

The spiritual warrior is not someone who seeks out conflict or who enjoys fighting. The spiritual warrior is someone who has learned to set healthy boundaries, defend what is sacred, say "no" when necessary, and channel anger into constructive, protective action.

In our modern world, we have largely lost the understanding of what it means to be a spiritual warrior. We have confused warriorship with aggression, strength with domination, and boundaries with cruelty. We have been taught, especially in certain streams of Christianity, that to be spiritual is to be passive, to be endlessly accommodating, to "turn the other cheek" no matter what. And while there is profound truth in Jesus' teaching about non-retaliation and forgiveness, there is also profound danger in misunderstanding it as a call to be a doormat, to allow ourselves and others to be exploited, to refuse to defend what is sacred.

The Holly teaches us a different way. It teaches us that there is a time for gentleness and a time for fierceness. There is a time to open the door and a time to close it. There is a time to say "yes" and a time to say "no" with the full force of our being. The Holly teaches us that love is not weak, that compassion is not passive, and that the spiritual life requires not only the softness of the dove but also the sharpness of the thorn.

CHRIST CLEANSING THE TEMPLE: THE NECESSITY OF HOLY DISRUPTION

One of the most striking and misunderstood moments in the Gospels is when Jesus enters the Jerusalem temple and finds it transformed into a marketplace. The sacred space, meant to be a house of prayer for all nations, has become a den of thieves, a place where the poor are exploited, and the divine encounter is commodified. And what does Jesus do? He does not write a letter of complaint. He does not organise a committee. He does not pray quietly in a corner. He makes a whip of cords, overturns the tables of the money-changers, drives out the merchants, and declares with fierce authority: "Take these things away; do not make my Father's house a house of trade" (John 2:16).

This is the ultimate Holly-energy act. It is not gentle. It is not passive. It is not "nice." It is fierce, disruptive, and absolutely necessary. It is the energy of righteous anger, of holy indignation, of the spiritual warrior who will not tolerate the desecration of sacred space.

For too long, the Christian tradition—particularly in its more modern, Western forms—has been uncomfortable with this aspect of Jesus. We prefer the gentle shepherd, the compassionate healer, the one who says, "Turn the other cheek." And those images are true and essential. But they are not the whole truth. Jesus was also the one who called the religious leaders "whitewashed tombs" and "a brood of vipers." He was the one who said, "I have not come to bring peace, but a sword" (Matthew 10:34). He was the one who wept over Jerusalem and then marched into the temple with a whip.

The Holly teaches us that this fierce, protective, boundary-setting energy is not a departure from love; it is an expression of love. It is the love that refuses to stand by while the vulnerable are exploited. It is the love that will not allow the sacred to be profaned. It is the love that knows when to say "no" with the full force of one's being.

Righteous Anger: The Spiritual Necessity of Holy Fire

We live in a culture that is deeply confused about anger. On the one hand, we are told that anger is always destructive, a "negative emotion" to be avoided or suppressed. On the other hand, we are drowning in toxic anger— rage on social media, road rage, political rage, the constant low-level irritation that characterises so much of modern life. We have lost the ability to distinguish between destructive anger and righteous anger, between the anger that tears down and the anger that protects.

The Holly invites us to reclaim the ancient understanding of righteous anger as a spiritual gift, a necessary energy for protecting what is sacred.

Let us be clear about what righteous anger is not:

Righteous anger is not anger that seeks revenge or personal satisfaction. It is not anger that is rooted in wounded ego or pride. It is not anger that lashes out indiscriminately, harming the innocent. It is not anger that is held onto and nursed into bitterness or resentment.

Righteous anger is anger on behalf of others, particularly the vulnerable and the voiceless. It is anger that arises from a clear perception of injustice or violation of the sacred. It is anger that is channelled into constructive, protective action. It is anger that is released once the boundary has been set or the injustice addressed.

Righteous anger is the emotional energy that fuels the prophet, the reformer, the defender of the weak. It is the fire that burns away complacency and apathy. It is the force that says, "This is not acceptable. This must change. I will not stand by."

In the Christian tradition, this energy is not foreign or pagan; it is deeply biblical. The prophets of the Hebrew Bible are filled with righteous anger at the exploitation of the poor, the corruption of the priests, and the idolatry of the people. Amos thunders against those who "trample on the needy and bring the poor of the land to an end" (Amos 8:4). Isaiah cries out, "Woe to those who decree iniquitous decrees, and the writers who keep writing oppression" (Isaiah 10:1). Jesus himself stands in this prophetic tradition, embodying the holy anger of God against all that dehumanizes, exploits, and destroys.

The Holly teaches that refusing to feel righteous anger in the face of injustice is not a sign of spiritual maturity; it is a sign of spiritual numbness. It is a failure to love. The opposite of love is not hate; it is indifference. To see suffering and to feel nothing, to witness injustice and to remain unmoved, to watch the sacred being violated and to shrug—this is not holiness. This is the death of the soul.

The Holly invites us to find the middle way: to feel the fire of righteous anger without being consumed by it, to channel it into protective action without allowing it to become a destructive force in our own souls. This is the art of the spiritual warrior. This is the wisdom of the Holly.

THE ARMOUR OF GOD: THE HOLLY AS SHIELD AND SWORD

In his letter to the Ephesians, St. Paul writes one of the most famous passages on spiritual warfare in the entire New Testament:

"Finally, be strong in the Lord and in the strength of his might. Put on the whole armour of God, that you may be able to stand against the schemes of the devil. For we do not wrestle against flesh and blood, but against the rulers, against the authorities, against the cosmic powers over this present darkness, against the spiritual forces of evil in the heavenly places.

Therefore, take up the whole armour of God, that you may be able to withstand in the evil day, and having done all, to stand firm. Stand therefore, having fastened on the belt of truth, and having put on the breastplate of righteousness, and, as shoes for your feet, having put on the readiness given by the gospel of peace. In all circumstances take up the shield of faith, with which you can extinguish all the flaming darts of the evil one; and take the helmet of salvation, and the sword of the Spirit, which is the word of God." (Ephesians 6:10-17)

The Holly is the living embodiment of this spiritual armour. Its spiky leaves are the shield of faith, deflecting the "flaming darts" of negativity, manipulation, and spiritual attack. Its red berries are the fire of the Spirit, the life-force that endures even in the darkest times. Its wood, strong and resilient, is the sword of the Spirit, the tool we use to cut through lies and illusions and to defend the truth.

Paul's language here is important: we do not wrestle against flesh and blood. Our battle is not against other people, but against the spiritual forces that seek to diminish, divide, and destroy. The Holly teaches us to be fierce in our defence of the sacred, but never cruel. It teaches us to set boundaries, but not to dehumanise those on the other side of the boundary. It teaches us to fight, but to fight with love.

This is the paradox of the spiritual warrior: the fiercest fighters are often the most compassionate, because they know what they are fighting for. They are not fighting out of hatred, but out of love. They are not attacking; they are defending. They are not seeking to destroy; they are seeking to protect the space where life can flourish.

THE HOLLY AND THE CROSS: THE THORNS THAT PROTECT

There is one more profound connection between the Holly and the Christian faith that we must explore: the crown of thorns. In the Passion narrative, the Roman soldiers mock Jesus by weaving a crown of thorns and placing it on his head, a cruel parody of a king's crown. The Gospels do not specify what kind of thorns were used, but Christian tradition has long associated them with the Holly, whose sharp spikes and association with kingship (the Holly King) make it a fitting symbol.

But here is the deeper truth: what was meant as an instrument of mockery and torture becomes, in the mystery of the Cross, an instrument of protection and redemption. The thorns that pierce Christ's head are the same thorns that guard the sacred. They are the boundaries that evil cannot cross. They are the price that love pays to create a safe space for the world.

The Holly, with its thorns, teaches us that protection always comes at a cost. Setting a boundary entails risking rejection. To defend the sacred is to invite conflict. To say "no" to what is harmful is to face the anger of those who benefit from the harm. But this is the cost of love. This is the price of discipleship. This is the way of the Cross.

The Holly invites us to wear our own crown of thorns—not as a burden, but as a badge of honour. It invites us to embrace the discomfort of setting boundaries, the loneliness of standing firm, and the cost of defending what is sacred. And it promises that, like Christ, we will find that the thorns that wound us are also the thorns that protect us, that the boundaries we set in love become the walls of a sacred garden where life can flourish.

THE PRACTICE: A MEDITATION ON HEALTHY BOUNDARIES

Find a quiet place and sit comfortably. If possible, sit near a Holly tree or hold a sprig of Holly in your hands (carefully, respecting its thorns). Close your eyes and take several deep, slow breaths.

Step 1: Envision Your Sacred Circle

Imagine that you are standing in the centre of a circle. This circle is your sacred space, your inner sanctuary, the place where your soul dwells. Now, imagine that around the perimeter of this circle, a ring of Holly trees begins to grow. They grow quickly, their branches intertwining, their leaves forming a protective barrier, their thorns facing outward. This is your boundary, your shield, your protection.

Step 2: Identify What Needs to Stay Out

Now, bring to mind a person, situation, or energy in your life that is draining you, harming you, or violating your sacred space. It might be a toxic relationship, a demanding job, a negative thought pattern, or a spiritual influence that is leading you away from God. See this energy approaching your circle of Holly trees, and watch as the trees hold firm. The thorns do not attack; they say, "You may not enter here. This space is sacred."

Step 3: Practice Saying "No"

Now, speak aloud (or in your heart) a firm but loving "no" to this energy. You might say: "I do not permit you to drain my energy. I do not allow you to violate my sacred space. I set a boundary here, in love, for the protection of my soul." Feel the strength of the Holly filling you, giving you the courage to stand firm.

Step 4: Breathe and Integrate

Take a few deep breaths, feeling yourself safe within your circle of Holly. Know that you have the right to protect yourself, that setting boundaries is an act of love, and that the Holly will always be there to help you. When you are ready, gently open your eyes.

Journaling Prompts:

• Where in my life do I need to set a firmer boundary?

• What am I afraid will happen if I do?

• What sacred part of myself am I called to defend?

• How can I channel my anger into constructive, protective action?

THE HAWTHORN (HÚATH): THE GUARDIAN OF THE THRESHOLD AND THE WISDOM OF PATIENCE

If the Rowan teaches us to see and the Holly teaches us to act, the Hawthorn teaches us to wait. If the Rowan is the lantern and the Holly is the shield, the Hawthorn is the gate, the threshold, the boundary between the known and the unknown, the sacred and the profane, the human world and the Otherworld. The Hawthorn is the most feared and the most revered tree in the entire Celtic landscape, and for good reason: it is the guardian of the liminal spaces, the keeper of the mysteries, the tree that stands at the edge of the sacred and says, "You may not pass—unless you are ready."

The Hawthorn is a tree of paradox. In late spring, it blooms, covered with clusters of white flowers so abundant and so fragrant that the entire countryside seems to glow with their beauty. It is a tree of joy, of fertility, of the promise of summer. But beneath those delicate blossoms are thorns—long, sharp, unforgiving thorns that can tear flesh and draw blood. In autumn, those blossoms give way to small red berries, called "haws," which are edible but tart, a reminder that the gifts of the sacred are not always sweet.

This is the essence of the Hawthorn: beauty and danger, invitation and warning, opening and closing. It is the tree that says, "Come closer, but not too close. Approach, but with respect. Enter, but only when you are ready." The Hawthorn is the guardian of the threshold, and it teaches us one of the most difficult and most necessary lessons of the spiritual life: the wisdom of patience, the art of waiting, the discipline of preparation.

The Faerie Tree: Gateway to the Otherworld

In Irish and Scottish folklore, the Hawthorn is known as the "faerie tree," and it is regarded with both reverence and terror. To cut down a Hawthorn, especially one that stands alone in a field (a "lone bush"), is to invite catastrophe. The stories are legion: farmers who cut down a Hawthorn and then lost their livestock, their health, or even their lives. Builders who attempted to move a Hawthorn to make way for a road found their equipment breaking down, their workers falling ill, and their projects plagued by inexplicable delays. Even in modern Ireland, there are documented cases of roads being rerouted to avoid disturbing a sacred Hawthorn.

To the modern, rationalist mind, this might seem like superstition, like a primitive fear of the unknown. But to the Celtic soul, it was something far deeper: it was a recognition that there are boundaries in the world that must not be crossed lightly, that there are sacred spaces that demand our respect, and that the Otherworld—the realm of the spirits, the ancestors, the divine—is not a fantasy or a metaphor, but a real dimension of existence that intersects with our own at certain places and certain times. The Hawthorn marks those places. It stands at the threshold, and it says, "Be careful. Be respectful. Be prepared."

The Hawthorn is associated with the Sidhe (pronounced "shee"), the faerie folk, the ancient gods and spirits of Ireland who retreated into the hollow hills and the hidden places when the human world became too loud, too busy, too disrespectful. The Hawthorn is their tree, their guardian, their gatekeeper. To approach a Hawthorn is to approach the edge of the Otherworld, and you do not do that casually. You do not do that with arrogance or entitlement. You do it with humility, with patience, with a willingness to wait until you are invited in.

The Thorn of Challenge: Preparation and Initiation

The Hawthorn's thorns are not as aggressive as the Holly's. The Holly's thorns are sharp and outward-facing, designed to repel actively. The Hawthorn's thorns are more subtle, more passive. They create a thicket, a

114

tangle, a barrier that is difficult to penetrate. They do not attack; they impede passage. They slow you down. They force you to be careful, to be intentional, to pay attention to every step.

This is the Hawthorn's great teaching: the sacred is not easily accessed. It requires preparation. It requires patience. It requires a willingness to be slowed down, challenged, and tested. The Hawthorn is the tree of initiation, and initiation is never easy. It is the process by which we are transformed from who we were into who we are meant to be, and that transformation always involves a threshold, a passage, a moment of fear and uncertainty when we do not yet know what lies on the other side.

In ancient mystery traditions, initiates were required to undergo trials, confront their fears, and demonstrate readiness before being permitted to enter the inner sanctum and receive the sacred teachings. This was not cruelty; it was wisdom. It was a recognition that the sacred is powerful, that it can overwhelm an unprepared soul, and that to approach it without proper preparation is dangerous—not because the sacred is hostile, but because it is so utterly other, so far beyond our ordinary experience, that we need to be strengthened, purified, and made ready before we can bear its presence.

The Hawthorn embodies this wisdom. Its thorns are not there to keep us out forever; they are there to make sure we are ready before we enter. They are there to test our sincerity, our patience, our humility. They are there to ask us: "Do you really want this? Are you willing to pay the price? Are you prepared to be changed?"

THE PARADOX OF FEAR AND BEAUTY: THE MAY BLOSSOMS

But the Hawthorn is not only a tree of fear and challenge. It is also a tree of extraordinary beauty. In May, the Hawthorn blooms, and the transformation is breathtaking. The thorny, forbidding tree becomes a cloud of white blossoms, so abundant that they seem to glow in the spring sunlight. The fragrance is sweet and heady, filling the air with the promise of summer, of fertility, of life renewed.

This is the paradox of the Hawthorn, and it is the paradox of the spiritual life itself: the most sacred things are often guarded by our greatest fears. The most beautiful experiences lie on the other side of the most difficult thresholds. The deepest joy is found only by those who are willing to wait, to prepare, to face the thorns.

In the Celtic calendar, May was the month of Bealtaine, the great fire festival that marked the beginning of summer. It was a time of celebration, of fertility rites, of the marriage of the earth and the sky. And the Hawthorn, blooming in all its glory, was the symbol of this sacred union. The May blossoms were gathered and woven into garlands, hung over doorways, and used to decorate the Maypole. They were a sign that the threshold had been crossed, that the dark half of the year was over, and that the light had returned.

But—and this is crucial—the Hawthorn only blooms for those who wait. If you try to force it, if you cut it down or damage it in your impatience, you will never see the blossoms. The Hawthorn teaches us that there is a right time for everything, a sacred timing that cannot be rushed, and that the greatest gifts come to those who are willing to wait with patient, respectful attention.

CHRISTIAN INTEGRATION: THE SACRED ENCLOSURE AND THE MONASTIC THRESHOLD

In the Christian tradition, the Hawthorn's wisdom finds its perfect expression in the concept of the claustrum, the sacred enclosure of the monastery. The walls of a monastery were not a prison; they were a boundary, a threshold, a protective space that separated the inner world of prayer and contemplation from the outer world of noise and distraction. Entering a monastery was to cross a threshold, and it was not undertaken lightly. Those who sought to become monks or nuns underwent a long period of preparation, a novitiate, during which they were tested, taught, and gradually initiated into the rhythms and disciplines of the monastic life.

This was not because the monastery sought to keep people out; rather, monastic life is demanding, and those who enter it must be prepared. The sacred enclosure is not a place to escape from the world; it is a place to encounter God in his fullness, and that encounter requires a prepared soul. The Hawthorn, with its thorny thicket surrounding the sacred space, is the natural version of the monastery wall. It says, "This space is set apart. If you wish to enter, you must be prepared. You must wait. You must prove your sincerity."

St. Brigid, when she founded her monastery at Kildare, understood this wisdom. She created a sacred enclosure, a space set apart for prayer, for study, for the cultivation of the inner life. But she did not make it a fortress. She made it a threshold, a place where the sacred and the ordinary could meet, where those who were ready could cross over and encounter the divine. The Hawthorn teaches us to do the same in our own lives: to create sacred spaces, sacred times, and sacred practices set apart from the noise and busyness of the world, and to guard those spaces with patience and respect.

"KNOCK, AND THE DOOR WILL BE OPENED": THE HUMILITY OF APPROACH

Jesus himself taught the wisdom of the threshold. He said, "Ask, and it will be given to you; seek, and you will find; knock, and the door will be opened to you" (Matthew 7:7). Notice the progression: ask, seek, knock. We do not demand. We do not force. We do not break down the door. We approach with humility. We ask. We seek. We knock, and then we wait for the door to be opened from the other side.

This is the Hawthorn's wisdom. The sacred is not something we can seize by force or access at will. It is a gift, and it is given to those who approach with the right spirit—with humility, with patience, with a willingness to wait until the time is right. The Hawthorn stands at the threshold and teaches us to knock, not to barge in. It teaches us to wait, not to force. It teaches us to respect the boundary, knowing that when we are ready, when the time is right, the door will open, and we will be invited into the sacred space.

This is especially important in our modern world, where we have become accustomed to instant gratification, to having everything we want at the click of a button. We have lost the capacity to wait, to be patient, to allow things to unfold in their own time. We want the spiritual life to be easy, convenient, and to fit into our busy schedules. But the Hawthorn teaches us that the sacred does not work that way. It has its own timing, its own rhythms, and if we want to experience it in its fullness, we must learn to wait.

THE PRACTICE: A MEDITATION ON THE SACRED THRESHOLD

Find a quiet place and sit comfortably. If possible, sit near a Hawthorn tree, or hold a sprig of Hawthorn (carefully, respecting its thorns). Close your eyes and take several deep, slow breaths.

Step 1: Identify Your Threshold

Bring to mind a threshold in your own life—a big decision you need to make, a new relationship you are considering, a spiritual calling you are discerning, a change you are contemplating. This is a doorway, a passage from one state of being to another, and you are standing before it, uncertain whether to cross.

Step 2: Sit Before the Hawthorn Gate

Now, imagine that this threshold is guarded by a beautiful Hawthorn tree, covered in white blossoms, but also surrounded by thorns. You cannot force your way through. You cannot rush. You must sit before the gate and wait. As you sit, ask yourself: Am I ready to cross this threshold? What preparation is still needed? What fears do I need to face? What lessons do I need to learn before I can safely pass through?

Step 3: Ask for Guidance

Now, speak to the Hawthorn, to the guardian of the threshold, to the Holy Spirit who guides us into all truth. Say: "Show me what I need to know. Help me to be patient. Give me the wisdom to wait until the time is right. And when the door opens, give me the courage to step through." Then, sit in silence, listening, waiting, trusting.

Step 4: Trust the Timing

When you feel complete, thank the Hawthorn for its wisdom. Know that the door will open when you are ready, and not a moment before. Trust the sacred timing. Take a few deep breaths, and when you are ready, gently open your eyes.

Journaling Prompts:

• What threshold am I currently facing in my life?

• Am I trying to force it open, or am I waiting with patient respect?

• What preparation is needed before I can safely cross?

• How can I cultivate the virtue of patience in my spiritual life?

CONCLUSION: THE COMPLETE GUARDIAN

We have now met the three great guardians of the Celtic grove. We have learned from the Rowan how to see with clarity and discernment, to trust our intuition, and to recognise truth and danger before they overtake us. We have learned from the Holly how to act with courage and conviction, to set firm boundaries, to defend what is sacred, and to channel our righteous anger into constructive, protective force. We have learned from the Hawthorn how to wait with patience and respect, to honour sacred thresholds, to prepare ourselves for spiritual initiation, and to trust in the divine timing that governs all things.

These are not three separate lessons; they are three dimensions of a single, unified wisdom. They are the three movements of the spiritual dance of protection, and we need all three to navigate the spiritual life with grace, strength, and wisdom. Let us now see how they work together, how they complement and complete one another, and how they form a complete system of spiritual self-defence that is both ancient and urgently relevant for our time.

THE TRINITY OF PROTECTION: SEE, ACT, WAIT

The Rowan, the Holly, and the Hawthorn together form a trinity of protection, a three-fold strategy for guarding the soul. And like all true trinities, they are not three separate things, but three aspects of one reality, three movements of one dance.

The Rowan teaches us to SEE. This is the first movement, the foundation of all protection. If we cannot see clearly, if we are blind to the truth, if we are deceived by appearances or manipulated by lies, then no amount of action or patience will save us. We will walk blindly into danger. We will give our energy to those who do not deserve it. We will mistake the voice of the enemy for the voice of God. The Rowan awakens the seer within us, the one who can perceive what is hidden, who can discern between the spirit of truth and the spirit of error, who can recognise the subtle signs of danger or blessing before they become obvious. This is the gift of spiritual sight, the first line of defence.

The Holly teaches us to ACT. This is the second movement, the necessary follow-through. Seeing alone is not enough. We can see the truth clearly, we can recognise danger, we can discern what is harmful—but if we do not act on that knowledge, if we do not set boundaries, if we do not defend what is sacred, then our seeing is useless. The Holly gives us the courage to act, to say "no" when necessary, to stand firm in the face of opposition, to channel our righteous anger into protective force. This is the gift of spiritual warriorship, the second line of defence.

The Hawthorn teaches us to WAIT. This is the third movement, the wisdom of restraint. Acting alone is not enough. We can be courageous, we can be fierce, we can be willing to fight—but if we do not know when to act, if we rush in unprepared, if we force thresholds that are not yet ready to be crossed, then our action becomes reckless and destructive. The Hawthorn gives us the patience to wait, to prepare, to honour sacred timing, to approach the divine with humility and respect. This is the gift of spiritual discernment, the third line of defence.

Together, these three movements form a complete cycle, a spiritual rhythm that we can return to again and again in our lives:

1. See the truth with the clarity of the Rowan.

2. Act on that truth with the courage of the Holly.

3. Wait for the right timing with the patience of the Hawthorn.

This is the dance of the guardian. This is the way of protection. This is how we keep our souls safe in a dangerous world.

Protection as an Act of Love

We must understand spiritual protection not as a fearful act of walling ourselves off from the world, but as a loving act of self-care that allows us to serve the world from a place of fullness rather than depletion. This distinction is often lost in our culture, which tends to see boundaries as selfish and self-care as indulgent. But the truth is exactly the opposite.

If we do not protect ourselves, if we allow our energy to be drained by toxic relationships and harmful situations, if we give ourselves away to everyone and everything without discernment, then we will have nothing left to give to those who truly need us. We will burn out. We will become bitter, resentful, and depleted. We will lose our capacity for joy, for creativity, for love. And in that state, we are no good to anyone—not to ourselves, not to our loved ones, not to the world, and not to God.

The guardians teach us that protection is not the opposite of love; it is the prerequisite for love. We cannot love well if we are depleted. We cannot serve well if we are exhausted. We cannot give generously if we have nothing left to give. The Rowan, the Holly, and the Hawthorn teach us to guard our energy, to set boundaries, to create sacred space, so that we can be a source of light and life for others rather than a burned-out shell.

This is what Jesus meant when he said, "Love your neighbour as yourself" (Mark 12:31). Notice: as yourself. Not instead of yourself. Not more than yourself. As yourself. The love we give to others must be rooted in a healthy love of self, a proper care for our own souls, and a wise stewardship of our own energy. The guardians teach us how to do this. They teach us that self-care is not selfish; it is sacred.

THE INTEGRATED GUARDIAN: DISCERNMENT, COURAGE, AND RESPECT

A mature spiritual person, one who has learned the lessons of the guardians, embodies all three energies simultaneously. They are discerning like the Rowan, courageous like the Holly, and respectful like the Hawthorn. They know when to see, when to act, and when to wait. They are neither naive nor cynical, neither passive nor aggressive, neither reckless nor paralysed. They have found the middle way, the balanced path, the integrated life.

Such a person can walk through the world with their eyes wide open, seeing the truth of every situation without being overwhelmed by it. They can set firm boundaries without being cruel, defend the sacred without being self-righteous, and say "no" without guilt or apology. They can also wait patiently, honour the sacred timing of events, and approach the divine with humility and awe. They are, in short, a guardian—not just of their own soul, but of the souls of others, of the sacred spaces in the world, of the light that must not be allowed to go out.

This is the goal of the spiritual life: not to be invulnerable, not to be untouchable, not to be isolated, but to be integrated. To be whole. To be fully alive, fully awake, fully present, fully protected, and fully available to love and to serve.

THE BRIGIDINE LENS: THE THREE GUARDIANS AND THE THREE ASPECTS OF BRIGID

As we have seen throughout this book, the Brigidine tradition offers us a powerful lens for understanding the integration of Celtic and Christian wisdom. And once again, we find that the three guardian trees correspond beautifully to the three aspects of St. Brigid.

The Rowan is Brigid the Poet. The poet is the one who sees, who perceives the hidden patterns, who reads the signs, who listens to the whispers of the divine in the rustling of leaves and the flight of birds. The poet is the seer, the prophet, the one who speaks truth to power and who illuminates what is hidden. The Rowan, with its bright red berries shining like lanterns in the forest, is the tree of the poet, the tree of vision, the tree of the inner eye that sees what others cannot.

The Holly is Brigid the Smith. The smith is the one who acts, who forges, who shapes, who takes raw materials and transforms them into tools of power and beauty. The smith is the warrior, the defender, the one who uses fire and force to create and to protect. The Holly, with its sharp thorns and its enduring green, is the tree of the smith, the tree of action, the tree of the forge where boundaries are set and the sacred is defended.

The Hawthorn is Brigid the Healer. The healer is the one who waits, who listens, who honours the body's own timing, who knows that healing cannot be rushed. The healer is the gatekeeper, the one who guards the threshold between sickness and health, between life and death, between the human and the divine. The Hawthorn, with its thorny barrier and its beautiful blossoms, is the tree of the healer, the tree of patience, the tree of the sacred threshold where transformation happens in its own time. Together, these three aspects of Brigid—Poet, Smith, and Healer—form a complete picture of the spiritual guardian. We need the poet's vision, the smith's courage, and the healer's patience. We need to see, to act, and to wait. We need to be discerning, fierce, and respectful all at once. This is the Brigidine way. This is the way of integration. This is the way of the grove.

Bridge to the Next Chapter

We have now established the foundation (Chapter 5: Oak, Ash, Yew) and learned how to protect it (Chapter 6: Rowan, Holly, Hawthorn).

We have been given the three pillars of strength, connection, and eternity, and we have been taught the three strategies of seeing, acting, and waiting.

We are rooted. We are guarded. We are ready.

And now, finally, we can seek the deepest treasures of the grove: the gifts of wisdom and inspiration. In the next chapter, we will meet the trees of knowledge—the Hazel, the Apple, and the Elder—the ancient teachers who guard the wells of wisdom, who offer the fruit of the Otherworld, and who whisper the secrets of the ages.

We will learn how to drink from the Well of Wisdom, how to journey to the Isle of Apples, and how to sit at the feet of the Crone who knows all things.

But for now, rest in this: you are protected. You have the Rowan's sight, the Holly's courage, and the Hawthorn's patience. You are a guardian of your own soul, and you are ready for the journey ahead.

The guardians have spoken.

The way is clear. The journey continues.

Chapter 7:

The Well of Wisdom: Trees of Knowledge and Inspiration

THE THREE STREAMS OF WISDOM

We have walked a long and fruitful path through the sacred grove. We have sat at the feet of the three great elders—the Oak, the Ash, and the Yew—and learned the foundational lessons of Strength, Connection, and Eternity. We have then sought out the three great guardians—the Rowan, the Holly, and the Hawthorn—and learned the practical arts of spiritual protection: how to See, how to Act, and how to Wait. We are rooted. We are guarded. We are ready.

And now, finally, we arrive at the heart of the grove, the place where the deepest treasures are hidden. We come to the well of wisdom itself. Having established our foundation and secured our boundaries, we are now prepared to receive the gifts of knowledge, inspiration, and deep knowing that the Celtic tradition has to offer. This is the goal of the spiritual journey: not just to be strong, not just to be safe, but to be wise. To see the world with the eyes of God, to understand the hidden patterns of creation, and to be filled with the creative fire of divine inspiration.

In this chapter, we will meet the three great teachers of wisdom in the Celtic grove: the Hazel, the Apple, and the Elder.

These are not just trees; they are living conduits of the three great streams of wisdom that flow from the heart of the divine:

• **The Hazel (Coll)** is the guardian of the Well of Wisdom. It represents the stream of knowledge that comes from deep within, from the hidden source of all things. It is the wisdom of contemplation, of intuition, of the direct, unmediated encounter with the divine. It is the wisdom of the mystic.

• **The Apple (Quert)** is the guardian of the Silver Branch. It represents the stream of knowledge that comes from the Otherworld, from the realm of the spirits, the ancestors, and the divine beings. It is the wisdom of the shamanic journey, of the quest for vision, of the courage to travel beyond the veil of ordinary reality to bring back gifts for the community. It is the wisdom of the visionary.

• **The Elder (Ruis)** is the guardian of the Sacred Earth. It represents the stream of knowledge that comes from experience, from the cycles of nature, from the wisdom of the body, and from the deep, practical knowing of the Crone who has seen it all. It is the wisdom of the herbalist, the midwife, the storyteller, the one who knows the secrets of life and death because she has lived them. It is the wisdom of the elder.

Together, these three trees offer a complete education in the ways of knowing. They teach us that wisdom is not just one thing; it is a river with many streams. It is not merely about intellectual knowledge but also about intuitive insight, visionary experience, and embodied, practical knowing. To be truly wise is to drink from all three streams, to honour the mystic, the visionary, and the elder within ourselves.

So, let us now approach the well. Let us prepare to taste the fruit of the Otherworld. Let us sit at the feet of the ancient Crone. The journey into the heart of wisdom begins now.

THE HAZEL (COLL): THE WELL OF WISDOM AND THE SALMON OF KNOWLEDGE

If you walk through an Irish woodland in late summer or early autumn, you will find them: small, elegant trees with smooth grey bark and heart-shaped leaves, bearing clusters of nuts enclosed in leafy green husks. These are the Hazel trees, and their nuts—hazelnuts—are one of the great treasures of the forest. They are sweet, rich, and nourishing, packed with oils and proteins that have sustained humans and animals for millennia. But in the Celtic tradition, the Hazel is not valued merely for its physical nourishment. It is revered for its spiritual nourishment, as hazelnuts are said to contain not only calories but also wisdom.

The Hazel is the tree of the Well of Wisdom, the guardian of the deepest source of knowledge in the Celtic cosmos. It is the tree of contemplation, of meditation, of the inward journey to the still point at the centre of the soul where the divine voice can be heard most clearly. The Hazel teaches us that the greatest wisdom does not come from books, from teachers, or from external authorities. It comes from within, from the deep well of the soul where we are connected to the source of all knowing.

THE NINE HAZELS AND THE WELL OF SEGAIS: THE SOURCE OF ALL KNOWLEDGE

At the heart of Celtic mythology is a sacred well, Tobar Segais (the Well of Segais), which is said to be the source of all the rivers of Ireland and, by extension, of all knowledge and inspiration. This well is located in the Otherworld, in a hidden place accessible only to those who are ready, who have prepared themselves through spiritual discipline and inner work.

Around this well grow nine sacred Hazel trees. These are not ordinary trees; they are the primordial Hazels, the first trees, the source from which all other Hazels descend. At certain times of the year, these trees drop their nuts into the well, and the nuts sink to the bottom. There, they are eaten by a sacred salmon—the Salmon of Knowledge—who absorbs the wisdom contained in the nuts and becomes the wisest creature in all of creation.

The salmon's body becomes covered with spots, one spot for each nut of wisdom it has consumed. To catch this salmon, to taste its flesh, is to receive all the knowledge of the universe in a single, overwhelming flash of illumination. This is the ultimate goal of the Celtic seeker: to drink from the Well of Wisdom, to taste the hazelnuts of knowledge, and to be transformed by the encounter with the divine source of all knowing.

This myth is not merely a charming fairy tale; it is a profound teaching about the nature of wisdom and its acquisition. The well represents the deep, hidden source of all things—what the Christian mystics would call the Godhead, the ground of being, the infinite mystery from which all creation flows. The Hazels represent the divine ideas, the logoi, the patterns and principles that structure reality. The salmon represents the soul, purified and prepared to receive these divine ideas. And the act of eating the salmon represents the mystical union, the moment when the soul is flooded with sacred knowledge and sees all things as they truly are.

THE STORY OF FIONN MAC CUMHAILL: THE ACCIDENTAL ENLIGHTENMENT

The most famous story of the Salmon of Knowledge involves the great Irish hero Fionn mac Cumhaill (Finn McCool). As a young man, Fionn was sent to study with a poet named Finnegas, who had spent seven years trying to catch the Salmon of Knowledge from the River Boyne. It was prophesied that whoever ate the salmon would receive all the wisdom of the world, and Finnegas believed that he was destined to be that person.

One day, Finnegas finally caught the salmon. Overjoyed, he instructed young Fionn to cook it for him, but warned him sternly: "Do not eat any of it. Not even a taste." Fionn obeyed. He carefully cooked the salmon over the fire, turning it slowly so that it would be perfectly done. But as he cooked, a blister rose on the salmon's skin, and without thinking, Fionn pressed his thumb against it to flatten it. The hot oil burned his thumb, and he instinctively put it in his mouth to soothe the pain.

In that instant, all the wisdom of the salmon flooded into him. When Finnegas saw the change in the boy's eyes, he knew immediately what had happened. The prophecy had been fulfilled, but not in the way he had expected. It was not Finnegas, but Fionn, who was destined to receive the wisdom. And so, with great humility and grace, Finnegas gave the rest of the salmon to Fionn to eat, and from that day forward, whenever Fionn needed wisdom or insight, he would put his thumb in his mouth, and the knowledge would come to him.

This story teaches us several profound truths.

First, it teaches that wisdom often comes to us unexpectedly, not through our striving and effort, but through grace, through accident, through the mysterious workings of providence. Finnegas spent seven years trying to catch the salmon, but it was the young apprentice, acting without intention, who received the gift. This is the paradox of the spiritual life: we must prepare ourselves and do the work, but ultimately, enlightenment is a gift, not an achievement.

Second, it teaches that wisdom is not something we possess; it is something we taste. Fionn did not eat the entire salmon in one sitting and then have all knowledge forever. He tasted it, and from that moment on, he could access the wisdom whenever he needed it by putting his thumb in his mouth—a gesture of remembering, of returning to the source, of reconnecting with the moment of illumination. This is the practice of contemplation: not to grasp at wisdom, but to return again and again to the well, to taste again and again the sweetness of divine knowledge.

THE HAZEL WAND: DIVINATION AND THE ART OF DOWSING

The Hazel is not only associated with the Well of Wisdom in mythology; it has also been used for centuries as a practical tool for finding hidden sources of water and knowledge. Hazel wood is the traditional material for dowsing rods, the Y-shaped sticks used to locate underground springs and wells. The dowser holds the two ends of the Y, and when they walk over a hidden source of water, the rod is said to dip or twitch, pulled down by an invisible force.

This practice, which continues to this day in rural Ireland and other Celtic lands, is not mere superstition. It is a form of intuitive knowing, a way of listening to the subtle signals of the earth and the body. The Hazel wand does not magically find water; instead, it amplifies the dowser's intuitive sense, their ability to perceive what lies beneath the surface. It is a tool for accessing the deep, unconscious knowing that we all possess but often ignore in our modern, rational culture.

The Hazel wand is also used in divination, to seek guidance from the spirit world, and to connect with the ancestors. To carry a Hazel wand is to declare yourself a seeker of hidden knowledge, a walker between the worlds, one who trusts that the answers we seek are not always found on the surface, but must be drawn up from the depths.

CHRISTIAN INTEGRATION: THE HOLY SPIRIT AS THE WELL OF LIVING WATER

In the Christian tradition, the image of the well of wisdom finds its ultimate fulfilment in Jesus' encounter with the Samaritan woman at the well (John

4:1-42). Jesus, tired from his journey, sits by the well and asks the woman for a drink. In the conversation that follows, he tells her:

"Everyone who drinks of this water will be thirsty again, but whoever drinks of the water that I will give him will never be thirsty again. The water that I will give him will become in him a spring of water welling up to eternal life." (John 4:13-14)

This is the Christian version of the Well of Wisdom. Jesus is not offering mere intellectual knowledge or esoteric secrets. He is offering living water, the Holy Spirit, the indwelling presence of God that becomes a perpetual source of wisdom, guidance, and life within the soul. To drink from this well is not to acquire information, but to be transformed, to have the very life of God flowing through you like a spring that never runs dry.

The Hazel teaches us that this well is not far away, not in some distant heaven or hidden Otherworld. It is within us. Jesus says the water will become "in him a spring of water." The well is in the depths of the soul, and to access it, we must go inward, we must be still, we must listen. This is the practice of contemplative prayer, of meditation, of sitting in silence and allowing the divine wisdom to rise up from the depths like water from a well.

St. Teresa of Ávila, the great Spanish mystic, used the image of the interior castle to describe the soul's journey to God. At the centre of the castle, in the innermost chamber, is the well of living water, the place where the soul encounters God directly, without mediation, without words. This is the goal of the contemplative life: to reach the centre, to drink from the well, to be filled with the wisdom that comes not from books or teachers, but from the direct experience of the divine presence.

The Hazel invites us to make this inward journey. It invites us to trust that the wisdom we seek is not outside us, but within us, waiting to be discovered. It invites us to sit in silence, to listen, to wait for the still, small voice of God to speak in the depths of our hearts.

THE PRACTICE: A MEDITATION ON THE INNER WELL

Find a quiet place where you will not be disturbed. If possible, sit beneath a Hazel tree, or hold a hazelnut in your hand. Close your eyes and take several deep, slow breaths.

Step 1: Descend to the Well

Imagine that you are standing at the top of a stone staircase that spirals down into the earth. This staircase leads to the well of wisdom at the centre of your soul. With each breath, take one step down. Feel yourself descending deeper and deeper, leaving behind the noise and distraction of the surface world, moving into the silence and stillness of the depths.

Step 2: Arrive at the Well

After many steps, you arrive at the bottom. Before you is a stone well, ancient and sacred. The water in the well is clear and still, reflecting the light from above. Around the well, nine Hazel trees grow, their branches heavy with nuts. This is the Well of Segais, the source of all wisdom, and it is within you.

Step 3: Drink from the Well

Now, approach the well. Kneel beside it. Cup your hands and draw up the water. It is cool, sweet, and clear. Drink deeply. As you drink, feel the wisdom of God flowing into you, filling you, becoming a spring of living water within you. Ask the Holy Spirit: "What do I need to know? What wisdom do I need for this moment of my life?" Then, simply listen. Wait. Be open to whatever comes—a word, an image, a feeling, a deep knowing.

Step 4: Return with the Gift

When you feel complete, give thanks for the gift of wisdom. Know that this well is always here, always within you, and that you can return to it whenever you need guidance. Slowly, climb back up the staircase, bringing the wisdom with you. When you reach the top, gently open your eyes.

Journaling Prompts:

• What wisdom did I receive from the well?

• How can I cultivate a regular practice of contemplative silence?

• What does it mean to trust that the answers I seek are within me?

• How can I become a "dowser" of my own inner knowing?

THE APPLE (QUERT): THE SILVER BRANCH AND THE JOURNEY TO AVALON

If the Hazel teaches us to go inward to find wisdom, the Apple teaches us to go outward—or rather, beyond. If the Hazel is the tree of contemplation and stillness, the Apple is the tree of adventure and vision. It is the tree that invites us to leave the safety of the known world and to journey into the Otherworld, the realm of spirits, ancestors, and divine beings, to seek knowledge that cannot be found in ordinary reality. The Apple is the tree of the visionary, the shaman, the mystic traveller who dares to cross the threshold and bring back gifts for the community.

In the Celtic tradition, the Apple tree is one of the most sacred and mysterious of all trees. It is not native to Ireland—settlers brought it in ancient times—but it was so quickly and so deeply integrated into the spiritual landscape that it became inseparable from the Celtic imagination. The Apple is the tree of the Otherworld, the tree of Avalon (the "Isle of Apples"), the tree of immortality, healing, and divine beauty. To eat an apple from the Otherworld is to be transformed, to be granted eternal youth, to be filled with joy and inspiration that transcends all earthly sorrow.

THE SILVER BRANCH: THE PASSPORT TO THE OTHERWORLD

In Irish mythology, there is a magical object called the Silver Branch, a branch from an apple tree that bears silver apples or golden apples, depending on the story. This branch is not just a beautiful ornament; it is a key, a passport, a sacred tool that grants the bearer safe passage into the Otherworld. When the branch is shaken, it produces the most beautiful music, a sound so enchanting that it can lull people to sleep, heal the sick, and ease all sorrow.

The Silver Branch appears in many of the great Irish voyage tales, the Immrama, where heroes are called to journey to the Otherworld. In the story of The Voyage of Bran, a mysterious woman appears to the hero Bran mac Febal, holding a silver branch covered in white blossoms. She sings to him of a beautiful island across the sea, a place of eternal youth and joy, where there is no sickness, no sorrow, and no death. When she finishes her song, the branch leaps from her hand into Bran's, and he knows that he has been chosen for the journey. He gathers a crew and sets sail, and after many adventures, he reaches the Isle of Women, a paradise in the Otherworld where time moves differently and all desires are fulfilled.

The Silver Branch is a symbol of divine invitation. It represents the call to the spiritual journey, the summons to leave behind the ordinary world and to seek a deeper, more expansive reality. But it is also a symbol of protection and guidance. The music of the branch soothes and heals; it is the voice of the divine singing to us, guiding us through the dangers of the journey, reminding us that we are not alone, that we are held in the love of God even as we venture into the unknown.

AVALON: THE ISLE OF APPLES AND THE LAND OF ETERNAL YOUTH

The most famous Otherworld destination in Celtic mythology is Avalon, the "Isle of Apples," also known as *Emain Ablach* in Irish tradition. This is a mystical island, sometimes located in the western sea, sometimes in a hidden valley, sometimes in a dimension that exists alongside our own but is normally invisible to mortal eyes. It is a place of extraordinary beauty, where apple trees grow in perpetual bloom, where the fruit never rots, and where those who eat it are granted eternal youth and freedom from all suffering.

Avalon is most famous as the place where King Arthur was taken after his final battle, to be healed of his wounds and to await the time when he will return to save Britain in its hour of greatest need. But Avalon is more than just a resting place for wounded heroes; it is a symbol of the soul's ultimate destination, the place of healing and wholeness that we all long for, the paradise that exists beyond the veil of death and suffering.

In the Christian tradition, Avalon echoes the Garden of Eden and the New Jerusalem, the heavenly city described in the Book of Revelation. Both are places of perfect beauty, where the Tree of Life grows and bears fruit for the healing of the nations (Revelation 22:2). Both are places where there is no more death, no more mourning, no more pain, for the old order of things has passed away (Revelation 21:4). The Apple tree, with its connection to both

Eden and Avalon, becomes a bridge between the two traditions, a symbol of the paradise that was lost and the paradise that will be restored.

THE APPLE IN THE GARDEN: TEMPTATION, KNOWLEDGE, AND REDEMPTION

We cannot speak of the Apple without addressing the most famous apple in Western culture: the fruit of the Tree of Knowledge of Good and Evil in the Garden of Eden. In the Genesis story, the serpent tempts Eve to eat the forbidden fruit, promising that it will make her "like God, knowing good and evil" (Genesis 3:5). Eve eats, Adam eats, and they are expelled from the garden, condemned to a life of toil, suffering, and death.

This story has been interpreted in many ways, but in the context of the Celtic Apple tradition, we can see it not as a simple tale of disobedience and punishment, but as a profound meditation on knowledge, desire, and the spiritual journey. The Apple in Eden represents the human longing to know, to understand, to transcend our limitations and to become more than we are. This longing is not inherently evil; it is part of what makes us human, part of the divine image within us. But the story warns us that there is a right way and a wrong way to seek knowledge.

The wrong way is to grasp, to take, to seek knowledge as a means of power and control, to want to be "like God" in the sense of being autonomous, self-sufficient, needing no one. This is the path of pride, and it leads to exile, to separation from the source of life. The right way is to receive knowledge as a gift, to approach the tree with humility and reverence, to seek wisdom not for our own glory but for the healing of the world.

The Celtic tradition, with its emphasis on the Apple as a gift from the Otherworld, as a fruit that must be sought through a dangerous journey and received with gratitude, offers a corrective to the Genesis story. It reminds us that the desire for knowledge and transformation is holy, but it must be pursued in the right spirit—not with grasping and pride, but with humility, courage, and a willingness to be changed by what we discover.

And here is the great mystery: in Christian theology, the Apple of Eden, the fruit of the fall, is redeemed by another tree, the Cross. Where the first Adam grasped at the fruit and brought death, the second Adam, Christ, freely gave himself on the tree and brought life. The tree that was a symbol of temptation and exile becomes, in the Cross, a symbol of redemption and return. And in the New Jerusalem, the Tree of Life grows again, and its fruit is freely given to all who hunger for it (Revelation 22:14).

The Apple, then, is a tree of paradox: it is both the tree of the fall and the tree of restoration, both the tree of exile and the tree of return. It teaches us that the spiritual journey is not a straight line but a spiral, one that takes us through darkness and light, through loss and recovery, through death and resurrection.

THE VISIONARY JOURNEY: CROSSING THE THRESHOLD

The Apple tree invites us to undertake the visionary journey, to cross the threshold into the Otherworld and to seek the wisdom that can only be found there. This is not a literal, physical journey (though it can be), but a journey of consciousness, a willingness to enter into altered states of awareness—through prayer, through meditation, through ritual, through dreams, through the creative imagination—and to encounter the divine in forms and images that transcend our ordinary, rational understanding.

This is the path of the mystic, the poet, the artist, the prophet—those who are willing to leave behind the safety of conventional thinking and to venture into the unknown. It is a dangerous path, because the Otherworld is not a safe place. It is a place of power, of beauty, of terror, of transformation. Those who journey there are changed by what they see, and they can never fully return to the ordinary world as they were before.

But it is also a necessary path, because the wisdom of the Otherworld is the wisdom that our world desperately needs. The visionary brings back gifts: new songs, new stories, new ways of seeing, new possibilities for healing and transformation. The Apple tree teaches us that we must be willing to take this journey, to eat the fruit of the Otherworld, to be changed by the encounter with the divine, and to bring back what we have learned for the benefit of all.

CHRISTIAN INTEGRATION: THE TRANSFIGURATION AND THE BEATIFIC VISION

In the Christian tradition, the visionary journey finds its ultimate expression in the Transfiguration of Christ (Matthew 17:1-9). Jesus takes Peter, James, and John up a high mountain, and there, before their eyes, he is transformed. His face shines like the sun, his clothes become dazzling white, and Moses and Elijah appear beside him, speaking with him about his coming death and resurrection.

This is a moment of Otherworldly vision, a glimpse into the true nature of Christ, a revelation of the glory that is normally hidden beneath the veil of his humanity. The disciples are terrified and overwhelmed. Peter, not knowing what to say, babbles about building three tents, trying to hold on to the moment, to make it permanent. But a cloud overshadows them, and the voice of God speaks: "This is my beloved Son, with whom I am well pleased; listen to him" (Matthew 17:5).

The Transfiguration is the Christian equivalent of the journey to Avalon. It is a moment when the veil between the worlds is lifted, when the divine reality breaks through into ordinary consciousness, when the disciples are given a taste of the heavenly realm. And like the heroes of the Celtic voyage tales, they are changed by what they see. They come down from the mountain different from how they went up, carrying within them a vision that will sustain them through the darkness to come.

The Apple tree invites us to seek our own moments of transfiguration, our own glimpses of the divine glory. It invites us to climb the mountain, to cross the sea, to enter into the silence and the darkness where God dwells in unapproachable light. It invites us to be open to visions, to dreams, to the creative imagination, to all the ways that the divine breaks through the veil of ordinary reality and speaks to us in images and symbols that transcend words.

THE PRACTICE: A GUIDED VISIONARY JOURNEY

Find a quiet place where you will not be disturbed. If possible, sit beneath an Apple tree or hold an apple in your hand. Close your eyes and take several deep, slow breaths.

Step 1: Receive the Silver Branch

Imagine that you are standing on a shore, looking out over a vast, misty sea. Before you, a figure appears—it may be an angel, a saint, or a mysterious woman from the Otherworld. In her hand, she holds a silver branch covered in white blossoms. She shakes it, and the most beautiful music fills the air, a sound that makes your heart ache with longing. She offers the branch to you, and as you take it, you know that you have been called to make a journey.

Step 2: Cross the Water

Now, a boat appears at the shore, waiting for you. Step into the boat and sit down. The boat begins to move under its own power, gliding across the water. As you travel, the mist grows thicker, and you lose sight of the shore behind you. You are crossing the threshold, leaving the ordinary world behind, entering the Otherworld. Trust the journey. You are safe.

Step 3: Arrive at the Isle of Apples

After a time, the mist clears, and you see before you a beautiful island. The shore is green and welcoming, and in the centre of the island grows a grove of apple trees, their branches heavy with golden fruit. The boat comes to rest on the shore, and you step out onto the land. Walk into the grove. Feel the peace, the beauty, the sense of being in a place where time moves differently, where all sorrow is healed.

Step 4: Receive the Gift

In the centre of the grove, you see a single apple tree, more beautiful than all the others. Beneath it stands a figure—it may be Christ, it may be a saint, it may be a wise elder. This figure offers you a golden apple. As you take it and bite into it, you taste not just fruit, but wisdom, healing, and inspiration.

Ask: "What vision do I need for my life? What gift am I meant to bring back to the world?" Listen. Wait. Be open to whatever comes.

Step 5: Return with the Gift

When you feel complete, thank the figure for the gift. Know that you carry this vision within you now. Walk back to the boat and step in. The boat carries you back across the water, through the mist, to the shore where you began. When you arrive, step out of the boat and gently open your eyes.

Journaling Prompts:

• What vision or insight did I receive on the Isle of Apples?

• How can I bring this gift back to my ordinary life?

• What does it mean to be a visionary, a traveller between worlds?

• How can I cultivate openness to the Otherworld in my daily life?

THE ELDER (RUIS): THE CRONE'S TREE AND THE WISDOM OF THE EARTH

If the Hazel teaches us to seek wisdom in the depths of contemplation, and the Apple teaches us to seek wisdom in the heights of visionary experience, the Elder teaches us to seek wisdom in the ground beneath our feet, in the cycles of the earth, in the body, in the lived experience of birth, growth, decay, and death. The Elder is the tree of the Crone, the wise woman who has lived through all the seasons of life and who knows, in her bones and in her blood, the great truths that cannot be learned from books or visions, but only from living, suffering, loving, and letting go.

The Elder is a tree of paradox and power. It grows quickly, almost aggressively, in hedgerows and waste places, thriving where other trees struggle. Its wood is hollow, pithy, and soft, yet it has been used for centuries to make flutes and whistles, instruments that produce hauntingly beautiful music. Its flowers are creamy white and fragrant, and they are used to make elderflower cordial and wine. Its berries are dark purple to almost black and must be cooked before consumption, as they are mildly toxic when raw. The

Elder gives generously, but it demands respect. It is a tree that stands at the boundary between life and death, between medicine and poison, between the sacred and the profane.

In the Celtic tradition, the Elder is associated with the Cailleach, the ancient Crone goddess who rules over winter, death, and the wild, untamed forces of nature. She is not a gentle, nurturing figure; she is fierce, uncompromising, and terrifying. But she is also wise, deeply wise, with the wisdom that comes from having seen everything, endured everything, and survived. The Elder is her tree, and to seek its wisdom is to seek the wisdom of the Crone: the wisdom of endings, of letting go, of facing the darkness, and of trusting that death is not the final word.

THE CAILLEACH: THE HAG OF WINTER AND THE KEEPER OF THE LAND

The Cailleach (pronounced "KAL-yakh") is one of the most ancient and influential figures in Celtic mythology. Her name means "the veiled one" or "the old woman," and she is often depicted as a giant hag with blue-grey skin, one eye, and a staff that can freeze the ground with a single touch. She is the bringer of winter, the one who covers the land with snow and ice, who strips the trees of their leaves, and who drives all living things into hibernation and retreat.
But the Cailleach is not a villain.

She is a necessary force, a part of the natural cycle that must be honoured. Without winter, there can be no spring. Without death, there can be no rebirth. Without the Crone, there can be no Maiden. The Cailleach teaches us that destruction is not the opposite of creation; it is part of creation. The earth must rest. The old must die so that the new can be born. This is the wisdom of the Elder: the wisdom of the cycle, the wisdom of letting go, the wisdom of trusting the dark.

The Cailleach as Landscape Sculptor

In some of the most vivid accounts, the Cailleach is not merely a goddess of winter but the primal architect of the land itself. In Scottish tradition, she is said to have created the mountains and valleys by carrying rocks in her apron and dropping them as she strode across the landscape. The great peaks of

Scotland—Ben Nevis, the Paps of Jura, the mountains of Skye—are said to be rocks that fell from her apron or were thrown by her in anger or play.

In Ireland, she is associated with the Hag's Chair on the summit of Sliabh na Caillí (the Hag's Mountain) in County Meath, where she is said to sit and survey her domain. The landscape itself bears her mark: rocky outcrops are called "the Cailleach's stones," deep pools are "the Cailleach's wells," and certain mountains are known as her dwelling places. She is not a goddess who rules over the land; she is the land, ancient and enduring, shaped by her own hands in the time before time.

This identification of the Cailleach with the landscape itself is profoundly important. It teaches us that the earth is not a dead thing, not a resource to be exploited, but a living being, ancient and powerful, deserving of reverence and respect. The Cailleach is the voice of the land, and when we damage the earth, we damage her. When we honour the earth, we honour her.

THE BATTLE WITH BRIGID: THE TURNING OF THE SEASONS

One of the most important myths about the Cailleach concerns her relationship with Brigid, the goddess of spring, fertility, and new life. In this story, the Cailleach and Brigid are not enemies, but partners in the great dance of the seasons. The Cailleach rules from Samhain (November 1st) to Bealtaine (May 1st), the dark half of the year. During this time, she walks the land with her staff, freezing the ground, bringing snow and ice, keeping the earth in a state of dormant rest.

But on the eve of Bealtaine, Brigid returns. In some versions of the story, the Cailleach throws her staff beneath a holly bush or an elder tree and transforms into a stone, relinquishing her power until the next Samhain. In other versions, the Cailleach herself transforms into Brigid, the old woman becoming the young maiden, the winter becoming the spring. This is not a battle of good versus evil, but a sacred exchange, a passing of the torch, a recognition that both the dark and the light are necessary, that both the Crone and the Maiden are aspects of the same divine feminine.

This myth encodes a profound spiritual truth: that life is cyclical rather than linear. We move through seasons—seasons of growth and seasons of rest, seasons of light and seasons of darkness, seasons of youth and seasons of age. To resist the cycle, to cling to spring and refuse winter, is to live in denial of reality. The Cailleach teaches us to embrace the whole cycle, to honour the winter as much as the summer, to see the Crone as beautiful and necessary as the Maiden.

And here is the deepest mystery: in some traditions, the Cailleach and Brigid are not two separate beings, but two faces of the same goddess. The young woman who lights the sacred fire at Imbolc (February 1st) and the old woman who brings the snow at Samhain are one. This is the great teaching of the Elder: that we contain multitudes, that we are both young and old, both light and dark, both life and death. To be whole is to embrace all of these aspects, to honour the Crone within us as much as the Maiden.

The Cailleach as Guardian of Animals

The Cailleach is also known as the protector of wild animals, particularly deer, goats, and wolves. In Scottish tradition, she is known as Cailleach nan Cruachan (the Cailleach of the Mountains) and is said to herd the deer across the high peaks, protecting them from hunters. She is fierce in her defence of the wild creatures, and those who hunt without respect, who kill for sport rather than need, may find themselves cursed by her wrath.

This aspect of the Cailleach elucidates the proper relationship with the natural world. She is not opposed to hunting or to the taking of life for food—this is part of the cycle—but she demands that it be done with respect, with gratitude, with an understanding that every life taken is a sacred exchange. The hunter must honour the animal, must thank it for its sacrifice, must take only what is needed. This is the wisdom of the Crone: that life feeds on life, that death is necessary for life to continue, but that this must be done with reverence, not with greed or cruelty.

The Cailleach and the Wells

In many Irish stories, the Cailleach is associated with sacred wells and springs. One of the most famous stories recounts that she was the guardian of a sacred well at the summit of a mountain. Every evening at sunset, she was required to cover the well with a large stone slab to prevent overflow. One evening, exhausted from her labours, she fell asleep before covering the well. The water burst forth, flooding the valley below and creating Lough Neagh, the largest lake in Ireland.

This story can be read as a cautionary tale about the consequences of neglecting our responsibilities. Still, it can also be read as a story about the power of the wild, untamed forces of nature that cannot be controlled forever. The Cailleach, even in her great power, cannot hold back the waters forever. Eventually, the wild will break free, the repressed will emerge, and the hidden will be revealed. This is the wisdom of the Elder: that we cannot control everything, that we must learn to live with uncertainty, with wildness, with the knowledge that the earth has its own power and its own will.

The Cailleach in Christian Times

Remarkably, the Cailleach survived the coming of Christianity to Ireland and Scotland, though her role shifted. In some areas, she became associated with St. Brigid herself, the two figures blending together in the folk imagination. In other contexts, she became a more ambiguous figure, sometimes a witch, sometimes a wise woman, sometimes a fairy. But she never fully disappeared, because she represents something too fundamental, too ancient, too necessary to be erased: the power of winter, the wisdom of age, the inevitability of death, and the promise of renewal.

The Elder tree, as the Cailleach's tree, carries all of this wisdom. It is a tree that thrives in the liminal spaces, in the hedgerows and the waste places, in the boundaries between the cultivated and the wild. It is a tree that gives generously—flowers, berries, medicine—but demands respect. It is a tree that teaches us to honour the Crone, to honour the winter, to honour the endings that make new beginnings possible.

THE ELDER IN FOLK TRADITION: MEDICINE AND MAGIC

The Elder has been used for centuries in folk medicine throughout the Celtic lands. Every part of the tree has medicinal properties: the flowers can be made into a tea to treat colds and flu, the berries (when cooked) can be made into syrup to boost the immune system, the leaves can be used in poultices for bruises and sprains, and the bark has been used as a purgative. The Elder is a tree of healing, but it also demands respect. In many traditions, it is considered unlucky to cut down an Elder tree without first asking permission from the tree spirit, and offerings of milk or bread are often left at the base of the tree as a sign of gratitude.

This tradition of asking permission and making offerings reflects a deep understanding that the Elder is not merely a resource but a being with its own spirit and will. To take from the Elder without respect is to invite misfortune. But to approach the Elder with humility, to ask for what you need, to give thanks for what you receive—this is to enter into right relationship, to honour the wisdom of the Crone, to acknowledge that we are not the masters of nature, but participants in a sacred exchange.

CHRISTIAN INTEGRATION: THE WISDOM OF THE ELDERS AND THE COMMUNION OF SAINTS

In the Christian tradition, the wisdom of the Elder finds its expression in the concept of the "elders" of the faith—those who have gone before us, who have lived through trials and suffering, who have gained wisdom through experience, and who now serve as guides and teachers for those who come after. The Book of Proverbs is filled with the sayings of the elders, practical wisdom about how to live a good life, how to avoid folly, and how to walk in the fear of the Lord.

But the deepest Christian expression of the Elder's wisdom is found in the doctrine of the Communion of Saints. This is the belief that the Church is not only the living believers on earth but also includes all who have died in Christ and now dwell in the presence of God. The saints are not distant, unreachable figures; they are our elder brothers and sisters, our ancestors in the faith, who pray for us, who guide us, who cheer us on in our own journey.

To honour the Elder tree is to honour the elders of the faith, to seek their wisdom, to learn from their example, to ask for their prayers. It is to recognise that we are not alone, that we are part of a great cloud of witnesses (Hebrews 12:1). This communion extends back through the centuries to the apostles, the martyrs, the desert fathers and mothers, and to all those who have walked the path before us.

It is to recognise that one day we too will be elders. We, too, will be ancestors. The wisdom we gain, the love we give, the sacrifices we make— these will be our legacy, our gift to those who come after us. The Elder teaches us to live in such a way that we become good ancestors, that we leave the world better than we found it, and that we pass on wisdom, not just wealth, and love, not just possessions.

FACING DEATH: THE ELDER AS TEACHER OF MORTALITY

However, the Elder's deepest teaching concerns death itself. The Cailleach is not merely the bringer of winter; she stands at the threshold between life and death, helping souls transition from this world to the next. The Elder tree, with its hollow trunk and its dark berries, is a symbol of the grave, of the tomb, of the dark passage that we all must walk.

In our modern culture, we are terrified of death. We hide it away in hospitals and nursing homes. We use euphemisms to avoid speaking its name. We spend billions of dollars on anti-ageing treatments, trying to hold back the inevitable. But the Elder teaches us that this fear, this denial, is a form of spiritual sickness. Death is not the enemy; death is part of life. To deny death is to deny life, to live in a state of perpetual anxiety, always running, never resting, never at peace.

The Elder invites us to face our mortality, to sit with the Crone, to listen to her wisdom. She teaches us that death is not an ending, but a transformation. The seed must die to become the plant. The caterpillar must die to become the butterfly. The grain of wheat must fall into the earth and die to bear much fruit (John 12:24). This is the great mystery of the Christian faith: that death is the gateway to life, that the Cross is the tree of life, that resurrection comes through the tomb.

St. Paul writes: "For to me to live is Christ, and to die is gain" (Philippians 1:21). This is the wisdom of the Elder: that when we have lived fully, when we have loved deeply, when we have given ourselves away in service to God and to others, then death is not something to be feared, but something to be embraced as the final act of surrender, the final letting go, the final step into the arms of the One who has loved us from the beginning.

THE PRACTICE: A MEDITATION ON LETTING GO

Find a quiet place where you will not be disturbed. If possible, sit beneath an Elder tree, or hold a piece of Elder wood or a dried elderberry in your hand. Close your eyes and take several deep, slow breaths.

Step 1: Acknowledge What Must Be Released

Bring to mind something in your life that is ending, something that you need to let go of. It might be a relationship that has run its course, a job that no longer serves you, a dream that will not be fulfilled, a stage of life that is passing, or even the anticipation of your own death. Hold this gently in your awareness. Do not judge it, do not resist it. Simply acknowledge: "This is ending. This must be released."

Step 2: Meet the Crone

Now, imagine that you are standing in a winter landscape, bare and cold, before you stands an ancient Elder tree, its branches bare, its trunk hollow. At the base of the tree sits the Cailleach, the Crone, the wise woman of winter. Her face is old and weathered, but her eyes are kind. She holds out her hand to you, and you know that she is asking you to give her what you are holding, to release it into her care. She says, "I am the keeper of endings. I will take this from you. Trust me."

Step 3: Release into Her Hands

Now, imagine that you are placing what you need to let go of into the Crone's hands. It might feel heavy, it might hurt to release it, but you do it anyway. As you let go, you feel a weight lift from your shoulders. The Crone takes it, and as she does, it begins to dissolve, to return to the earth, to become compost for new growth. She says, "Death is not the end. What dies will feed what is to come. Trust the cycle."

Step 4: Rest in the Silence

Sit in silence for a few moments, feeling the emptiness, the space that has been created by letting go. This emptiness is not a void; it is a womb, a place of potential, a place where new life can grow. When you are ready, thank the Crone for her wisdom. Know that she is always there, ready to help you release what must be released. Gently open your eyes.

Journaling Prompts:

• What in my life is ending, and what am I being called to let go of?

• What does it mean to honour the wisdom of the body and the wisdom of ageing?

• How can I face my own mortality with courage and grace?

• What new life might grow from the endings I am experiencing?

CONCLUSION: THE THREE STREAMS OF WISDOM

We have now drunk from the three great wells of wisdom in the Celtic grove. We have tasted the hazelnuts of knowledge from the Well of Segais, learning from the Hazel the wisdom of contemplation, of going inward to the still point where the divine voice speaks most clearly. We have eaten the golden apples of Avalon, learning from the Apple the wisdom of vision, of crossing the threshold into the Otherworld to seek knowledge that transcends ordinary reality. And we have received the bitter medicine of the Elder, learning from the Crone the wisdom of the earth, of the body, of the cycles of life and death that govern all existence.

These are not three separate wisdoms; they are three streams flowing from a single source.

There are three ways of knowing, three dimensions of understanding, three paths to the same truth. And we need all three if we are to become truly wise, to live fully integrated lives, and to fulfil our calling as human beings made in the image of God.

Let us now see how these three streams work together, how they complement and complete one another, and how they form a complete system of spiritual education that is both ancient and urgently relevant for our time.

THE TRINITY OF KNOWING: INWARD, OUTWARD, EMBODIED

The Hazel, the Apple, and the Elder together form a trinity of wisdom, a three-fold path to knowledge that mirrors the very structure of reality itself. Just as the World Tree connects the three worlds—the Underworld, the Middle World, and the Upper World—so too do these three trees connect the three dimensions of human knowing:

The Hazel teaches us the wisdom of going inward, of contemplation, of descending into the depths of the soul to find the well of living water that springs up from within. This is the mystical path, the way of silence and stillness, the way of the hermit and the contemplative. It is the wisdom that comes from direct encounter with the divine, unmediated by words or images, a knowing that is deeper than thought, a union that transcends all separation.

The Apple teaches us the wisdom of going outward, of vision, of crossing the threshold into the Otherworld to seek knowledge that cannot be found in ordinary reality. This is the prophetic path, the way of the seer and the visionary, the way of dreams and imagination. It is the wisdom that comes from encounters with the divine in forms and images, in symbols and stories, in the creative imagination that opens us to realities beyond the visible world.

The Elder teaches us the wisdom of being embodied, of living in the world, of learning from experience, from the cycles of nature, from the body's own deep knowing. This is the practical path, the way of the herbalist and the midwife, the way of those who work with their hands and learn from the earth. It is the wisdom that comes from living, from suffering, from loving, from ageing, from facing death with courage and trust.

Together, these three paths form a complete education in the ways of knowing. We need the inward journey of the Hazel to ground us in the source, to connect us to the divine centre from which all wisdom flows. We need the outward journey of the Apple to expand our vision, to open us to new possibilities, to remind us that reality is far more vast and mysterious than we can imagine. We need the Elder's embodied journey to keep us rooted in the earth, in the body, and in the practical realities of daily life, reminding us that wisdom is not merely about knowing but about living.

The Three Streams in the Life of Christ

These three streams of wisdom are not just Celtic; they are universal, and they find their ultimate expression in the life of Christ himself. Christ embodies the wisdom of the Hazel in his practice of contemplative prayer. Repeatedly in the Gospels, we see Jesus withdrawing from the crowds, going up into the mountains or out into the wilderness to pray in solitude.

He goes inward to the deep well of communion with the Father, and from that well, he draws the wisdom and the power to fulfil his mission. He teaches his disciples to do the same: "But when you pray, go into your room and shut the door and pray to your Father who is in secret" (Matthew 6:6).

This is the wisdom of the Hazel: that the source of all wisdom is within, in the secret place where we meet God face to face.

Christ embodies the wisdom of the Apple in his visionary experiences. At his baptism, the heavens are opened, and he sees the Spirit descending like a dove (Matthew 3:16). At the Transfiguration, he is revealed in glory, conversing with Moses and Elijah about his coming death and resurrection (Matthew 17:1-9). In the Garden of Gethsemane, he sees the cup that he must drink, the path of suffering that lies before him (Matthew 26:39). Christ is a visionary, one who sees beyond the veil of ordinary reality, who walks between the worlds, who brings back from the Otherworld the knowledge of God's will and God's love.

Christ embodies the Elder's wisdom in his full embrace of human life, including suffering, ageing, and death. He is born as a baby, grows through childhood and adolescence, experiences hunger, thirst, fatigue, temptation, grief, and pain. He does not float above the human condition; he enters fully into it. And he faces death not with denial or fear, but with courage and trust, surrendering himself into the hands of the Father. "Father, into your hands I commit my spirit" (Luke 23:46). This is the wisdom of the Elder: that to be fully human is to embrace the whole cycle of life, including its end, and to trust that death is not the final word.

To follow Christ, then, is to walk all three paths. It is to cultivate the inward life of prayer and contemplation (the Hazel), to be open to visions and dreams and the creative imagination (the Apple), and to live fully in the body and in the world, embracing the cycles of life and death with courage and grace (the Elder).

The Three Streams in the Life of Brigid

These three streams of wisdom are also beautifully embodied in St. Brigid, the great patron saint of Ireland, whose life and legend we have encountered throughout this book. Brigid is the perfect example of the integrated spiritual life, the one who drinks from all three wells.

Brigid embodies the wisdom of the Hazel in her deep life of prayer and contemplation. She is known for her long hours of prayer, fasting, and vigil, and for her intimate communion with God. The stories recount how she would become so absorbed in prayer that she would lose track of time, how she would see visions of angels and saints, and how she would be filled with such love for God that her face would shine with light. She is a mystic, one who has descended to the well and drunk deeply of the living water.

Brigid embodies the wisdom of the Apple in her visionary gifts and her creative imagination. She is a poet, a storyteller, a weaver of words and images. She sees the world not just as it is, but as it could be, as it will be when God's kingdom comes in fullness. She crosses the threshold between the worlds, bringing back gifts of healing, of inspiration, of hope. She is a prophet, one who speaks the word of God into the present moment, calling people to transformation.

Brigid embodies the Elder's wisdom in her practical service to the poor, the sick, and the suffering. She is a healer, a midwife, a provider of food and shelter. She works with her hands; she tends the sick; she feeds the hungry; she welcomes the stranger. She does not retreat from the world into a life of pure contemplation; she engages fully with the messy, painful, beautiful realities of human life. She is an elder, one who has learned wisdom through experience, through living, through serving. She is the model of the complete human being.

BRIDGE TO THE NEXT CHAPTER

We have now completed our education in the fundamental principles of the Celtic spiritual path. We have learned the foundation (Chapter 5: Oak, Ash, Yew), the protection (Chapter 6: Rowan, Holly, Hawthorn), and the wisdom (Chapter 7: Hazel, Apple, Elder). We are rooted, guarded, and wise. We are ready to move into the final phase of our journey: the application of this wisdom to the practical challenges of daily life.

In the chapters that follow, we will explore the trees of healing, the trees of transformation, and the trees of celebration. We will learn how to work with the specific energies of each tree to address specific needs in our lives. We will learn how to create our own sacred grove, how to walk the forest as a spiritual practice, and how to live in right relationship with the earth and all its creatures.

But for now, rest in this: you have drunk from the three wells.

You have tasted the hazelnuts of contemplation, the apples of vision, and the elderberries of embodied wisdom.

You are no longer a beginner on the path.

You are a seeker who has been initiated into the mysteries.

You are ready for what comes next.

The three streams have converged.

The well is full.

The journey continues.

Chapter 8:

The Cross as the Ultimate Tree

Welcome, fellow traveller, to the heart of the grove. We have journeyed far together, through the ancient world of the Druids, into the vibrant faith of the Celtic saints, and deep into the rustling, whispering wisdom of the trees. We have learned to see the world not as a collection of inert objects, but as a living, breathing community of beings, each with its own voice, its own spirit, its own story to tell. We have begun to reclaim a way of seeing that is both ancient and new, a way that honours the immanence of God in all creation, a way that finds the sacred not only in churches and cathedrals but also in the dappled light of the forest floor and the steadfast strength of the ancient oak.

In our journey, we have encountered many sacred trees, each a profound archetype of spiritual truth. We have stood in awe before the mighty Ash, the World Tree that connects the three realms of existence. We have sought the wisdom of the Hazel, the tree of knowledge and contemplation. We have glimpsed the Otherworld through the branches of the Apple, the tree of vision and eternal life. We have honoured the cycle of death and rebirth in the Elder, the tree of transformation. We have learned of sovereignty and strength from the Oak, the king of the forest. We have sought discernment from the Rowan, the tree of protection and insight. We have respected the boundaries of the Holly, the warrior tree. And we have waited at the threshold with the Hawthorn, the tree of patience and union.

Each of these trees has offered us a piece of the puzzle, a glimpse into the deep mysteries of life, death, and the divine. But now, we come to the centre of the puzzle, to the image that gathers all these threads together, to the tree that stands at the very heart of the Celtic Christian vision: the Cross.

For the Celtic saints, the Cross was not a symbol of defeat, but of ultimate victory. It was not an instrument of torture, but the true Tree of Life. It was not a sign of God's absence, but the ultimate revelation of God's presence, a love so fierce and so tender that it would enter into the heart of suffering and death to bring forth new life. They saw in the Cross the fulfilment of all three archetypes they had known and revered. It was the true World Tree, the Crann Bethadh, the axis of the cosmos, the bridge between heaven and earth. It was the tree of wisdom, the tree of sovereignty, the tree of protection, the tree of eternal life.

In this chapter, we will undertake a profound theological and spiritual exploration. We will see how the Cross of Christ fulfils and deepens the wisdom of the Druidic sacred trees. This is not a process of replacement or conquest, but of integration and fulfilment. We will see how the Celtic mind, so attuned to the rhythms of the natural world, was able to see in the Cross the ultimate expression of the truths they had always known in their hearts. Our journey in this chapter will unfold in seven parts:

1. Introduction: The Tree at the Centre of the World: We will lay the groundwork for our exploration, framing the Cross as the fulfilment of the tree archetypes.

2. The Cross as the True World Tree: We will explore how the Cross functions as the ultimate Ash, connecting the three worlds and holding all of creation in its embrace.

3. The Cross as the Tree of Life and Wisdom: We will see the Cross as the fulfilment of the Apple and Hazel, the source of eternal life and the deepest wisdom.

4. The Cross as the Tree of Sovereignty and Protection: We will delve into the Cross as the ultimate Oak and Holly, the throne of the true king and the ultimate shield against all that would harm us.

5. The Irish High Crosses: Stone Sermons of the Tree of Life: We will encounter the magnificent stone crosses of Ireland, seeing them as theological and artistic masterpieces that proclaim the Cross as the Tree of Life.

6. The Practice: A Meditation on the Cross as World Tree: We will engage in a guided contemplative practice to experience the Cross not just as an idea, but as a living, transformative reality.

7. Conclusion: The Tree at the Centre of Your Grove: We will synthesise the chapter's themes, seeing the Cross as the living centre of our own spiritual lives and the bridge to a "cruciform" way of being in the world.

This chapter is the theological heart of our book. It is where the two streams of our exploration—the Druidic and the Christian—flow together and become one. It is my prayer that by the end of this chapter, you will see the Cross with new eyes, not as a symbol of sorrow, but as the ultimate tree, the tree that stands at the centre of the world, its branches reaching to the heavens, its roots deep in the earth, its arms outstretched to embrace all of creation in a gesture of infinite, unbreakable love. Let us begin.

THE CROSS AS THE TRUE WORLD TREE

In the spiritual cosmology of our ancestors, the world was not a random assortment of landscapes and objects, but a structured, living, and interconnected whole. At the very centre of this cosmos stood a great tree, an axis mundi or world axis, that bound all of existence together. For the Norse peoples, this was the mighty Ash, Yggdrasil. For our own Celtic forebears, it was the bile or sacred tree, often an ancient oak or ash, that stood as the spiritual and political centre of the tribe. This tree was a living ladder, a conduit of divine energy, connecting the three essential realms: the Underworld, the Middle World, and the Upper World.

The roots of this World Tree plunged deep into the earth, into the Underworld—the realm of the ancestors, of memory, of the collective unconscious. This was not a place of punishment, but a source of deep wisdom, the wellspring from which the waters of life emerged. The trunk of the tree stood firmly in the Middle World, our own plane of existence, the world of human community, of nature, of daily life. And its branches soared high into the heavens, into the Upper World—the realm of the divine, of spiritual beings, of the sun, moon, and stars, the source of inspiration and cosmic order.

To be a whole and integrated person in this worldview was to live in conscious relationship with all three realms. It was to honour the ancestors, to live well in community, and to seek the inspiration of the heavens. The World Tree was the symbol and the reality of this integration. It was the place where all three worlds met, where communication between them was possible. It was the centre of the world because it was the place where the whole world could be seen and understood.

When the first Christian missionaries arrived in Ireland, they did not find a spiritual vacuum. They found a people whose souls were already shaped by the deep patterns of the natural world, by the wisdom of the trees, by the threefold rhythm of the cosmos. And when they spoke of the Cross, the Celtic mind did not see an alien symbol of imperial power or a grim instrument of execution. They saw, with an astonishing flash of spiritual insight, the fulfilment of their most profound archetype. They saw in the Cross the true World Tree, the Crann Bethadh—the Tree of Life—that did not just symbolise the connection between the worlds, but was that connection, embodied in the person of Jesus Christ.

Let us explore this profound integration, seeing how the simple shape of the Cross becomes the map of the entire cosmos, a map that can guide our own spiritual journey.

THE VERTICAL BEAM: THE BRIDGE BETWEEN EARTH AND HEAVEN

The most immediate dimension of the Cross is its verticality. It is a line that connects the earth beneath our feet with the heavens above our heads. This single beam of wood fulfils the primary function of the World Tree: it is the bridge, the ladder, the pathway between the divine and the human.

The Root in the Underworld: The Cross is not a floating, ethereal symbol. It is planted firmly in the ground. Its root is driven into the soil of our world, into Golgotha, "the place of the skull." It is grounded in human history, in our suffering, our mortality, our earthiness. But it goes deeper still. In the theology of the early Church, and with particular resonance for the Celts, the root of the Cross plunges into the Underworld itself.

This is the meaning of the "harrowing of hell," the doctrine that between his death and resurrection, Christ descended to the dead. He journeyed into the realm of the ancestors, not as a captive, but as a liberator. He went to preach the good news to all those who had waited in hope, from Adam and Eve to the patriarchs and prophets. He broke down the gates of death and led the captives into the light. The Cross, therefore, is rooted in the redemption of all history. It honours the ancestors, it gathers up all the past, and it plants the seed of new life in the very heart of death. When we stand before the

Cross, we are connected to this deep root system, to the great cloud of witnesses, to all those who have gone before us in faith.

The Trunk Reaching to the Upper World: From this deep root, the vertical beam of the Cross soars upward, a straight, true line pointing to the heavens. It is the mast of the world-ship, the trunk of the cosmic tree, the ladder of ascent for the human soul. It is Jacob's ladder, upon which the angels of God ascend and descend. Through the Cross, humanity is no longer trapped in the Middle World, cut off from the divine. A way has been made. The heavens are opened. In Christ, who is both fully human and fully divine, the two realms are joined. He is the bridge. To journey up the trunk of the Cross in our prayer and contemplation is to ascend to the Upper World, to enter into communion with the Father, to be filled with the light and life of the Holy Spirit.

It is to move from the complexity of the world to the simplicity of divine union, to hear the words of Christ, "Father, into your hands I commit my spirit" (Luke 23:46), and to make them our own.

THE HORIZONTAL BEAM: THE EMBRACE OF ALL CREATION

If the vertical beam connects the worlds, the horizontal beam embraces them. Its arms stretch east and west, encompassing the entirety of the Middle World, from the rising to the setting of the sun. While the old bile tree stood for the unity of a single tribe, the Cross stands for the unity of all humanity. It is a gesture of radical, unconditional welcome.

As the arms of Christ were stretched out upon the wood, they formed an embrace that excludes no one. On his left and on his right were two thieves, the righteous and the unrighteous, the repentant and the unrepentant. In that moment, he held them both. His arms reach across all the divisions that we create: race, nation, religion, gender, politics. They reach out to our friends and to our enemies, to those we love and to those we find it impossible to love. The Cross is the great reconciliation, the place where all the walls of hostility are broken down (Ephesians 2:14).

This horizontal embrace is not only for humanity but also for all of creation. The Celtic saints knew that the redemption won on the Cross was cosmic in its scope. It was for the salmon and the stag, the mountain and the river, the oak and the ash. The entire created order, groaning in travail, was being renewed and restored through the loving sacrifice of its Creator. The Cross stands as a sign that this world, this Middle World, is not a place to be escaped from, but a place to be loved, healed, and transformed. It calls us to extend our arms in love and service to the world, to participate in its healing, to be agents of its reconciliation.

THE CENTRE: THE HEART OF THE NEW CREATION

At the intersection of the vertical and horizontal beams is the heart of the matter, both literally and figuratively. It is the point where the divine and the human meet, where the love of God for the world is made manifest, where the suffering of the world is taken into the heart of God.

This centre point is the heart of Christ.

This is the still point of the turning world, the hub of the cosmic wheel. It is the place of perfect balance, of perfect integration. Here, the upward reach for God and the outward reach for the world are held in perfect tension. Here, contemplation and action, being and doing, love of God and love of neighbour, become one. To live a "cruciform" life, a life shaped by the Cross, is to live from this centre. It is to find in the heart of Christ the source of our own integration. In this place, our own inner worlds—our own underworld of memory, our middle world of daily life, our upper world of spiritual aspiration—are brought into harmony.

The Cross, then, is not a static object, but a dynamic, living, cosmic event. It is the true World Tree, the engine of the new creation, the place where the love of God flows down into the world and the prayers of the world ascend to God. It fulfils the ancient dream of the bale tree, not by abolishing it, but by filling it with a new and deeper meaning. The Celtic Christians who carved the great High Crosses, which we will explore later in this chapter, understood this perfectly.

They covered their crosses not with images of suffering, but with the intricate knots and spirals of creation, with scenes from the Old and New Testaments, with the images of a cosmos redeemed and made new. They saw the Cross, and they saw the World Tree, and they knew, with the certainty of faith, that they were the same. And in seeing this, they have given us a key, a map, a way to see the Cross not as the end of the story, but as the beginning of a new and more wonderful one, a story in which we are all invited to take part.

THE CROSS AS THE TREE OF LIFE AND WISDOM

As we stand at the foot of the Cross, seeing it as the great World Tree that holds the cosmos together, we begin to perceive its even deeper mysteries. The Celtic soul, shaped by the stories of its land, knew of two other trees that were central to its spiritual quest: the Apple, the tree of the Otherworld and eternal life, and the Hazel, the tree of sacred wisdom. The Apple tree's silver branch was a passport to the land of eternal youth, a place of feasting, beauty, and joy. The Hazel tree stood over the Well of Segais, the well of wisdom, dropping its nine nuts of knowledge into the water for the Salmon of Knowledge to consume. To taste this salmon was to gain all the wisdom of the world.

Life and Wisdom. Are these not the two things the human heart longs for most deeply? We long for a life that is not cut short by death, a life that is abundant, joyful, and eternal. And we long for the wisdom to navigate this life, to understand its meaning, to know what is true, good, and beautiful. The Celtic tradition encoded these longings in the archetypes of the Apple and the Hazel. And in the Cross of Christ, the Celtic saints saw the ultimate fulfilment of both these desires. They saw that the Cross was not only the World Tree, but also the true Tree of Life and the ultimate Tree of Wisdom.

THE CROSS AS THE TREE OF LIFE: THE RESTORED GARDEN

The story of humanity begins in a garden, with two trees. The Book of Genesis tells us that in the centre of Eden, God planted the Tree of the Knowledge of Good and Evil and the Tree of Life (Genesis 2:9). The first tree was forbidden, a test of trust and obedience. The second was a gift, the source of immortality. By choosing to eat from the first tree, humanity was exiled from the garden and barred from the second. The way to the Tree of Life was blocked by a cherubim with a flaming sword. The story of our fallenness is the story of this exile, this loss of access to the source of eternal life.

From that moment on, the human story has been a quest to find our way back to that tree. In Celtic mythology, this quest took the form of voyages to the Otherworld, to Tír na nóg (the Land of the Young) or Avalon (the Isle of Apples), a paradise in which sickness and death did not exist. The passport to this land was often a silver branch of an apple tree, bearing blossoms and fruit at the same time, a sign of life's eternal newness.

When the Christian story reached Celtic lands, it brought an astonishing proclamation: the way back to the Tree of Life has been reopened. The flaming sword has been quenched. The garden is accessible once more. And the new Tree of Life is the Cross of Christ.

This is a theology of beautiful, poetic reversal. The first tree, in a garden, was a tree of temptation that led to death. The second tree, on a barren hill, is a tree of execution that leads to life. The instrument of our death has become the means of our salvation. The wood that was a sign of our curse has become the symbol of our blessing. As the ancient hymn Vexilla Regis proclaims, "Fulfilling what he so long foretold, / He reigns a King from a tree of wood."

Christ is the new Adam. Where the first Adam reached out his hand in disobedience to grasp the fruit of a tree, the new Adam, Christ, stretched out his hands in obedience to be nailed to a tree. That act of perfect, self-giving love transformed the very nature of the wood. It ceased to be dead timber, an instrument of Roman torture, and became a living, fruit-bearing tree, the source of a life that death cannot overcome. Jesus himself declared, "I am the resurrection and the life. The one who believes in me will live, even though they die" (John 11:25).

The fruit of this new Tree of Life is given to us freely. It is the Eucharist, the bread and wine that become the body and blood of Christ. When Jesus says, "Take, eat; this is my body" (Matthew 26:26), he is offering us the fruit of the new Tree of Life. He is inviting us to partake in his own divine life, to receive into ourselves the very substance of immortality. The Cross, then, is not just a historical artefact. It is a living, fruit-bearing tree whose branches extend through time and space to every altar where the Eucharist is celebrated. It is the ultimate Silver Branch, the true passport to the Otherworld, which is not a mythical island, but the very life of the Triune God.

THE CROSS AS THE TREE OF WISDOM: THE FOOLISHNESS OF GOD

If the Cross is the fulfilment of the Apple tree, it is just as surely the fulfilment of the Hazel. The Hazel, with its nuts of wisdom, represented the deepest knowledge attainable. This was not just factual information, but a profound, intuitive understanding of the nature of reality, the kind of wisdom that poets and seers possessed.

But what is the ultimate wisdom? What is the most profound truth about God, the universe, and ourselves? The Cross provides the definitive and shocking answer. The wisdom of the Cross is the wisdom of self-giving love. It is the revelation that true power is found in weakness, true exaltation in humility, true victory in surrender, and true life in death. This is the central paradox of the Christian faith, and it is a wisdom that completely upends the world's values.

To the world, the Cross is foolishness. The Apostle Paul understood this better than anyone.

He wrote to the church in Corinth:

"For the message of the cross is foolishness to those who are perishing, but to us who are being saved it is the power of God... For the foolishness of God is wiser than human wisdom, and the weakness of God is stronger than human strength." (1 Corinthians 1:18, 25)

This is the wisdom of the hazelnut, cracked open. The hard shell of worldly logic, of power politics, of self-preservation, is broken, and inside is the kernel of a truth so radical it can only be received by faith. The Cross reveals that God is not a distant, impassive monarch, but a vulnerable, suffering lover. It reveals that the fundamental law of the universe is not survival of the fittest, but the law of the gift, the law of self-emptying (kenosis). It teaches us that the way up is the way down, that to be great is to be a servant, that to save your life is to lose it for the sake of love.

To contemplate the Cross is to sit by the Well of Segais and to eat the Salmon of Knowledge. It is to drink deeply of a wisdom that cannot be found in books or lectures, but only in the silent, prayerful gaze upon the figure of the Crucified One. It is to allow the logic of the Cross to seep into our bones, to reshape our understanding of everything. It is to learn that forgiveness is stronger than revenge, that mercy is more powerful than justice, that love is, in the end, the only thing that is real.

The One Tree of Life and Wisdom

In the Cross, the archetypes of the Apple and the Hazel merge and become one. The Life it offers is not a mindless, vegetative existence; it is a life lived in accordance with the highest Wisdom. And the Wisdom it reveals is not a dry, abstract philosophy; it is the very path to Life, abundant and eternal.

To eat the fruit of the Tree of Life is to be filled with the wisdom of the Cross. To drink from the well of its wisdom is to receive the gift of eternal life. The two are inseparable. The Christian life is a journey of learning to live by this cruciform wisdom, and in doing so, to experience ever more deeply the reality of this divine life.

Therefore, when we look upon the Cross, we see more than an instrument of death. We see the flowering of a new Eden. We see the Tree of Life, its branches laden with the fruit of immortality, offered freely to all who will receive it. And we see the Tree of Wisdom, its leaves rustling with the secrets of the universe, revealing the beautiful, paradoxical, and life-giving truth of a God who is love. The Cross is the answer to the deepest longings of the Celtic soul, and of every human soul. It is the tree that nourishes and the tree that enlightens, the tree that saves and the tree that teaches. It is the one tree we need, the tree that stands at the centre of the restored garden of our own hearts.

THE CROSS AS THE TREE OF SOVEREIGNTY AND PROTECTION

Having seen the Cross as the cosmic axis and the source of eternal life and wisdom, we now turn to two of the most primal human needs: the need for just and stable order, and the need for safety and protection from harm. In the Celtic world, these needs were embodied by two powerful tree archetypes: the Oak, the king of the forest, the symbol of sovereignty and endurance; and the Holly, the evergreen warrior, the symbol of protection and the setting of sacred boundaries. The Oak represented the centre of the tribe, the source of law and authority. The Holly, with its prickly leaves, represented the defence of that sacred centre against all that would threaten it.

When the Celtic Christians looked at the Cross, they did not see a symbol of a defeated king or a failed protector. They saw, with the eyes of faith, the ultimate expression of both true sovereignty and perfect protection. They saw in the wood of the Cross the throne of the one true King and the shield of the one true Warrior. For them, the Cross became the ultimate Oak and the ultimate Holly, fulfilling and transforming these ancient archetypes in the person of Christ.

THE CROSS AS THE TREE OF SOVEREIGNTY: THE THRONE OF THE SERVANT KING

The Oak is the quintessential tree of strength, stability, and nobility. Its deep roots and mighty branches have made it a universal symbol of sovereignty. The king, like the Oak, was to be the stable centre of his people, a source of justice, wisdom, and strength. His rule was meant to create a space of order and flourishing for the tribe. This is a noble ideal, but one that has been tragically corrupted throughout human history. Worldly sovereignty almost inevitably becomes a matter of domination, of power over others, of wealth accumulated, and of enemies crushed. The throne becomes a seat of pride, not of service.

The Cross presents us with a radical and revolutionary redefinition of sovereignty. It is a throne, yes, but a throne unlike any other. The inscription that Pontius Pilate had placed above Jesus' head, intended as a final, cynical mockery, proclaims the profound truth: Iesus Nazarenus, Rex Iudaeorum— "Jesus of Nazareth, King of the Jews" (John 19:19). On the Cross, Christ reigns as King.

But what kind of a king is this? His crown is made of thorns. His royal robes have been stripped from him. His sceptre is a reed. His throne is an instrument of execution. His courtiers are two thieves. His subjects are a jeering mob and a small, weeping band of followers. This is a kingship that utterly subverts our every expectation of power. It is a sovereignty founded not on the ability to command and coerce, but on the capacity to love and to suffer. It is the sovereignty of the servant.

This is the king who, on the night before his death, knelt to wash his disciples' feet, an act reserved for the lowest of slaves. He told them, "You call me 'Teacher' and 'Lord,' and rightly so, for that is what I am. Now that I, your Lord and Teacher, have washed your feet, you also should wash one another's feet" (John 13:13-14). The sovereignty of the Oak is here transformed from the power to rule to the authority to serve.

The strength of the Cross is not the power to inflict violence, but the power to absorb it and transform it into love. It is the unshakeable, enduring strength of a love that will not be defeated by hatred, a life that will not be extinguished by death. This is a strength far greater than that of any earthly empire.

The kingdom that this King establishes is, as he told Pilate, "not of this world" (John 18:36). Its power does not come from armies or political manoeuvring, but from the irresistible force of self-giving love. To accept Christ as King, to live under the sovereignty of the Cross, is to enlist in this new kind of kingdom. It is to renounce the world's frantic and violent quest for power and to embrace the cruciform path of service, humility, and love for our enemies. The Cross is the true Oak, the unshakable centre of a new humanity, establishing an order based not on fear, but on love.

THE CROSS AS THE TREE OF PROTECTION: THE SHIELD OF THE VULNERABLE WARRIOR

If the Oak represents the stable centre, the Holly represents its fierce protection. With its evergreen leaves and sharp spines, the Holly was a symbol of defence, vigilance, and the establishment of sacred boundaries. It was the warrior tree, a living shield against negative influences. In a world full of real and perceived dangers—famine, disease, violence, malevolent spirits—the need for protection was paramount.

The Cross is the ultimate act of divine protection. It is the place where God himself, in the person of Christ, stands in the gap between humanity and all the forces of chaos, sin, and death that threaten to destroy us. Christ on the Cross is the ultimate warrior, but he fights the battle in a way that no earthly warrior ever could.

His strategy is not to meet violence with greater violence, but to absorb it into his own being. He takes upon himself all the hatred, all the fear, all the sin of the world, and he does not retaliate. He prays, "Father, forgive them, for they know not what they do" (Luke 23:34). In his own body, he exhausts the power of evil. He swallows up death in victory. The Cross is the shield that does not just deflect the blow, but absorbs its energy and renders it powerless. It is the ultimate act of spiritual jujitsu, using the enemy's own momentum to defeat him.

This means that the protection of the Cross is not a magical charm that saves us from all suffering. Christians still get sick, they still face hardship, they still die. The protection of the Cross is something far deeper. It is the unshakable promise that within our suffering, we are not alone. It is the certainty that nothing, not hardship or distress, not persecution or famine, not even death itself, can separate us from the love of God in Christ Jesus our Lord (Romans 8:38-39). The Cross does not protect us from the storm, but it is the unbreakable anchor in the storm.

The outstretched arms of the Cross create a sacred enclosure, a sanctuary of grace. To flee to the Cross for refuge is to place ourselves within this zone of ultimate safety, to know that whatever happens to us in this life, our ultimate destiny is secure in the loving hands of God. The Cross sets a final boundary against despair. It declares that while suffering is real, it does not get the last word. While death is real, it is not the end. Love gets the last word. Life gets the last word. This is the ultimate protection, the ultimate victory, won by the ultimate warrior on the battlefield of the ultimate Holly tree.

In the Cross, the King is the Warrior. Sovereignty is the protection. The one who rules is the one who saves, and he does both through the same act of radical, self-sacrificial love. The Cross is the strong tower of the new kingdom, the mighty Oak that is also the impenetrable Holly. It is the place where we find both our allegiance and our safety, our King and our shield. It is the tree under whose authority we live and within whose embrace we find our eternal home.

THE IRISH HIGH CROSSES: STONE SERMONS OF THE TREE OF LIFE

Nowhere is the Celtic understanding of the Cross as the Tree of Life, the Crann Bethadh, more powerfully and beautifully expressed than in the great stone High Crosses that still stand sentinel over the Irish landscape. These are not mere historical markers or simple grave decorations. They are magnificent works of art, profound theological statements, and enduring sermons carved in stone. To stand before one of these crosses—at Monasterboice, Clonmacnoise, or Kells—is to witness the culmination of the spiritual vision we have been exploring. It is to see the Cross not as a stark instrument of death, but as a vibrant, living tree, teeming with stories, symbols, and the promise of a cosmos redeemed.

These crosses, which began to appear in the 8th and 9th centuries, represent a uniquely Irish contribution to Christian art and thought. They are the ultimate synthesis of the pre-Christian and Christian worldviews, a testament to the genius of the Celtic church in integrating the new faith with the ancient wisdom of the land. They are, in essence, the physical embodiment of the theology we have been discussing: the Cross as the World Tree, the Tree of Life and Wisdom, and the Tree of Sovereignty and Protection.

THE FORM OF THE CROSS: THE RING OF LIFE

The most distinctive feature of the Irish High Cross is the ring that encircles the intersection of the shaft and the arms. This ring is a masterstroke of symbolic genius, and its meaning is manifold. What does it represent?

First, it is a cosmic symbol. The circle represents the cosmos, the entirety of creation, while the Cross represents the presence of Christ within it. The ring binds the arms of the Cross together, showing that the power of Christ holds the entire universe in being. It is a visual representation of St. Paul's words that in Christ "all things hold together" (Colossians 1:17). The Cross is not an intrusion into the world, but its very structure and support.

Second, it symbolises the sun. The pre-Christian Irish revered the sun as a source of life and light. The ringed cross can be seen as a Christianized sun-symbol, a way of saying that Christ is the true sun, the "sun of righteousness" (Malachi 4:2), the light of the world. It is a powerful act of baptismal imagination, taking a potent pagan symbol and filling it with new, Christian meaning.

Third, it is a halo or nimbus. The ring can be seen as a halo of light emanating from the centre of the Cross, from the heart of Christ. It signifies the glory, the divinity, and the holiness of the one who hangs upon it. It transforms the Cross from a place of shame into a place of radiant glory.

Fourth, and perhaps most importantly for our purposes, it is a wreath of victory. In the ancient world, a wreath of leaves was given to the victor in a contest or a triumphant general. The ring on the cross is a victory wreath, proclaiming that the Crucifixion is not a defeat, but the ultimate triumph over sin, death, and the devil. It is the crown of the victorious King.

This ring transforms the very nature of the Cross. It turns it from a simple crossing of two beams into a complex, integrated, and dynamic symbol. It makes the Cross look less like an instrument of execution and more like a cosmic diagram, a celestial key, or a great, stylised tree. The ring is the foliage of the Tree of Life, the vibrant, living crown of the King of the Universe.

THE CARVINGS ON THE CROSS: A LIBRARY IN STONE

If the form of the High Cross is symbolic, its content is narrative. The surfaces of these crosses are covered in intricately carved panels, each depicting a scene from the Bible. In an age when books were scarce and literacy was limited to monasteries, these crosses served as a public library of sacred narratives, a visual catechism for the people. They are truly "sermons in stone."

The choice of scenes is not random. They are carefully selected and arranged to tell the story of salvation history and to interpret the meaning of the Cross itself. On a typical High Cross, you might find:

• **Scenes from the Old Testament:** Adam and Eve (the story of the first tree and the fall), Cain and Abel (the first murder), Noah's Ark (salvation from the flood), Abraham's sacrifice of Isaac (a prefigurement of the Father's sacrifice of the Son), Moses striking the rock (a prefigurement of the life-giving waters flowing from Christ's side), David with his harp (the poet-king), and Daniel in the lion's den (salvation from certain death).

• **Scenes from the New Testament:** The Annunciation, the Baptism of Christ, the miracle at Cana, the feeding of the five thousand, the arrest of Christ, and, at the centre of it all, the Crucifixion.

• **The Central Panel:** The Crucifixion and the Last Judgment: The heart of the cross is almost always occupied by the Crucifixion on one side and the Last Judgment on the other. This is a profound theological statement.

The Crucifixion is the pivotal event of history, and the Last Judgment is its ultimate consequence. The King who reigns from the Cross is also the Judge who will come again in glory. But the judgment is always seen through the lens of the Cross, meaning it is a judgment of mercy and love.

What is most striking about these carvings is their depiction of the Cross. The central figure of Christ is not usually shown as a suffering, bleeding victim. He is often portrayed as a calm, majestic King, with his eyes open and his arms outstretched in a gesture of welcome rather than of agony. He is robed, not naked. He is the victorious King on his throne, not the defeated criminal on his gibbet.

Furthermore, the Cross itself is often depicted not as dead wood, but as a living tree. The panels' backgrounds are filled with intricate, swirling patterns of knotwork and spirals, symbols of eternity and the interconnectedness of all life. Vines, leaves, and animals are often carved into the very structure of the Cross, suggesting that it is the new Tree of Life, the source of a new creation.

The message is clear: the Cross is not an end, but a beginning. It is the tree from which the new Eden blossoms.

THE CROSS OF THE SCRIPTURES: A SERMON IN STONE

Let us take one example, the magnificent Cross of the Scriptures at Clonmacnoise. On its east face, at the centre, is Christ the King in glory, holding the sceptre and the cross-staff of the resurrection. Below him are scenes of the secular world being brought into submission to his gentle rule. On the west face, at the centre, is the Crucifixion.

The two soldiers flank Christ, one offering him the sponge soaked in vinegar, the other piercing his side with a spear. But even here, he is majestic, a figure of calm power. And all around this central scene, the story of salvation unfolds, from the Garden of Eden to the empty tomb.

The entire cross is a sermon on the meaning of the Crucifixion. It tells us that this event must be understood in the context of the whole story of God's love for humanity. It tells us that the one who died on the Cross is the King of the Universe. It indicates that his death was not a tragedy but a victory. It indicates that this victory brings about a new creation, a world filled with the vibrant, interconnected life of God.

The Irish High Crosses are the ultimate expression of the Celtic Christian vision. They are a testament to a faith that did not reject the natural world, but saw it as a sacrament of God's presence. They are a proclamation of a gospel that did not fear the ancient archetypes of the human soul, but saw them as signposts pointing the way to Christ. They are a powerful reminder that the Cross is not a symbol of death, but the ultimate Tree of Life, the Crann Bethadh, whose leaves are for the healing of the nations, and whose fruit is eternal life.

They stand today as an invitation to us, to read their stories, to contemplate their beauty, and to enter into the profound and life-giving mystery they so eloquently proclaim. They are the great trees of the Celtic Christian grove, and their roots run deep into the soil of faith, and their branches reach to the very heart of heaven.

THE PRACTICE: A MEDITATION ON THE CROSS AS WORLD TREE

We have journeyed far with our minds, exploring the rich theology of the Cross as the ultimate tree. We have seen it through the eyes of the Celtic saints as the World Tree, the Tree of Life, the throne of the true King. But theology, if it is to be truly life-giving, must move from the head to the heart. It must become not just a concept we understand, but a reality we experience. The time has come to leave the library of the intellect and enter the sacred grove of the heart.

This meditation is an invitation to encounter the Cross not as a historical artefact or a theological principle, but as a living, dynamic, spiritual reality. We will journey along its three dimensions, experiencing it as the Crann Bethadh, the great tree that connects the realms. Find a quiet and comfortable place where you will not be disturbed for fifteen to twenty minutes. You may wish to sit before a crucifix, an image of a High Cross, or simply a bare wall. Close your eyes, and take three slow, deep breaths.

With each exhale, release the busyness of your day and the chatter of your mind. Settle into the stillness of the present moment. You are on holy ground.

Step 1: Stand at the Foot of the Cross

In your mind's eye, allow an image of the Cross to form. It may be a simple wooden cross or an ornate High Cross. See it standing before you, planted firmly in the earth, its vertical beam reaching for the heavens, its horizontal arms open wide. Imagine yourself standing at its foot. Feel the ground beneath your feet. Smell the air. You are at the centre of the world, the axis of all time and space. Before you is the most powerful symbol in the universe, a symbol of a love so strong it willingly entered into death to conquer it.

Do not try to analyse or understand. Be present. Gaze upon the Cross in silence. Allow feelings of awe, reverence, or even sorrow to arise without judgment. You are standing at the intersection of heaven and earth. Be still, and know that God is here.

Step 2: Journey Down the Root—Honouring the Ancestors

Now, bring your attention to the base of the Cross, where it enters the earth. Imagine that you can follow it down, journeying along its deep taproot into the soil. You are descending into the Underworld, the realm of memory, the home of the ancestors. As you go deeper, feel the presence of all those who have gone before you. See the faces of your grandparents and their parents, stretching back through countless generations. They are the foundation upon which your life is built.

Go deeper still, and you feel the presence of the great cloud of witnesses—the saints, the martyrs, the prophets, and the patriarchs. You arrive in the great waiting place, the realm of the dead, before Christ's coming. And there, in the midst of them, is a great light. It is Christ himself, the Harrower of Hell, breaking the gates of death and setting the captives free. He is gathering all of history into his redemptive embrace. Feel the joy and liberation of this moment.

The root of the Cross redeems all that has been.

Take a moment to give thanks for your ancestors and for the communion of saints. Acknowledge their struggles and their faith.

Quietly in your heart, say to them: "I remember you. I honour you. Your story is part of my story." Feel yourself rooted in this great family of faith, held securely by the deep anchor of the Cross.

Step 3: Journey Across the Arms—Embracing the World

Slowly, allow your awareness to ascend back to the surface, to the foot of the Cross. Now, turn your attention to the horizontal beam, the arms of the Cross stretching out to embrace the whole of the Middle World. Imagine yourself journeying out along one of those arms. As you do, you encounter all of humanity in its beautiful and broken diversity. You see people of every race, nation, and creed. You see those you love and those you struggle with. You see your friends and your enemies.

Feel the unconditional embrace of these arms. They do not discriminate. They do not judge. They hold the victim and the perpetrator, the righteous and the sinner, in the same compassionate grasp. Hear the words whispered from the Cross: "Father, forgive them." Feel the walls of hostility and division dissolving in this radical act of love. The arms of the Cross create a new family, a new humanity, where all are welcomed, and all belong.

Now, extend your own arms in your imagination. Feel what it is like to hold the whole world in an embrace of forgiveness and compassion. Quietly in your heart, say: "I am part of this family. I forgive, and I am forgiven. We are all beloved." Rest in this horizontal embrace, the peace of universal reconciliation.

Step 4: Journey Up the Trunk—Ascending to the Father

Return your awareness to the centre of the Cross, to the heart of Christ. Now, begin your final journey, ascending the vertical beam, climbing the trunk of the great tree toward the Upper World, the realm of the divine. As you rise, you feel the pull of the earth lessening. The cares, anxieties, and fears of your life begin to fall away. You are rising into a realm of pure light, pure peace, pure love.

You are being drawn up into the very heart of God. Feel the intimacy of this ascent, the joy of returning home.

You hear the final words of surrender from the Cross: "Father, into your hands I commit my spirit."

Allow yourself to enter into that same surrender, that same perfect trust. You are not climbing by your own strength; you are being drawn up by a love that desires you completely.

At the summit of the Cross, you find yourself resting in the heart of the Father. There are no words here, only presence. You are held, known, and loved unconditionally. You are home. Rest in this silent, loving communion for as long as you wish.

Step 5: Return and Integration

When you are ready, begin your gentle descent. Bring the peace, the love, and the light of the Upper World back down with you, through the reconciling embrace of the Middle World, and into the deep, rooted strength of the Underworld. Come to rest once more at the foot of the Cross, the integrated centre of your being.

Become aware again of your body, of the chair beneath you, of the room around you. Take a final, deep breath and, when you are ready, slowly open your eyes.

Journaling Prompts:

• Which part of the journey—down, across, or up—resonated most deeply with you, and why?

• How does experiencing the Cross as a three-dimensional, living tree change your relationship with it?

• In what specific area of your life do you need to experience the reconciling embrace of the Cross's arms right now?

CONCLUSION: THE TREE AT THE CENTRE OF YOUR GROVE

We have arrived, dear friend, at the end of this chapter, but at the very heart of our journey. We have walked a path that has led us from the ancient groves of the Druids to the foot of a Roman cross, and we have discovered, with the Celtic saints, that this was no detour, but a homecoming. We have seen how the Cross, far from being a symbol of rupture from the natural world, is in fact the ultimate fulfilment of all the wisdom the trees have been whispering to us since the beginning of time.

Think back on the trees of our journey. The Cross is the ultimate Oak, for on it reigns the true King, whose sovereignty is not domination but service, whose strength is the enduring power of self-giving love. It is the ultimate Ash, the true World Tree, whose roots embrace the ancestors, whose branches reach to the heavens, and whose arms hold all of creation in a gesture of cosmic reconciliation. It is the ultimate Yew, the tree of death and resurrection, proclaiming that life is stronger than death and that every ending is a new beginning in disguise.

It is the ultimate Hazel, for it is the source of the most profound wisdom— the paradoxical, world-changing wisdom that power is perfected in weakness and that the foolishness of God is wiser than the wisdom of men. It is the ultimate Apple, the true Silver Branch, the Tree of Life whose fruit is immortality, offered freely to all who would come and eat. It is the ultimate Holly, the warrior tree that does not protect by violence but by absorbing all violence into itself and transforming it into forgiveness.
It is the ultimate Rowan, the tree of discernment that protects us from all illusion by showing us the ultimate reality: that God is love.

Every truth we have gleaned from the forest, every archetype we have explored in the Ogham, finds its final, deepest, and most beautiful expression in the tree of the Cross. It is the tree that contains all trees, the symbol that fulfils all symbols, the story that makes sense of all other stories.

The Cross in Your Inner Grove

But this is not just a grand, abstract theology. It is an intensely personal truth. In the introduction to this book, I invited readers to cultivate an inner landscape, a sacred grove within their own souls where they can meet with the divine. We have been planting that grove together, tree by tree. But a grove is not just a random collection of trees. It has a centre, a heartwood, a place of power from which the entire grove draws its life and meaning.

I invite you now to see that the centre of your inner grove is the Cross. It is the Crann Bethadh of your own soul. It is the tree that anchors your personal underworld of memory and loss, connecting you to your ancestors in a spirit of gratitude and healing. It is the tree that defines your middle world of relationships and work, calling you to extend your arms in a cruciform gesture of love and service to all you meet. It is the tree that guides your ascent into the upper world of divine communion, the ladder by which you climb into the heart of the Father.

To live a Christian life, in this Celtic sense, is to be a person of the grove, and to be a person of the grove is to be a person of the Cross. It is to live a "cruciform" life—a life shaped by the Cross. This means that in your moments of joy, you recognise the fruit of the Tree of Life. In your moments of sorrow, you cling to the wood of the Cross as your anchor in the storm. In your moments of confusion, you seek the wisdom of the Cross that clarifies all things. In your moments of weakness, you find your strength in the King who reigns from a tree. In your moments of fear, you take refuge in the protection of the warrior who laid down his life for you.

Living a cruciform life means that the pattern of the Cross—death and resurrection, self-giving and new life—becomes the rhythm of your own existence. You learn to let go of the old to make way for the new. You learn to forgive as you have been forgiven. You learn to serve as you have been served. You learn to love as you have been loved. The Cross ceases to be something you merely believe in; it becomes the very shape of your being.

The Journey Continues

This chapter has been the theological peak of our mountain climb together. But the view from the summit is not the end of the journey; it is the inspiration for the path that lies ahead. We do not simply gaze upon the Cross; we are called to live by its light. In the chapters that follow, we will carry this vision down from the mountain and into the valleys of our daily lives. We will explore the practical ways we can live as people of the grove, people of the Cross. We will learn how to create sacred space, how to walk the forest as a spiritual practice, how to honour the cycles of the seasons, and how to live in right relationship with all of God's creation.

But for now, let us rest here. Let us rest in the shade of this great tree. You have seen the Cross with new eyes. You have understood it not as a symbol of sorrow, but as the Tree of Life. You have recognised it as the fulfilment of the deepest truths whispered by the wind in the leaves. You have stood at its foot, journeyed along its dimensions, and, I pray, experienced its power to connect, to heal, and to transform.

The Cross stands at the centre of your grove. It is the tree that holds your life together. It is the tree that gives meaning to your joys and your sorrows. It is the tree that promises that love is stronger than death, that life will have the final word, that all things—even you, even me, even this broken and beautiful world—will be made new.

The great synthesis is complete. The Cross is the tree. The tree is the Cross. And you are invited to live beneath its branches, to eat its fruit, to rest in its shade, to draw your life from its roots, now and forever.

The journey continues.

The grove is waiting.

The Cross stands at the centre, its arms outstretched, welcoming you home.

Chapter 9:

The Grove of Your Life: Creating Sacred Space Within and Without

Welcome back, dear friend. We have just descended from a high mountain. In our last chapter, we stood at the theological summit of our journey, gazing upon the Cross as the ultimate Tree of Life, the axis of the cosmos, the fulfilment of all the wisdom the whispering trees have offered us. We saw it as the great synthesis, the point where the stream of Celtic nature mysticism and the river of Christian faith flow into one another and become a single, mighty torrent of love and grace. It was a breathtaking view, one that I hope has forever changed the way you see the central symbol of our faith.

But a vision from a mountaintop, however glorious, is not meant to be a permanent residence. We are not called to be hermits of the summit, forever contemplating the vista. We are called to be pilgrims of the valley, tasked with carrying the light of that vision down into the beautiful, messy, and often chaotic landscape of our daily lives. The journey continues, as it must. The question that now stands before us is a profoundly practical one: How do we put this into practice? How do we take the grand, cosmic truth of the cruciform life and make it our own, not just as a belief, but as a lived reality?

This is the task that will occupy us for the remainder of our book. We are moving from the what to the how, from theology to practice, from vision to dwelling. And the very first step in building a dwelling place for the spirit is to consecrate the ground. Before a house can be built, a foundation must be laid. Before a garden can be planted, the soil must be tilled. Before we can live a consecrated life, we must first learn to create sacred space.

The concept of sacred space is one of the most ancient and universal of human instincts. From the stone circles of our Neolithic ancestors to the great cathedrals of Europe, humanity has always felt the need to set aside certain places as special, as holy, as locations where the veil between the worlds is thin and the divine can be more readily encountered. The Celtic tradition is particularly rich in this regard. It speaks of "thin places," locations where the boundary between heaven and earth seems almost to disappear. It honours the bile, the sacred tree that marked the centre of the tribe. And it gave us the model of the cill, the small, simple, sacred cell of the hermit or monk, a place of quiet prayer and communion with God.

In this chapter, we will reclaim this ancient and vital practice. We will learn that creating sacred space is not an escape from the world, but a way of engaging with it more deeply. It is the act of creating a focal point for our spiritual lives, a sanctuary where we can be still, listen, and remember who we are. It is about making a conscious choice to invite the sacred into the very fabric of our daily existence.

Our exploration will be twofold. We will learn to tend to the inner grove, the sacred landscape of our own hearts, for it is here that the most important work is always done. But we will also learn to cultivate an outer grove, a physical manifestation of that inner reality in our homes and in the world around us. The inner and the outer are not separate; they are reflections of one another. A well-tended inner grove will naturally lead to the creation of outer sacred space, and a well-tended outer grove will, in turn, help to cultivate peace and order within.

Our journey in this chapter will unfold in seven practical steps:

1. Introduction: From Vision to Dwelling: We will frame our task as the practical application of the vision we received in the last chapter.

2. Tending the Inner Grove: The Landscape of the Heart: We will explore the essential practices for cultivating a rich inner life.

3. The Hearth of the Sacred: Creating a Home Altar: We will learn the practical art of building a small, personal altar in our homes.

4. The Fidchell Board of the World: Recognising Sacred Space Around Us: We will learn to see and honour the natural thin places in our own local environments.

5. Sanctifying Time: The Rhythm of the Hours: We will discover how to create sacred space not just in place, but in time, through the rhythm of daily prayer.

6. The Practice: Building Your Cill: We will engage in a guided practice to create our own sacred cell or home altar.

7. Conclusion: Living a Consecrated Life: We will see how the practice of creating sacred space can transform our entire lives, making every place a sanctuary.

This chapter is an invitation to become a builder, a gardener, a tender of the sacred. It is a call to take the glorious vision of the Cross as the Tree of Life and to plant a seed of that tree in the soil of your own life.

It is time to roll up our sleeves, to put our hands in the earth, and to begin the joyful work of building a home for our souls. Let us lay the first stone.

TENDING THE INNER GROVE: THE LANDSCAPE OF THE HEART

Before we build a single altar or light a single candle in our homes, we must begin our work in the place where all true sacredness is born: the inner grove of the heart.

All external acts of piety are but empty gestures if they do not flow from a well-tended inner landscape. The most beautiful cathedral is but a pile of stones if the hearts of the people within it are barren. The most ancient forest is just a collection of trees if the one walking through it has no eyes to see. Therefore, our first and most important task in creating sacred space is to turn inward and begin the patient, lifelong work of cultivating the garden of our own souls.

Your heart is a sacred grove. It is a landscape as real as any you might walk through. It has its sunlit clearings and its dark, tangled thickets. It has its ancient, wise oaks and its young, vulnerable saplings. It has its fallow seasons and its times of abundant growth. To live a spiritual life is to become a gardener of this inner landscape, a tender of this sacred grove. It is to learn the rhythms of your own soul, to know when to plant and when to prune, when to water and when to let the ground lie fallow. It is a gentle, attentive, and deeply personal art.

This may sound like a daunting task, especially in our modern world, which does everything in its power to distract us from this inner work. We are constantly pulled outward by the demands of work, the noise of the media, and the endless scroll of social connection. The path to the inner grove has become overgrown with the weeds of busyness and the thorns of anxiety.

But do not be discouraged. The path remains, awaiting rediscovery. The Celtic saints, the anamcharas or soul friends, have left us maps and tools. They teach us that the work of tending the inner grove is not about grand, heroic efforts, but about small, consistent, and loving practices. Let us explore some of these essential practices, framing them as the sacred tasks of a gardener of the soul.

THE FIRST TASK: CLEARING THE GROUND WITH SILENCE

No gardener can begin their work until they have first cleared the ground. The weeds, the brambles, the accumulated debris of winter must be removed to make way for new life. In the inner grove, the tool for this clearing is silence. Silence is the practice of intentionally stepping away from the noise of the world and the even greater noise of our own minds to be present to the stillness that lies beneath it all.

In our culture, silence is often seen as an absence, an emptiness, a void to be filled as quickly as possible. But in the spiritual tradition, silence is a presence. It is the presence of God, who most often speaks in what the prophet Elijah called the "still, small voice" (1 Kings 19:12).

Entering silence creates a space in which that voice can be heard. It is to say to God, "I am here. I am listening."

How do we practice silence in a world that is never quiet? We must be gentle with ourselves. It is not about achieving a perfectly blank mind; that is impossible.

It concerns the intention to remain still. Here is a simple way to begin:

1. Find a Time and Place: Set aside just five or ten minutes in your day. It may be early in the morning before the house awakes, or during your lunch break, or just before you go to sleep. Find a comfortable chair in which you can sit upright yet relaxed.

2. Set Your Intention: Begin by saying a simple prayer, such as, "Lord, I offer you this time. Help me to be still and to listen for your voice."

3. Focus on Your Breath: Close your eyes and bring your attention to your breath. Do not try to change it. Notice the sensation of the air entering and leaving your body. Your breath is a sacred rhythm, a gift of life in every moment. Let it be your anchor to the present.

4. Welcome Distractions as Guests: Your mind will wander. This is not a sign of failure; it is the nature of the mind. When a thought, a worry, or a memory arises, do not fight it. Acknowledge it gently, as you might nod to a stranger passing on the street, and then gently, lovingly, return your attention to your breath. Do this 100 times if necessary. The practice is not in never wandering, but in always returning.

5. Rest in the Stillness: There will be moments, even if fleeting, of deep stillness between your thoughts. These are the clearings in your inner grove. Rest in them. Savour them. This is the fertile ground where new life can begin to grow.

Practising silence is the act of clearing the undergrowth. It creates space. It allows the soil of your heart to breathe. It is the essential first step in tending your inner grove.

THE SECOND TASK: TILLING THE SOIL WITH THE PRAYER OF EXAMEN

Once the ground is cleared, the gardener must till the soil, turning it over to aerate it and prepare it for planting. The spiritual tool for this tilling is the ancient practice of the Prayer of Examen. Developed by St. Ignatius of Loyola, but with roots in the earliest days of the Church, the Examen is a simple, prayerful review of your day, a way of looking back to see where God has been present and active.

To practice the Examen is to believe that your life, even on its most ordinary days, is a sacred text, a story being co-written by you and God. It is to take the raw material of your day—the joys and the sorrows, the successes and the failures, the moments of connection and the moments of frustration—and to hold it all up to the light of God's love. This practice tills the soil of your heart, breaking up the hard clumps of indifference and revealing the nutrients of grace that were there all along.

The Examen consists of five simple steps, usually practised for ten or fifteen minutes at the end of the day:

1. Become Aware of God's Presence: Begin by remembering that you are in the presence of God, who loves you unconditionally. Give thanks for the gift of this day and for this opportunity to be with the One who created you.

2. Review the Day with Gratitude: Ask God to help you see your day as God sees it. Then, review the events of your day, from morning to evening. Where did you feel most alive? What brought you joy? What are you most grateful for? Savour these moments of light and give thanks for them.

3. Pay Attention to Your Emotions: As you review your day, pay attention to your feelings. Where did you feel consolation—a sense of peace, joy, and connection to God? Where did you feel desolation—a sense of anxiety, sadness, and disconnection? These feelings are the movements of the spirit within you, guiding you toward what gives life and away from what brings death.

4. Choose One Feature of the Day and Pray from It: From all the moments you have reviewed, choose one that particularly stands out. It may be a moment of great joy or a moment of significant struggle. Hold this moment before God in prayer. If it was a moment of joy, give thanks. If it was a moment of struggle, ask for forgiveness, healing, or guidance.

5. Look Toward Tomorrow: Finally, look toward the day to come. Ask God for the grace you will need for its challenges and opportunities. End with a simple prayer, such as the Our Father.

The daily practice of the Examen is like turning over the soil of your inner grove. It keeps your heart soft and receptive. It prevents the ground from becoming hard and compacted. It makes you an attentive observer of the subtle ways God is at work in your life, preparing the ground for the seeds of wisdom and love to be planted.

THE THIRD TASK: PLANTING SEEDS WITH SACRED READING (LECTIO DIVINA)

With the ground cleared and the soil tilled, it is time to plant. The gardener of the soul plants seeds of truth, beauty, and goodness. The classic method for this sacred planting is the ancient monastic practice *of Lectio Divina*, or "sacred reading." This is a way of reading a short passage of scripture, poetry, or other sacred text, not for information, but for formation.

It is a slow, prayerful, and receptive way of reading, allowing the words to sink deep into the soil of your heart and take root.

Lectio Divina has four traditional movements, like the four seasons of a plant's life:

1. Lectio (Reading): Choose a short passage of scripture or another text that speaks to you. Read it slowly, perhaps even aloud. Listen for a word or a phrase that shimmers, that seems to stand out and call to you. Do not analyse it. Receive it as a gift.

2. Meditatio (Meditation): Reread the passage. This time, gently ponder the word or phrase that caught your attention. What does it mean to you, in this moment of your life? What images, feelings, or memories does it evoke? This is not intellectual analysis, but a gentle, loving rumination, like a bee buzzing around a flower.

3. Oratio (Prayer): Read the passage a third time. Now, let your meditation turn into prayer. Speak to God from your heart about what has been stirred within you. It may be a prayer of praise, of petition, of sorrow, or of gratitude. Let the text be the bridge between your heart and God's.

4. Contemplatio (Contemplation): Finally, let go of all words and thoughts. Simply rest in the presence of God. This is the fruit of the practice, a moment of silent, loving communion. It is a moment of simply being with the Beloved, beyond words and ideas.

Practising *Lectio Divina* is like planting a seed in the prepared soil of your heart. You do not make the seed grow; you create the conditions for it to take root and bear fruit in its own time. These sacred words, planted in the silence and tilled by the Examen, will begin to grow within you, shaping your thoughts, your feelings, and your actions from the inside out.

By faithfully practising these three tasks—clearing the ground with silence, tilling the soil with the Examen, and planting seeds with sacred reading—you become a true gardener of your soul.

You create within yourself a sacred space, an inner grove that is fertile, vibrant, and alive. It is from this inner sanctuary that all our outer acts of creating sacred space derive their meaning and power. For when the grove within is flourishing, the whole world begins to look like a garden.

THE HEARTH OF THE SACRED: CREATING A HOME ALTAR

As we diligently tend to the soil of our inner grove, a natural desire arises to see that inner reality reflected in our outer world. The human person is not a disembodied spirit; we are a mysterious and beautiful union of body and soul. We experience the world and God through our senses. It is, therefore, a deeply human and holy instinct to want to create a physical space that honours and facilitates our connection to the divine.

We need a place to stand, a place to kneel, a place to be in the presence of the sacred. In the Christian tradition, this place is often called an altar. And while we may think of altars only as the grand stone tables in our churches, the tradition of the home altar is equally ancient and equally vital. It is the practice of creating a hearth for the sacred in the very centre of our daily lives.

Think of the hearth in an old Celtic home. It was the heart of the house. It provided warmth, light, and a fire for cooking food. It was the place where the family gathered to share stories, to pray, and to be together. It was the centre of life. A home altar is the spiritual hearth of your home. It is a small, dedicated space that serves as a focal point for your prayer and a constant, gentle reminder of the sacred reality that underpins all of life. It is a declaration, in physical form, that this home is a place where God is honoured and welcomed.

Creating a home altar is not about building a stage for a performance, nor is it about idolatry. The objects on the altar are not worshipped. Instead, they are pointers, symbols, and reminders. They are tools that help us to focus our minds and open our hearts. They are sacraments, in the small "s" sense of the word: outward signs of an inward grace. They are the physical vocabulary of our prayer. In this section, we will explore the practical art of creating your own home altar, a sacred hearth that will bring warmth and light to your entire home.

CHOOSING THE GROUND: LOCATION, LOCATION, LOCATION

Your first step is to choose a location. This need not be a large or dramatic space. In fact, a small, quiet corner is often best. The key is that it should be a place that you can, to some degree, set apart. It might be the top of a bookshelf, a small side table, a windowsill, or even a dedicated shelf in a closet that can be opened for prayer. Consider a place that is out of the main flow of household traffic, a place where you can be still for a few moments without being disturbed.

Traditionally, Christian churches were built facing east, toward the rising sun, the symbol of the resurrected Christ. You might consider this in choosing your location, but it is not essential. What is essential is that the place feels right to you. It should be a place that invites you into stillness, not a place that adds to your stress. Once you have chosen your spot, clean it thoroughly. This act of cleaning is itself a prayer, a preparation of the space for a holy purpose.

LAYING THE FOUNDATION: THE ALTAR ITSELF

The base of your altar can be very simple. A small piece of beautiful cloth, perhaps in a colour that reflects the current liturgical season (green for Ordinary Time, purple for Advent and Lent, white for Christmas and Easter), can serve to define the space and set it apart. This cloth is like the clearing in the grove, the prepared ground upon which the sacred can appear. Upon this cloth, you might place a simple wooden board, a flat stone, or nothing at all. The surface itself is less important than the intention with which it is set. This is your holy ground, your personal "thin place."

THE ELEMENTS OF THE GROVE: WHAT TO PLACE ON YOUR ALTAR

Now we come to the joyful task of populating your sacred space. What do you place on your altar? The answer is deeply personal, but here are some traditional and meaningful elements, seen through the lens of our Celtic Christian journey. Think of this as gathering sacred treasures for the hearth of your soul.

1. The Centrepiece: The Tree of Life. At the centre of your altar, just as at the centre of your inner grove, should stand the Cross. This is the focal point, the ultimate symbol that encompasses all the others. It could be a small standing crucifix, a simple wooden cross you have made yourself, or an image of a Celtic High Cross. This is your Crann Bethadh, your Tree of Life, the primary reminder of God's self-giving love.

2. The Four Elements: The Building Blocks of Creation Our ancestors understood the world to be composed of four sacred elements: Earth, Air, Fire, and Water. Placing a symbol of each on your altar is a way of honouring the goodness of creation and inviting the God of creation into your prayer. It connects your small, personal space to the vastness of the cosmos.

• **Earth:** A symbol of grounding, stability, and our connection to the land. This could be a beautiful stone from a beach or a forest walk, a small bowl of soil from your garden, or a piece of wood with interesting grain. An acorn is a perfect symbol of the Oak's strength and potential.

• **Air:** A symbol of the Holy Spirit (the Ruach, the breath of God), of prayer ascending, and of communication. This could be a feather you have found, which, for the Celts, was a sign of celestial messages. Or you might use incense, whose fragrant smoke has symbolised prayer rising to heaven for millennia.

• **Fire:** A symbol of Christ as the Light of the World, of illumination, of passion, and of the divine presence. The most straightforward and most powerful symbol of fire is a candle. Lighting the candle at the beginning of your prayer time is a powerful ritual act, a signal to your soul that you are now entering sacred time.

• **Water:** A symbol of baptism, of cleansing, of the emotions, and of the Well of Wisdom. This can be a small seashell or a simple bowl of water. You might use this water to bless yourself, making the sign of the cross on your forehead as a reminder of your baptism.

3. Echoes of the Grove: Connecting to the Trees. Your altar can also be a place to honour the wisdom of the specific tree archetypes we have explored. You might place a hazelnut or a smooth river stone to remind you of the quest for wisdom. A small, polished apple could symbolise your longing for the eternal life of the Otherworld. A sprig of holly at Christmas or a branch of yew can connect you to the turning of the seasons and the cycles of life and death.

4. The Communion of Saints: Your Heavenly Family. An altar is a place where the veil between heaven and earth is thin. It is a wonderful place to remember that you are part of a great family of faith. You might include an icon or a small statue of a favourite saint, particularly a Celtic saint like Patrick, Brigid, or Columba. You could also have small, framed photographs of loved ones who have passed away, your personal "saints," as a way of honouring their memory and remembering that they are still with you in the communion of saints.

A LIVING SPACE: TENDING THE HEARTH FIRE

Your altar is not a static museum display. It is a living, breathing space that should change and evolve with your own spiritual journey and with the rhythms of the year. You might change the cloth for the liturgical seasons. You might add a flower in the spring, a colourful leaf in the autumn, a sprig of evergreen in the winter. If a particular scripture verse or poem speaks to you during your Lectio Divina, you might write it on a small card and place it on your altar for a week.

Tend to your altar as you would a small garden. Keep it clean and uncluttered. Refresh the water. Replace the candle when it burns down. The physical act of tending to your altar is a prayer in itself, a way of honouring the sacred space you have created.

Creating a home altar is a simple but profound act of spiritual resistance against the noise and chaos of the modern world. It is the creation of a "thin place" in your own home. It is the building of a hearth for your soul, a place of warmth and light where you can come to be nourished, to be comforted, and to be reminded of the great and beautiful truth that you are a beloved child of God, dwelling always in the sacred grove of God's presence. It is the first and most important step in carrying the vision of the mountain down into the valley of your daily life.

THE FIDCHELL BOARD OF THE WORLD: RECOGNISING SACRED SPACE AROUND US

Once we begin tending our inner grove and establish a sacred hearth within our homes, a remarkable transformation in our perception begins. The boundary between the "sacred" and the "secular" starts to dissolve. The grace that we cultivate in our times of prayer begins to seep out into the rest of our lives, and we start to see the world with new eyes. We begin to realise that the sacred is not confined to our churches, our altars, or our moments of quiet contemplation. The entire world, if we have the eyes to see it, is a sacred landscape, a vast and intricate temple where God is perpetually present and at work.

Our Celtic ancestors had a profound sense of this. They did not see the world as a uniform, homogenous space. They saw it as a landscape of varying spiritual intensity, a place of power points, energy lines, and sacred centres. In the old Irish myths, the land is often compared to a great fidchell board. Fidchell was a complex board game, similar to chess, played by the nobility. To see the world as a fidchell board was to see it as a strategic and meaningful landscape, where every feature—every hill, every well, every ancient tree—had its own unique significance and power. The gods and heroes moved across this landscape, and their stories were woven into the very fabric of the land itself.

For the Celtic Christian, this vision was not abolished, but baptised. The world is indeed a sacred board, but the game being played upon it is the great game of salvation history, and the chief player is Christ himself, the King who moves across the land, healing, blessing, and making all things new. To learn to see the world in this way is to move from being a passive observer of nature to an active participant in its sacred drama. It is to learn to recognise the "thin places" in our own environment, the places where the divine presence seems to break through with particular clarity and power.

THIN PLACES: WHERE HEAVEN AND EARTH KISS

The most beautiful and enduring concept in Celtic spirituality is the "thin place." A thin place is a location where the veil between this world and the Otherworld, between heaven and earth, is especially permeable. It is a place where the sacred is not just a belief, but a palpable presence. These are not necessarily dramatic or spectacular locations. A thin place might be a great pilgrimage site like Iona or Glendalough, but it is just as likely to be a quiet corner of your local park, a particular bend in a river, an ancient tree standing alone in a field, or even the spot on your daily walk where the light falls in a certain way.

What makes a place "thin"? It is a mystery, a confluence of many factors: natural beauty, historical memory, the prayers of those who have gone before, and the subtle energies of the land itself. But most importantly, a place becomes thin for you when you approach it with a thin heart—a heart that is open, receptive, and attentive. The thinness is as much in the perceiver as it is in the place itself.

Learning to identify and honour the thin places in your own life is a vital part of living a Celtic-inspired faith. It is the practice of rooting your spirituality in the soil of your own particular place. It is a way of saying that God is not just a God of the Bible lands or of the great saints, but the God of your own backyard, your own neighbourhood, your own city. How, then, do we find these places?

READING THE LANDSCAPE: A PRACTICAL GUIDE TO FINDING YOUR THIN PLACES

Finding your thin places is not a science, but an art of holy attention. It requires that you slow down, unplug from your devices, and engage your senses. It is a form of Lectio Divina for the book of creation.

Here are some practical steps to guide you on your quest:

1. Walk with Intention: Choose a familiar route for a walk, perhaps one you take every day. But this time, walk with a new intention. Before you set out, say a simple prayer: "Lord, open my eyes to see your presence in this place. Show me the thin places." Walk more slowly than you usually would. Resist the urge to listen to music or a podcast. Your only soundtrack is the world around you.

2. Engage All Your Senses:

• **See:** Look for patterns of light and shadow. Notice the texture of a tree's bark, the intricate design of a leaf, the colour of the sky reflected in a puddle. Look for places that seem to have a special quality of light.

• **Hear:** Listen to the symphony of sounds. Can you distinguish the songs of different birds? Can you hear the rustle of the wind in the leaves, the hum of traffic, the laughter of children? Listen for the silence that lies beneath all the sounds.

• **Smell:** What are the scents of your neighbourhood? The smell of damp earth after a rain, of freshly cut grass, of woodsmoke in the autumn air? Scent is a powerful trigger for memory and emotion.

• **Touch:** Feel the rough bark of a tree, the coolness of a stone, the warmth of the sun on your skin. Let the world touch you back.

3. Look for the Markers of the Sacred: As you walk, keep your eyes open for the traditional markers of a sacred place, the places that would have caught the eye of an ancient Celt:

• **Ancient Trees:** Is there a particularly old or large tree in your area? A tree that has witnessed generations of human life? Such trees have a gravitas and a presence that make them natural sacred centres.

• **Sources of Water:** A spring, a well, a river, a lake. Water is a universal symbol of life and cleansing. Places where water emerges from the earth were considered especially sacred.

• **High Places:** A hill, a lookout point, a place that offers a wide perspective. High places have always been associated with revelation and a sense of closeness to the heavens.

• **Thresholds and Boundaries:** A gateway, a bridge, a shoreline where land and water meet. These are liminal spaces, places of transition, where the veil between the worlds is naturally thin.

• **Places of Memory:** A historic battlefield, an old cemetery, the ruins of an old building. These are places saturated with the stories and emotions of those who have gone before.

4. Trust Your Intuition: More important than any external marker is your own inner response. Pay attention to the feelings that arise in you as you walk. Is there a place where you consistently feel a sense of peace?

A place that seems to quiet your mind?

A place that evokes a sense of awe or wonder?

A place that feels "right"? This is your heart recognising a thin place.

Trust that feeling. It is the Holy Spirit guiding you.

HONOURING YOUR THIN PLACES: BECOMING A GUARDIAN OF THE SACRED

Once you have identified a thin place, what do you do? You become its guardian. You honour it. This need not be a dramatic act. It is a simple, loving relationship that you build with the place over time.

• **Visit Regularly:** Return to your thin place often. Let it become a regular part of your spiritual rhythm. Your repeated, prayerful presence will, in turn, make the place even "thinner."

• **Pray There:** Your thin place is a natural oratory, an outdoor chapel. You can say your daily prayers there, practice your Lectio Divina, or simply sit in silence.

• **Leave a Small Offering:** This is an ancient practice. It is not a bribe to a nature spirit, but a simple gesture of gratitude and respect. It could be a prayer, a song, or a small, biodegradable offering, such as a beautiful stone or a sprinkle of cornmeal. The most important offering is your attention.

• **Care for the Place:** If your thin place is a natural one, become its steward. Pick up any litter you find. Learn about the native plants and animals. Your care for the place's physical well-being is a powerful prayer.

By learning to recognise and honour the thin places in your own life, you are participating in the great work of re-sacralizing the world.

You are pushing back against the modern tendency to see the world as a mere resource to be exploited.

You are reclaiming the ancient Christian and pre-Christian vision of the world as a sacrament, a living icon of its Creator.

You are learning to play your part on the great fidchell board of the world, moving with grace and intention across a landscape charged with the grandeur and intimacy of God.

Your home altar becomes the hearth, and these thin places become the outer chapels of the great cathedral of your life.

SANCTIFYING TIME: THE RHYTHM OF THE HOURS

We have journeyed inward to tend the grove of the heart, and we have journeyed outward to establish a sacred hearth in our homes and to recognise the thin places in the world around us. We have learned to create sacred space. But space is only one of the two great dimensions of our existence. The other is time. If our lives are to be truly consecrated, we must learn not only to sanctify the where of our lives, but also the when. We must learn to weave the sacred not just into the places we inhabit, but into the very rhythm of the hours we are given. This is the practice of sanctifying time.

In our modern world, we tend to think of time as a commodity. It is "clock time," a linear, relentless, and finite resource that we spend, save, waste, or manage. The ticking of the clock rules us, the deadlines on our calendars, and the constant pressure to be productive. This view of time can easily lead to anxiety, burnout, and a sense of spiritual emptiness. It is a flat, one-dimensional experience of time.

Our Celtic ancestors, however, lived in a different temporal world. They experienced time not as a straight line, but as a series of nested cycles and rhythms. There was the rhythm of the day, from sunset to sunset. There was the rhythm of the moon, from new to full and back again. And there was the great rhythm of the year, the turning of the wheel through the seasons and the great fire festivals. This was "sacred time," a deep, cyclical, and meaningful experience, in which each moment was part of a larger, holy pattern. For them, time was not a resource to be managed, but a mystery to be inhabited.

One of the most powerful ways in which the early Christian church, and particularly the Celtic monastic tradition, engaged with this mystery was through the Liturgy of the Hours, also known as the Divine Office. This is the ancient practice of pausing at specific times throughout the day and night to offer prayers of praise, thanksgiving, and petition. It is a way of fulfilling St. Paul's injunction to "pray without ceasing" (1 Thessalonians 5:17), not by being in a constant state of formal prayer, but by weaving moments of prayer into the fabric of the entire day, thereby consecrating all of our time— our work, our rest, our joy, our sorrow—to God.

While the full monastic cycle of seven or eight prayer times a day may be impractical for most of us living in the world, we can adopt the spirit of this practice and create our own simplified rhythm. By pausing at the great "hinges" of the day, we can create our own sacred rhythm, our own personal Liturgy of the Hours. This practice transforms time from a tyrant into a teacher, from a source of stress into a source of grace.

The Three Great Hinges of the Day

Let us focus on three key moments that form the day's primary hinges: morning, midday, and evening. By anchoring our day with these three simple pauses for prayer, we create a sacred structure that can hold and sanctify all the hours in between.

1. The Morning Hinge: At Sunrise (Lauds)

For the Celts, the day began not at midnight, but at sunset. The darkness was the womb from which the new day was born. The morning, therefore, was a time of birth, of resurrection, of the victory of light over darkness. To pray at sunrise is to align ourselves with this powerful cosmic drama.

• **The Theme:** The primary theme of morning prayer is resurrection and new beginnings. We celebrate the rising of the sun as a symbol of the rising of Christ, the true Sun of Righteousness. We give thanks for the gift of a new day, a fresh start, a page yet unwritten. We consecrate the work of our hands and the intentions of our hearts to God, asking for strength and guidance for the hours to come.

• **The Practice:** Your morning prayer does not need to be long. Even five minutes of intentional prayer can set the tone for your entire day. Find a place where you can see the morning light, perhaps near a window facing east. You might light the candle on your home altar. A simple structure could be:

• **A Psalm of Praise:** Begin with a psalm that captures the spirit of the morning, such as Psalm 63 ("O God, you are my God, I seek you, my soul thirsts for you") or Psalm 148 ("Praise the Lord from the heavens").

• **A Prayer of Consecration:** Offer the day to God. You might use a traditional prayer, such as the Lorica (Breastplate) of St. Patrick, which begins, "I arise today, through a mighty strength, the invocation of the Trinity." Or you can pray in your own words: "Lord, I offer you this day. May all that I do bring you glory."

• **A Moment of Intention:** Hold before God the main tasks and encounters of the day ahead. Ask for the specific graces you will need: patience, wisdom, courage, or love.

• **The Lord's Prayer:** Conclude with the prayer that Jesus taught us, the prayer that contains all prayers.

Praying at the morning hinge is like setting the rudder of your ship for the day. It establishes your direction and your destination, ensuring that no matter what winds may blow, you are oriented toward the safe harbour of God's will.

2. The Midday Hinge: At Noon (Sext)

The sun is at its highest point. The day is in full swing. We are busy, distracted, and perhaps beginning to feel the strain of our work. This is the perfect moment to pause, to take a single, conscious breath, and to re-centre ourselves. The traditional time for this prayer is noon, the "sixth hour," which in the Gospels is the hour when Jesus was crucified. It is the moment when the light of the world seemed to be extinguished.

• **The Theme:** The theme of midday prayer is remembrance and perseverance. We pause to remember the Cross, the great act of love at the centre of history and of our faith. We remember that our work is not the ultimate reality. We draw strength from the one who persevered to the end, asking for the grace to continue our own work with love and faithfulness.

• **The Practice:** This is the shortest of the three hinges. It is a moment of sacred interruption. You can do it at your desk, in your car, or wherever you happen to be. Stop what you are doing for sixty seconds.

• **The Sign of the Cross:** Begin and end by making the sign of the cross, consciously remembering your baptism and your identity as a child of God.

• **A Simple Phrase:** Repeat a short, centring prayer, known as a "breath prayer." It could be the Jesus Prayer ("Lord Jesus Christ, Son of God, have mercy on me"), or simply the word "Maranatha" ("Come, Lord").

• **A Moment of Gratitude:** Give thanks for the food you are about to eat, for the work you have been given to do, or for a single, small blessing you have experienced that morning.

The midday pause is a spiritual reset button. It is a small act of resistance against the tyranny of busyness. It reminds us of who we are and whose we are, right in the middle of the muddle of our day.

3. The Evening Hinge: At Sunset (Vespers)

The sun is setting. The work of the day is done. The light gives way to the gentle embrace of the darkness. This is a time for gathering, reflection, and giving thanks. In the monastic tradition, this is the hour of Vespers, one of the most beautiful and beloved of the prayer times.

• **The Theme:** The theme of evening prayer is gratitude and trust. We look back on the day with gratitude, thanking God for the blessings seen and unseen. And we look forward to the night, entrusting ourselves, our loved ones, and the entire world to God's loving protection. It is a time of surrender, of letting go of the day's burdens and resting in the peace of God.

• **The Practice:** This prayer can be a little longer and more reflective than the morning prayer. The light is fading, and the soul is naturally inclined toward quiet contemplation.

• **The Prayer of Examen:** The evening is the perfect time to practice the Prayer of Examen, as we explored in the previous section. This prayerful review of your day is the heart of evening prayer.

• **A Hymn of Light:** Many beautiful evening hymns exist, such as the ancient Phos Hilaron ("O Gladsome Light") or "Abide with Me." Singing or reciting one of these connects you to centuries of Christians who have prayed at this hour.

• **Prayers of Intercession:** The evening is a natural time to pray for others. Hold before God the needs of your family, your community, and the world. You might light a candle on your altar for each person or situation you are praying for.

• **The Nunc Dimittis:** Conclude with the beautiful canticle of Simeon from the Gospel of Luke: "Lord, now you let your servant go in peace, your word has been fulfilled..." (Luke 2:29-32). This is the ultimate prayer of trust, a peaceful surrender into God's hands.

Praying at the evening hinge is the act of bringing your day to a holy close. It is the gathering of the harvest of the day's graces. It allows you to enter into the night not with anxiety, but with a peaceful and trusting heart, ready for the restorative gift of sleep.

By building your day around these three sacred hinges, you transform your experience of time. Your day is no longer a frantic race against the clock, but a graceful dance with the rhythms of the sacred. You create a cathedral in time, a structure of prayer that can house your entire life. You learn to live in kairos, not just chronos. You learn that every hour is holy, and every moment is an opportunity to encounter the God who is the Lord of all time.

THE PRACTICE: BUILDING YOUR CILL (YOUR SACRED CELL)

My dear friend, we have discussed the theory of sacred space at length. We have explored the inner grove, the home altar, the thin places of the world, and the sacred rhythm of the hours. Now, the time has come to put our hands to the holy work. This section is a practical, step-by-step guide to building your own cill—your own small, sacred cell or home altar. The Irish word cill is related to the Latin *cella* and gives rise to the modern term "cell." But this is not a cell of imprisonment; it is a cell of incubation, a womb for the soul, a place where new life can be nurtured in peace.

This practice is not about creating a perfect, Instagram-worthy display. It is about creating a space that is authentic to you, a space that will call you to prayer, a space that will be a wellspring of grace in your daily life. I invite you to undertake this practice not as a chore, but as a joyful, creative act of devotion. Set aside an hour or so for this activity. Put on some quiet, contemplative music if you wish. Move slowly and with intention. This is a prayer in motion.

Step 1: The Gathering (Anam Cara Walk)

Your first task is to become a holy collector, a seeker of sacred objects. We will begin with a walk. This is not merely a walk; it is a prayerful pilgrimage through your local environment to find the elements for your altar. Think of it as an Anam Cara walk—a walk where you are befriending your own soul and the soul of the place where you live.

Before you leave your home, take a moment to be still. Close your eyes and pray:

"Generous God, Creator of all that is beautiful and good, open my eyes to see your presence in the world around me. Please guide me to the small treasures you have left for me to find. May this walk be a prayer, and may the objects I gather be a sign of my love for you."

Now, take a small bag and go outside. Walk slowly. Pay attention. You are looking for one or two small items that represent the four sacred elements: Earth, Air, Fire, and Water.

• **For Earth:** Look for a stone that feels good in your hand, a uniquely shaped piece of wood, a handful of rich soil, or an acorn, pinecone, or seed pod. Don't just grab the first thing you see. Wait for something to "call" to you. Pick it up. Feel its texture, its weight. Give thanks for its solidity, its rootedness.

• **For Air:** You may find a feather on the ground. This is a classic symbol of the Holy Spirit. If you don't find one, don't worry. The air itself is the element. Your intention is enough.

• **For Water:** If you live near a stream, a river, or the sea, you might find a smooth, water-worn stone or a seashell. If not, you may use a small bowl of tap water, which is equally sacred when blessed with intention.

• **For Fire:** You will not find fire on your walk, but you can look for a symbol of it. Perhaps a red or orange leaf, or a piece of flint. Or you can simply hold the intention of finding a candle later.

As you gather your items, do so with reverence. You are not taking; you are receiving a gift. For each item, say a silent "thank you." When you have your small collection, return home.

Step 2: Preparing the Space

Go to the location you have chosen for your altar. Clean the surface and the surrounding area. This is a ritual act of purification. As you wipe away the dust, imagine that you are also clearing away the inner clutter of your mind and heart, making a clean space for God.

Lay down your altar cloth. Smooth it out with your hands. As you do, pray:

"Lord, may my heart be a clean and humble space, ready to receive you."
This cloth now defines your sacred ground.

Step 3: Assembling the Altar

Now comes the creative part. Arrange the items you have gathered on your altar. There is no right or wrong way to do this. Trust your intuition. This is your unique conversation with God.

Here is a possible arrangement to get you started:

1. Place the Cross: First, place your cross or crucifix at the centre or the back of the altar. It is the heart of your cill. It is the Tree of Life that gives meaning to everything else.

2. Arrange the Four Elements: Place your symbols of the four elements around the cross. Many traditions place Earth (the stone or wood) in the North, Air (the feather) in the East, Fire (the candle) in the South, and Water (the seashell or bowl) in the West. This creates a sacred compass, orienting your space to the whole cosmos. As you place each item, recall its meaning and give thanks.

3. Add Personal Touches: Now, add any other items that are meaningful to you. An icon of a beloved saint? A photo of a grandparent? A flower from your garden? A Bible or a book of prayers? Your altar should be a reflection of your own story, your own family of faith.

Take your time. Move things around. Step back and look. Does the arrangement feel balanced? Does it feel peaceful? Does it feel like you? Your altar should bring you a quiet sense of joy and rightness when you look at it.

Step 4: The Consecration

Once your altar is assembled, it is time to formally consecrate it, to set it apart for its holy purpose. This is a simple but powerful act of prayer.

Stand or kneel before your newly created altar. Take a few deep breaths. Light the candle.

As the flame flickers to life, say:

"In the name of the Father, and of the Son, and of the Holy Spirit, I set apart this space as a sanctuary of prayer and peace. May it be a hearth for my soul, a wellspring of grace, a thin place where heaven and earth may meet."

Next, take your bowl of water. Dip your fingers in it and make the sign of the cross on your forehead, saying: "I am a beloved child of God." Then, sprinkle a few drops of water on the altar, saying: "I bless this altar in the name of the Triune God."

Finally, spend a few moments in silent prayer before your new altar. Gaze upon the objects. Look at the flickering candlelight. Rest in the sacred space you have created. Offer a prayer of thanksgiving for this gift.

Step 5: Living with Your Cill

Your cill is now complete. It is ready to become a part of your daily life.

Here are a few suggestions for living with your new sacred space:

• **Visit it daily:** Make it the place where you pause for your three sacred hinges: morning, midday, and evening prayer.

• **Let it be your anchor:** When you feel stressed, anxious, or overwhelmed, come to your altar. Light the candle, take a few deep breaths, and rest in its presence for a moment.

• **Let it evolve:** Remember that your altar is a living space. Add to it, subtract from it, and rearrange it as your spirit moves you and as the seasons change.

Journaling Prompts:

• Describe the experience of gathering your sacred objects. What surprised you? What did you learn?

• Look at your completed altar. What does it say about you and your spiritual journey right now?

• How do you hope this sacred space will change your daily life and your relationship with God?

CONCLUSION: LIVING A CONSECRATED LIFE

We have come to the end of our chapter on creating sacred space, but I hope it is the beginning of a new way of living for you. We have journeyed from the vast, cosmic vision of the Cross as the Tree of Life to the small, intimate act of placing a stone upon a windowsill. We have seen that the sacred is not something distant or reserved for a spiritual elite. It is here, now, woven into the very fabric of our existence, waiting only for us to open our eyes and our hearts to its presence.

The practices we have explored—tending the inner grove through silence and prayer, building a hearth for the sacred in our homes, recognising the thin places in our world, and sanctifying the rhythm of our days—are not separate, disconnected activities. They are an integrated whole, a symphony of practices that work together to create what the Celtic tradition would call a consecrated life. To consecrate something is to set it apart for God. To live a consecrated life is to live a life that is, in its entirety, set apart for and offered to God.

This does not mean that we must all become monks or hermits, retreating from the world into a life of perpetual prayer. On the contrary, it is a call to engage with the world more deeply, more lovingly, and more intentionally than ever before. The purpose of creating a sacred space, such as a home altar, is not to build a fortress in which we can hide from the messiness of the world. The purpose is to create a wellspring from which we can draw the grace, the strength, and the love we need to go out into that messy world and be a source of healing and light. Your cill is not a destination; it is a starting point. It is the training ground for the heart, the armoury where you are equipped with the spiritual weapons of love, forgiveness, and peace.

Similarly, the purpose of sanctifying the hours of our day is not to fill our lives with rigid obligation, but with grace. The pauses for prayer at morning, noon, and night are not interruptions of our "real" lives; they are the moments that give our real lives meaning and direction. They are the nails that hold our day's structure together, preventing it from collapsing under the weight of stress and distraction. They are the moments when we remember who we are—beloved children of God—so that we can live out that identity in all the other moments of the day.

And the purpose of seeking out thin places in the world around us is not to become spiritual tourists, collecting experiences of the sacred. It is to train our eyes to see that every place is potentially a thin place, that God is whispering to us not just in the grand cathedrals of nature, but in the cracks in the pavement, in the face of a stranger, in the quiet heroism of ordinary life. The whole world is a burning bush, but only those who have learned to take off their shoes will see it.

To live a consecrated life is to erase the line between the sacred and the secular. It is to understand that washing the dishes can be as much of a prayer as reciting a psalm. It is to see that a difficult conversation with a colleague is as much a spiritual practice as sitting in silent meditation. It is to know that our work, our relationships, our joys, and our sorrows are all part of the great, unfolding drama of God's love for the world. It is to live with a constant, low-humming awareness of the divine presence in all things.

This is the great gift of the Celtic Christian vision. It is a faith that is earthy, embodied, and deeply connected to the rhythms of the natural world. It does not ask us to reject the world, but to love it into holiness. It does not ask us to escape our bodies, but to see them as temples of the Holy Spirit. It does not ask us to abandon our traditions, but to see how Christ fulfils their deepest longings.

As you proceed with this chapter, I encourage you to be gentle with yourself. Do not attempt to implement all these practices simultaneously. Choose one that resonates with you and begin there. Perhaps you will start by simply finding a stone and placing it on your desk. Perhaps you will commit to pausing for sixty seconds at noon each day. Perhaps you will take a slow, attentive walk once a week. Start small. The path to a consecrated life is not a sprint; it is a slow, patient, and joyful pilgrimage. The great Oak grows from a tiny acorn.

The grove of your life is waiting. The soil of your heart is rich with possibility. The Cross, the ultimate Tree of Life, stands at the centre, offering you its shade, its fruit, and its unwavering strength. You have the tools. You have the maps. You have the desire.

Now, begin the holy and beautiful work of building your sacred dwelling, a place where you can live in intimate and constant communion with the God who is, and was, and is to come, the Lord of the grove and the King of your heart.

Chapter 10:

The Way of the Pilgrim: Walking the Forest as a Spiritual Practice

FROM DWELLING TO JOURNEYING

Welcome back, my friend, to the path. In our last chapter, we devoted ourselves to the beautiful and necessary work of creating a home for the soul. We learned to tend the inner grove of the heart, to build a sacred hearth in our homes, and to sanctify the rhythms of our days. We learned the art of dwelling, of creating a consecrated space where our roots can grow deep into the soil of God's presence. This work is the foundation of a spiritual life. It gives us a centre, an anchor, a place to return to for nourishment and peace. It is the vital practice of being at home in our own lives and in our relationship with God.

But a healthy spiritual life, like any living thing, requires a balance between two complementary movements: the inward movement toward rootedness and the outward movement toward journeying. A tree that is all root and no branch will never reach for the sun or bear fruit. A river that pools and never flows becomes stagnant. So it is with the soul. Having established our sacred dwelling, our cill, we are now called to step out from its doorway and embark on the next phase of our adventure. We are called to move from dwelling to journeying, from being rooted to being a pilgrim.

The idea of pilgrimage is deeply embedded in the Celtic Christian soul. The Irish saints were famous for their peregrinatio pro Christo—their "wandering for Christ." They would set out in small, flimsy boats, casting themselves upon the mercy of the waves, with no destination in mind other than the place where God would lead them. They understood that the spiritual life is not just about finding a home, but also about the courage to leave home, to embrace the unknown, and to find God in the journey itself. As one of the most famous Irish blessings says, "May the road rise up to meet you." It is a culture that regards the road itself as a place of blessing.

For most of us, setting out in a coracle into the North Atlantic is not a practical option. But the spirit of the peregrinatio is not about the scale of the journey; it is about the intention of the heart. We can embrace the way of the pilgrim not by abandoning our lives, but by transforming one of our most ordinary, everyday activities into a profound spiritual practice: the simple act of walking. This chapter is dedicated to the sacred art of walking. We will learn how to transform any walk—whether it is a hike through a dense forest, a stroll through a city park, or a simple walk around your own neighbourhood—into a pilgrimage, an opportunity to encounter God, and a journey into the heart of the living world.

We will discover that walking is not just good for the body; it is good for the soul. It is a practice that slows us down, reconnects us to the rhythms of our own bodies and the earth, and opens our senses to the subtle beauty of the world around us. To walk with the heart of a pilgrim is to see the world as a cathedral, a vast and holy book in which God has written the story of God's love in the language of trees, stones, rivers, and light.

Our pilgrimage in this chapter will follow a path of seven steps:

1. Introduction: From Dwelling to Journeying: We will explore the vital balance between rootedness and journeying in the spiritual life.

2. The Pilgrim's Pace: Rediscovering the Art of Walking: We will learn to slow down and walk with a new quality of attention that connects us to our bodies and the earth.

3. Peregrinatio pro Christo: The Soul-Friendship of the Path: We will delve into the Celtic concept of pilgrimage and apply its spirit to our daily walks.

4. The Forest as Cathedral: Reading the Book of Nature: We will learn to engage with the natural world as a sacred text, a source of divine revelation.

5. The Stations of the Grove: Encounters on the Path: We will discover how to see the events of our walk as "stations" for prayer and reflection.

6. The Practice: A Celtic Tree Walk: We will undertake a guided walk to find and reflect upon the tree archetypes in our own environment.

7. Conclusion: Bringing the Journey Home: We will reflect on how to integrate the lessons of the pilgrim's path into our daily lives.

So, my friend, lace up your walking shoes. The door of your cill is open. The path is waiting. The great cathedral of the world is ready to reveal its secrets. It is time to step outside and begin the journey. May the road indeed rise up to meet you.

THE PILGRIM'S PACE: REDISCOVERING THE ART OF WALKING

Before we can embark on a pilgrimage, even one that goes around our own block, we must first learn to walk like a pilgrim. This may sound strange. Walking, after all, is one of the first things we learn to do, an act so automatic that we rarely give it a second thought. But it is precisely because it is so automatic that we have forgotten its sacred potential. For most of us, most of the time, walking is not an experience in itself; it is merely a means to an end. It is the thing we do to get from the car to the office, from the kitchen to the bedroom, from Point A to Point B. It is a necessary, but largely unconscious, form of transit.

The tyranny of speed rules our modern world. We value efficiency, productivity, and haste. We drive fast, we talk fast, we eat fast. And when we walk, we often walk fast, our minds already at our destination, our bodies merely machines for locomotion. We walk with our heads down, staring at our phones, our ears plugged with headphones, our minds lost in a fog of worries, plans, and digital distractions. In this mode of walking, we are not fully present. Our bodies are in one place, but our minds are somewhere else entirely. We are, in a very real sense, dis-embodied. We have forgotten that we have bodies and the wisdom they hold.

To walk as a pilgrim is to declare a gentle rebellion against this tyranny of speed. It is to rediscover the ancient and holy art of walking for its own sake. It is to reclaim walking as a spiritual practice, a form of embodied prayer, a way of connecting our souls to the world through the soles of our feet. It is to learn what I call the Pilgrim's Pace.

THE BODY: A TEMPLE, NOT A TAXI

The foundation of the Pilgrim's Pace is a radical shift in how we view our own bodies. Our culture tends to treat the body as a machine to be optimised or a vehicle to be used—a taxi for the mind. But the Christian tradition, at its heart, offers a much more profound and beautiful vision.

The central mystery of our faith is the Incarnation: that God, the infinite, eternal, and unseeable Spirit, chose to become flesh and blood in the person of Jesus Christ. God did not despise the body; God embraced it, sanctified it, and made it a dwelling place for the divine.

St. Paul picks up this theme when he asks the Corinthians, "Do you not know that your bodies are temples of the Holy Spirit, who is in you, whom you have received from God?" (1 Corinthians 6:19). This is a staggering thought. Your body, with all its aches and pains, its strengths and its weaknesses, its beauty and its imperfections, is a holy place. It is a sanctuary where God has chosen to dwell.

To walk, therefore, is not just to move a machine from one place to another. It is to move a temple through the world. Every step is a sacred act. Every breath is a prayer. Walking, in this light, becomes a form of worship, a way of honouring the God who dwells within us and the God who created the world through which we move.

THE RHYTHM OF THE WALK, THE RHYTHM OF THE WORLD

When we slow down and pay attention, we discover that walking has a deep, primal rhythm. There is the steady, two-beat rhythm of our feet upon the earth: left, right, left, right. There is the gentle swing of our arms, a counterpoint to the movement of our legs. And there is the constant, life-giving rhythm of our breath, flowing in and out, a ceaseless tide of air and life.

This simple, repetitive rhythm is one of the most powerful meditative tools we possess. It has a profoundly calming effect on the nervous system. The steady beat of our footsteps acts like a mantra, a gentle drumbeat that can quiet the frantic chatter of the anxious mind. It is no accident that so many spiritual traditions have incorporated rhythmic movement into their practices, from the walking meditation of Buddhists to the ecstatic dance of Sufis. The rhythm of the walk lulls the analytical, controlling part of our brain—the ego—to sleep, allowing a deeper, more intuitive, and more receptive part of ourselves to awaken.

This inner rhythm also connects us to the great rhythms of the world around us. The beat of our heart echoes the pulse of the tides. The rhythm of our breath echoes the turning of the seasons. The cadence of our steps echoes the ancient, slow rhythm of the earth itself. To walk at a Pilgrim's Pace is to attune ourselves to this great symphony of creation. We cease to be a frantic, isolated soloist, and we find our place in the vast and beautiful orchestra of the cosmos. We begin to feel, in our very bones, that we are not separate from the world, but a living, breathing part of it.

THE QUALITIES OF THE PILGRIM'S PACE

The Pilgrim's Pace is not a specific speed; it is a quality of attention. It is a way of walking that is characterised by three essential qualities: slowness, silence, and attentiveness.

• **Slowness:** This is the most obvious and the most challenging quality. It means intentionally walking at a pace slower than your usual hurried gait. It is a pace that allows you to feel each footstep, notice the shifting of your weight, and be aware of your body's movement. It is a pace that says, "I am not in a hurry. I have time to be here, now."

• **Silence:** This means walking without the distractions of headphones, phone calls, or even conversation. It is an invitation to listen to both the world around you and the world within you. It is in the silence that we begin to hear the subtle whispers of the Spirit.

• **Attentiveness:** This is the heart of the practice. It is a gentle, open, non-judgmental awareness of the present moment. It is paying attention to the sensations of your body, the sights and sounds of your environment, and the thoughts and feelings that arise within you, all without getting carried away by them. It is a state of relaxed alertness, of being fully present to the gift of the moment.

A SIMPLE PRACTICE: FINDING YOUR PACE

I invite you to try this simple exercise. Find a place where you can walk back and forth for just a few yards, either indoors or outdoors. For the first minute, walk at your normal, hurried pace.

Notice how it feels in your body. Notice the quality of your thoughts. Are you already thinking about what you need to do next?

Now, for the next five minutes, intentionally slow your pace by half. Feel the sole of your foot as it makes contact with the ground. Feel the roll of your foot from heel to toe. Feel the gentle push-off into the next step. Pay attention to the subtle shifts in balance. Notice the feeling of the air on your skin. Listen to the sounds around you. When your mind wanders (which it will), gently and without judgment, bring your attention back to the simple sensation of your foot touching the earth.

How does this feel? It may feel strange, awkward, or even frustrating at first. That is normal. We are so conditioned to hurry that slowing down can feel like a radical act. But if you persist, you may begin to notice a shift. A sense of calm. A feeling of being more grounded, more present in your own body. A new awareness of the world around you. This is the beginning of the Pilgrim's Pace.

This is the pace that can transform a simple walk into a sacred journey. It is the pace that opens the door to the cathedral of the world.

PEREGRINATIO PRO CHRISTO: THE SOUL-FRIENDSHIP OF THE PATH

Having rediscovered the sacred rhythm of the Pilgrim's Pace, we are now ready to infuse our walking with a powerful and uniquely Celtic intention: the spirit of peregrinatio. This Latin term, which translates as "pilgrimage" or "wandering," held a profound significance for early Irish Christians. It was not just a journey to a holy place, such as Rome or Jerusalem, to venerate relics or seek a specific miracle.

It was something far more radical, more existential, and, in many ways, more terrifying. It was the practice of leaving home, kin, and country, not for a specific destination, but for the love of Christ alone. It was a pilgrimage of radical unknowing, a casting of oneself into the arms of divine providence.

This was the famous "white martyrdom" of the Irish saints. While the "red martyrdom" was to die for the faith, and the "green martyrdom" was to retreat into the forest for a life of asceticism, the "white martyrdom" was to become a pilgrim, an exile for Christ. Saints such as Columba, who left his native Ireland for the remote island of Iona, and Columbanus, who wandered through the wilds of pagan Europe, founding monasteries, were not merely missionaries in the modern sense.

They were *peregrini,* pilgrims whose primary goal was not to convert others but to deepen their own souls by embracing a life of total dependence on God. Their wandering was their prayer. Their homelessness was their home.

This may seem like a strange and extreme form of spirituality, far removed from our comfortable modern lives. And yet, the spirit of the peregrinatio holds a vital and liberating truth for us today. It is the truth that our ultimate security is not found in our homes, our jobs, our relationships, or our plans, but in the unwavering love of God. It is true that letting go of our need for control and adopting a posture of trust can lead to a profound sense of freedom and adventure.

We can practice our own form of peregrinatio not by selling our homes and setting sail into the ocean, but by bringing the intention of the pilgrim to our daily walks. We can learn to walk not to get somewhere, but to be with Someone. We can make the path itself our anam cara, our soul-friend.

The Three Intentions of the Peregrinus

What does it mean to walk with the intention of a peregrinus?

It means embracing three core principles that guided the ancient Irish pilgrims: detachment, attentiveness, and companionship.

1. Detachment: Leaving the Shore

The most fundamental act of the peregrinus was the act of leaving. They left the security of their tribe, the comfort of their homeland, and the predictability of their lives. They embraced a life of voluntary exile. For us, this does not mean abandoning our families or our responsibilities. It entails practising a form of inner detachment while walking. It means, for the duration of our walk, consciously leaving behind our worries, to-do lists, ambitions, and anxieties. It is a small act of letting go, of creating an inner space of freedom.

Before you begin your walk, take a moment to stand at your doorway. See it as the shore of your own private Iona. On this side of the door is your life, with all its demands and complexities. On the other side is the open road, the path of pilgrimage. As you step across the threshold, make a conscious intention to leave your burdens behind, just for a little while. You can say a simple prayer, such as: "Lord, I leave my cares at this threshold. For this short time, let me be an exile for you. Let my only destination be your presence."

This act of detachment is not an act of irresponsibility. It is an act of profound trust. It is the recognition that the world will continue to turn without our constant, anxious management. It is believed that God's hands are large enough to hold our concerns while we take a brief sabbatical to walk with Him. This practice of detachment creates a space of lightness and freedom in our walk. We are no longer walking to solve a problem or to figure something out. We are walking simply to be.

2. Attentiveness: Charting the Inner Sea

The Irish pilgrims, having set sail without a map, had to become exquisitely attentive to the signs of the sea: the movement of the stars, the direction of the wind, the flight of the birds. Their outward attentiveness mirrored their inner attentiveness to the movements of the Holy Spirit. They were constantly watching and listening for God's subtle guidance.

When we walk as pilgrims, we too are called to a new level of attentiveness. As we explored in the previous section on the Pilgrim's Pace, this begins with an attentiveness to our own bodies and to the world around us. But it also extends to the inner world. A pilgrimage walk is an opportunity to become a gentle observer of the sea of your own soul. What thoughts are arising? What feelings are surfacing? What memories are being stirred?

The key here is to be an observer, not a judge. You are not trying to fix your thoughts or to eliminate your feelings. You are simply noticing them, as you might notice the clouds passing in the sky. You are creating a space of loving awareness for your own inner life. You might find that as you walk, the rhythm of your steps and the beauty of your surroundings help to untangle the knots in your mind.

A solution to a problem you have been wrestling with may suddenly appear. A new perspective on a complicated relationship may emerge. A feeling of gratitude or joy may bubble up for no apparent reason. This is the fruit of attentive walking. It is the Spirit of God, the great Anam Cara, whispering to you in the gentle breeze and the steady rhythm of your own heart.

3. Companionship: Walking with the Trinity

The peregrini were not alone on their journeys. They travelled with a deep and abiding sense of the Trinity's companionship. The Celtic imagination was profoundly Trinitarian. They saw the presence of the Father, the Son, and the Holy Spirit in all of creation. The Father was the great, unseeable ground of all being, the Creator of the landscape through which they moved. The Son, Jesus Christ, was the anam cara, the soul-friend, the fellow pilgrim walking beside them on the path, sharing their hardships and their joys. And the Holy Spirit was the wild goose, the unpredictable, guiding presence, the wind in their sails, the inner compass that pointed the way.

To walk as a peregrinus is to cultivate this sense of divine companionship. It is to know, in your bones, that you are not walking alone. You are walking with God.

• **Walk with the Father:** As you walk, look at the world around you—the trees, the sky, the birds, the people—and see it as a manifestation of the creative love of the Father. Let your walk be a prayer of praise and thanksgiving for the sheer gift of existence. "Father, thank you for this beautiful, broken world."

• **Walk with the Son:** Imagine Jesus walking beside you on the path. He is not a distant historical figure, but a living, breathing presence. Talk to him as you would to your closest friend. Share your joys, your fears, your hopes, your regrets. Ask for his guidance. Listen for his response in the events of your walk and the movements of your heart. Let him be the true anam cara of your journey.

• **Walk with the Spirit:** Be open to the surprising, unpredictable guidance of the Holy Spirit. Perhaps you feel a sudden urge to turn down a street you have never explored before. Perhaps a particular bird catches your eye. Perhaps a line of a song or a verse of scripture pops into your head. These are the "wild goose" moments, the gentle nudges of the Spirit. Follow them. See where they lead. The Spirit is the divine adventurer, inviting you to step off the beaten path and discover something new.

By embracing the three intentions of the peregrinus—detachment, attentiveness, and companionship—we transform our daily walk from a mundane chore into a sacred adventure. We become pilgrims in our own neighbourhood, exiles for Christ in our own city. We learn that the most profound journeys are not the ones that cover the greatest distances, but the ones that take us deepest into the heart of God. The path itself becomes our soul-friend, teaching, guiding, and leading us, step by step, closer to home.

THE FOREST AS CATHEDRAL: READING THE BOOK OF NATURE

As we walk the path of the pilgrim, with a heart detached from its anxieties and attentive to the divine companionship, our senses begin to open in a new way. The world, which once seemed ordinary or even inert, begins to reveal itself as a place of wonder and profound meaning. We are now ready to engage in one of the most ancient and beautiful practices of the Celtic Christian tradition: the reading of the Book of Nature.

The early church fathers, and the Celtic saints in particular, spoke of God's revelation as coming to us through Two Books. The first book is the Book of Scripture, the Holy Bible, which tells us the specific story of God's relationship with humanity, culminating in the life, death, and resurrection of Jesus Christ. This is the book of special revelation, and it is our primary and indispensable guide to the faith.

But there is also a second book, the Book of Nature. This is the vast, beautiful, and complex book of the created world, which reveals the general truths of God's power, wisdom, and goodness.
As St. Paul writes in his letter to the Romans, "Ever since the creation of the world his invisible nature, namely, his eternal power and deity, has been

clearly perceived in the things that have been made" (Romans 1:20). For the Celtic saints, living in a world that was not yet scarred by industrialization, this second book was not a poor substitute for the first, but its beloved companion and confirmation.

They believed that the same God who inspired the prophets and evangelists also shaped the mountains, breathed life into the forests, and painted the wings of the butterfly. To study nature, therefore, was to study the mind of God.

To walk as a pilgrim is to become a student of this second book. It is to enter the forest not as a hiker or a naturalist, but as a reader entering a great library, or a worshipper entering a vast cathedral.

The Architecture of the Forest Cathedral

Imagine you are standing at the edge of an old forest. As you step across the threshold from the open field into the dappled light of the trees, you are entering a sacred space. Let your imagination, sanctified by prayer, see this forest as a great, green cathedral, built by the hand of God himself.

• **The Trees as Pillars:** Look at the tall, straight trunks of the trees rising around you. They are the pillars of this cathedral, holding up the sky. Feel their strength, their rootedness, their patient endurance. They have stood in this place for decades, perhaps centuries, in silent, ceaseless prayer. They are the elders of this place, the silent monks of the forest.

• **The Canopy as a Vaulted Ceiling:** Look up at the canopy of leaves, where the branches of the trees interlace high above you. This is the vaulted ceiling of the cathedral. See how the light filters through it, creating a living, breathing mosaic of green and gold. It is a ceiling that changes with the seasons, from the bare tracery of winter to the lush fullness of summer.

• **The Light as Stained Glass:** Notice the shafts of light that pierce the canopy and fall to the forest floor. These are the stained-glass windows of the forest cathedral. They are not static images of saints and angels, but living, moving beams of light that dance and shift with the wind. They illuminate a patch of moss here, a delicate flower there, drawing your attention to the small, hidden beauties of the forest floor.

• **The Birdsong as Choir:** Close your eyes for a moment and listen. The birdsong that fills the air is the choir of this cathedral. It is a liturgy that has been sung here since the dawn of time. There are solos and choruses, calls and responses. It is a song of praise, of warning, of courtship, of life itself, offered up to the Creator without ceasing.

• **The Wind as the Breath of the Spirit:** Feel the wind as it moves through the trees. Hear the rustle of the leaves, the whisper of the pines. This is the breath of the Holy Spirit, the Ruach, the wild and untameable presence of God, animating this sacred space, making it live and breathe.

By seeing the forest in this way, we are not engaging in a childish fantasy. We are engaging in a profound act of spiritual perception. We are learning to see the world sacramentally, as an outward sign of an inward grace. We are recognising that the patterns of the sacred are written everywhere, if only we have the eyes to see them.

LEARNING THE LANGUAGE: THE SERMONS OF STONE, WATER, AND TREE

Every cathedral is filled with symbols and stories, carved into its stones and depicted in its windows. To understand the cathedral, you must learn to read its language.

So, it is with the forest cathedral. The elements of nature are the words, the sentences, the parables of the Book of Nature. They are constantly preaching silent sermons to those who have learned to listen.

• **The Sermon of the Stone:** Find a stone on your path. Pick it up. Feel its weight, its coolness, its texture. This stone has a sermon to preach. It speaks of patience, of having been shaped by the slow, inexorable forces of water, ice, and time. It speaks of endurance, of being able to withstand the storm and the heat. It speaks of deep time, of a history that stretches back long before your own small life. And it speaks of Christ, the Cornerstone, the solid rock upon which our lives are built. To hold a stone in your hand is to hold a reminder of the steadfast, unchanging nature of God.

• **The Gospel of the Water:** If you come across a stream or a river, pause and listen to its gospel. A flowing stream speaks of the unceasing flow of grace, always moving, always giving, always making its way around obstacles. It speaks of letting go, of not clinging to any one place, but trusting the journey. A still pond, by contrast, connotes clarity and reflection. It teaches us that only when we are still can we accurately reflect the beauty of the heavens above. Water speaks of cleansing, of the baptism that has washed us clean, and of the living water that Jesus promises, which quenches the deepest thirst of our souls.

• **The Theology of the Tree:** Every tree you meet is a theologian, a teacher of divine truth. As we have explored throughout this book, the different trees embody different aspects of the divine character. The Oak teaches of strength and hospitality. The Ash teaches of connection and the three worlds. The Yew teaches of resurrection and eternal life. The Birch teaches of new beginnings. As you walk, do not just see "trees." See individuals. See teachers. Approach a particular tree with a question in your heart. "What do you have to teach me today, old friend?" Stand before it in silence and listen, not with your ears, but with your heart.

The answer may not come in words, but in a feeling, a sense of peace, a new insight, a quiet strengthening of your own soul.

THE ART OF CONTEMPLATIVE SEEING

Reading the Book of Nature is not an intellectual exercise. It is a contemplative art. It is the art of seeing things not just for what they are, but for what they signify. It is seeing with the heart as well as the eyes. The medieval spiritual writers called this practice visio divina, or "divine seeing." It is the practice of gazing upon an object in nature until it becomes a window into the divine.

Here is a simple way to practice visio divina on your walk:

1. Choose an Object: Let something on your path choose you. It could be a leaf, a flower, a patch of moss, a spider's web. Don't search for something spectacular. The humblest objects often have the most profound lessons.

2. Gaze upon it: Stop walking. Stand or sit before your chosen object. For a few minutes, gaze upon it. Notice its details: its colour, its shape, its texture. Let your eyes drink in its form without naming or analysing.

3. Reflect upon it: Ask a few gentle questions. "What is this object's life like?" "What is its purpose in the great web of being?" "What quality does it most embody?" "What does it remind me of in my own life, or in the life of God?"

4. Respond in Prayer: Let your reflection turn into prayer. Offer a prayer of thanksgiving for the existence of this small miracle. Offer a prayer for the grace to embody the quality you have seen in it. Offer a prayer that connects this object to a need in your own life or in the world.

5. Rest in Communion: Finally, let go of all thoughts and words. Be present with the object in a moment of silent, loving communion. Recognise that the same God who created this object also created you, and that you are both held in the same loving embrace.

By practising the art of reading the Book of Nature, we learn that the world is not a collection of dead objects, but a community of living subjects, each with its own voice, its own wisdom, and its own sermon to preach. We learn that the forest is indeed a cathedral, and that worship is not something that is confined to an hour on Sunday morning. It is a way of life, a way of walking, a way of seeing.

Every step becomes a prayer, and every walk becomes a pilgrimage into the heart of God.

THE STATIONS OF THE GROVE: ENCOUNTERS ON THE PATH

As we learn to walk as pilgrims and to read the Book of Nature, our journey through the world assumes a new, interactive quality. It ceases to be a monologue in which we are simply observing a beautiful but static landscape. It becomes a dialogue, a conversation, a series of encounters. The path begins to speak to us, to challenge us, to comfort us, and to surprise us. To give structure to this dialogue, we can borrow a beautiful and ancient practice from the church's devotional life: the Stations of the Cross.

The Stations of the Cross is a traditional Christian devotion that commemorates the final journey of Jesus from his condemnation by Pilate to his burial in the tomb. It is a mini-pilgrimage, a walk through the story of the Passion, with fourteen "stations" or stopping points for prayer and reflection. At each station, the pilgrim pauses to contemplate a specific event—Jesus falls the first time, Jesus meets his mother, Jesus is stripped of his garments—and to find a personal connection to that moment of suffering and love. It is a powerful practice that makes the story of the Passion immediate, personal, and deeply moving.

We can adapt the spirit of this practice to our walks in nature. We can create our own devotional journey, not with fourteen pre-determined stops, but with a series of spontaneous encounters that become our own unique Stations of the Grove. In this practice, the events of our walk—the things we see, hear, and experience—become the stations. They are not merely random occurrences; they are invitations from God to pause, reflect, and pray. They are the curriculum of our pilgrimage, the specific lessons that the Divine Teacher has prepared for us on this particular day.

The Unfolding Narrative of the Path

Unlike the traditional Stations of the Cross, the Stations of the Grove are not fixed. We do not know what they will be when we set out. This is the practice's adventure. We must walk with a heart that is open and attentive, trusting that the path will provide the stations we need. One day, the theme of our walk might be joy and gratitude, with stations of birdsong and wildflowers. Another day, it might be a more sombre journey, with stations of fallen trees and gathering storm clouds. The path becomes a mirror of our own inner landscape and a vehicle for God's specific word to us in that moment.

What can serve as a station? Anything. Absolutely anything that catches your attention and makes you pause. The key is to trust that the things that draw your eye or your ear are not random. They are gentle nudges from the Holy Spirit, invitations to a deeper conversation. Let us explore some possible stations you might encounter on your path and how you might pray with them.

Examples of Stations

1. The Station of the Ancient Tree

You come across a tree that is clearly much older and larger than the others around it. Its bark is gnarled and deeply furrowed. Its branches are thick and spreading. A great elder accompanies it.

• **Pause:** Stand before it in silence. Feel its presence.

• **Observe:** Notice its deep roots, its strong trunk, its vast canopy. See the signs of its history—the broken branches, the hollows, the scars. It has weathered many storms.

• **Reflect:** This tree is a symbol of endurance, wisdom, and rootedness. It reminds you of the long, slow work of growth. It connects you to the generations that have passed under its branches. It stands as a silent witness to history. It is an image of the Cross, the ancient tree of salvation.

• **Pray:** "Lord, grant me the patience and endurance of this tree. Help me to sink my roots deep into the soil of your love, so that I may weather the storms of my life. Thank you for the wisdom of the elders, and for the great, ancient story of salvation of which I am a part."

2. The Station of the Flowing Stream

Your path leads you alongside a stream or a river. You pause to watch the water as it flows over the rocks.

• **Pause:** Sit by the water's edge. Listen to its sound.

• **Observe:** Notice how the water is always moving, always letting go. See how it navigates obstacles, finding its way around them without force. Notice the clarity of the water and the life it supports.

• **Reflect:** The stream is a symbol of grace, cleansing, and the passage of time. It speaks of the need to let go of resentments and regrets, to allow the river of God's mercy to wash us clean. It reminds us that life is a journey, not a destination.

• **Pray:** "Jesus, you are the Living Water. Wash me clean of all that holds me back. Grant me the grace to let go of what I cannot control and to trust the flow of my life, knowing that you are guiding me to the great sea of your love."

3. The Station of the Soaring Bird

You hear a cry above you and look up to see a hawk or an eagle soaring on the wind currents, high above the earth.

• **Pause:** Watch it until it disappears from view.

• **Observe:** Notice the effortless grace of its flight. It is not flapping its wings frantically; it is resting on the power of the unseen wind. See the world from its perspective—vast, interconnected, and whole.

• **Reflect:** The soaring bird is a classic symbol of the Holy Spirit, who lifts us up and gives us a new perspective. It speaks of freedom from earthly attachments and the ability to view our problems from a higher, more expansive perspective.

• **Pray:** "Come, Holy Spirit, you who are the wild goose of the Celtic saints. Lift my heart above my worries. Give me the gift of your perspective, that I may see my life and my world with your eyes. Grant me the freedom to rest in your power."

4. The Station of the Fallen, Decaying Log

You encounter a large fallen tree that is now in a state of decay. It is covered in moss and fungi, and insects are burrowing into its soft wood.

• **Pause:** Sit gently on the log, if you can.

• **Observe:** Notice the signs of death and decay. But look closer. See also the signs of new life. The fungi are breaking the log down into rich soil. The insects are creating homes. Small saplings may be sprouting from the decaying wood.

• **Reflect:** This log is a powerful sermon on the paschal mystery: the cycle of death and resurrection. It teaches that in God's economy, nothing is wasted. Death is never the final word. It is the necessary precondition for new life, new growth, new possibilities. It is a reminder that our own failings and "deaths" can become fertile ground for God's grace.

• **Pray:** "Lord of Life, you who brought life from the dead wood of the Cross, I offer you the dead and decaying parts of my own life—my failures, my sins, my sorrows. Break them down. Transform them into fertile soil, that new life may grow in me. Help me to trust that every death is a doorway to a resurrection."

5. The Station of the Discarded Litter

Amidst the beauty of the path, you come across a discarded plastic bottle, a candy wrapper, or a rusty can.

• **Pause:** Stop and look at this object.

• **Observe:** Notice how it clashes with its surroundings. It is out of place, a sign of brokenness and carelessness. It cannot be reabsorbed into the life of the forest.

• **Reflect:** This piece of litter is a symbol of human sin and brokenness. It is a small sign of our disconnection from the natural world and from our responsibility as its stewards. It is a wound in the body of the earth. It is a call to repentance and to action.

• **Pray:** "Father, forgive us for the ways we have wounded your beautiful creation. Forgive me for my own carelessness, my own consumption, my own contribution to the brokenness of the world. Grant me a new heart, a heart of a loving steward, that I may work to heal and protect this sacred home you have given us." (And then, if you are able, pick up the litter and carry it with you to the next trash can. This is prayer in action.)

The Rhythm of the Stations

As you can see, any encounter can become a station. A patch of wildflowers, a spider's web, a sudden rain shower, the laughter of children in the distance—all are potential invitations to prayer.

The practice is simple:

1. Pause: Stop walking. Give your full attention to the encounter.

2. Observe: Look and listen with your senses. What is really here?

3. Reflect: What does this remind you of? What quality does it embody? What is its sermon for you today?

4. Pray: Turn your reflection into a conversation with God.

5. Move On: Give thanks for the encounter and continue your walk, carrying the lesson with you.

By practising the Stations of the Grove, your walk becomes a dynamic and unpredictable liturgy. The path becomes your priest, the encounters become your scripture readings, and your heart becomes the altar where the world is offered back to God in a sacrifice of praise.

You learn that God is not a distant, silent deity, but a living, speaking presence who is constantly seeking to communicate with you through the rich and beautiful language of the created world.

Your pilgrimage becomes a treasure hunt, and the prize is a deeper, more intimate, and more joyful friendship with the God who walks with you every step of the way.

THE PRACTICE: A CELTIC TREE WALK

My dear pilgrim, we have spent much of this book together exploring the wisdom of the trees. We have learned their stories, their symbolism, and their unique theological voices. We have seen how the Oak speaks of strength, the Ash of connection, the Yew of resurrection. Now, it is time to move from learning about the trees to learning from them directly. This practice is a guided pilgrimage, a Celtic Tree Walk, designed to help participants encounter the archetypal wisdom of the trees in their local environment.

You do not need to live in an ancient Celtic forest to do this practice. The archetypes of the trees are universal, and you can find their echoes in the parks, gardens, and even the street corners of your own neighbourhood. The goal is not to find the exact species of every tree we have studied, but to find trees that embody their spirit. A mighty Maple can be your Oak. A graceful

Willow by a stream can be your Hazel. The key is to walk with an open heart and attentive eyes.

Set aside at least an hour for this walk. Go alone, and leave your phone behind, or at least turn it off.

This is a journey of soul-friendship, and the friends you will meet are the quiet, rooted beings who have been patiently waiting to share their wisdom with you.

Step 1: The Pilgrim's Prayer

Before you begin, stand at the trailhead, the park gate, or your own front door.

Close your eyes, take a few deep breaths, and offer this prayer:

"God of the Grove, Father, Son, and Holy Spirit, I set out on this path today not as a tourist, but as a pilgrim. I come seeking not information, but communion. Open my eyes to see your face in the faces of the trees. Open my ears to hear your voice in the whisper of the leaves. Open my heart to receive the wisdom you have planted in this place for me. Jesus, my Anam Cara, walk with me now. Amen."

Step 2: The Walk Begins - Seeking the Birch

Begin your walk at the Pilgrim's Pace—slow, silent, and attentive. Your first quest is to find a tree that speaks to you of new beginnings. The traditional tree for this is the Birch, with its slender, white trunk and delicate leaves, often the first tree to colonise a barren piece of land.

Look for a young tree, a sapling, or a tree that has a quality of lightness and grace.

When you find your tree, pause before it. This is your first station.

• **Observe:** Notice its youth, its flexibility. If it is a Birch, notice the paper-like quality of its bark, a surface for a new story to be written.

• **Reflect:** This tree is a symbol of a fresh start, of purification, of the courage to begin again. It is the grace of baptism, the promise of a clean slate. What in your life needs a new beginning? What old skin do you need to shed?

• **Pray:** "Lord of all beginnings, thank you for the gift of this new day and the promise of this young tree. Grant me the courage to let go of my past failures and to begin again in your grace. Purify my heart, that I may be a clean page on which you can write a new story of love."

Step 3: The Heart of the Walk - Seeking the Oak

Continue your journey, and now seek out a tree that embodies strength and endurance. The archetype here is the mighty Oak. Look for the largest, strongest, most established tree you can find. It may be an Oak, or it could be a Maple, a Beech, or a great Pine.

You are looking for a tree with a sense of gravitas and sovereignty.

This is your central station. Stand beneath its branches.

• **Observe:** Feel the sense of stability and power it exudes. Look at its thick trunk, its deep roots (if you can see them), and its wide, hospitable canopy. Imagine the storms it has weathered, the seasons it has endured.

• **Reflect:** This tree is a symbol of Christ's kingship, a sovereignty based not on domination, but on steadfast love and protection. It is a symbol of faith, of the strength that comes from being deeply rooted in God. It is also a symbol of hospitality, its branches providing shelter for the birds and shade for the weary pilgrim.

• **Pray:** "Christ our King, you who reign from the Tree of the Cross, I rest here in the shadow of your strength. Make me strong in faith, rooted in love, and steadfast in the face of life's storms. Grant me a hospitable heart, that I may offer shelter and comfort to others. Be the unshakeable Oak at the centre of my life's grove."

Step 4: The Turn of the Path - Seeking the Yew

As you continue your walk, let your intention turn to the mystery of endings and beginnings. Seek out a tree that holds this paradox. The classic tree is the Yew, an evergreen often found in old churchyards, whose drooping branches can root themselves and form new trees, a living symbol of resurrection.

You might find a Yew, or perhaps another evergreen like a Holly or a Pine, or even a fallen log that is sprouting new life (as in our previous chapter).

Pause before this station of mystery.

• **Observe:** Notice the deep darkness of the evergreen's foliage, a colour of solemnity and depth. If it is a Yew, notice its ancient, gnarled appearance. If it is a decaying log, notice the interplay of death and life.

• **Reflect:** This station speaks of the Paschal Mystery. It reminds you that every ending is a doorway to a new beginning, that death does not have the final word, and that in every loss, there is the seed of a future resurrection. What in your life needs to die so that something new can be born?

• **Pray:** "God of eternal life, you who are the Resurrection and the Life, I bring to you my fears of endings, my griefs, and my losses. Help me to trust that you are present in the darkness as well as the light. Grant me the faith to believe that in every death, your resurrecting power is at work, bringing forth a life that is stronger than I can imagine."

Step 5: The Way Home - Seeking the Rowan

As you begin to turn your steps toward home, your final quest is to find a tree that speaks of protection and discernment. The archetype is the Rowan (Mountain Ash), with its bright red berries, traditionally planted by the door of a house to ward off evil. Look for a tree that has a protective feel, perhaps one that stands by a gateway, or one that has beautiful berries or flowers.

This is your final station before you complete your pilgrimage.

• **Observe:** Notice the tree's location. Does it seem to be guarding a threshold? Notice its details—the delicate leaves, the bright berries. The berries are a warning to some birds (they are bitter) but a source of food for others, a symbol of discernment.

• **Reflect:** This tree is a symbol of the protection that God offers us on our journey. It is not a magical charm, but the protection that comes from wisdom, from discerning what is life-giving and what is harmful. It is the protection of the Cross, which guards our hearts and minds in Christ Jesus.

• **Pray:** "Lord, my protector and my guide, thank you for the gift of this walk. As I prepare to re-enter my daily life, I ask for your protection. Guard my heart from all that is not of you. Grant me the gift of discernment, that I may choose the path of life, the path of love, and the path of wisdom. May the blessing of this pilgrimage surround me and my home, now and always."

Step 6: Closing the Circle

When you return to your starting point, pause one last time. Close your eyes and offer a simple prayer of thanksgiving for the journey, for the path, and for the wisdom of the trees.

Journaling Prompts:

• Which tree on your walk spoke to you most powerfully, and why?

• Did you have any unexpected encounters or "stations" on your walk? What was their message for you?

• How did it feel to walk with the intention of a pilgrim? How was it different from your usual way of walking?

• How can you carry the wisdom of the trees you met today into the week ahead?

CONCLUSION: BRINGING THE JOURNEY HOME

And so, our path for this chapter comes to an end. We have journeyed together from the doorway of our sacred dwelling, our cill, out into the great, green cathedral of the world. We have slowed our pace, opened our senses, and learned to walk not as commuters, but as pilgrims. We have befriended the path, seeing it not as a means to an end, but as an anam cara, a soul-friend. We have learned to read the sermons of the stones and the gospels of the water.

We have paused at the stations of the grove, allowing the ordinary encounters of our walk to become extraordinary moments of grace. We have, in short, learned to walk as a spiritual practice, a prayer in motion.

But what happens now? What happens when the walk is over, when we step back across the threshold of our homes and re-enter the world of emails, deadlines, and dirty dishes? Is the pilgrimage just a temporary escape, a brief holiday from our "real" lives? Or can it be something more?

The great secret of the pilgrim's way is this: the goal of the journey is not to arrive at a destination, but to be transformed by the journey itself. The purpose of the pilgrimage is not to leave our lives behind, but to return to them with new eyes, a new heart, and a new way of being. The goal is to bring the journey home.

To bring the journey home means that the qualities we have cultivated on the path—the slowness, the silence, the attentiveness, the sense of divine companionship—begin to permeate the rest of our lives. It means that the Pilgrim's Pace does not end when we take off our walking shoes. It becomes our way of being in the world.

How do we do this? We do so by recognising that our whole life is a pilgrimage. The walk is simply the training ground. It is the place where we practice, in a concentrated way, the skills we need to navigate the much longer and more complex journey of our one, precious life.

• **Bring home the slowness.** Can you bring a little of the Pilgrim's Pace to your work? Can you resist the urge to multitask for just a few minutes and give your full, unhurried attention to a single task? Can you eat a meal without rushing, savouring each bite? Can you listen to a friend or a family member without already formulating your reply?

• **Bring home the silence.** Can you create small pockets of silence in your day? Can you drive to work without the radio on? Can you take a five-minute break from your computer to sit and breathe? Can you resist the constant lure of the screen and allow your mind to be still?

• **Bring home the attentiveness.** Can you look at the face of your child, your spouse, or your colleague with the same gentle, loving attention you gave to the leaf or the stone on your walk? Can you see them not just for the role they play in your life, but as a unique and unrepeatable miracle of God's creation? Can you see your own home, your own office, your own backyard as a potential "thin place," a place where the sacred might be revealed?

• **Bring home the companionship.** Can you carry the sense of walking with Jesus, your Anam Cara, into the most challenging parts of your day? Can you speak to him during a difficult meeting? Can you feel his presence as you comfort a crying child? Can you trust the guidance of the Holy Spirit, the wild goose, in the unexpected twists and turns of your day?

To bring the journey home is to understand that there is no separation between the sacred path and the ordinary street. Every street is a potential pilgrim's path. Every encounter is a potential station of the grove. Every moment is an invitation to walk with God.

This is the ultimate fruit of the Celtic Christian vision. It is a faith that does not divide the world into sacred and secular, but consecrates the whole of creation to God. It is a faith that is lived not just in the church, but in the forest, in the home, in the workplace, and in the heart. It is a faith that is as earthy as the soil under our feet and as transcendent as the stars above our heads.

So do not be discouraged if your life does not feel like a pilgrimage.

Do not worry if your walks are often distracted and your prayers feel dry. The path is not about perfection; it is about intention. It is about the simple, repeated act of setting out, of putting one foot in front of the other, of trusting that the road will rise to meet you. The trees will be your teachers, the stones will be your guides, and the Spirit will be your constant companion.

The journey continues.

The path is always waiting.

And Christ, the eternal pilgrim, the one who is himself the Way, walks with you, every step of the journey home.

Chapter 11:

The Wheel of the Year: Walking Through the Seasons

THE SACRED CIRCLE OF TIME

My dear fellow pilgrim, we have learned to walk. We have slowed our pace, opened our senses, and transformed the simple act of putting one foot in front of the other into a sacred pilgrimage. We have learned to see the world as a cathedral and to read the sermons of the stones and the trees. We have discovered that the path itself can be our soul-friend, our anam cara, leading us ever deeper into the heart of God. Our journey so far has been linear, a path stretching out before us.

However, we are now invited to take a turn. We are invited to see that the pilgrim's path is not just a straight line; it is also a circle. The spiritual life, especially in the Celtic tradition, is not just about moving forward; it is also about participating in the great, cyclical dance of time. It is about learning to walk not only through space but also through the seasons.

In this chapter, we will step onto the Wheel of the Year, the sacred calendar of our Celtic ancestors, and discover how our practice of pilgrimage deepens and changes as we journey through the great, recurring rhythm of winter, spring, summer, and autumn.

In our modern, urbanised world, many of us have become disconnected from the seasons. We live in climate-controlled homes and offices, we eat food that is shipped from halfway around the world, and we can turn on a light to banish the darkness at any time. We have, in many ways, flattened the year into a uniform, monotonous experience, marked only by commercial holidays and the occasional change of wardrobe. We have forgotten the profound spiritual wisdom that is embedded in the turning of the seasons.

Our Celtic Christian ancestors, however, lived in intimate and constant dialogue with the seasons. Their lives, their work, their celebrations, and their prayers were all shaped by the great wheel of the year. They knew that each season had its own unique character, its own spiritual lessons, and its own special invitations from God. They understood that God speaks not just through the words of scripture, but through the language of the turning earth: the stark silence of a snow-covered field, the irrepressible joy of the first spring blossoms, the glorious abundance of a summer meadow, and the melancholy beauty of the autumn leaves.

To walk through the seasons as a spiritual practice is to re-synchronise our own souls with the great, God-given rhythms of creation. It is to learn the wisdom of the tree, which does not fight against the seasons, but gracefully adapts to each one, knowing that each has its purpose in the great cycle of life. It is to discover that our own spiritual lives also have their seasons: times of quiet and withdrawal, times of new growth, times of fruitfulness, and times of letting go.

In this chapter, we will explore the spiritual meaning of the four great seasons, seeing each one as a different kind of pilgrimage, a different way of walking with God. We will also touch upon the eight great festivals of the Celtic year—the four solar festivals (the solstices and equinoxes) and the four fire festivals (Imbolc, Beltane, Lughnasadh, and Samhain)—which mark the turning points of the great wheel. Our journey will be structured as follows:

1. Introduction: The Sacred Circle of Time: We will transition from the linear path of the pilgrim to the cyclical journey of the seasons.

2. The Celtic Wheel: The Eight Fire Festivals: We will briefly explore the eight-spoked wheel of the Celtic year, the framework for our seasonal pilgrimage.

3. Winter's Wisdom: The Season of the Yew: We will learn to walk in winter as a pilgrimage into the holy darkness, a practice of rest, waiting, and trust.

4. Spring's Promise: The Season of the Birch: We will walk in spring as a pilgrimage of resurrection, a celebration of new life, hope, and the power of God to make all things new.

5. Summer's Abundance: The Season of the Oak: We will walk in summer as a pilgrimage of abundance, a practice of strength, generosity, and joyful praise.

6. Autumn's Harvest: The Season of the Hazel: We will walk in autumn as a pilgrimage of wisdom, a practice of gratitude, harvesting, and letting go.

7. The Practice: A Seasonal Walking Ritual: We will learn a simple, adaptable ritual to mark the turning of each season on our walks.

8. Conclusion: Living in Rhythm with Creation: We will reflect on how aligning our lives with the seasons can bring a new sense of peace, balance, and rootedness to our faith.

This chapter is an invitation to step out of the flat, monotonous time of the clock and into the deep, meaningful time of the cosmos. It is an invitation to become a student of the seasons, to let the turning of the earth turn your own soul more deeply toward the God who is the Lord of all time and all seasons.

Let us begin our walk around the sacred wheel.

THE CELTIC WHEEL: THE EIGHT FIRE FESTIVALS

To walk through the seasons as a spiritual practice, it helps to have a map. The map our Celtic ancestors gave us is the Wheel of the Year, a beautiful and elegant model of sacred time. Unlike our modern, linear calendar, which often appears arbitrary and disconnected from the natural world, the Celtic calendar is cyclical. This wheel is constantly turning, always returning, and yet always new. It is a calendar based not on the decrees of emperors, but on the movements of the sun and the subtle shifts in the life of the land.

The Wheel of the Year is marked by eight great festivals, which together create an eight-spoked wheel. These festivals were the pivotal moments of the year, occasions of communal celebration, spiritual reflection, and deep connection to the rhythms of the cosmos. They are not arbitrary dates on a calendar; they are moments of profound energetic and spiritual significance, windows in time when the veil between the worlds is thin and the lessons of the season are most potent.

These eight festivals can be divided into two groups: the four Solar Festivals and the four Fire Festivals (also known as cross-quarter days).

• The Solar Festivals are determined by the position of the sun. They are the two Solstices (the longest and shortest days of the year) and the two

Equinoxes (the days of equal light and darkness). These are the great hinges of the solar year, the moments of maximum light, maximum darkness, and perfect balance.

• The Fire Festivals fall roughly halfway between the solar festivals. They are ancient, pastoral holidays that marked the key moments in the agricultural year: the beginning of spring, the coming of summer, the start of the harvest, and the descent into winter. They were often celebrated with great bonfires, which symbolised the cleansing, protective, and life-giving power of the sun.

When the Celtic lands embraced Christianity, these ancient festivals were not always abolished. Instead, they were often "baptised" or re-imagined in a Christian light. The old festivals acquired new layers of meaning, and their dates often became associated with the feasts of major saints or with events in the life of Christ. This process of integration created a rich and uniquely Celtic Christian calendar, one that honoured both the Book of Scripture and the Book of Nature.

As we embark on our pilgrimage through the seasons, this eight-spoked wheel will be our guide. It identifies eight specific moments in the year to pause, reflect, and align our own spiritual journey with the Earth's great journey. We briefly introduce the eight festivals that will serve as the backdrop for our seasonal walks.

Festival Name	Approximate Date	Type	Core Theme	Christian Connection
Samhain	October 31st	Fire	Endings & Beginnings, Ancestors	All Saints'/All Souls' Day
Winter Solstice (Yule)	December 21st	Solar	Rebirth of the Sun, Holy Darkness	Christmas
Imbolc	February 1st	Fire	Quickening of Life, Purification	St. Brigid's Day, Candlemas
Spring Equinox (Ostara)	March 21st	Solar	Balance, New Growth, Fertility	Annunciation, Easter
Beltane	May 1st	Fire	Fullness of Life, Union, Vitality	Feasts of St. Philip & St. James
Summer Solstice (Litha)	June 21st	Solar	Peak of Light, Abundance, Power	Feast of St. John the Baptist
Lughnasadh	August 1st	Fire	First Harvest, Gratitude, Sacrifice	Lammas, Transfiguration
Autumn Equinox (Mabon)	September 21st	Solar	Second Harvest, Balance, Letting Go	Michaelmas (Feast of St. Michael)

A Living Calendar

It is important to remember that this is a living, natural calendar, not a rigid, man-made one. The exact dates can vary slightly from year to year, and the "feel" of the season will be different depending on where you live. The key is not to become a slave to the dates, but to use them as invitations to pay attention. The Wheel of the Year is not a set of rules; it is a set of reminders. It is a tool to help us notice what is happening in the world around us and to connect that outer reality to the inner landscape of our souls.

In the sections that follow, we will not explore each of the eight festivals in detail. Instead, we will focus on the four great seasons that these festivals define: Winter, Spring, Summer, and Autumn. We will see how each season has its own unique spiritual character, its own "pilgrim's path," and its own profound lessons to teach us. The eight festivals will serve as our signposts, the markers on our journey around the sacred wheel. Let us begin our pilgrimage in the place where the Celtic year begins: the holy darkness of winter.

WINTER'S WISDOM: THE SEASON OF THE YEW

Our pilgrimage around the Wheel of the Year begins, as the Celtic year itself begins, not in the light, but in the darkness. We start our journey at Samhain (October 31st), the great festival that marks the end of the harvest and the beginning of winter. For the ancient Celts, this was the most significant night of the year. The veil between the worlds was at its thinnest, the ancestors were close, and the new year was born out of the womb of the growing darkness. This is a profound and counter-cultural truth: life begins not in a burst of light, but in a quiet, hidden, and mysterious gestation in the dark.

Our modern culture is terrified of the dark. We fear it literally, filling our nights with artificial light, and we fear it metaphorically. We fear the "dark" emotions of sadness and grief. We fear the darkness of unknowing, of not having a plan. We fear the darkness of the tomb, of death itself. But the Celtic Christian tradition invites us to a different relationship with the darkness. It invites us to see the darkness not as an enemy to be vanquished, but as a holy and necessary part of the great cycle of life. It is the season of the Yew, the tree of death and resurrection, which teaches us that the path to new life leads directly through the heart of the tomb.

Walking in winter, therefore, is a unique and powerful spiritual practice. It is a pilgrimage into the holy darkness. It is a journey that teaches us the wisdom of rest, the grace of waiting, and the courage of trust.

THE PILGRIM'S PATH IN WINTER: A JOURNEY INWARD

As the land around us sheds its leaves, as the sap of the trees retreats deep into the roots, as the animals enter hibernation, so too are we invited on an inward journey. A winter walk is not about covering great distances or seeing spectacular sights. It is a quiet, contemplative, and often starkly beautiful practice. The landscape is stripped bare, its essential structure revealed. The sky is often grey, the air is cold, and the world is quiet.

This outer quiet invites an inner quiet. It is a time to walk with our own thoughts, memories, and souls.

The Wisdom of Rest: In our productivity-obsessed culture, rest is often seen as a sign of weakness or laziness. But nature teaches us a different lesson. Winter is the great Sabbath of the year. It is the time when the land rests, when the soil replenishes its nutrients, when the seeds lie dormant, gathering their strength for the great explosion of spring. To walk in winter is to permit ourselves to rest. It is about letting go of the need to constantly achieve, produce, and strive. It is to embrace the fallow time in our own lives, recognising that it is not empty but a time of deep, hidden, and essential preparation.

As you walk on a cold winter's day, notice the stillness of the trees. They are not dead; they are resting. They are conserving their energy, trusting that the light will return. Let their quiet dignity be your teacher. Are you allowing yourself seasons of rest in your own life? Or are you trying to live in a perpetual summer of activity? A winter walk can be a prayer for the grace to embrace our own need for rest, for Sabbath, for holy inactivity.

The Grace of Waiting: Winter is the season of waiting. The farmer waits for the seed to germinate. The pregnant mother waits for the birth of her child. The world waits for the return of the sun. In the Christian story, this is the season of Advent, the four weeks of patient waiting for the coming of Christ, the Light of the World, at the Winter Solstice (around December 21st). The solstice is the longest night of the year, the moment of maximum darkness. But it is also the turning point. It is the moment when, in the heart of the darkness, the light begins its slow, almost imperceptible, return. Christmas is the celebration of this great truth: that the Light shines in the darkness, and the darkness has not overcome it (John 1:5).

To walk in the deep mid-winter is to enter into this mystery of waiting. It is to walk in hope, even when the world around us seems bleak and lifeless. It is to cultivate the spiritual virtue of patience. On your walk, look for the subtle signs of life waiting to be born. Look for the tight, hard buds on the tips of the branches, each one a tiny, packed promise of a future leaf. Look for animal tracks in the snow, evidence of the hidden life that continues even in the coldest of times. A winter walk teaches us to trust the process, to know that even when we cannot see it, God is at work, preparing a new creation in the secret, silent darkness.

The Courage of Trust: Finally, a winter walk is a pilgrimage of trust. It requires a certain courage to venture out into the cold and the dark. It requires trust that the path remains, even when it is covered in snow. It requires a trust that the sun will rise again, even on the greyest of days. It requires trust that the spring will eventually come.

This is the season of the Yew tree, which remains green even in the depths of winter, a living symbol of eternal life. It is a reminder that our hope is not in the fleeting warmth of a summer's day, but in the God who is the Lord of all seasons, the one who is with us in the darkness as well as the light. As you walk, feel the cold air on your face. Let it be a bracing reminder of the world's reality. But also feel the warmth of your own breath, the steady beat of your own heart, the life that persists within you. Your walk becomes an act of faith, a declaration that you will not be overcome by the darkness, but will continue to put one foot in front of the other, trusting in the one who has promised to be your light in the darkness.

As winter begins to wane, we reach the festival of Imbolc (February 1st), which means "in the belly." It is the time when the first stirrings of new life are felt in the belly of the earth. The snowdrops appear, the ewes are pregnant with their lambs, and the light is noticeably returning. In the Christian calendar, this is the feast of St. Brigid of Kildare, one of Ireland's greatest saints, whose story is deeply interwoven with the themes of fire, light, and new life. It is also the time of Candlemas, the feast of the Presentation of the Lord, when the candles for the entire year are blessed, a beautiful symbol of the light of Christ that will guide us through the coming year.

A walk at Imbolc is a walk of budding hope. It is a time to look for the very first signs of spring, to celebrate God's faithfulness, and to give thanks that we have made it through the holy darkness of winter, carrying its quiet wisdom in our hearts.

SPRING'S PROMISE: THE SEASON OF THE BIRCH

Out of the holy darkness of winter, life erupts. The sun grows stronger, the earth softens, and a great, green wave of new life overcomes the world. This is the season of spring, the great festival of resurrection. It is the time when the promise that was whispered at the Winter Solstice is gloriously and undeniably fulfilled. The light has returned, and life is triumphant. For the pilgrim walker, spring is a season of pure joy, a pilgrimage of hope, new beginnings, and irrepressible life.

The first great marker of the spring is the Spring Equinox (around March 21st), the moment of perfect balance when day and night are of equal length. From this point on, the light will triumph over the darkness. This is a time of powerful, surging energy. You can feel it in the air. The birds are singing with a new intensity, the buds on the trees are swelling to the bursting point, and the first brave flowers are pushing their way up through the cold earth. In the Christian calendar, this is the season of Lent, a time of preparation that culminates in the explosive joy of Easter, the greatest feast of the Christian year, the celebration of the ultimate victory of life over death.

Walking in the spring is a profoundly different experience from walking in the winter. The energy is different. The world is no longer quiet and withdrawn; it is loud, vibrant, and highly active. A spring walk is a symphony for the senses, a feast of sights, sounds, and smells. It is a journey that teaches us about the power of resurrection, the courage of new beginnings, and the sheer, unadulterated joy of being alive.

THE PILGRIM'S PATH IN SPRING: A JOURNEY OF RESURRECTION

As the world awakens around us, so too are our own souls invited to awaken from their winter slumber. A spring walk is an antidote to cynicism and despair. It is a powerful reminder that no matter how long or how dark the winter may have been, the spring will always come. Life is stronger than death. Love is stronger than hate. Hope is stronger than despair. This is the core message of the Christian faith, and it is written in the great, green letters of the spring landscape.

The Power of Resurrection: To walk in the spring is to be a witness to a million tiny resurrections. Every unfurling leaf, every blooming flower, every blade of grass pushing its way through the soil is a testament to life's power to overcome the tomb. The great, cosmic drama of Easter is played out in miniature all around you.

On your walk, attune your eyes to these signs of new life. Don't just see a flower; see a miracle. Consider the journey that this small blossom has taken. It has lain dormant as a seed in the cold, dark earth all winter, and now, in response to the call of the sun, it has broken open, pushed its way through the darkness, and opened itself in a glorious act of praise. This is the pattern of your own life in Christ. You, too, have been buried with him in the waters of baptism, and you, too, have been raised with him to a new life. A spring walk is a renewal of your baptismal vows. It is a joyful remembrance that you are a creature of the resurrection.

The Courage of New Beginnings: Spring is the season of the Birch, the pioneer tree, the first to colonise the barren ground. It is a symbol of the courage it takes to start again. Every spring is a new beginning for the world, and it is an invitation for us to make a new beginning in our own lives. Perhaps the winter has been a difficult one for you, a season of loss, of grief, or of spiritual dryness. Spring comes as a messenger of hope, a promise that your own inner winter will not last forever.

As you walk, look for the Birch trees with their slender, white trunks. They appear fragile, yet they are highly resilient. They teach us that the courage to begin again does not require brute strength, but flexibility and a willingness to be vulnerable. A spring walk can be a prayer for such courage. It is an opportunity to ask God: "What new thing are you wanting to bring to birth in my life right now? Where are you calling me to be a pioneer, to step out in faith into a new and unknown territory?"

The Joy of Being Alive: Above all, a spring walk is a pilgrimage of joy. After the quiet introspection of winter, spring is a time of exuberant celebration. The world is throwing a party, and you are invited. The sheer, profligate beauty of the spring is a manifestation of the divine generosity, the overflowing, superabundant love of God.

On your walk, allow yourself to be infected by this joy. Let your senses be filled with the beauty around you. Take off your shoes and feel the cool, damp earth beneath your feet. Breathe in the scent of the blossoms and the rain-washed air. Listen to the riotous chorus of the birds. Let your walk become a dance, a song of praise. This is not a time for deep, sombre reflection. It is a time for simple, childlike delight in the goodness of creation. It is a time to remember that joy is not a frivolous emotion, but a core characteristic of the Kingdom of God.

As spring progresses, we come to the great fire festival of Beltane (May 1st). This was the traditional start of summer in the Celtic world, a time when the cattle were driven out to their summer pastures between two great bonfires to be purified and protected. It is a festival of fertility, of passion, and of the full, unbridled power of life. It is the moment when the promise of spring is consummated in the glorious fullness of the green world.

A walk at Beltane is a walk of ecstatic praise. It is a time to celebrate the sheer, raw power of life, the sacredness of our bodies, and the goodness of the physical world. It is a time to give thanks for the love that brought the world into being and sustains it in every moment. It is a pilgrimage into the fiery heart of God's own creative joy.

SUMMER'S ABUNDANCE: THE SEASON OF THE OAK

The wheel turns, and the vibrant, youthful energy of spring matures into the glorious, confident fullness of summer. This is the season of maximum light, the time when the sun is at the height of its power, and the world is clothed in a magnificent garment of deep, verdant green. If spring was the promise, summer is the fulfilment. It is a season of abundance, strength, and joyful generosity. For the pilgrim walker, a summer walk is a journey into the heart of God's own magnanimity, a celebration of the glorious, overflowing, and unconditional love that sustains the universe.

The great turning point of the summer is the Summer Solstice (around June 21st), the longest day of the year. This is the moment of the sun's greatest triumph, the peak of its power. From this day forward, though the days will remain warm for many weeks, the darkness will begin its slow, almost imperceptible return. The Solstice is therefore a bittersweet moment, a celebration of fullness and a gentle reminder that nothing in this world lasts forever.

It is a call to savour the present moment of abundance, to drink deeply from the cup of life, and to live with a generous and open heart. In the Christian calendar, the Summer Solstice is closely associated with the feast of St. John the Baptist, the great prophet who prepared the way for Jesus. John famously said, "He must increase, but I must decrease" (John 3:30). This is the wisdom of the Solstice: the light reaches its peak and then begins to wane, making way for the coming harvest and the necessary descent into darkness.

Walking in the summer is a pilgrimage of the senses. The air is thick with the scent of flowers and warm earth. The trees are in their full glory, their leaves creating a dense canopy of shade. The world is humming with the sound of insects and alive with the frantic activity of birds feeding their young. A summer walk is a journey that teaches us about the strength of maturity, the beauty of generosity, and the simple, profound joy of being fully alive.

THE PILGRIM'S PATH IN SUMMER: A JOURNEY OF FULLNESS

As the world around us reaches its peak of growth and vitality, we too are invited to celebrate the fullness of our own lives. A summer walk is an opportunity to give thanks for the blessings we have received, to recognise our own strength and capacity, and to share the abundance of our lives with others.

The Strength of Maturity: Summer is the season of the Oak, the king of the forest. The Oak, which began as a vulnerable sapling in the spring, is now in its full power. Its trunk is thick and strong, its leaves are a deep, leathery green, and its vast canopy provides a generous shelter from the summer sun. It is a symbol of mature strength, of a power that is not brittle or aggressive, but deep, rooted, and life-giving.

On your summer walk, seek out a great Oak or another tree that embodies this sense of mature strength. Stand under its branches and feel the quality of its shade. It is a cool, deep, and welcoming shade. This is the image of a mature faith. It is a faith that is neither anxious nor defensive, but rather confident, peaceful, and generous. The storms of life have tested it and has grown stronger as a result. A summer walk is a time to reflect on our growth, on the ways we have matured in our faith and in our lives. It is a time to pray for the grace to become like the Oak, a source of strength, stability, and shelter for others.

The Beauty of Generosity: Summer is a season of extravagant generosity. The flowers are not content to produce just one or two blossoms; they produce a riot of colour. The trees are not content with just a few leaves; they are covered in lush abundance. The sun does not ration its light; it pours it down upon the just and the unjust alike. The whole of the summer landscape is a sermon on the divine generosity.

This is a powerful antidote to the scarcity mindset that so often governs our lives. We are taught to compete, to hoard, to worry that there is not enough to go around. But a summer walk teaches us the truth of the Gospel: that we serve a God of abundance, a God who gives good gifts to his children, pressed down, shaken together, and running over. As you walk, notice the sheer, unnecessary beauty of it all. The intricate pattern on a butterfly's wing, the sweet scent of a wildflower, the cool feel of the moss on a stone. None of this is strictly necessary for survival. It is a free, unmerited gift. It is grace. A summer walk is a pilgrimage of gratitude, a time to train our hearts to notice and to give thanks for the thousands of small, beautiful gifts that we receive every day.

The Joy of Being Fully Alive: Summer is a season of intense, vibrant life. It is a time of long days and warm nights, of outdoor gatherings and shared meals, of play and celebration. It is a season that invites us to inhabit our bodies and to enjoy the simple, physical pleasures of being alive. It is a time to remember that God created the physical world and called it "good."

On your summer walk, allow yourself to enter into this bodily joy. Walk barefoot in the grass. Wade in a cool stream. Lie on your back and watch the clouds drift by. Let the sun warm your skin. A summer walk is a sensual experience, a feast for the body as well as the soul. It is a time to let go of our overly spiritualized ideas of faith and to remember that we are creatures of flesh and blood, made to delight in the goodness of God's creation. This is not hedonism; it is a holy and grateful enjoyment of the gifts of the Creator.

As summer begins to wane, we reach the festival of Lughnasadh (August 1st), the first of the three harvest festivals. The name comes from the god Lugh, a master of all arts and skills, but it was Christianized as "Lammas," from the Anglo-Saxon for "loaf-mass," the day when the first loaves of bread from the new wheat harvest were blessed in the church. It is a time of gratitude for the abundance of the summer, but also a time of sacrifice.

The grain must be cut down, threshed, and ground into flour to provide life for the community. A walk at Lughnasadh is a walk of thanksgiving, a time to begin to gather the harvest of our own summer's growth and to ask ourselves: "What is the fruit of my life? And how can I offer it as a gift for the nourishment of others?"

AUTUMN'S HARVEST: THE SEASON OF THE HAZEL

The wheel turns once more, and the high, green glory of summer begins its graceful descent into the gold and crimson of autumn. This is the season of harvest, a time of gathering in, of giving thanks, and of letting go. The air grows crisp, the light takes on a golden, slanted quality, and the world is filled with a sense of poignant, bittersweet beauty. If winter is a pilgrimage of rest, spring a pilgrimage of resurrection, and summer a pilgrimage of abundance, then autumn is a pilgrimage of wisdom, gratitude, and surrender.

The great turning point of the autumn is the Autumn Equinox (around September 21st), the second moment of perfect balance in the year, when day and night are once again of equal length. From this point on, the darkness will begin to triumph over the light, leading us back toward the holy darkness of winter. This is the time of the second harvest, the harvest of fruits and nuts. In the Christian calendar, it is the time of Michaelmas, the feast of St. Michael and All Angels, a celebration of the unseen spiritual world and the great cosmic battle between good and evil.

It is a time to take stock, to weigh things in the balance, and to prepare for the coming darkness.

Walking in the autumn is a pilgrimage of profound and gentle beauty. The world is not dying; it is performing its final, most glorious act of the year. The trees, which were a uniform green all summer, now reveal their unique and individual characters in a breathtaking display of colour. A walk in the autumn is a journey that teaches us about the wisdom of maturity, the importance of gratitude, and the liberating grace of letting go.

THE PILGRIM'S PATH IN AUTUMN: A JOURNEY OF WISDOM

As the world around us begins to shed its summer growth, we, too, are invited to enter a season of reflection and release. An autumn walk is a time to look back over our own year's journey, to gather the harvest of our experiences, and to let go of what we no longer need to carry. It is a pilgrimage into the heart of wisdom.

The Wisdom of Maturity: Autumn is the season of the Hazel, the tree of wisdom and poetic inspiration. In Celtic mythology, the Hazel tree grew over the Well of Wisdom, and its nuts would fall into the water, where the Salmon of Knowledge ate them. To eat the hazelnut was to gain all the wisdom of the world. Autumn is the time when the hazelnuts ripen. It is the season when the fruits of the year's growth, both literal and metaphorical, are ready to be harvested. It is a time of mature wisdom, a wisdom that is not just about knowing facts, but about understanding the deeper patterns and meanings of life.

On your autumn walk, look for the fruits of the forest: the acorns, the chestnuts, the bright red berries of the hawthorn. Each one is a small, packed container of life and potential, the result of a whole season of growth. They are a symbol of the wisdom that we gain from our own experiences. An autumn walk is a time to reflect on the year that has passed. What have you learned? How have you grown? What are the "hazelnuts" of wisdom that you have gathered from your joys and your sorrows? It is a time to honour the journey and to recognise that all of it, the easy and the difficult, has been a source of learning and growth.

The Importance of Gratitude: Autumn is, above all, a season of thanksgiving. It is the time when we gather in the harvest that will sustain us through the winter. This spirit of gratitude is central to a healthy spiritual life. It is the conscious choice to focus not on what we lack, but on what we have been given. Gratitude is the soil in which joy grows.

As you walk through the autumn landscape, let your walk be a litany of thanksgiving. Give thanks for the beauty of the leaves, for the crispness of the air, for the warmth of the sun on your face. Give thanks for the harvest of your own life: for your family, your friends, your home, your work. Give thanks for the challenges that have made you stronger and the joys that have made you sing. An autumn walk is a powerful practice of counting your blessings, of training your heart to see the grace that is all around you. This spirit of gratitude culminates in the final harvest festival of Samhain (October 31st), the end of the old year and the beginning of the new, when thanks were offered to the ancestors and the spirits of the land for the harvest that had been safely gathered.

The Grace of Letting Go: The most poignant and powerful lesson of autumn is letting go. The trees, in a final, glorious act of surrender, release the leaves that have served them all summer. They do not cling to them.

They let them fall, trusting that this act of letting go is necessary for their survival and for the possibility of new growth in the spring. The fallen leaves, in turn, do not go to waste. They decompose and become the rich, fertile soil that will nourish the next generation of life.

This is one of the most difficult and most important of all spiritual practices. We all have things that we need to let go of: old resentments, past hurts, outdated ideas about ourselves, our attachment to success or to being right. We cling to these things, fearing that without them, we will be diminished. But the trees teach us a different truth. They teach us that letting go is not an act of loss, but an act of profound trust and liberation. It is only by releasing what is old and dead that we make space for the new thing that God wants to do in our lives.

On your autumn walk, pay special attention to the falling leaves. Watch them as they dance and spiral in the wind. See their surrender not as a death, but as a graceful and necessary dance. As you walk, ask yourself: "What do I need to let go of in my own life? What old leaves am I clinging to that are preventing new growth?" Let your walk be a prayer for the grace to surrender, to trust, and to let go, knowing that in every act of release, there is the promise of a future spring.

THE PRACTICE: A SEASONAL WALKING RITUAL

My dear friend, we have journeyed in our imaginations around the great Wheel of the Year. We have explored the unique wisdom and spiritual invitations of each of the four seasons. Now, it is time to ground this wisdom in a simple, repeatable practice. This section offers a Seasonal Walking Ritual that you can adapt and use to mark the turning of the seasons in your own life and on your pilgrimage.

This ritual is designed to be done four times a year, at or near the great turning points: the Winter Solstice, the Spring Equinox, the Summer Solstice, and the Autumn Equinox. These are the four great hinges of the year, the moments of maximum darkness, maximum light, and perfect balance. By pausing to mark these moments with a special, intentional walk, you can consciously align your own spiritual life with the great rhythms of God's creation.

This ritual has four parts: Preparation, The Threshold, The Walk, and The Return. It is a basic structure that you can and should adapt to your own environment and your own spiritual temperament.

1. Preparation

In the days leading up to the solstice or equinox, begin to prepare your heart. Pay attention to the subtle shifts in the world around you. Notice the quality of the light, the temperature of the air, and the state of the trees and plants.

Read back over the section of this chapter that corresponds to the coming season. What are its key themes? What is its spiritual invitation?

On the day of your walk, find a small object from nature that represents the season for you.

• **For Winter:** A piece of evergreen (like Yew or Holly), a smooth, dark stone, or a bare twig.

• **For Spring:** A budding branch, a feather, a resilient flower like a crocus or a snowdrop.

• **For Summer:** A fragrant, fully opened flower, a deep green leaf from an Oak tree, a piece of sun-warmed quartz.

• **For Autumn:** A brightly coloured leaf, an acorn or a hazelnut, a piece of harvested grain.
Hold this object in your hand. It will be your touchstone, your focal point for the walk.

2. The Threshold

Go to the starting point of your chosen walk. Before you begin, stand at the threshold—the gateway, the trailhead, your own front door. Hold your seasonal object in your hand. Take a few deep breaths and call to mind the specific qualities of the season you are entering.

Then, offer this prayer, adapting it for the season:

For a Winter Solstice Walk (Prayer for Light in the Darkness): "God of the Holy Darkness, as I stand at this threshold of the longest night, I give you thanks for the gift of winter's rest. I bring to you my own inner darkness, my fears, and my unknowings. I ask for the grace to trust that your light is being born in me, even when I cannot see it. Jesus, Light of the World, be my companion on this path."

For a Spring Equinox Walk (Prayer for New Life): "God of Resurrection, as I stand at this threshold of perfect balance, I give you thanks for the promise of spring. I bring to you the parts of my life that feel barren or dead. I ask for the courage to break open, to grow, and to embrace the new thing you are doing in me. Jesus, the Firstborn from the Dead, be my companion on this path."

For a Summer Solstice Walk (Prayer for Abundance): "God of Abundant Life, as I stand at this threshold of the longest day, I give you thanks for the glory of summer. I bring to you my joys and my blessings, my strengths and my gifts. I ask for a generous heart, that I may share the abundance you have given me with others. Jesus, the True Vine, be my companion on this path."

For an Autumn Equinox Walk (Prayer for the Harvest): "God of the Wise Harvest, as I stand at this threshold of perfect balance, I give you thanks for the beauty of autumn. I bring to you the fruits of my year's journey, my learnings, and my accomplishments. I also bring you what I need to release. I ask for a grateful heart and the grace to let go. Jesus, the Bread of Life, be my companion on this path."

After the prayer, step across the threshold and begin your walk.

3. The Walk: Four Stations

As you walk at the Pilgrim's Pace, your task is to find four "stations" that speak to you of the season. These can be anything that catches your attention. At each station, you will pause for a brief reflection and prayer, using your seasonal object as a focus.

Station 1: A Gift of the Season

Your first station perfectly embodies the beauty and character of the current season.

• **Pause and Observe:** Gaze upon this gift with loving attention (visio divina).

• **Reflect:** What does this object teach you about the season? What quality does it most represent?

• Pray: Offer a simple prayer of thanksgiving for the beauty of the season and the specific gift you have found.

Station 2: A Sign of the Previous Season

Your second station is something that reminds you of the recently passed season. In winter, it might be a single, stubborn brown leaf still clinging to a branch. In spring, it might be a patch of melting snow. In summer, it might be a flower that has already gone to seed. In autumn, it might be a still-green leaf on a tree that is mostly gold.

• **Pause and Observe:** Look at this sign of the past.

• **Reflect:** What were the gifts and the challenges of the season that has gone? What have you brought with you from that time?

• **Pray:** Offer a prayer of gratitude and release. Give thanks for the lessons of the past season, and consciously release them, letting them go with love.

Station 3: A Promise of the Coming Season

Your third station is a sign of the season that is yet to come. In winter, it is the tightly closed bud on a branch. In spring, it is the first sign of a fruit beginning to form. In summer, it is the first hint of colour on a single leaf. In autumn, it is the tree's bare, skeletal form that signals the coming winter.

• **Pause and Observe:** Look closely at this promise of the future.

• **Reflect:** What does the coming season ask of you? What do you hope for? What do you fear?

• **Pray:** Offer a prayer of hope and trust. Entrust the future to God, asking for the specific graces you will need to meet the coming season with faith.

Station 4: A Personal Connection

Your final station addresses your current life directly. It could be anything: a fork in the path, a tangled root, a soaring bird, a piece of litter. Trust that the Spirit has guided you to this place for a reason.

• **Pause and Observe:** Give your full attention to this object or event.

• **Reflect:** How is this a mirror of your own inner state? What is its personal message for you today?

• **Pray:** Offer a prayer of petition or intercession. Talk to God honestly about what is on your heart, using the object as a prompt. Offer this situation, this feeling, this person to God's loving care.

4. The Return

As you walk back toward your starting point, do so in silence, carrying the lessons of your four stations in your heart. When you arrive back at the threshold, pause one last time. Hold your seasonal object and offer a final prayer of thanksgiving.

"God of all seasons, thank you for this journey. Thank you for the wisdom of the path and the companionship of Christ. May the lessons of this walk take root in my heart and bear fruit in my life. May I live in harmony with your creation, in tune with your sacred rhythms, and in the constant joy of your presence. Amen."

When you get home, place your seasonal object on your home altar. Let it be a reminder of your pilgrimage until the wheel turns and it is time for the next journey.

CONCLUSION: LIVING IN RHYTHM WITH CREATION

We have come to the end of our pilgrimage around the Wheel of the Year. We began in the holy darkness of winter, walked through the explosive joy of spring and the glorious abundance of summer, and have arrived now in the wise, gentle beauty of autumn, ready to begin the cycle once more. We have learned that each season has its own unique spiritual wisdom, its own character, and its own special invitation from the God who is the Lord of all seasons. We have discovered that to walk through the seasons is to walk through the great, unfolding story of our own faith: a story of waiting, of resurrection, of abundance, and of letting go.

To live in rhythm with creation, to align our own small lives with this great, cosmic dance, is to find a new sense of peace, balance, and rootedness. In a world that is increasingly frantic, fragmented, and disconnected from the natural world, this is not just a pleasant idea; it is an essential spiritual practice. It is a form of resistance against the tyranny of the urgent and the shallow. It is a way of sinking our roots deep into the soil of a faith that is as ancient and as reliable as the turning of the earth itself.

What does it mean to live this way, day in and day out? It means that we begin to see our own lives not as a linear, relentless climb toward some distant goal, but as a series of seasons. It means that we learn to honour the seasons of our own souls.

• It means we permit ourselves to have winters. There will be times in our lives of fallowness, of grief, of unknowing, when all we can do is rest and wait in the dark. To live in rhythm with creation is to know that these times are not failures, but a holy and necessary part of the journey. It is to trust that the seed of new life is gestating in the darkness, and that the light will, in God's good time, return.

• It means we learn to recognise and celebrate our springs. There will be times of new beginnings, of fresh starts, of creative energy. To live in rhythm with creation is to embrace these moments with courage and joy, to step out in faith, and to allow the new thing that God is doing in us to blossom.

• It means we learn to savour and to share our summers. There will be times of strength, of abundance, of fruitfulness, when our lives are whole, and our gifts are in high demand. To live in rhythm with creation is to inhabit these times with gratitude and generosity, to share the abundance we have been given, and to offer our strength as a shelter for others.

• And it means we learn the graceful art of our autumns. There will be times when we are called to let go: of a job, of a relationship, of a dream, of our own youthful energy. To live in rhythm with creation is to learn that this letting go is not a tragedy, but a wise and beautiful surrender. It is to trust that in every act of release, we are making space for a new and deeper wisdom to take root.

To walk the Wheel of the Year is to discover that you are a part of a story that is much bigger than your own. You are a part of the great, unfolding story of creation, a story that is filled with beauty, with sorrow, with joy, and with an unshakeable hope.

It is the story of a God who so loved the world that he entered into its rhythms, its seasons, its very soil. He is the seed that dies in the winter of the tomb, the green shoot that bursts forth on Easter morning, the glorious, fruit-laden vine of summer, and the harvested grain that gives its life to become our bread.

My prayer for you, dear pilgrim, is that you will continue to walk this sacred wheel.

Let the seasons be your teachers. Let the path be your guide.

And may you find, in every season of the year and in every season of your own soul, the faithful, loving, and ever-present companionship of Christ, the Lord of the Dance.

Chapter 12:

The Community of the Grove: Walking with Others

My dear friend and fellow pilgrim, we have walked a long and beautiful path together. We have learned to create sacred space in our homes and in our hearts. We have learned to walk as a spiritual practice, transforming every journey into a pilgrimage. We have learned to align our lives with the great, sacred rhythms of the seasons. So far, our journey has been largely solitary. We have focused on the practices that we, as individuals, can undertake to deepen our connection with God. This is good and necessary. A strong and vibrant spiritual life must be rooted in a deep, personal, and intimate relationship with the Divine. We must, as the mystics say, be able to be alone with the Alone.

But this is not the whole story. A faith that remains purely individualistic is incomplete. It is like a tree with deep roots but no branches, unable to provide shade or fruit to the world. The Christian life, and especially the Celtic Christian life, is not a solo performance; it is a choral symphony. It is a life lived in community. The solitary path of the pilgrim must, eventually, lead to the joyful company of the pilgrim band. In this chapter, we will take that crucial step. We will move from the solitude of the individual grove to the shared life of the Community of the Grove. We will examine what it means to walk not only with God but also with one another.

In our modern Western culture, the very idea of community is in crisis. We are, as many sociologists have noted, more connected and more lonely than at any other time in human history. We have thousands of "friends" on social media, but we may not know the name of our next-door neighbour. We prize our independence, our autonomy, and our personal freedom above all else. The idea of belonging to a community, with all the obligations, compromises, and messiness that it entails, can feel threatening to our sense of self. We prefer to keep our spirituality private, a personal matter between ourselves and God.

But the Celtic Christian tradition offers us a powerful and attractive alternative. It presents a way of being in community that is not about conformity but about mutual flourishing. It is a vision of community rooted like the Triune God, who is not a solitary monarch but a perfect, eternal community of love—Father, Son, and Holy Spirit. To be created in the image of this God is to be created for community. We are, as the African proverb says, people through other people. We need each other to become ourselves fully.

In this chapter, we will explore the rich and life-giving Celtic vision of community. We will learn about the central importance of the anam cara, the soul-friend, and how this ancient practice can transform our relationships. We will discover how the simple act of walking together can become a profound spiritual practice. We will explore the practical steps we can take to form our own small, life-giving spiritual communities. And we will rediscover the radical and world-changing practice of Celtic hospitality.

Our journey will be structured as follows:

1. Introduction: From Solitude to Community: We will make the crucial transition from the individual spiritual life to the life lived in community.

2. The Celtic Vision of Community: The Monastic Family: We will explore the model of the early Celtic monasteries, not as institutions, but as spiritual families.

3. The Anam Cara: The Soul Friend: We will delve into the beautiful and profound practice of spiritual friendship.

4. Walking Together: The Practice of Communal Pilgrimage: We will learn how walking with others can deepen both our faith and our friendships.

5. The Sacred Circle: Creating a Celtic Christian Small Group: We will explore practical ways to form our own life-giving spiritual communities.

6. Hospitality and the Hearth: Welcoming the Stranger: We will rediscover the radical Celtic practice of hospitality as a core spiritual discipline.

7. The Practice: A Group Tree Walk and Sharing Circle: We will learn a simple, guided practice for walking and reflecting together as a small group.

8. Conclusion: The Grove is a Community: We will reflect on the truth that we need both solitude and community to live a full and balanced spiritual life.

This chapter is an invitation to step out of the isolation of the modern world and into the warm, messy, and beautiful embrace of Christian community. It is an invitation to discover that the path of the pilgrim is not meant to be walked alone. It is a journey we are meant to take together, hand in hand, heart to heart, walking each other home.

THE CELTIC VISION OF COMMUNITY: THE MONASTIC FAMILY

To understand the Celtic vision of community, we must return to the great monastic settlements that were the vibrant heart of the early Irish church. When we hear the word "monastery," we might picture a silent, gloomy, and rigid institution, a place of strict rules and joyless asceticism. But the great Celtic monasteries—places like Clonmacnoise, Iona, and Kildare—were something quite different.

They were not so much institutions as they were spiritual families, bustling villages of faith, learning, and art. They were the spiritual, cultural, and social centres of their time, and they offer us a powerful and inspiring model of what Christian community can be.

Unlike the highly structured and hierarchical Benedictine monasteries of continental Europe, the Celtic monasteries were organised more like traditional Irish tribes or clans. The abbot or abbess was not a distant, authoritarian ruler, but a spiritual father or mother, a chieftain of the soul. The community was known as their *muintir*, their family or their people. This was a community based not on rigid rules, but on relationships of loyalty, affection, and mutual service. It was a family, with all the messiness, intimacy, and unconditional love that the word implies.

What can these ancient monastic families teach us about building community in our own time? They teach us that a true spiritual community is characterised by three essential qualities: a shared centre, a common rhythm, and a deep sense of belonging.

A SHARED CENTRE: THE HEARTH OF CHRIST

Every healthy family has a centre, a place where they gather for warmth, for nourishment, and for connection. In the traditional Irish home, this was the hearth, the central fire that was kept burning day and night. The great Celtic monasteries also had a centre, a spiritual hearth around which their entire life revolved. That centre was Christ, made present in the Word and the Sacraments.

The life of the monastic community was centred on the church, where it gathered several times a day for the liturgy of the hours. This regular, communal prayer was the heartbeat of the monastery. It was the constant, rhythmic return to their shared centre. It was the fire that sustained their love for God and for one another. In addition to prayer, the study of scripture was a central practice. The monks and nuns of the Celtic world were famous for their love of the Bible. They memorised vast portions of it, copied it in their beautiful, intricate script, and meditated on it day and night. The Word of God was the primary source of their spiritual nourishment.

This is the first and most important lesson for any community that seeks to be a "community of the grove." It must have a shared centre. It must be a community that is gathered around the spiritual hearth of Christ. This does not mean that everyone must believe exactly the same things or have the same kind of spiritual experience. But it does mean that there must be a shared commitment to seeking Christ together, to listening for his voice in the scriptures, and to encountering his presence in prayer and worship. A community without a spiritual centre is just a social club. A community centred on Christ is a powerhouse of grace.

A COMMON RHYTHM: THE DANCE OF WORK AND PRAYER

The Celtic monastic family was not a place of idleness. It was a bustling hive of activity. The monks and nuns were farmers, scholars, artists, and craftspeople. They ran farms, taught schools, copied manuscripts, and created the magnificent high crosses and illuminated gospels that are the treasures of Irish art. Their life was a beautiful, integrated dance of work and prayer, of *ora et labora*.

This rhythm of work and prayer was essential to the community's health. The work of their hands grounded their prayer in the real world, and their prayer infused their work with a sense of sacred purpose. They did not see a separation between the holy and the secular. All of life was an opportunity to glorify God. Tilling the soil was a form of prayer. Copying a manuscript was an act of worship. Caring for a sick person was an encounter with Christ.

This suggests that a healthy spiritual community is not merely a group of people who gather to talk about God. It is a community that does things together. It is a community that finds a common rhythm of service and celebration. This might mean tending a community garden, volunteering at a local charity, or creating art together. It might mean establishing a regular rhythm of meeting for prayer and study. The specific activities are less important than the underlying principle: that a true community is built not just on shared beliefs, but on a shared life, a common rhythm of doing and being that integrates the spiritual and the practical.

A DEEP SENSE OF BELONGING: THE CIRCLE OF THE ANAM CARA

Perhaps the most attractive and challenging aspect of the Celtic monastic family was its profound sense of belonging. In a world that was often violent and unstable, the monastery was a place of peace, of refuge, and of deep, committed relationships. To be a member of the community was to be known, loved, and held. It was to have a place where you belonged, no matter what.

This sense of belonging was fostered by the practice of the anam cara, or soul-friend, which we will explore in the next section. A deep commitment to mutual accountability and forgiveness also fostered it. The Celtic monks had a practice known as "the chapter of faults," where members of the community would openly confess their failings to one another and ask for forgiveness and prayer.

This was not a shaming exercise; it was an act of profound humility and trust. It was the recognition that we are all broken, we all make mistakes, and we all need the grace of God and the support of our community to grow.

This is a radical challenge to our modern individualism. We are taught to be self-sufficient, to hide our weaknesses, and to project an image of success. But the Celtic vision of community invites us into a place of vulnerability, a place where we can take off our masks and be our true selves, warts and all. It is only in such a place that we can experience the true grace of belonging. A true spiritual community is not a showcase for saints; it is a hospital for sinners. It is a place where we can be honest about our struggles, where we can find forgiveness when we fail, and where we can be cheered on in our journey toward wholeness.

To build a community of the grove in our own time is to take these three principles to heart. It is to create a community with a shared centre in Christ, a common rhythm of work and prayer, and a deep sense of belonging, where we can be our true, broken, and beloved selves. It is to create a spiritual family, a muintir, a place to call home.

THE ANAM CARA: THE SOUL FRIEND

At the very heart of the Celtic vision of community lies one of its most beautiful and enduring gifts to the world: the practice of anam cara. The phrase, in Irish, literally means "soul friend." An anam cara is more than just a best friend, a mentor, or a confidant, though they may be all of those things. The anam cara is the person with whom you can share the deepest secrets of your heart, the person who knows your soul, and the person who is committed to helping you on your journey toward God. The great St. Brigid of Kildare, one of the most powerful figures in the early Irish church, is quoted as saying, "A person without an anam cara is like a body without a head." For Celtic Christians, having a soul friend was not a luxury; it was an absolute necessity for a healthy spiritual life.

This ancient practice of spiritual friendship is a powerful antidote to the loneliness and isolation of our modern world. It is a call to move beyond the superficiality of many of our relationships and to cultivate friendships of real depth, intimacy, and spiritual significance. It is a rediscovery of the truth that we cannot make the journey of faith alone. We need companions, guides, and mirrors. We need soul friends.

What does it mean to have an anam cara? And how can we cultivate this kind of friendship in our own lives? The practice of soul friendship is built on three foundational pillars: intimacy, honesty, and spiritual companionship.

INTIMACY: THE MEETING OF TWO SOULS

The relationship of the *anam cara* is, above all, a relationship of profound intimacy. The Irish writer and poet John O'Donohue, in his beautiful book Anam Cara: A Book of Celtic Wisdom, describes it this way: "In the Celtic tradition, there is a beautiful understanding of love and friendship.

It's the Gaelic term *anam cara*. Anam is the Gaelic word for soul, and cara is the word for friend. So anam cara in the Celtic world was the 'soul friend.' In the early Celtic church, a person who acted as a teacher, companion, or spiritual guide was called an anam cara. It originally referred to someone to whom you confessed, revealing the hidden intimacies of your life. With the *anam cara*, you could share your innermost self, your mind and your heart. This friendship was an act of recognition and belonging. When you had an *anam cara*, your friendship cut across all conventions, morality, and categories. You were joined anciently and eternally with the "friend of your soul."

This is a friendship that goes beyond shared interests or common backgrounds. It is a meeting of two souls. It is the experience of being truly seen and truly known by another person, and of seeing and understanding them in return. This kind of intimacy is rare and precious. It requires time, commitment, and a willingness to be vulnerable. It cannot be rushed or forced. It grows slowly, in the soil of trust and mutual respect.

In our fast-paced and transient world, we are often starved for this kind of deep, abiding connection. We may have many acquaintances, but few true friends. The practice of anam cara invites us to slow down, to be present, and to invest in the relationships that matter most. It invites us to seek out those people in our lives with whom we feel a sense of spiritual resonance, a sense of coming home. It might be a spouse, a sibling, a long-time friend, or someone new that God has brought into our lives. The key is to recognise the sacred potential in that relationship and to nurture it with intention and care.

Honesty: The Mirror of the Soul

The second pillar of the anam cara relationship is a radical and loving honesty. The soul friend is the person to whom you can tell the whole truth about yourself, without fear of judgment or rejection. They are the person who has seen you at your worst and still loves you. This is why the anam cara was originally the person to whom one would confess. In the early Celtic church, the practice of confession was not a formal, juridical act, but a personal, therapeutic, and healing conversation with a trusted soul friend.

The anam cara serves as a mirror for the soul. They reflect back to us not only our beauty and gifts but also our blind spots, self-deceptions, and areas for growth. This is not always comfortable. A true soul friend is not someone who simply tells us what we want to hear. They are someone who loves us enough to tell us the truth, even when it is difficult.

As the book of Proverbs says, "Faithful are the wounds of a friend" (Proverbs 27:6).

This kind of honesty requires immense trust and a deep commitment to the other person's well-being. The anam cara is not a critic or a judge. They are a compassionate witness. They listen with a heart of love, and they speak with a spirit of gentleness and encouragement. Their goal is not to condemn, but to heal. They help us see ourselves more clearly, take responsibility for our lives, and grow more fully into the person God created us to be.

To have a soul friend is to have a safe place to be imperfect. It is to have someone who can hold our brokenness without trying to fix us, and who can gently guide us toward the healing and wholeness found only in God.

Spiritual Companionship: Walking the Path Together

Finally, the anam cara relationship is a partnership in the spiritual journey. It is a commitment to walk together on the path toward God. The soul friend is a fellow pilgrim, a companion on the way. They are the person who encourages us when we are weary, who challenges us when we are complacent, and who celebrates with us when we experience moments of grace.

This spiritual companionship can take many forms. It might involve praying for and with one another, reading and discussing Scripture or other spiritual books, or simply sharing stories of how God is at work in one's life. It might involve holding one another accountable for spiritual commitments, such as a daily prayer practice or a commitment to a particular form of service. It might involve embarking on actual pilgrimages together, whether to a holy site or simply a walk in the woods.

The role of the anam cara is not to be a spiritual guru or a director who has all the answers. It is to be a companion who walks alongside us, asks good questions, listens deeply, and points us back to the true spiritual director: the Holy Spirit. The soul friend helps us discern the voice of God in our lives and respond to it with courage and faith.

In a world that often sees the spiritual journey as a private, individualistic pursuit, the practice of anam cara reminds us that we are not meant to make this journey alone. We need the wisdom, the support, and the love of our fellow travellers. We need friends who can help us see God more clearly, love God more dearly, and follow God more nearly, day by day.

How do you find an anam cara?

You do not find a soul friend by putting out an advertisement.

You find a soul friend by becoming a soul friend.

You begin by practising the qualities of soul friendship in your existing relationships: the intimacy of deep listening, the courage of gentle honesty, and the commitment of spiritual companionship.

You pray for the gift of soul friendship. And you trust that God, who knows the deepest longings of your heart, will provide you with the companions you need for the journey. For as Jesus himself promised, "where two or three are gathered in my name, I am there among them" (Matthew 18:20).

The journey of the soul is a journey we are meant to take together, in the company of friends, and in the presence of the one who is the friend of all souls.

WALKING TOGETHER: THE PRACTICE OF COMMUNAL PILGRIMAGE

We have learned to walk as a solitary spiritual practice, a pilgrimage into the heart of God through the cathedral of nature. We have also rediscovered the ancient and beautiful practice of anam cara, the soul friend, who accompanies us on our spiritual journey. Now, we bring these two powerful streams of the Celtic tradition together. We learn to walk not just alone, and not just with a single soul friend, but as a small community of pilgrims. We discover the unique and transformative power of communal pilgrimage.

The history of pilgrimage, in almost every tradition, is a history of walking together. From the great medieval pilgrimages to Santiago de Compostela to the annual Hajj to Mecca, people have always sought God in the company of others. There is a profound wisdom in this. To walk together is to share not just a path, but a purpose. It is to create a temporary community, a mobile monastery, in which the journey itself becomes a crucible for spiritual growth and deep human connection.

To walk with others as a spiritual practice is very different from simply going for a hike with a group of friends. It is a practice that requires intention, structure, and a shared commitment to a spiritual purpose. It is not about covering a certain distance or reaching a particular destination. It is about creating a space in which God can be encountered in the landscape, in the silence, and in the faces of our fellow pilgrims.

A communal pilgrimage is a powerful practice that weaves together the threads of solitude, conversation, and shared worship.

THE RHYTHM OF THE WALK: WEAVING SOLITUDE AND CONVERSATION

A successful group pilgrimage is not a non-stop conversation. It is a carefully orchestrated dance between times of silence and times of sharing. Both are essential. The silence allows for individual reflection and a personal encounter with God in nature. The conversation allows for the sharing of those encounters, the building of community, and the weaving of individual stories into a common narrative.

A simple and effective structure for a communal walk is to alternate between periods of walking in silence and periods of walking in conversation.

For example, you might agree to walk the first twenty minutes in silence, then the next twenty minutes in conversation, and so on. This rhythm allows for a natural ebb and flow. The silence creates a space for each person to have their own experience, to notice what is stirring in their own heart, and to listen to the voice of God in the world around them. The conversation then becomes a time of harvest, a time to share the fruits of that silence.

"This is what I saw." "This is what I felt." "This is what I was reminded of."

This is very different from the kind of conversation we usually have when we walk with others. It is not idle chatter or gossip. It is a focused and intentional form of sharing, a kind of communal visio divina. We are helping one another see the world with spiritual eyes. We are bearing witness to how God is speaking to us through the Book of Nature. This kind of sharing is a profound act of community building. It creates a space of trust and intimacy, where we can share our spiritual lives without fear of judgment. It is the practice of anam cara expanded to the level of the small group.

THE FOCUS OF THE WALK: A SHARED INTENTION

A communal pilgrimage is more than just a walk; it is a prayer in motion. And like any prayer, it is helpful to have a focus, a shared intention. This intention can be straightforward. It might be a theme for reflection, a question to ponder, or a particular person or situation to hold in prayer. The leader or facilitator of the walk can propose an intention at the beginning of the journey, or the group can decide on one together.

Here are some examples of intentions for a communal walk:

• **A Walk of Gratitude:** The intention is to notice and to name the things for which you are grateful. During the conversation, each person shares something they saw on the walk that sparked a feeling of gratitude.

• **A Walk of Lament:** The group walks in solidarity with a particular suffering in the world—a war, a natural disaster, an injustice. The intention is to be present to the brokenness of the world and to offer that brokenness to God in prayer. The conversation might be a time to share feelings of grief, anger, or helplessness.

• **A Walk of Discernment:** The group is walking with a shared question or decision. It might be a question facing the community as a whole, or a common question that each member is wrestling with individually (e.g., "What is God calling me to let go of in this season of my life?"). The silence is a time of listening for guidance, and the conversation is a time of sharing the wisdom that emerges.

• **A Themed Walk:** The walk is focused on a particular spiritual theme, such as one of the seasons from the previous chapter, or one of the tree archetypes. For example, a "Birch Tree Walk" in the spring might be focused on the theme of new beginnings.

A shared intention gives the walk a sense of purpose and unity. It transforms a group of individuals into a community of pilgrims, walking together with a common heart and a common mind.

THE RITUAL OF THE WALK: CREATING SACRED SPACE ON THE MOVE

Even a simple walk can be made more sacred by including small, intentional rituals. These rituals help mark the walk as a special, set-apart time. They create a container for the spiritual experience.

• **The Threshold Prayer:** As we learned in the previous chapter, it is powerful to begin any pilgrimage with a prayer at the threshold. When walking as a group, you can gather in a circle at the starting point. The leader can state the intention for the walk, and then everyone can join in a simple prayer, either a set prayer or a spontaneous one.

• **The Reading of a Text:** At some point during the walk, perhaps at a beautiful stopping place, the group can pause to listen to a short reading. It could be a passage of scripture, a poem, or a reading from a Celtic prayer book. The text should be aligned with the purpose of the walk. After the reading, the group can stand in silence for a few minutes, allowing the words to sink in.

• **The Sharing Circle:** The heart of the communal pilgrimage is the practice of sharing. This can be done while walking, as described above, or in a more formal way by stopping at one or more points along the journey to gather in a circle. In a sharing circle, a simple talking piece (like a stone or a stick) can be used. Only the person holding the talking piece speaks. Everyone else listens with silent, loving attention. There is no cross-talk, no advice-giving, no discussion.

It is simply a space for each person to share what is on their heart. This is a powerful practice of deep listening and mutual respect.

• **The Blessing:** The walk should end as it began, with a prayer. Gather in a circle at the end of the path. The leader can offer a prayer of thanksgiving for the journey. Then you can provide a blessing for one another.

A beautiful and straightforward Celtic practice is for everyone to extend their hands toward the centre of the circle and to say together a prayer of blessing, such as the famous Celtic blessing:

"May the road rise up to meet you, may the wind be always at your back, may the sun shine warm upon your face, the rains fall soft upon your fields, and until we meet again, may God hold you in the palm of His hand."

To walk together in this way is to experience a taste of what the church is called to be: a pilgrim people, a community of friends, walking together through the beauty and the brokenness of this world, bearing witness to the presence of God in our midst, and encouraging one another on the journey home.

THE SACRED CIRCLE: CREATING A CELTIC CHRISTIAN SMALL GROUP

We have explored the beautiful and inspiring vision of community that the Celtic Christian tradition offers us. We have seen how the ancient monastic families were centres of faith, learning, and art, and how the practice of anam cara and communal pilgrimage can transform our relationships. But how do we translate this ancient vision into our modern lives? How do we move from being inspired by the idea of community to actually experiencing it?

This section is a practical guide to forming your own Celtic Christian small group, your own "community of the grove."

Many of us have had mixed experiences with small groups in a church context. They can sometimes feel forced, superficial, or overly structured. However, a small group founded on Celtic principles is distinct. It is not primarily a Bible study, a prayer group, or a social club, though it will contain elements of all three. It is a sacred circle, a small, committed group of fellow pilgrims who gather regularly to share their lives, to support one another on the spiritual journey, and to seek the face of God together. It is a modern-day expression of the *muintir*, the spiritual family.

Creating such a group does not require a charismatic leader or a complex curriculum. It requires a small group of willing souls, a shared commitment, and a simple, flexible structure. Here are some practical steps and principles for creating your own sacred circle.

1. The Invitation: Gathering the Circle

Everything begins with an invitation. The first step is to prayerfully consider who you might invite to join you on this journey. A Celtic small group is most effective when it is small, typically comprising three to eight people. This is large enough to provide a diversity of perspectives, but small enough to allow for real intimacy and for everyone to have a chance to share.

Who should you invite? Look for people with whom you already have a sense of connection and trust. Look for people who have a genuine hunger for a deeper spiritual life and a curiosity about the Celtic way. They need not be experts in Celtic Christianity. They need to have an open heart. It is often best to start with one or two other people, your potential *anam caras*, and to discern together who else to invite. Pray about it. Ask God to show you who belongs in this circle. Then, extend a simple, personal invitation.

Explain that you are hoping to form a small group to explore the spiritual path together, inspired by the wisdom of the Celtic tradition.

2. The Commitment: Setting the Container

Once you have a small group of interested people, the next step is to agree on a shared commitment. A sacred circle is not a drop-in group. It is a community that is built on trust and consistency. This requires a commitment from each member to be present, both physically and spiritually.

At your first gathering, have an open conversation about the shape of your commitment.

Here are some key things to discuss:

• **Frequency and Duration:** How often will you meet? Every two weeks is a good rhythm for many groups. How long will each meeting be? 90 minutes to 2 hours is usually sufficient.

• **Timeframe:** Agree to commit to meeting for a specific period of time, for example, for six months or a year. At the end of that period, you can re-evaluate and decide whether to continue. This creates a clear container and commits feel manageable.

• **Confidentiality:** This is absolutely essential. Agree as a group that whatever is shared in the circle stays in the circle. This creates the safety that is necessary for genuine vulnerability and honesty.

• **Shared Leadership:** A Celtic small group is not a class with a teacher. It is a circle of equals. While one person may need to act as a facilitator to manage time and guide the process, leadership should be shared. Different members can take turns leading the opening prayer, choosing a reading, or facilitating the sharing circle.

3. The Rhythm: A Simple Structure for Your Gatherings

A simple, predictable rhythm for your meetings can help to create a sense of sacred space and time. A good structure allows for both connection with God and connection with one another.

Here is a simple, three-part structure that you can adapt:

Part 1: The Gathering (Connecting with God)

Begin each meeting by consciously creating a sacred space. You might light a candle, have a moment of silence, or listen to a piece of contemplative music. Then, open with a prayer. This could be a prayer from a Celtic prayer book, a psalm, or a simple, spontaneous prayer. The goal of this first part of the meeting is to shift your attention from the busyness of your day and to centre yourselves in the presence of God. This is the "hearth" of your gathering.

Part 2: The Reading (Engaging with Wisdom)

Next, spend some time engaging with a piece of wisdom. This is not a heavy academic study, but a contemplative reading. You might choose a passage of scripture, a chapter from a book you are reading together (perhaps this one!), a poem, or the life story of a Celtic saint. Read the text aloud, slowly. Then, sit in silence with it for a few minutes. After the silence, you can have a time of open reflection. This is not a debate or a discussion, but a time for each person to share what resonated with them in the text.

A good way to frame this is to use the question: "What word or phrase in this reading is shimmering for you right now?"

Part 3: The Sharing (Connecting with One Another)

This is the heart of the gathering. It is time to practice anam cara in a group setting. The most effective way to structure this is as a sharing circle, as described in the previous section. Gather in a circle. Use a talking piece. Agree that only the person holding the piece speaks, and that everyone else listens with loving, non-judgmental attention. There is no feedback, no advice, no cross-talk.

The facilitator can propose a simple, open-ended question to guide the sharing. The question should be an invitation to share from the heart, not the head.

Good questions include:

• "How is your soul today?"

• "Where have you seen God at work in your life since we last met?"

• "What are you grateful for, and what are you struggling with?"

This practice of deep listening is one of the greatest gifts you can give to one another. It creates a space where people can be sincere, where they can share their joys and their sorrows, their doubts and their hopes, without fear. It is in this space of shared vulnerability that the bonds of true community are forged.

4. The Extension: Living as a Community

A sacred circle is more than just a meeting. It is a community that begins to spill out into the rest of your lives. Look for ways to extend your connection beyond your regular gatherings.

• **Go on pilgrimage together.** Use the practice of communal pilgrimage we explored in the last section. Go for walks together. The simple act of walking side by side can facilitate conversations that might not occur when you are sitting face to face.

• **Share meals together.** The breaking of bread has been a central act of Christian community since the very beginning. Sharing a simple meal together is a powerful way to build friendship and intimacy.

• **Serve together.** Find a way to serve others as a group. This moves your community from being purely inward-focused to being a source of blessing for the world.

• **Pray for each other.** Hold each other in prayer throughout the week. A simple text message or email can be a powerful way of reminding someone that they are not alone.

Creating a sacred circle is a beautiful and counter-cultural act.

It is a declaration that you are not meant to make this journey alone. It is a commitment to creating a small pocket of grace, of trust, and of love in a world that is often graceless, suspicious, and lonely. It is the practice of building the grove, not just in your own heart, but in the heart of a community.

HOSPITALITY AND THE HEARTH: WELCOMING THE STRANGER

A true community of the grove is not a closed circle. It is not a holy huddle, a private club for the spiritually elite. A healthy community, like a healthy tree, must be open to the world. It must have branches that extend to offer shelter and fruit to those in need. A Celtic Christian community is, by its very nature, hospitable. In this section, we examine one of the central and challenging virtues of the Celtic tradition: the radical practice of hospitality.

In the ancient Celtic world, hospitality was not just a social grace; it was a sacred duty. In a society where there were no hotels or inns, a traveller's life depended on the willingness of strangers to offer them food, shelter, and protection. To refuse hospitality to a traveller was one of the most shameful things a person could do. The ancient Irish laws, known as the Brehon Laws, had detailed regulations about the obligations of hospitality. Every person of a certain standing was required to have a guest house and to welcome anyone who came to their door, without asking their name or business until they had been fed and warmed by the fire.

This cultural value was enthusiastically embraced and deepened by the early Celtic Christians. They saw in the practice of hospitality a direct reflection of the Gospel. Did not Abraham and Sarah entertain angels unawares (Hebrews 13:2)? Did not Jesus himself say, "I was a stranger, and you welcomed me" (Matthew 25:35)? For the Celtic saints, to welcome the stranger was to welcome Christ himself. The guest was regarded as a sacrament, an outward sign of Jesus's presence. St. Brigid of Kildare, who was renowned for her extravagant hospitality, is said to have seen Christ in every guest who came to her door.

This is a profound and challenging vision. It calls us to move beyond our natural fear of the stranger and to see every person, especially the person who is most different from us, as a potential bearer of divine grace. It calls us to open not only our homes but also our hearts. What does this radical hospitality look like in our modern world? It is a practice that unfolds in three concentric circles: hospitality to the guest, hospitality to the stranger, and hospitality to the enemy.

HOSPITALITY TO THE GUEST: TENDING THE HEARTH

The practice of hospitality begins at home. It begins with the way we welcome those we have invited into our lives—our friends, our family, our fellow members of our sacred circle. It is the practice of creating a space where people feel not just entertained, but truly seen, heard, and cherished.

This kind of hospitality is not about having a perfect home, serving a gourmet meal, or impressing our guests with our cleverness. It is about something much simpler and much more profound. It is about presence. It is about putting away our distractions, turning off our screens, and giving the person in front of us the gift of our full, undivided attention. It is about listening with a generous heart. It is about creating a space of warmth, of safety, and of grace.

The hearth was the centre of the ancient Irish home. It was the place of warmth, of light, and of nourishment. To practice hospitality is to tend the hearth of our homes and our communities, to make them places where people can come in from the cold and find not only physical warmth but also the warmth of human connection and divine love. It is important to remember that when we share a meal, we are participating in a profoundly sacred act, an echo of the Last Supper, a foretaste of the heavenly banquet.

HOSPITALITY TO THE STRANGER: OPENING THE DOOR

The second circle of hospitality is more challenging. It is the practice of welcoming the stranger, the person we do not know. In our world, we are taught to be suspicious of the stranger. We are warned about "stranger danger." We lock our doors and avoid eye contact with people we pass on the street. However, the Celtic tradition and the Gospel itself call us to a different way.

To practice hospitality toward the stranger is to intentionally move beyond our circles of comfort and open ourselves to the lives of those who are different from us. This might take many forms. It might mean volunteering at a homeless shelter or a refugee centre. It might mean getting to know our actual neighbours, the people who live on our street. It might mean striking up a conversation with the person who serves us our coffee or checks out our groceries. It might mean joining a club or a group where we will meet people from different backgrounds, cultures, and belief systems.

This practice requires courage and humility. It requires us to set aside our stereotypes and prejudices. It requires us to be willing to be uncomfortable, to listen more than we speak, and to learn from those we might be tempted to dismiss. But the reward is immense. To welcome the stranger is to have our own world expanded. It is to discover the beautiful diversity of God's creation. And it is to discover, again and again, that in the face of the stranger, we can, if we have the eyes to see, catch a glimpse of the face of Christ.

HOSPITALITY TO THE ENEMY: THE ULTIMATE CHALLENGE

This is the third and most radical circle of hospitality. It is the one that takes us to the very heart of the Gospel. Jesus, in the Sermon on the Mount, gives us this breathtaking command: "Love your enemies and pray for those who persecute you" (Matthew 5:44). The Celtic saints took this command with utmost seriousness. There are many stories of the saints showing extraordinary kindness and forgiveness to those who had wronged them. St. Aidan of Lindisfarne was famous for his gentle and respectful engagement with the pagan kings of Northumbria. St. Columba is said to have prayed for the pirates who raided his monastery.

To practice hospitality to the enemy is the ultimate test of our faith. It is believed that no one is beyond the reach of God's love and that every person, no matter how broken or how hostile, is created in the image of God. This does not mean that we condone their actions or that we put ourselves in harm's way. It means that we refuse to return hatred for hatred. It means that we pray for their conversion and their well-being. It means that we hold open the possibility of reconciliation, no matter how remote it may seem.

In our deeply polarised world, where we are constantly encouraged to demonise those who disagree with us politically, religiously, or ideologically, this practice of hospitality to the enemy is more needed than ever. It is a powerful act of spiritual resistance. It is a witness to a different kind of kingdom, a kingdom in which enemies can become friends, the stranger is welcomed as a sibling, and every person is treated with the dignity of a beloved child of God.

The practice of hospitality, in all its forms, is the practical expression of a life lived in community. It is the way that our small, sacred circle opens itself to the needs of the world. It is the way that the love we have received from God and from our soul friends overflows to bless others. It is the way that our grove becomes a place of shelter, of healing, and of hope for a weary and fragmented world. It is the way that we, like the saints before us, learn to welcome Christ himself, disguised as the guest, the stranger, and even the enemy.

THE PRACTICE: A GROUP TREE WALK AND SHARING CIRCLE

My friends, we have explored the beautiful and challenging landscape of the Celtic Christian community. We have dreamed of the monastic family, the soul friend, and the open door of hospitality. Now, let us ground these ideas in a simple, embodied practice that you can do with your own sacred circle. This is a Group Tree Walk and Sharing Circle, a practice that weaves together our love for the trees, our practice of pilgrimage, and our commitment to walking together as a community of the grove.

This practice is an ideal activity for a Celtic small group, but it can also be done with a group of friends, a church committee, or even as a family. It is a wonderful way to get to know one another on a deeper level and to experience the presence of God in creation and in community. You will need about 90 minutes to two hours for the full practice.

1. The Gathering and the Invitation

Gather your group at the starting point of your chosen walk—a park, a forest trail, or even a tree-lined street. Stand in a circle. The facilitator for the day begins by welcoming everyone and creating a sacred space.

Facilitator: "Welcome, fellow pilgrims. Let us take a moment to arrive in this place. Feel the ground beneath your feet. Feel the air on your skin. Listen to the sounds around you. Let us take three deep breaths together, breathing in God's peace and breathing out the busyness of our day."

(The facilitator leads the group in three slow, deep breaths.)

Facilitator: "Today, we are going on a pilgrimage together. Our theme for this walk is 'The Trees of Our Lives.' We will be walking in silence for a time, and each of us is invited to find a tree that speaks to us, a tree that feels like a mirror of our own soul in this season of our lives. After our silent walk, we will gather to share the stories of our trees. Let us begin with a prayer."

(The facilitator or another member of the group can offer a prayer, such as this one:)

"God of the Grove, you who speak in the whisper of the leaves and who made your home on the wood of the Cross, we thank you for the gift of these trees and for the gift of this community. Open our eyes to see. Open our ears to hear. And open our hearts to receive the wisdom you have for us today. Jesus, our Anam Cara, walk with us now. Amen."

2. The Silent Walk: Finding Your Tree

Facilitator: "We will now walk in silence for the next 20 to 30 minutes. As you walk, I invite you to be attentive. Notice the trees around you. Don't search anxiously, but walk with a quiet heart, and allow a particular tree to choose you. It might be large or small, beautiful or broken. When you have found your tree, I invite you to pause with it. Use the practice of visio divina. Gaze upon it. Notice its details. Ask it, 'What do you have to teach me today?' Listen with your heart. After about 20 minutes, I will give a gentle signal, and we will all gather back at this spot."

The group now disperses and walks in silence. This is a time for individual contemplation. Each person finds their own tree and spends time with it, as we have practised in previous chapters. They are not just looking at a tree; they are looking for a mirror of their own inner state. One person might be drawn to a tall, strong Oak, feeling a sense of stability and strength in their life. Another might be drawn to a weeping Willow, feeling a sense of grief or sadness.

Another might be drawn to a tree that is scarred or broken, but still growing, a symbol of their own resilience. There is no right or wrong tree to choose. The important thing is the sense of personal connection.

3. The Sharing Circle: The Stories of the Trees

After the silent walking period, the facilitator signals (e.g., by a quiet bell or a soft call), and everyone returns to the starting point or another designated location. The group sits in a circle.

Facilitator: "Welcome back. We will now enter into a time of sharing. This is a sacred circle of listening. We will use this stone (or leaf, or stick) as our talking piece. Only the person holding the stone speaks. Everyone else has the great privilege of listening with a heart of love. We do not comment, ask questions, or offer advice. We simply receive the gift of each person's story. The question for our sharing is this: "Tell us about the tree you found and what it has to say about your life right now."

The facilitator begins by sharing about their own tree, modelling the personal and reflective sharing that is invited. Then, they pass the talking piece to the person next to them. The sharing continues around the circle.

This is the heart of the practice. As each person shares, a beautiful and intricate tapestry is woven. The stories of the trees become the stories of the people. The person who was drawn to the strong oak reports a newfound sense of purpose in their work. The person who was drawn to the weeping Willow shares about their grief over a recent loss. The person who was drawn to the broken tree shares about their journey of healing from a past wound.

In this space of deep, nonjudgmental listening, something sacred occurs. People feel seen and heard. The masks come off. The burdens are shared. The joys are multiplied. The group ceases to be a collection of individuals and becomes a true community, a muintir, a spiritual family. The trees have become the confessors, the spiritual directors, the *anam caras* for the group.

4. The Closing: A Circle of Blessing

After everyone who wishes to share has had a chance to do so, the facilitator takes the talking piece back.

Facilitator: "Thank you all for the gift of your stories. We have been in a sacred place. Let us take a moment of silence to hold all that has been shared in the heart of God."

(The group sits in silence for a minute or two.)

Facilitator: "Let us close our time together by offering a blessing to one another. Let us extend our hands toward the centre of our circle and pray together."

(All extend their hands and pray a blessing, such as the one from the previous section, or this one:)

"May the strength of the Oak be your foundation. May the wisdom of the Hazel be your guide. May the resilience of the Birch be your inspiration. May the hope of the Yew be your comfort. And may the blessing of the Three-in-One God, the God of the Grove, be with you now and always. Amen."

This simple practice is a powerful way to build a community of the grove. It is a practice that can be repeated in every season. Each time you do it, you will learn something new about the trees, about yourself, and about the people with whom you walk. You will discover that the grove is not just a place of solitude; it is a place of deep and life-giving communion.

CONCLUSION: THE GROVE IS A COMMUNITY

We began this chapter with a journey from the solitary grove of the individual heart to the shared life of the community. We have seen how the Celtic tradition offers us a rich and life-giving vision of what it means to be the people of God together. We have explored the monastic family, the soul friend, the communal pilgrimage, and the open-hearted welcome of hospitality. We have discovered that the spiritual journey is not a solo flight, but a shared pilgrimage, a walk we are meant to take in the company of friends.

But as we conclude this chapter, it is important to remember that the path of community does not replace the path of solitude. It fulfils it. A healthy spiritual life is not a choice between solitude and community. It is a rhythmic dance between solitude and community. We need both to be whole. We need the deep, personal connection with God that we find in the silence of our own hearts, and we need the love, support, and challenge of our fellow pilgrims to help us live out that connection in the world.

Think, once more, of the image of the grove. A grove is not a single, isolated tree. It is a community of trees, standing together. Their roots are intertwined beneath the soil, drawing nourishment from the same earth and sharing it. Their branches may touch, offering shade and shelter to each other and to the creatures that make their home among them. But each tree also stands alone. Each tree has its own unique shape, its own history, its own relationship with the sun and the wind. Each tree is both an individual and a member of a community.

This is a beautiful image of the Christian life. We are each called to be a strong, healthy, and unique tree, deeply rooted in the love of God. We must take responsibility for our own spiritual growth, for our own practices of prayer, and for our own relationship with our Creator. No community, no matter how wonderful, can do this for us. This is the work of solitude.

But we are also called to be part of a grove. We are called to intertwine our roots with our brothers and sisters in Christ, to draw strength from one another, and to share the nourishment we have received. We are called to offer the shade of our compassion and the fruit of our gifts for the good of the whole. We are called to stand together against the storms of life, protecting and supporting one another. This is the work of the community.

A spiritual life that is all solitude can become sterile, self-absorbed, and disconnected from the needs of the world. A spiritual life that is entirely communal can become shallow, busy, and devoid of deep personal conviction. The Celtic way is a way of balance, a way of rhythm. It is the rhythm of the monk who prays alone in his cell and then gathers with his brothers for the liturgy. It is the rhythm of the pilgrim who walks for miles in silence and then shares the story of her journey around the evening fire. It is the rhythm of the anam cara relationship, which honours both the sacredness of the individual soul and the holy bond that unites two souls in friendship.

My prayer for you, as you continue on your own pilgrim path, is that you will cultivate this holy rhythm in your life. I pray that you will find the courage to enter into the solitude of your own heart, to meet God in the silence and the stillness. And I pray that you will find the courage to reach out your hand to others, to build your own sacred circle, to become an anam cara to someone else, and to discover the profound joy of walking together.

For the grove is not a place of isolation. The grove is a community. And you, my friend, have a place within it.

You have a place to stand, a place to grow, and a place to belong.

You have a place in the great, green, and ever-growing forest of the people of God.

Chapter 13:

The Wounded Grove: Healing and Reconciliation with Creation

THE CRY OF THE LAND

My dear friend, we have walked a long and beautiful road together. We have learned to build a grove in our hearts, to walk the pilgrim's path, to dance to the rhythm of the seasons, and to share the journey with soul friends. We have, I hope, rediscovered a faith that is rooted, embodied, and communal.

But our journey is not yet complete. A faith that is truly rooted in the earth cannot ignore the fact that the earth itself is groaning. A spirituality that draws its wisdom from the grove cannot turn a blind eye to the fact that the groves of our world are being destroyed. We cannot, in good conscience, speak of the beauty of creation without also speaking of its brokenness. In this chapter, we must turn our faces toward a difficult and painful truth: the grove is wounded, and we, its keepers, have been complicit in its wounding.

We live in an era of an unprecedented ecological crisis. We see it in the headlines every day: rising temperatures, melting glaciers, raging wildfires, devastating floods, and the heartbreaking loss of countless species. We feel it in our bodies, in the air we breathe and the water we drink. The land itself is crying out.

The ancient Celts, who lived in such intimate communion with the natural world, would be horrified. They would see our modern way of life—our relentless consumption, our disposable culture, our exploitation of the earth's resources—as a form of madness, a profound spiritual sickness.

For too long, the Christian church has been either silent or, worse, complicit in this crisis. A distorted theology that viewed the earth as a mere backdrop for the drama of human salvation and interpreted the Genesis command to "have dominion" as a license to exploit has contributed to our current predicament. We have forgotten that we are not the owners of this earth, but its caretakers. We are not its masters, but its servants. We are, as the book of Genesis also tells us, the gardeners, placed in the garden "to work it and take care of it" (Genesis 2:15).

The Celtic Christian tradition offers us a powerful and timely corrective to this spiritual amnesia. It reminds us of a faith in which creation is not a thing to be used, but a sacrament to be revered. It is a faith that sees the presence of God shimmering in every leaf and every stone. It is a faith that recognises our own healing is inextricably bound to the healing of the earth. It is a faith that calls us not just to be admirers of creation, but to be its healers, its protectors, and its advocates.

This chapter will be a journey into the heart of this ecological calling. It will not be an easy journey. It will require us to face our own complicity in the wounding of the grove. It will require us to lament, to repent, and to change. But it will also be a journey of profound hope. It is a journey that will lead us to the foot of the Cross, where we will find a God who so loved the world—the cosmos—that he entered into its suffering in order to redeem it. It is a journey that will empower us to become, in our own small way, co-workers with Christ in the great project of the restoration of all things.

Our journey through this wounded grove will be structured as follows:

1. Introduction: The Cry of the Land: We will face the painful reality of the ecological crisis as a spiritual crisis.

2. The Celtic Vision of Creation: All Things Bright and Beautiful: We will rediscover the Celtic understanding of creation as sacred and filled with the presence of God.

3. The Fall of the Grove: Sin Against Creation: We will examine how our disconnection from creation is a form of sin.

4. The Cross in the Wounded Grove: Christ the Healer: We will explore how the Cross stands in solidarity with a suffering creation.

5. Becoming Healers: Practices of Ecological Reconciliation: We will learn practical ways to live in a more just and sustainable relationship with the earth.

6. The Practice: A Healing Walk and Act of Restoration: We will engage in a guided practice of lament, prayer, and practical action for the healing of a wounded place.

7. Conclusion: Hope for the Wounded Grove: We will ground ourselves in the Christian hope for the renewal of all creation.

This chapter is a call to action. It is a call to roll up our sleeves and to put our hands in the soil. It is a call to become the people of the grove in a new and deeper way—not just as contemplatives, but as healers; not just as pilgrims, but as restorers of the breach. It is a call to love the earth as God loves it, and to give our lives for its healing. For the whisper of the oak in our time is not just a whisper of peace; it is a cry for help.

THE CELTIC VISION OF CREATION: ALL THINGS BRIGHT AND BEAUTIFUL

Before we can understand the wounding of the grove, we must first remember its original beauty. Before we can become healers of the earth, we must first learn to see the earth as the Celtic saints saw it: not as a collection of resources to be exploited, but as a sacred icon, a living testament to the goodness and the glory of its Creator. The Celtic Christian tradition is one of profound and joyful immanence, the belief that God is not a distant, detached deity but a living, breathing presence who fills every corner of creation. To recover this vision is the first and most crucial step in our journey of ecological reconciliation.

This vision is beautifully captured in the famous hymn, "All Things Bright and Beautiful," written by the Irish poet Cecil Frances Alexander.

The lyrics of this hymn are a perfect summary of the Celtic view of nature:

All things bright and beautiful, All creatures great and small, All things wise and wonderful, The Lord God made them all.

For the Celtic Christians, the world was not a fallen, godless place. It was a place that was charged, as the poet Gerard Manley Hopkins would later write, "with the grandeur of God." They believed in what has been called the "Book of Nature." They believed that God had revealed Himself in two great books: the Book of Scripture and the Book of Creation. To learn to read the Book of Nature was to learn to see the fingerprints of God on every leaf, every stone, and every creature. The natural world was a source of theological insight, a primary means of knowing and loving God.

This belief is everywhere in the poetry of the early Celtic saints. St. Columba, the great missionary of Iona, was known for his deep love of nature.

A poem attributed to him contains these beautiful lines:

Delightful it is to stand on the peak of a rock, in the bosom of the isle, gazing on the face of the sea. That I might see its heavy waves over the glittering ocean, as they chant a melody to their Father on their eternal course.

For Columba, the waves of the sea were not just a natural phenomenon; they were a choir, singing a hymn of praise to their Creator. This is the heart of the Celtic vision. The world is not a silent, inanimate object. It is a vibrant, living community of praise. The wind is the breath of the Spirit. The sun is a symbol of Christ, the light of the world. The birds are a choir of angels. To walk through the world with Celtic eyes is to walk through a world that is alive with the presence of God.

This sense of the sacredness of creation was rooted in a deep understanding of the doctrine of the Trinity. The Celtic Christians had a strong sense of the distinct roles of each person of the Trinity in creation. God the Father is the transcendent source of all being, the one who spoke the world into existence. God the Son, the eternal Word, is the one through whom all things were made (John 1:3).

He is the inner logic, the pattern, the divine blueprint of creation. The beauty and the order of the natural world are a reflection of his mind. And God the Holy Spirit is the immanent, life-giving presence of God within creation, the one who "brooded over the waters" at the dawn of time (Genesis 1:2). The Spirit is the wild, untamed energy of God that animates all living things.

This Trinitarian understanding of creation has profound implications. It means that there is no such thing as "mere nature." Every part of creation is a gift from the Father, a reflection of the Son, and a dwelling place of the Spirit. To honour creation is to honour the Triune God who created it and who sustains it every moment.

This vision also gave the Celtic Christians a profound sense of kinship with all created things. They did not see themselves as separate from or superior to the rest of creation. They saw themselves as part of a great, interconnected family. They were fellow creatures, sharing a common home and a common Creator. This is beautifully expressed in the prayers and poems of the *Carmina Gadelica*, a collection of traditional Scottish Gaelic prayers and hymns. In these prayers, the people speak of "Brother Sun" and "Sister Moon," much like St. Francis of Assisi would later do. They saw the animals as their kin.

There are countless stories of the Celtic saints having deep and loving relationships with animals: St. Kevin of Glendalough allowing a blackbird to nest in his outstretched hand, St. Ciaran of Clonmacnoise making friends with a fox, a badger, and a stag.

These stories are not just charming fairy tales. They are expressions of a deep theological truth: that in Christ, the original harmony of creation is restored. They are a vision of a world in which humanity lives not as a tyrant but as a gentle and loving older sibling to the rest of creation. They are a reminder of our true vocation: to be the priests of creation, those called to gather the praises of all created things and to offer them back to God.

Finally, the Celtic vision of creation was a vision of thin places. The Celts believed that the veil between heaven and earth is thin. There are certain places and times when this veil is especially thin, when the spiritual world seems to break through into the physical world. These are the "thin places." A thin place could be a holy well, an ancient mountain, a remote island, or a quiet grove of trees. These were places where people went to pray, to seek healing, and to encounter the living God.

But in a deeper sense, the Celtic vision is that all of creation is a thin place. The whole world is a sacrament, a visible sign of an invisible grace. The whole world is a burning bush, filled with the fire of God's presence, if only we have the eyes to see and the humility to take off our shoes. To live the Celtic way is to live in constant expectation of encountering the holy in the ordinary, the divine in the everyday, the eternal in the midst of time.

This is the vision that we must recover if we are to become healers of the wounded grove. We must learn to see the world not as a commodity, but as a communion. We must learn to walk the earth not as its owners, but as its lovers. We must learn to listen, once again, to the song of the waves, the whisper of the trees, and the cry of the wild goose. For in these sounds, if we listen closely, we will hear the voice of the one who made them, the one who loves them, and the one who is calling us to love them too.

THE FALL OF THE GROVE: SIN AGAINST CREATION

To hold the beautiful Celtic vision of a world shimmering with the presence of God in one hand and the painful reality of our ecological crisis in the other is to experience profound dissonance. It is to ask the heartbreaking question: How did we get here? How did we fall from a state of communion with creation to a state of alienation and exploitation? How did the sacred grove become a wounded grove? The Christian tradition has a name for this kind of rupture, this broken relationship. It is called sin.

For too long, we have thought of sin in purely personal and individualistic terms. We have regarded it as a violation of the rules and a private matter between ourselves and God. However, the biblical understanding of sin is broader and more cosmic. Sin is not just a personal failing; it is a power, a force in the world that sets itself against the good purposes of God. It is the force of disintegration, of alienation, of death. And one of the most tragic and overlooked dimensions of sin is our sin against creation. It is the story of the Fall, not just of humanity, but of the entire grove.

This story begins, of course, in the Garden of Eden. In the Genesis story, the first humans are placed in a garden of delight, in perfect harmony with God and with all of creation. Their vocation is to be gardeners, to "work it and take care of it" (Genesis 2:15). But the serpent's lie tempts them, the lie that they can be "like God" (Genesis 3:5), that they can be the masters of their own reality, that they can take what they want without regard for the limits that God has set.

This act of disobedience, this grasping for a power that is not theirs to have, shatters the harmony of the garden. It results not only in their alienation from God but also from one another and from the earth itself. The ground is cursed, and they are driven out of the garden, into a world of toil and sorrow.

This is not just an ancient story. It is our story. It is the story of a humanity that has, again and again, chosen the path of the serpent. We have chosen to see ourselves as gods, as the masters of creation, rather than as its humble servants. We have chosen to believe the lie that the earth is just a collection of resources for us to use, to consume, and to discard as we see fit. We have chosen to live as if we are separate from and superior to the rest of creation, rather than as members of a great, interconnected family. This is the original sin against creation, and it has manifested in three key ways: pride, greed, and sloth.

THE SIN OF PRIDE: THE MYTH OF HUMAN SUPREMACY

The first sin against creation is the sin of pride, the sin of Adam and Eve in the garden. It is the belief that we are the centre of the universe, that the world revolves around us, and that all other created things exist solely for our benefit. This is the myth of human supremacy. It is a form of species-level narcissism.

This pride has been fueled by a distorted reading of scripture, particularly the command in Genesis 1:28 to "fill the earth and subdue it. Rule over the fish in the sea and the birds in the sky and over every living creature that moves on the ground." For centuries, this verse has been used to justify a relationship of domination and exploitation. But this is a profound misreading.

The Hebrew word for "rule" used here, *radah*, is the same word used to describe the rule of a wise and benevolent king, a shepherd-king who cares for his flock. Our calling is not to be tyrants, but to be viceroys, to rule the earth on God's behalf, with the same love, care, and justice with which God rules. Our dominion is meant to be a dominion of service, not a dominion of destruction.

Our pride has led us to see the natural world as an "it" rather than a "thou." We have disenchanted the world, stripping it of its sacredness and its intrinsic value. We have treated it as a machine to be engineered, a resource to be managed, and a commodity to be bought and sold. We have forgotten that we are but one small part of a vast and intricate web of life, and that our well-being is inextricably bound up with the well-being of the whole.

THE SIN OF GREED: THE INSATIABLE HUNGER FOR MORE

The second sin against creation is the sin of greed, or avarice. This is the insatiable desire for more—more wealth, more power, more pleasure, more stuff. It is the spiritual sickness of a consumer culture that is never content, always seeking the next purchase, the next experience, the next dopamine hit. Greed is a form of idolatry. It is the worship of the creature rather than the Creator. It is the attempt to fill the infinite longing of our hearts with finite things.

Our collective greed has fueled an economic system based on the untenable premise of infinite growth on a finite planet. This system requires us to extract resources at an unsustainable rate, to produce goods designed for disposal, and to foster a culture of perpetual dissatisfaction. We are clear-cutting ancient forests, strip-mining mountains, polluting our rivers and oceans, and driving countless species to extinction, all to feed our addiction to more. We are, as the prophet Isaiah wrote, those who "add house to house and join field to field till no space is left and you live alone in the land" (Isaiah 5:8).

The sin of greed has obscured the true meaning of abundance. True abundance is not found in the accumulation of possessions. It is found in the joyful reception of the gifts of God. It is found in the beauty of a sunset, the taste of fresh-picked berries, the sound of birdsong, and the love of friends and family. The Celtic saints, who often lived lives of radical material simplicity, were rich in this true abundance. They knew that the best things in life are not things. Our greed has made us spiritually impoverished amid our material wealth.

THE SIN OF SLOTH: THE FAILURE TO CARE

The third sin against creation is the sin of sloth, or acedia. This is not just laziness. It is a kind of spiritual apathy, a failure to care, a refusal to take responsibility. It is the sin of the priest and the Levite in the parable of the Good Samaritan, who saw the wounded man on the side of the road and "passed by on the other side" (Luke 10:31-32).

When it comes to the ecological crisis, many of us are guilty of the sin of sloth. We know that the earth is wounded. We see the evidence all around us. But the problem feels too big, too overwhelming, too inconvenient. We feel powerless to effect change. And so, we look away. We change the channel. We distract ourselves with the trivialities of our daily lives.

We tell ourselves that it is someone else's problem to solve—the government's, the corporations', the scientists'. We pass by on the other side.

This failure to care is a failure of love. It is a failure to love our neighbour, especially our poorest neighbours worldwide, who bear the brunt of the ecological crisis. It is a failure to love our children and our grandchildren, who will inherit the damaged world that we are creating. And it is a failure to love God, because we cannot claim to love the Creator while we are actively participating in the destruction of his creation.

To name our sin against creation is not to wallow in guilt. It is the first necessary step toward repentance and healing. It is to wake up from our slumber, to confess our pride, our greed, and our sloth, and to turn back to the God of the garden. It is to ask for forgiveness, not just from God, but from the earth itself and from the generations to come. And it is to ask for the grace to begin again, to learn once more what it means to be the humble and loving keepers of the grove.

THE CROSS IN THE WOUNDED GROVE: CHRIST THE HEALER

To confront the reality of our sin against creation is to stand in a place of profound grief and helplessness. We have wounded the grove, and we do not, on our own, have the power to heal it. If the story ended here, it would be a story of despair. But for the Christian, the story does not end with the Fall. It leads us to the Cross. It is at the foot of the Cross, the true Tree of Life, that we find the hope for the healing of our wounded world. The Cross is not just the symbol of our personal salvation; it is the symbol of God's cosmic reconciliation. It is a sign that God has not abandoned his creation but has entered into its suffering to redeem it.

This is a truth that the Celtic Christians understood deeply. As we saw in Chapter 8, they saw the Cross as the fulfilment of all three archetypes, the true World Tree that reconnects heaven and earth. But they also saw it as a profoundly ecological symbol. The Cross, made from the wood of a tree, stands in solidarity with a suffering creation. It is the ultimate symbol of God's love for the material world. The God who became incarnate in a human body, who lived and breathed and walked on this earth, is the same God who allowed his body to be nailed to a piece of wood, a piece of his own creation. In the Cross, God takes the violence, the brokenness, and the sin of the world into himself, and he transforms it into a source of life and healing.

This cosmic and ecological understanding of the Cross is rooted in the New Testament itself. The Apostle Paul, in his letter to the Colossians, writes of Christ: "For in him all things were created: things in heaven and on earth, visible and invisible... all things have been created through him and for him. He is before all things, and in him all things hold together... For God was pleased to have all his fullness dwell in him, and through him to reconcile to himself all things, whether things on earth or things in heaven, by making peace through his blood, shed on the cross" (Colossians 1:16-20).

This is a breathtaking vision. The work of the Cross is not just for humanity. It is for "all things." It is a work of cosmic reconciliation. The broken harmony of the garden is restored at the Cross. The alienation between God, humanity, and creation is overcome. The Cross is the great act of peace-making, the healing of the broken relationships that are the source of all our suffering. To be a Christian is to be a person of the Cross, and to be a person of the Cross is to be an agent of this cosmic reconciliation. It is to be a peacemaker, not just between people, but between people and the rest of creation.

Paul expresses this same idea in his letter to the Romans, in one of the most powerful and poignant passages in all of scripture:

"I consider that our present sufferings are not worth comparing with the glory that will be revealed in us. For the creation waits in eager expectation for the children of God to be revealed. For the creation was subjected to frustration, not by its own choice, but by the will of the one who subjected it, in hope that the creation itself will be liberated from its bondage to decay and brought into the freedom and glory of the children of God. We know that the whole creation has been groaning as in the pains of childbirth right up to the present time." (Romans 8:18-22)

Here, Paul personifies creation. He describes it as a conscious being that suffers, groans, and waits. It is suffering because of human sin. It has been "subjected to frustration," to a "bondage to decay." This is a perfect description of our ecological crisis. The earth is groaning under the weight of our pride, our greed, and our sloth. The clear-cut forests are groaning. The polluted rivers are groaning. The extinct species are groaning. The whole creation is in labour, awaiting the birth of something new.

And what is it waiting for? It is waiting for "the children of God to be revealed." It is waiting for us. It is waiting for the church to wake up and remember its true identity and vocation. We are the children of God, the heirs of the new creation. We are the ones who have been reconciled to God through the Cross. And because we have been reconciled, we are called to be agents of reconciliation. We are called to be the midwives of the new creation. We are called to work with God to help liberate creation from its bondage to decay and to bring it into the glorious freedom that is its birthright.

This is our ecological calling. It is neither new nor optional in the Christian faith.

It is at the very heart of the Gospel. To be a follower of Jesus is to be a healer of the wounded grove. It is to stand in solidarity with a suffering creation, to hear its groaning, and to respond with compassion and with action. It is to live our lives in such a way that we become a sign of hope for a wounded world, a foretaste of the new creation where the wolf will live with the lamb, the leopard will lie down with the goat, and "they will neither harm nor destroy on all my holy mountain, for the earth will be filled with the knowledge of the Lord as the waters cover the sea" (Isaiah 11:9).

This is the hope that the Cross offers us. It is not a cheap or an easy hope. It is a hope that is born out of suffering, a hope that looks the brokenness of the world square in the face and does not despair. It is the hope that the God who raised Jesus from the dead is at work in our world, bringing life out of death, healing out of brokenness, and a new creation out of the ruins of the old. It is the hope that the wounded grove can, and will, be healed. And it is the invitation to us, the children of God, to be a part of that healing.

Becoming Healers: Practices of Ecological Reconciliation

To be a person of the Cross is to be an agent of cosmic reconciliation. To be a child of God is to be a healer of the wounded grove. This is our high and holy calling. But what does it look like in practice? How do we move from the beautiful theology of ecological reconciliation to the nitty-gritty reality of our daily lives? The task can feel overwhelming. The forces of destruction are so large and so powerful, and we are so small. What difference can one person, one family, or one small community possibly make?

The answer is: more than we can possibly imagine. The kingdom of God, Jesus tells us, is like a mustard seed. It is the smallest of all seeds, but when it is planted, it grows into a great tree, and the birds of the air come and make their nests in its branches (Matthew 13:31-32). Every small act of healing, every choice to live more simply, more justly, and more lovingly, is a mustard seed. It is a sign of the new creation, a foretaste of the kingdom, a witness to the hope that is in us. We are not called to save the world. That is God's job. We are called to be faithful, to plant our mustard seeds, and to trust that God will make them grow.

So, what are some of these mustard seeds? What are the practical, everyday ways that we can begin to live as healers of the wounded grove? The journey of ecological reconciliation is a journey of a thousand small steps. It is a journey that involves our heads, our hearts, and our hands. It is a journey of learning, of loving, and of living differently.

Learning: The Education of a Healer

The first step in becoming a healer is to understand the nature of the wound. We cannot heal what we do not understand. This requires us to educate ourselves. We must be willing to learn about the ecological challenges facing our planet and our local communities. This is not always pleasant. It can be painful to read about the realities of climate change, plastic pollution, or habitat loss. But we cannot afford to look away. To be a healer is to be willing to look at the wound without flinching.

So, where do we begin?

• **Read.** Read books and articles about the ecological crisis from a variety of perspectives—scientific, economic, political, and theological.

• **Watch.** Watch documentaries that explore the beauty of creation and the challenges it faces.

• **Listen.** Listen to the voices of those most affected by environmental degradation—indigenous communities, low-income communities, and young people. Listen to the scientists who are studying the problems and proposing solutions. Listen to the theologians and spiritual leaders who are articulating a faith-based response.

• **Learn your place.** This is perhaps the most important and most Celtic way of learning. Get to know the place where you live. What is the name of the river that flows through your town? What are the names of the trees that grow in your local park? What is the history of the land on which your house is built?

To become a healer of a place, you must first become a student of that place.

You must fall in love with its unique beauty and become familiar with its unique wounds.

LOVING: THE MOTIVATION OF A HEALER

Information alone is not enough. We can have all the facts and figures about the ecological crisis, but if we do not have love, we will not be moved to act. The motivation of a healer is not guilt, or fear, or even a sense of duty. It is love. It is a deep, abiding, and compassionate love for God's creation. It is the love that we see in the Celtic saints, who saw every creature as their kin and every place as holy ground. This is a love that we must cultivate.

How do we grow in our love for creation?

• **Spend time in it.** This is the most essential practice of all. You cannot love what you do not know. Make it a regular practice to spend time in nature, not as a consumer or a tourist, but as a pilgrim. Walk, sit, listen, and observe. Use the *Visio Divina* practices we have learned. Allow yourself to be filled with a sense of wonder and awe. Let the beauty of creation capture your heart.

• **Lament.** To love something is to be willing to grieve its wounding. Allow yourself to feel the pain of the wounded grove. Do not be afraid of your anger, your sadness, or your fear. These are signs that you are paying attention. Lament is a form of prayer. It is a way of standing in solidarity with a suffering creation and crying out to God for healing. You can do this alone or with your sacred circle.

• **Give thanks.** Gratitude is the foundation of a loving relationship. Make it a daily practice to give thanks for the gifts of creation. Give thanks for the food you eat, the water you drink, the air you breathe, and the beauty that surrounds you. Gratitude opens our eyes to God's goodness and fuels our desire to protect the gifts we have been given.

LIVING DIFFERENTLY: THE WORK OF A HEALER

Love, if it is real, must lead to action. A faith that does not change the way we live is not genuine. To be a healer of the wounded grove is to make conscious, intentional choices to live in a way that is more gentle, more just, and more sustainable. This is the work of repentance, of turning our lives around. This work operates at three levels: personal, communal, and political.

• **Personal Choices:** We can begin by examining our own patterns of consumption. This is the practice of asking, "What is the story of the things I buy? Where did they come from? Who made them? What will happen to them when I am finished with them?" We can make small, incremental changes in our daily lives:

• **Reduce, Reuse, Recycle:** This is the classic environmental mantra, and it is still a good one. Reduce your consumption of single-use plastics. Reuse what you can. Recycle what you can't.

• **Eat Mindfully:** Pay attention to the food you eat. Where possible, choose food that is locally grown, organic, and seasonal. Reduce your consumption of meat, especially factory-farmed meat, which has a huge environmental impact.

• **Conserve Energy and Water:** Be mindful of your use of electricity and water. Turn off the lights. Take shorter showers. Drive less and walk, bike, or use public transport more.

• **Simplify:** Resist the siren song of consumer culture. Buy less stuff. Choose experiences over possessions. Discover the joy and the freedom of a simpler life.

• **Communal Action:** We are more effective when we act together. Your sacred circle can become a community of practice, a place to support and encourage one another in making these changes.

You can also work together on larger projects:

• Start a community garden.

• Organise a litter clean-up in your local park or river.

• Work with your church to make your building more energy-efficient and to incorporate creation care into your worship and education.

• Support local farmers and businesses that are committed to sustainable practices.

• **Political Engagement:** Many of the most significant environmental challenges we face cannot be solved by personal choices alone. They require systemic change. This means that we must also be engaged citizens. We must use our voices and our votes to advocate for policies that protect our common home.

• Stay informed about environmental issues and legislation.

• Contact your elected officials and let them know that you care about creation care.

• Support environmental organisations that are working for systemic change.

• Speak up. Use your voice in your church, your workplace, and your community to advocate for the Earth.

To become a healer is a lifelong journey. It is a journey of a thousand small steps. We will not do it perfectly. We will stumble and fail. But we are not alone. We are walking with Christ, the great Healer, and with a great cloud of witnesses, the saints who have gone before us. And we are walking with one another.

Let us, therefore, take the next small step, plant the next mustard seed, and trust that God will use our fumbling efforts to bring healing and hope to his wounded and beloved, and our wounded and beloved world.

THE PRACTICE: A HEALING WALK AND ACT OF RESTORATION

My dear friend, we have journeyed through some difficult territory in this chapter. We have looked at the wound of our world, and we have named our own complicity in it. This is heavy work. It can leave us feeling sad, angry, and overwhelmed. Now, it is time to take all that we have learned and all that we are feeling and to bring it into a concrete, embodied practice. This is a Healing Walk and Act of Restoration. It is a practice that you can do on your own or with your sacred circle. It is a way of bringing the healing power of the Cross to a small, wounded corner of God's creation.

This practice has three parts:

The Walk of Lament, The Prayer of Confession and Hope, and The Act of Restoration.

1. The Walk of Lament: Seeing the Wounds

The first part of this practice is to go on a walk with the specific intention of seeing the wounds of the earth. Choose a place in your local community that is in need of healing. It could be a polluted stream, a neglected park, a piece of waste ground, or even a street filled with litter. This is not a walk for seeing beauty. This is a walk for seeing brokenness.

As you walk, do so in silence. Pay attention. Notice the signs of disrespect and degradation. Notice the litter, the pollution, the graffiti, the dead or dying trees. Note the absence of birdsong and biodiversity. As you walk, allow yourself to feel the sadness of this place.

Do not rush to fix it or to explain it away. Be present to its woundedness. This is the practice of lament. It is a form of prayer, a way of sharing in the groaning of creation.

If you are doing this with a group, you can walk in silence for a set period (e.g., 20 minutes), then gather in a circle to share what you have observed and how you feel. Use a talking piece.

Let each person share a word or a phrase that describes the wound they have witnessed.

"I saw a plastic bag tangled in the branches of a tree." "I saw a stream that was brown and lifeless." "I felt a sense of hopelessness."

By sharing your lament, you are bearing witness together to the suffering of the earth.

2. The Prayer of Confession and Hope: Standing at the Cross

After the Walk of Lament, find a place to stand or sit together in the midst of this wounded place. This is the time to bring this brokenness to the foot of the Cross.

This is a prayer in two parts: confession and hope.

First, lead the group in a prayer of confession. Acknowledge your own part in the wounding of creation. This is not about shaming or blaming, but about taking responsibility. You can use a set prayer or pray spontaneously.

Here is an example:

"God of all creation, we stand before you in this wounded place, and we confess our sin. We confess our pride, which has led us to see ourselves as masters of the earth rather than its servants. We confess our greed, which has led us to consume more than our share and to value things more than we value you and your creatures. We confess our sloth, which has led us to look away from the wounds of the earth and to fail to act. Forgive us, we pray. Forgive us for the ways we have harmed this place and all places. Forgive us for our complicity in the groaning of creation. Have mercy on us, and have mercy on our wounded world."

After the prayer of confession, pause for a moment of silence. Then, move to a prayer of hope. This is the time to remember the promise of the Cross, the promise of cosmic reconciliation and the renewal of all things. Remind yourselves that the story does not end in brokenness.

It ends in healing.

Here is an example:

"God of the Resurrection, we stand before you in this wounded place, but we do not despair. We look to the Cross, the tree of life, and we find our hope. We thank you for not abandoning your creation, but for entering into its suffering to redeem it. We thank you that through Christ, you are reconciling all things to yourself. We place our hope in your promise to make all things new. We ask you to fill us with your Holy Spirit, the Spirit of life and renewal. Make us signs of your hope in this place. Make us agents of your healing. Give us the courage, the wisdom, and the love to become the healers of this wounded grove. Amen."

3. The Act of Restoration: Planting a Mustard Seed

Prayer must lead to action.

The final part of this practice is to engage in a small, concrete act of restoration. This is your mustard seed. It is a tangible expression of your prayer and your hope.

It is a way of saying, "We will not just talk about healing; we will be a part of it."

The restoration process should be appropriate to the context and your group's abilities.

Here are some ideas:

• **Clean up litter.** This is the simplest and most obvious act of restoration. Bring gloves and trash bags, and spend 30 minutes to an hour cleaning the area where you have been praying. As you pick up each piece of trash, you can offer a silent prayer of blessing for the land.

• **Remove invasive species.** If you are in a park or natural area, you may be able to collaborate with local authorities to remove invasive plants that are displacing native species. This is a powerful act of restoring a place's biodiversity.

• **Plant something.** If appropriate and permitted, plant a native tree, shrub, or wildflower. This is a beautiful and hopeful act, a sign of your commitment to the future flourishing of this place.

• **Create a small piece of beauty.** Even if you cannot do a large-scale restoration project, you can create a small moment of beauty. You could build a small cairn of stones as a memorial to the place's woundedness and a sign of your prayer for its healing. You could create a small nature mandala out of leaves, petals, and twigs. This is a way of offering a gift of beauty back to a place that has been dishonoured.

As you engage in your act of restoration, do so with a spirit of prayer and mindfulness. You are not just cleaning up a mess. You are tending the garden. You are participating in God's healing work. You are being the hands and feet of Christ in a wounded world.

When you have finished, gather one last time in a circle. Look at what you have done. It may be small, but it is not insignificant. It is a sign, a sacrament, a mustard seed. Close your time with a prayer of blessing for the land and for one another.

This practice of a Healing Walk and Act of Restoration is a powerful way to integrate the head, the heart, and the hands in our ecological calling. It is a way to move from despair to hope, from apathy to action, from being a part of the problem to being a part of the healing. It is a way to live out our identity as the children of God, for whom all creation is waiting in eager expectation.

CONCLUSION: HOPE FOR THE WOUNDED GROVE

We have walked a difficult path in this chapter. We have looked into the heart of the wound that afflicts our world, and we have named our own complicity in it. We have stood in the place of lament, and we have begun the slow, hard work of repentance and restoration. It would be easy, at the end of such a chapter, to feel overwhelmed, discouraged, or even hopeless. The scale of the ecological crisis is so vast, and our own small efforts can feel like a single drop of rain in a raging fire.

But we are people of the Resurrection. We are people of the empty tomb. We believe the story of the world does not end in death, but in life. As

Christians, our ecological activism is not fueled by a desperate, last-ditch effort to save a dying planet. It is fueled by a joyful and confident hope in the God who is, even now, making all things new. The final word is not destruction. The final word is redemption.

This is the hope beautifully depicted in the final chapters of the Bible. The book of Revelation ends not with a disembodied, spiritual heaven, but with a new heaven and a new earth. It is a vision of a renewed and transfigured creation, a world where God himself will come to dwell with his people. The story that began in a garden ends in a city, the New Jerusalem, but it is a city that is also a garden. Through the middle of the city flows the river of the water of life, and on either side of the river stands the tree of life, bearing twelve crops of fruit, and "the leaves of the tree are for the healing of the nations" (Revelation 22:2).

This is the ultimate vision of the healed grove. It is a world where the wounds of sin and death have been healed, where the nations are reconciled, and where all of creation flourishes in the life-giving presence of God. This is not a future we must build on our own. It is a future God has promised and is already bringing into being. The resurrection of Jesus from the dead is the down payment on this promise. It is the first fruits of the new creation, the sign that the long winter of our world is coming to an end and that an eternal spring is about to dawn.

Our work of healing and reconciliation, then, is not a desperate attempt to turn back the clock or to fix a broken world on our own. It is a joyful and hopeful participation in the work that God is already doing. Every time we choose to live more simply, every time we plant a tree, every time we raise our voice for justice for the poor and for the earth, we are not just performing a good deed. We are planting a signpost. We are establishing a small outpost of the new creation in the midst of the old. We are bearing witness to the truth that the kingdom of God is at hand. We are living as if the resurrection is true.

This is what it means to be a people of hope. It is not naive optimism to believe that everything will be okay. It is a rugged and resilient faith that God is faithful to his promises, even in the face of overwhelming evidence to the contrary. It is the faith of the farmer who plants a seed in the cold, dark earth, trusting that the sun and the rain will come and that life will, miraculously, emerge. It is the faith of the Celtic saints, who built their monasteries in the wild and desolate places, trusting that these places could become centres of light, of learning, and of life.

My prayer for you, my dear friend, is that you will be filled with this rugged and resilient hope. I pray that you will not be paralysed by despair, but that you will be energised by love. I pray that you will find the courage to take the next small step, to plant your own mustard seed of healing in the wounded grove of your own community. And I pray that you will do so with a joyful and confident heart, knowing that you are not alone. You are working with the grain of the universe. You are participating in the great, cosmic project of the Triune God. And you are a beloved child of the one who has promised, "Behold, I am making all things new" (Revelation 21:5).

Let us go forth, then, as people of hope. Let us go forth as healers of the wounded grove. And let us go forth with the song of the new creation on our lips, a song of praise to the Father who created the grove, the Son who redeemed it on the tree, and the Holy Spirit who is, even now, breathing new life into it.

Chapter 14:

The Grove in the City: Celtic Spirituality in Urban Life

Introduction: The Concrete Grove

My dear friend, we have spent a great deal of time in this book wandering through the green and beautiful landscapes of the Celtic world. We have walked through ancient forests, stood on lonely islands, and felt the sacred rhythm of the seasons. It is a beautiful and inspiring vision. But I am keenly aware that for many of you, this world may feel very far away. You may be reading these words not in a quiet cottage surrounded by a grove of trees, but in a high-rise apartment, a bustling coffee shop, or on a crowded commuter train. You may be thinking, "This is all very lovely, but what does it have to do with my life? How can I find the whisper of the oak in a world of concrete, steel, and glass?"

This is a vital question. For the majority of the world's population, most people now live in cities. If Celtic Christianity is to be a living tradition, not just a historical curiosity, it must speak to the reality of urban life. It must be a spirituality that can be practised not just in the wild and beautiful places, but in the messy, noisy, and often overwhelming reality of the modern city. This chapter explores that possibility. It is a journey to find the grove in the midst of the town or city, to discover that the sacred is not confined to the countryside, but can be found in the most unexpected of places.

It is easy to see the city as a spiritual wasteland. The city is often loud, chaotic, and anonymous. It is a place of commerce, of competition, and of constant stimulation. It can feel like a place that is cut off from the natural world, a place where it is difficult to hear the voice of God. In the previous chapter, we confronted the painful reality of the wounded grove—how human greed, exploitation, and disconnection have scarred creation. The city, with its concrete covering the earth and its consumption of vast resources, can seem to be the ultimate expression of that wounding.

And yet, the city is not beyond redemption. It is not outside the reach of God's love. The city has also always been a place of intense spiritual energy. The great religious movements of history have often been born and nurtured in cities. The early Christian church was an urban movement, spreading from city to city throughout the Roman Empire. The city, with its density of human life, its diversity of cultures, and its concentration of both human creativity and human suffering, is a powerful crucible for the spiritual life. The city, like all of creation, bears the wounds of human sin. But it is also a place that God loves, a place where millions of his children live, and therefore a place where we are called to be a healing presence. We do not romanticise the city, but neither do we abandon it.

The Celtic tradition, which we often associate with the rural and the wild, also has a profound and often overlooked urban dimension. The great Celtic monasteries were, in many ways, the first cities of Ireland, centres of population, of learning, and of culture. And the Celtic missionaries, like St. Columbanus, were not afraid to take their faith into the heart of the great cities of Europe. They knew that God is not just the God of the hills and the glens, but also the God of the marketplace and the crowded street.

In this chapter, we will follow in their footsteps. We will learn to see our cities not as spiritual deserts, but as potential groves, as places where God is present and at work. We will learn to find the "green in the grey," the moments of grace and beauty that are hidden in the midst of the urban landscape. We will explore how to sanctify our work, how to build community in the crowd, and how to walk the city streets as a form of pilgrimage.

Our journey will be structured as follows:

1. Introduction: The Concrete Grove: We will address the challenge and the promise of practising a nature-based spirituality in an urban context.

2. The Celtic Saints in the City: Historical Precedents: We will explore the often-overlooked urban dimension of the Celtic Christian tradition.

3. Finding the Green in the Grey: Urban Thin Places: We will learn to recognise the sacred spaces that are hidden in our cities.

4. The Office as Monastery: Sanctifying Work: We will apply the Celtic rhythm of work and prayer to our modern professional lives.

5. Community in the Crowd: Building Urban Sacred Circles: We will explore the unique challenges and opportunities of building community in a transient and anonymous urban world.

6. The Practice: An Urban Tree Walk: We will engage in a guided practice of finding and honouring the trees of our city.

7. Conclusion: Every Place is a Thin Place: We will embrace the truth that God's presence is not limited to the beautiful and the wild, but can be found everywhere, even in the heart of the city.

This chapter is an invitation to a new way of seeing your city. It is an invitation to fall in love with the place where you live, not for what you wish it were, but for what it is. It is an invitation to discover that the whisper of the oak can be heard not just in the forest, but in the rustle of a single tree in a city park, in the kindness of a stranger on the subway, and in the quiet longing of your own heart. It is an invitation to find the grove, and to find God, right where you are.

THE CELTIC SAINTS IN THE CITY: HISTORICAL PRECEDENTS

To practice Celtic spirituality in the city is not to invent something new. It is to recover a lost part of our own tradition. While we rightly associate the Celtic saints with the wild, beautiful, and remote landscapes of Ireland, Scotland, and Wales, we often forget that they were also pioneers of urban mission. They were not afraid of the city. They saw it as a place of opportunity, a place where the Gospel could be planted and where new communities of faith could take root. By looking back at their example, we can find inspiration and guidance for our own urban pilgrimage.

The Monastic "City"

First, it is important to remember that the great Celtic monasteries were themselves a form of city. Places like Clonmacnoise in Ireland, Iona in Scotland, and Llandaff in Wales were not quiet, isolated hermitages. They were bustling centres of population, commerce, and culture. They were often larger and more influential than the secular settlements of their time. The

Irish word for a monastery is cathair, which is also the word for a city. For the early Irish, the monastery was the city.

These monastic cities were laid out to reflect a sacred geography. At the centre was the church, the spiritual heart of the community. Around it were the cells of the monks, the scriptorium where manuscripts were copied, the workshops of the artisans, the guesthouse for pilgrims, and the fields and gardens that sustained the community.

It was a fully integrated world, a place where the sacred and the secular, work and prayer, solitude and community were held together in a creative tension. This vision of a sacred city, a city centred on the presence of God and ordered toward the flourishing of all its members, is a powerful model for our own thinking about urban life.

St. Columbanus: The Pilgrim in the City

Perhaps the greatest example of a Celtic saint who was at home in the city is St. Columbanus. Born in Ireland in the 6th century, Columbanus was a monk who was seized by the spirit of peregrinatio, the wandering pilgrimage for the love of Christ. He left his homeland and, with a small band of companions, travelled across Europe, founding monasteries in what is now France, Switzerland, and Italy.

Columbanus was not a country hermit. He was a sophisticated intellectual, a gifted poet, and a fearless prophet who spoke truth to power. He engaged with kings and bishops and founded his monasteries near the major urban centres of his day. His most famous monastery, Luxeuil in France, became one of the most important centres of learning and culture in all of Europe.

Columbanus demonstrates that Celtic spirituality is not a fragile, delicate flower that can only survive in pristine wilderness. It is a robust and adaptable faith that can be transplanted into new and challenging environments. He did not try to recreate a perfect copy of an Irish monastery in the heart of Europe. He adapted the principles of Celtic monasticism to a new context. He shows us that the core values of Celtic Christianity—a deep love of scripture, a commitment to community, a rhythm of prayer and work, and a passion for mission—can be lived out anywhere, even in the heart of a bustling and often hostile city.

St. Aidan: The Gentle Evangelist

Another powerful example is St. Aidan of Lindisfarne. In the 7th century, Aidan was sent from the monastery of Iona to be a missionary to the pagan kingdom of Northumbria in northern England. The king, Oswald, gave him the island of Lindisfarne as a base for his mission, but Aidan did not stay on his holy island. He was a tireless traveller, a pilgrim bishop who walked the roads of his diocese, engaging with people from all walks of life.

The historian Bede, in his Ecclesiastical History of the English People, provides a vivid portrait of Aidan. He tells us that Aidan was a man of great humility, gentleness, and compassion. He was not a fiery preacher who condemned the pagan culture of the Northumbrians. He was a patient and respectful listener who sought to find common ground and to build relationships of trust. Bede reports that Aidan would often enter the royal court and engage the king and his nobles in conversation. But he was equally at home with the poor and the marginalised. He would often use the money that was given to him by the rich to buy the freedom of slaves.

Aidan's approach to mission was deeply incarnational. He did not stand apart from the culture he was trying to reach. He entered into it. He learned the language, he respected the customs, and he loved the people. He shows us that to be a Christian in the city is not to retreat into a holy ghetto, but to be a gentle and loving presence in the midst of the city's life. It is to be a person who is willing to cross boundaries, to build bridges, and to see the image of God in every person, regardless of their rank or their beliefs.

Lessons from the Urban Saints

What can we learn from these urban saints? They teach us several important lessons for our own practice of Celtic spirituality in the city.

1. Adaptability: They teach us that our faith must be adaptable. We cannot simply try to import a rural, nature-based spirituality into the city without modification. We must be creative and discerning, finding new ways to live out the ancient principles in a new context.

2. Engagement: They teach us that we are called to be engaged with the life of our city, not to retreat from it. We are called to be a leaven in the lump, a light in the darkness. This means being informed about the issues facing our city, being involved in our local communities, and being a voice for justice and compassion.

3. Incarnation: They teach us that our mission is to be incarnational. We are called to be the hands and feet of Christ in our cities. This means being present to the people around us, listening to their stories, sharing their joys and their sorrows, and serving their needs.

4. Hope: Above all, they teach us that the city is not a godless place. It is a place filled with the presence and promise of God. Our task is not to bring God to the city, but to discover where God is already at work and to join in.

To be a Celtic Christian in the city is to be a Columbanus, a pilgrim who is not afraid to venture into new and challenging territory.

It is to be an Aidan, a gentle and compassionate presence who builds bridges of love and respect. It is to be a builder of monastic cities, a creator of small oases of prayer, of community, and of peace in the midst of the urban jungle. It is a high calling, but, as the saints have shown us, it is not impossible.

FINDING THE GREEN IN THE GREY: URBAN THIN PLACES

To be a Celtic Christian in the city is to be a seeker of thin places.

In Chapter 9, we explored the practice of recognising sacred space in our local environment—those places where the veil between heaven and earth seems especially thin. We learned that these thin places can be found in a particular tree, a bend in a river, or a quiet park.

We must now ask: how does this practice of seeking thin places assume a distinct character in the urban context? In the countryside, thin places are often obvious: an ancient stone circle, a holy well, a majestic mountain peak. But where are the thin places in the city? How do we find the green in the grey, the sacred in the midst of the secular? It requires us to adapt what we have learned, to train our spiritual senses to perceive the presence of God in the urban landscape, where the sacred often hides in unexpected ways.

An urban thin place is any place where the love, the beauty, or the justice of God becomes tangible. It is a place where we are reminded of our connection to God, to one another, and to the earth. These places are all around us, hidden in plain sight. We have only to open our eyes and our hearts to them. Let us explore some of the forms that these urban thin places might take.

The City Park: The Urban Grove

The most obvious thin place in any city is the city park. These green oases are the lungs of the city, places where we can go to breathe, to rest, and to reconnect with the natural world. A city park is a curated grove, a place where nature and culture meet. It may not be a wild and untamed wilderness, but it is a place where we can encounter the beauty and the resilience of creation.

To treat a city park as a thin place is to enter it not as a consumer of recreation, but as a pilgrim. It is to walk its paths with reverence and attention. It is to see its trees not just as landscaping, but as living beings, each with its own story and its own wisdom. It is to listen to the birdsong, to feel the wind on your face, and to give thanks for this gift of green in the midst of the grey. Your local park can become your urban grove, your place of prayer, of contemplation, and of renewal.

The Community Garden: The New Eden

A community garden is a particularly powerful kind of urban thin place. It is a place where a neglected parcel of land has been transformed into a source of life and nourishment. It is a modern-day Eden, a place where people are once again living out their vocation as gardeners, working the earth and caring for it.

A community garden is a place of resurrection. It is a sign that life can spring forth from the most unlikely of places. It is a place of community, where people from different backgrounds come together to share in the work and the harvest. It is a place of justice, where fresh, healthy food is made available to those who might not otherwise have access to it. To spend time in a community garden, to put your hands in the soil, to talk to the people who are tending it, is to experience a powerful foretaste of the new creation.

The Wayside Shrine: The Unexpected Holy Place

Urban thin places are not always green. They can be found in the most unexpected of locations. A wayside shrine is any small, often unofficial, place that has been set aside for prayer or remembrance. It could be a mural of a saint on the side of a building, a collection of candles and flowers left at the site of a tragic accident, or a small, lovingly tended statue of Mary in someone's front yard.

These wayside shrines are powerful reminders that the sacred is not confined to our official religious buildings. They are expressions of a grassroots spirituality, a testament to the enduring human need to connect with the holy in daily life. When you encounter one of these places, do not rush by. Pause for a moment. Read the inscriptions. Say a prayer. Make a small offering of a flower or a silent blessing. These are places where the heart of the city is made visible, where its joys and its sorrows are brought before God.

The Library and the Museum: The Keepers of the Story

The Celtic tradition has long been characterised by learning and storytelling. The ancient monasteries were the great libraries and museums of their time, preserving the wisdom of the past for the future. In our own time, the public library and the art museum can be powerful urban thin places.

A library is a sanctuary of silence and of knowledge. It is a place where the voices of generations are gathered, waiting to speak to us. To sit in the quiet of a library, to hold a book in your hands, is to participate in a sacred act of communion with the past and the future. An art museum is a temple of beauty. It is a place where we can encounter the human capacity for creativity, for imagination, and for transcendence. To stand before a great work of art is to have a thin place experience, to be lifted out of the ordinary and into a realm of wonder and of awe.

The Place of Suffering: The Urban Calvary

Some thin places are not beautiful or peaceful. They are places of suffering. They are the urban Calvaries, the places where the world's brokenness is most painfully visible. A homeless shelter, a soup kitchen, a hospital emergency room, a prison, a place of protest against injustice—these are all thin places. They are thin because they are places where Christ is present in a special way. Jesus tells us that whatever we do for the "least of these," we do for him (Matthew 25:40). When we enter into these places of suffering, when we are present to the pain of our brothers and sisters, we are meeting Christ.

These are not easy places to be. They challenge our comfort and our complacency. But they are essential places for the urban pilgrim. They are the places where our faith is tested and where our compassion is deepened. They are the places where we are reminded of the cost of discipleship and the radical love of the God who emptied himself and took on the form of a servant.

To find the green in the grey is to train our spiritual eyes to see the world as God sees it. It is to see the potential for holiness in every place and in every person. It is believed that our cities, for all their brokenness, are beloved by God and are filled with the seeds of the new creation. Our task as urban pilgrims is to find those seeds, to water them with our prayers, and to help them grow.

THE OFFICE AS MONASTERY: SANCTIFYING WORK

For many of us who live in cities, the place where we spend the majority of our waking hours is not a park or a garden, but an office. Our days are filled not with the rhythm of the seasons, but with the rhythm of meetings, emails, and deadlines. It can be easy to feel that our work life is completely separate from our spiritual life, that we leave God at the door when we enter the office and pick him up again on our way out. However, the Celtic tradition offers a different perspective. It is a vision of an integrated life, a life in which work and prayer are not two separate activities, but two dimensions of a single, consecrated life. It is the office's vision as a monastery.

This may sound like a strange and even impossible idea. The modern office, with its focus on productivity, competition, and profit, seems to be the very antithesis of a monastery. But the heart of Celtic monasticism was not the place, but the rhythm. It was the rhythm of ora et labora, prayer and work. The monks did not see their work as a distraction from their prayer, but as a form of prayer itself. They believed that any work, no matter how humble, could be sanctified and offered to God as an act of worship. This is a revolutionary idea, and it has the power to transform our experience of work.

To see the office as a monastery is to see it as a place of spiritual practice. It is to see our colleagues not just as co-workers, but as fellow members of a community. It is to see our daily tasks not merely as a means of earning a living, but as a way to serve God and our neighbour. How can we begin to cultivate this vision? It begins with creating a personal "rule of life" for our workday, a simple set of practices that can help us stay centred and connected to God amid our busy lives.

The Morning Offering: Consecrating the Day

Your monastic workday begins before you even arrive at the office. It begins with a morning offering. As you wake up, before checking your email or social media, take a few moments to consecrate your day to God.

You can use a simple prayer like this one, adapted from the Carmina Gadelica:

"God, bless me this day. Bless to me my work and my rest. Blessed to me my colleagues and my clients. Bless me with my hands and my mind. God, bless to me this day."

This simple act of consecration changes everything. It frames your workday not as a series of tasks to be completed, but as a gift to be received and to be offered back to God. It reminds you that you are not alone, but that God is with you, in you, and working through you.

The Commute as Pilgrimage: The Journey to the Monastery

For many of us, the daily commute is a source of stress and frustration. However, it can also be a form of pilgrimage, a sacred journey to our workplace. Whether you are walking, biking, driving, or taking public transport, you can use this time to prepare your heart and mind for the day ahead.

If you are walking or biking, pay attention to the world around you. Notice the sky, the trees, the faces of the people you pass. Offer a silent blessing for your city. If you are on a bus or a train, resist the temptation to distract yourself with your phone. Look out the window. Listen to a piece of sacred music. Read a psalm or a short passage of scripture. If you are driving, you can listen to a spiritual podcast or drive in silence, offering the time to God. The commute is a threshold, a liminal space between home and work. By treating it as a pilgrimage, you can arrive at your office centred, peaceful, and ready to serve.

The Cubicle as Cell: Creating a Sacred Workspace

Your desk, your cubicle, or your office is your monastic cell. Just as we created a Cill, a sacred cell in our homes (Chapter 9), we can also sanctify our workspace as a kind of monastic cell. It is the place where you will do your sacred work. Take a few moments to make this space a place of prayer. You don't need to build a full-scale altar, but you can have a few small, simple reminders of the sacred.

• A small, beautiful stone or shell that you found on a walk.

• A postcard of a favourite piece of sacred art.

• A single flower in a small vase.

• A short, handwritten prayer or verse of scripture taped to your computer monitor.

These small objects are not just decorations. They are anchors. They are focal points for your attention. When you feel stressed or distracted, you can glance at your sacred object and take a deep breath, remembering that you are in the presence of God.

The Rhythm of the Hours: Weaving Prayer into the Day

In Chapter 9, we examined the ancient practice of sanctifying time through the hours—Lauds at dawn, Sext at midday, and Vespers at evening. The Celtic monks structured their entire day around this rhythm of prayer, the Liturgy of the Hours. They would pause at regular intervals to pray, to recenter themselves, and to remember the presence of God. Here, we adapt that principle to the specific context of the modern workplace. We may not be able to stop for a full prayer service every three hours, but we can create a simple rhythm of "prayer pauses" that honour the spirit of the hours while fitting into the realities of our work environment.

• **The Morning Pause (9:00 AM):** As you begin your work, take one minute to pray for the day ahead. Pray for wisdom, for patience, and for a spirit of service. Pray for your colleagues and for the people you will serve through your work.

• **The Midday Pause (12:00 PM):** Before you eat your lunch, pause for a moment of gratitude. Give thanks for your food, for your work, and for the gift of life. You can use the traditional grace or a simple prayer of your own.

• **The Afternoon Pause (3:00 PM):** The afternoon can often be a time of low energy and distraction. Take a moment to stand up, to stretch, and to offer a simple "breath prayer." As you breathe in, say a name for God (e.g., "Jesus"). As you breathe out, say a simple petition (e.g., "have mercy"). This simple practice can help to clear your mind and to re-centre your heart.

• **The End-of-Day Pause (5:00 PM):** Before you leave your office, take a moment to review your day with God. This is a simplified version of the Prayer of Examen. Give thanks for the moments of grace and of joy. Ask for forgiveness for the moments when you failed to love. Offer all of your work, your successes and your failures to God.

This simple rhythm of prayer pauses can transform your workday.

It can weave a thread of sacredness through the most ordinary of days, reminding you that every moment is an opportunity to encounter the living God.

The Meeting as Council: Seeing Christ in the Other

One of the most challenging parts of any workday is the meeting. Meetings can often be a source of conflict, ego, and wasted time. But they can also be a place of encounter, of collaboration, and of shared wisdom. The Celtic monastic tradition placed strong emphasis on the council, the community's meeting to discern the will of God.

To see the meeting as a council is to enter it with a spirit of prayer and of humility. It is to see your colleagues not as competitors, but as fellow seekers of the truth. It is to listen respectfully to every voice, believing that the Holy Spirit can speak through anyone. It is to seek consensus rather than victory. It is to practice the art of holy conversation. Before your next meeting, take a moment to pray for a spirit of wisdom, of charity, and of peace.

To see the office as a monastery is not to escape from the realities of the modern workplace. It is to engage with them in a new way. It is believed that our work, no matter how secular it may seem, can be a path to holiness. It is thought that the whisper of the oak can be heard even over the hum of the fluorescent lights. It is to believe that our daily labour can be a prayer, a sacrament, and a participation in the creative and a participation in the creative and redemptive work of God.

COMMUNITY IN THE CROWD: BUILDING URBAN SACRED CIRCLES

One of the great paradoxes of modern urban life is that millions of people surround us, yet we often feel profoundly alone. We live in a state of "lonely crowdedness," sharing sidewalks and subways with countless strangers but rarely forming deep, lasting connections. The city, for all its energy and excitement, can be a place of profound anonymity and isolation. This is perhaps the greatest spiritual challenge for the urban pilgrim.

In Chapter 12, we explored the principles of building a sacred circle—a community rooted in the Celtic vision of the monastic family, soul friendship, and shared pilgrimage. We learned about the importance of intentionality, rhythm, hospitality, and vulnerability. These principles are universal, but they must be adapted to address the unique challenges of urban life. The question before us is not whether to build community, but how to do so in a context that appears designed to prevent it. How do we create sacred circles in the midst of the transient and anonymous urban crowd?

It is not easy. The city presents a unique set of challenges to the formation of an authentic community. The sheer anonymity of urban life means that we can go through our days without really knowing or being known by anyone. The transience of many urban populations means that just as we begin to build a connection, our friend may move to a new apartment, a new job, or a new city. The sheer busyness of our lives, filled with long commutes and demanding careers, can leave us with little time or energy for the slow, patient work of building relationships. And the privatisation of our lives, lived out in individual apartments and curated online profiles, can make it difficult to find spaces for genuine, face-to-face encounters.

But the challenges are not insurmountable. The human heart was made for community, and the Holy Spirit is at work in our cities, drawing people together. To build a sacred circle in the city requires us to be intentional, creative, and courageous. It requires us to adapt the ancient principles of Celtic community to our modern urban context.

Intentionality: The Art of the Invitation

In a small village, a community may happen organically. In a large city, it rarely does.

The urban community must be intentional. It begins with an invitation. It begins with one person having the courage to say to another, "I would like to share this journey with you."

Who do you invite into your sacred circle? It may be a friend from church, a colleague from work, a neighbour from your apartment building, or someone you met in a coffee shop. The key is to be open to the surprising connections that God is making in your life. Don't wait for the "perfect" group of people. Start with one or two others who share a similar longing for a deeper spiritual life.

The invitation can be simple: "I've been reading this book about Celtic spirituality, and I was wondering if you'd be interested in getting together to talk about it." Or, "I'm trying to build a more regular rhythm of prayer in my life. Would you be willing to be my prayer partner?"

Rhythm: Finding a Sacred Time in a Busy Schedule

Once you have a small group, the next step is to establish a rhythm. In a busy and chaotic urban world, a regular, predictable meeting schedule is essential. It creates a sense of stability and commitment. Your group might decide to meet weekly, bi-weekly, or monthly. The important thing is to choose a rhythm that is sustainable for everyone and to stick to it.

You will also need to be creative about finding a time to meet. The traditional 7:00 PM weeknight meeting may not accommodate individuals with long commutes or family responsibilities. You might consider a morning meeting before work, a lunchtime gathering, or a weekend brunch. The key is to find a time that feels like a sacred pause in the midst of the week, a time to breathe, to connect, and to be renewed.

Hospitality: The Apartment as Monastery

The Celtic tradition places a high value on hospitality. But how do you practice hospitality when you live in a small apartment? Urban hospitality is not about having a large and impressive space. It is about creating a warm and welcoming atmosphere. It is about the spirit of generosity and acceptance.

Your sacred circle can meet in one another's apartments, rotating from week to week. This is a beautiful way to practice hospitality and to enter into one another's lives. The host doesn't need to provide an elaborate meal. A simple pot of tea and a plate of biscuits is more than enough. The focus is not on entertaining, but on creating a safe and sacred space for sharing. If meeting in homes is not possible, you can find a quiet corner of a coffee shop, a public library meeting room, or even a corner of a city park on a nice day. The place is less important than the quality of your presence.

Vulnerability: The Antidote to Anonymity

The greatest gift that a sacred circle can offer in an anonymous city is a space for vulnerability. It is a place where we can take off our masks, where we can share our true selves, our joys and our sorrows, our hopes and our fears, without fear of judgment. In a world of curated online personas, this is a radical and life-giving act.

To create this kind of space, the group must commit to maintaining confidentiality, practising respectful listening, and avoiding judgment. Using a talking piece can be a helpful practice, ensuring that each person has an opportunity to speak and to be heard. The questions you discuss should be open-ended and focused on the heart. "Where did you see God at work in your life this week?" "What are you struggling with?" "What are you grateful for?" By sharing our stories, we break down the walls of our isolation, and we discover that we are not alone.

The Neighbourhood as Parish: Blooming Where You Are Planted

Finally, an urban sacred circle can help us to redefine our understanding of "parish." For many of us, our parish is the church we drive to on Sunday morning. But in the Celtic tradition, your parish is the geographical area where you live. It is your neighbourhood. Your sacred circle can become a community that is committed to being a loving and prayerful presence in your specific corner of the city.

You can walk the streets of your neighbourhood together, praying for the people and the places you see. You can volunteer at a local school or a homeless shelter. You can support your local businesses. You can organise a neighbourhood block party or a community clean-up day. By rooting your spiritual practice in the concrete reality of your neighbourhood, you begin to see it not as a random collection of buildings, but as a sacred grove, a place that God loves and to which you are called to be a blessing.

Building community in the crowd is not easy, but it is essential. It is the antidote to the loneliness and the anonymity of modern urban life. It is a powerful witness to a different way of being human, one rooted in love, vulnerability, and mutual care. It is the way of the sacred circle, the way of the Celtic saints, and the way of Jesus himself, who called a small group of friends to share his journey. For in the end, the grove is not a place you find, but a community you build, a community you build, one intentional, courageous, and loving relationship at a time.

THE PRACTICE: AN URBAN TREE WALK

My dear friend, it is time to put on our walking shoes and to take our urban pilgrimage out onto the streets. In Chapter 10, we learned the practice of the Celtic Tree Walk, in which participants seek out trees that embody the sacred archetypes of Oak, Ash, Yew, and Rowan. We now adapt this practice to the city's unique landscape.

This Urban Tree Walk is a way of weaving together all the threads of this chapter. It is a way of finding the green in the grey, of treating the city as a sacred text, and of honouring the presence of God in the most overlooked and yet most noble of our urban neighbours: the city tree.

Trees in the city are miracles of resilience. They grow in cramped and often polluted conditions, their roots navigating a hidden world of pipes and cables. They are living symbols of hope, of life, and of a wildness that cannot be entirely tamed. To go on an urban tree walk is to go on a pilgrimage of gratitude, to pay homage to these silent witnesses to the life of our city. You can do this practice on your own or with your sacred circle.

1. Preparation: The Pilgrim's Intention

Before you begin your walk, take a moment to set your intention. Find a quiet place on a park bench or a doorstep, and take a few deep breaths. Remind yourself that this is not just a walk to get from one place to another. It is a sacred journey. You are a pilgrim, and the city is your cathedral.

Offer a simple prayer of intention.

You might pray:

"God of the city and of the grove, open my eyes to see your beauty in this place. Open my ears to hear the whisper of the oak in the midst of the city's noise. Open my heart to feel your presence in the trees that share this city with me. Make this walk a prayer, and make me a blessing to this place. Amen."

2. The Walk: Seeking the Trees

Now, begin to walk. Your destination is not a place, but a series of encounters. Your goal is to find and honour three different trees. Walk slowly, at a pilgrim's pace. Pay attention to the world around you. Notice the details that you usually rush past.

As you walk, be on the lookout for trees. Don't just look in the parks and the green spaces. Look for the single tree growing in a tiny square of dirt in the sidewalk. Look for the row of trees planted along a busy street. Look for the old, gnarled tree in a churchyard or a cemetery. Let the trees find you. Be open to the ones that seem to call to you.

When you find your first tree, stop. This is your first station on your urban pilgrimage.

3. The Encounter: The Three Stations

At each of your three trees, you will engage in a simple three-part practice of Observing, Reflecting, and Blessing.

Station 1: The Tree of Resilience

• Find a tree that is growing in a difficult place. It might be a tree whose roots are buckling the sidewalk, or a tree that is hemmed in by buildings and power lines. This is your Tree of Resilience.

• Observe: Spend a few minutes simply observing this tree. Notice its shape, its bark, its leaves. Notice the signs of its struggle and the signs of its life. How has it adapted to its difficult environment? What does its very existence in this place say to you?

• Reflect: Reflect on the resilience of this tree. It is a living symbol of life's capacity to persist under the most challenging circumstances. Where in your own life do you need this kind of resilience? What challenges are you facing that require you to dig your roots down deep and to keep on growing?

• Bless: Place your hand on the trunk of the tree (if you can do so without looking too strange!) and offer a silent prayer of blessing. Give thanks for its resilience and for its witness. You might pray: "God of all life, I thank you for this tree. Thank you for your strength, your patience, and your stubborn refusal to give up. May its resilience inspire me in my own struggles. Bless this tree, and bless all who pass by it. Amen."

Station 2: The Tree of Community

• Find a tree that is a gathering place. It might be a large, shady tree in a park where people are sitting, or a tree outside a coffee shop or a school. This is your Tree of Community.

• Observe: Watch the life that is happening around this tree. Who is gathered here? What are they doing? How is this tree serving as a silent host, a provider of shade and of beauty? Notice how the tree creates a space for community to occur.

• Reflect: Reflect on the role of this tree as a centre of community. It is a living symbol of the importance of rootedness, of shelter, and of shared space. Where in your own life do you find this kind of community? Who are the people who gather with you under the branches of a shared life? Give thanks for them.

• Bless: Offer a prayer of blessing for this tree and for the community that gathers around it. You might pray: "God of all community, I thank you for this tree. Thank you for the gift of its shade and its beauty. Thank you for the way it brings people together. Bless this tree, and bless all who find rest and fellowship in its presence. May my own life be a source of shelter and of community for others. Amen."

Station 3: The Hidden Tree

• Find a tree that is hidden or overlooked. It might be a small, young tree in a back alley, or a tree in a neglected corner of a park. This is your Hidden Tree.

• Observe: This tree may not be as majestic as the others, but it is no less precious in the eyes of God. Notice its smallness, its vulnerability. Observe the details of its leaves and bark. See it not as a weed, but as a beloved child of God.

• Reflect: Reflect on the hiddenness of this tree. It is a symbol of all that is small, overlooked, and marginalised in our world. It is a reminder of the God who sees and loves those whom the world ignores. Where in your own life do you feel hidden or overlooked? Who are the hidden people in your city that you are called to see and to love?

• Bless: Offer a prayer of blessing for this hidden tree. You might pray: "God of the hidden and the small, I thank you for this tree. Thank you for its quiet and faithful life. Forgive me for the times I have failed to see the beauty in the small and the overlooked. Help me to see the world, and the people in it, with your eyes of love. Bless this tree, and bless all that is hidden and precious in this city. Amen."

4. The Return: Carrying the Grove in Your Heart

After you have visited your three trees, it is time to return. As you walk back, do so with gratitude. You have been on a pilgrimage. You have encountered the sacred in the midst of the city. You have found a grove in the concrete jungle.

When you return home, take a moment to journal about your experience. What did you see? What did you feel? What did you learn? How might this practice change the way you see your city?

This Urban Tree Walk is a simple practice, but it can be profound. It is a way of training your eyes to see the green in the grey, to find the thin places in the midst of your daily life. It is a way of remembering that the whisper of the oak can be heard anywhere, if only we have the ears to hear it. It is a way of carrying the grove in your heart, so that every walk can become a pilgrimage, and every street can become a sacred path.

CONCLUSION: EVERY PLACE IS A THIN PLACE

We began this chapter with a question: How can we live a Celtic, nature-based spirituality in a world of concrete, steel, and glass? We have wandered the streets of our cities, seeking an answer. We have found it in the example of the urban saints, in the hidden beauty of urban thin places, in the sanctification of our daily work, and in the courageous building of community in the crowd. The answer, my dear friend, is both more straightforward and more profound than we might have imagined. The answer is that the city itself is a grove. The city itself is a thin place.

The great Celtic theologian John Scotus Eriugena, writing in the 9th century, made a radical claim. He said that "every visible and invisible creature is a theophany, or appearance of God."

A theophany is a manifestation of the divine. What Eriugena was saying is that everything—every tree, every stone, every person, every star, every city—is a place where God is revealing himself to us. The whole world is a burning bush. The whole world is a thin place. The question is not whether God is present. The question is whether we are paying attention.

This is the ultimate gift of a Celtic Christian spirituality for urban life. It is a spirituality that trains us to pay attention. It is a spirituality that gives us new eyes to see the sacred in the midst of the ordinary. It teaches that we need not leave the city to find God. We can find God right where we are, in the glorious, messy, beautiful, broken, and beloved reality of our urban lives.

To live this way is to become a "contemplative in the city." It is to be a person who is deeply engaged in the life of the world, but who is also deeply rooted in the presence of God. It is to be a person who can hear the whisper of the oak over the roar of the traffic. It is to be a person who can see the image of God in the face of a stranger on the subway. It is to be a person who can find a moment of sabbath rest in the midst of a frantic workday. It is to be a person who knows, in their bones, that the ground beneath their feet, whether it is soft earth or hard concrete, is holy ground.

This is not a spirituality of escape. It is a spirituality of incarnation. It is a spirituality that takes seriously the stunning truth that God so loved the world, the whole world, the urban world and the rural world, the beautiful world and the broken world, that he became a part of it. He became a human being, a citizen of a particular place and a particular time. He walked the dusty streets of first-century Palestine.

He ate and drank with friends. He worked with his hands. He knew the joys and the sorrows of a fully human life. And in his resurrection, he did not abandon this world. He affirmed it. He redeemed it. And he promised to be with us in it, always, to the very end of the age.

My prayer for you, as we conclude this chapter, is that you will fall in love with your city. I pray that you will see it not as a place to be endured, but as a place to be embraced. I pray that you will become a student of its stories, a connoisseur of its hidden beauties, and a healer of its wounds. I pray that you will find your own urban grove, your own sacred circle, your own rhythm of prayer and of work. And I pray that you will, in your own unique and beautiful way, become a thin place in your city, a person through whom the love, the beauty, and the justice of God become tangible for others.

For the great secret of the Celtic saints is this: the thin place is not ultimately a location. It is a way of being. It is a heart that is open, an attentive mind, and a life that is consecrated to the God who is not far from any one of us, the God in whom we, and our cities, live and move and have our being.

Chapter 15:

The Grove Through the Seasons of Life: Celtic Spirituality for the Human Journey

The Seasons of the Soul

My dear friend, we have come to the final chapter of our journey together in this book. We have explored the sacred archetypes of the trees, we have stood at the foot of the Cross as the true Tree of Life, and we have learned to cultivate a grove in our hearts, in our homes, and in our communities. We have learned to walk as pilgrims through the world, marking the rhythm of the seasons in the great Wheel of the Year. Now, we turn to the most intimate landscape of all: the landscape of our own lives. For each human life is itself a sacred journey, a pilgrimage through its own unique seasons.

In Chapter 11, we explored how our spiritual practice can be enriched by aligning ourselves with the great cycle of the seasons in the natural world. We saw how winter, spring, summer, and autumn can become our teachers, guiding us into a deeper understanding of the mysteries of death, resurrection, growth, and wisdom. Now, we will apply that same framework to the seasons of our own souls. Our lives, like the year, have their own spring of new beginnings, their own summer of growth and fruitfulness, their own autumn of maturity and letting go, and their own winter of ageing and of death.

Celtic spirituality is not a faith that is detached from the realities of human life. It is a deeply embodied and earthy spirituality that honours the sacredness of every stage of the human journey. It does not shy away from the messiness, the joy, the sorrow, and the beauty of a life lived in a human body. It provides us with rituals, prayers, and a way of seeing that can help us navigate the significant transitions of our lives with grace, courage, and a deep sense of God's presence.

In this final chapter, we will walk through the seasons of a human life, from the cradle to the grave, and we will discover how the wisdom of the Celtic tradition can be a lamp to our feet and a light to our path.

We will explore:

1. Introduction: The Seasons of the Soul: We will frame the human life as a pilgrimage through four great seasons, each with its own unique spiritual tasks and gifts.

2. Spring: Birth, Baptism, and New Beginnings: We will look at the season of childhood and youth, exploring the Celtic understanding of birth, the practice of baptism, and the celebration of new beginnings.

3. Summer: Growth, Marriage, and Fruitfulness: We will explore the season of adulthood, with its challenges of growth, its celebration of love and marriage, and its call to a life of fruitful service.

4. Autumn: Maturity, Wisdom, and Letting Go: We will look at the season of mid-life and beyond, exploring the journey into a deeper wisdom, the grace of letting go, and the beauty of a mature faith.

5. Winter: Ageing, Death, and the Ars Moriendi: We will confront the final season of our lives, exploring the spiritual gifts of ageing and the Celtic art of dying well (ars moriendi).

6. The Practice: A Ritual for Life Transitions: We will learn a simple, adaptable ritual for marking the major passages of our lives in a sacred and meaningful way.

7. Conclusion: The Eternal Spring: We will end our journey by looking beyond the winter of death to the Christian hope of resurrection and the promise of an eternal spring.

This chapter invites you to view your own life story as a sacred text, a story written by the hand of God. It is an invitation to honour the season you are in, with its unique challenges and beauty. And it is an invitation to trust that the God who guides the great dance of the cosmos is also guiding the small and precious dance of your own life, leading you, season by season, home to himself.

Spring: Birth, Baptism, and New Beginnings

The human journey begins in spring. It is the season of birth, of childhood, and of youth. It is a time of wonder, of vulnerability, and of explosive growth. Like the natural world in springtime, the young human person is a miracle of new life, a bundle of potential awaiting its unfolding. The Celtic tradition, with its deep reverence for the sacredness of creation, offers a profound understanding of the first season of our lives.

The Sacredness of Birth

In the modern world, we have often medicalised birth, treating it as a clinical procedure rather than a sacred event. But for the Celtic Christians, the birth of a child was a theophany, a manifestation of God. It was a moment when the veil between the worlds was drawn back, and a new soul, fresh from the hand of God, entered into the world. The prayers and blessings for childbirth in the Carmina Gadelica are filled with a sense of awe and wonder. They speak of the child as a "jewel of God," a "gift from the King of all."

This reverence for the sacredness of birth has profound implications for how we view children. It means that every child, regardless of the circumstances of their birth, is a beloved child of God, bearing the divine image. It means that childhood is not just a waiting room for adulthood, but a sacred season in its own right, a time of unique spiritual sensitivity and openness. Jesus himself reminded us of this when he said, "Let the little children come to me, and do not hinder them, for the kingdom of heaven belongs to such as these" (Matthew 19:14). To be a Celtic Christian is to see the face of God in the face of a child, and to treat every child with the reverence and the tenderness that is due to a messenger from the heavenly court.

Baptism: The Soul's Anointing

The central ritual of this springtime of life is baptism. In the Celtic tradition, baptism was not just a legalistic washing away of original sin. It was a rich and multi-layered sacrament, an anointing of the soul for the journey of life. It was a moment of incorporation into the great family of the church, the community of the grove.

The Celtic practice of baptism was often a full immersion, a symbolic drowning and rising again that powerfully enacted the mystery of dying and rising with Christ. The water of baptism was seen as a holy well, a place of healing and of new life. The anointing with oil was a sign of the Holy Spirit, a setting apart of the person for a life of sacred service. The giving of a new white garment symbolised the new identity the person had received in Christ.

But perhaps the most distinctive feature of Celtic baptism was the Caim, or encircling prayer. The priest or parent would circle the child with their finger or a staff, praying that God's protection surround the child on every side. This beautiful and powerful ritual is a tangible expression of the belief that from the very beginning of our lives, we are held and protected in the loving embrace of God. The Caim is a prayer that can be used not only at baptism but also at any time of transition or danger, a reminder that we are never outside the circle of God's love.

The Anam Cara and the Nurturing of the Soul

In the Celtic tradition, the spiritual formation of a child was not the responsibility of parents alone, but of the whole community. The concept of the Anam Cara, the soul friend, was central to this process. Every child would have a godparent, an Anam Cara who was chosen to be a spiritual guide and mentor for the child. This was not just a ceremonial role. The Anam Cara was expected to take an active and ongoing interest in the child's spiritual life, to pray for them, to teach them the stories of the faith, and to be a model of Christian living.

This practice is a powerful reminder that we are not meant to walk the spiritual path alone. We need wise and trusted companions to guide us, to encourage us, and to hold us accountable. In our time, we can revive this practice by intentionally cultivating intergenerational relationships in our churches and communities. We can be Anam Caras to the young people in our lives, and we can seek out older and wiser mentors for ourselves.

The Blessing of the Senses

The Celtic tradition has a deep appreciation for the goodness of the created world and for the body as a vehicle for spiritual experience. The spiritual formation of a child, therefore, was not just about teaching them doctrines and prayers. It was about awakening their senses to the presence of God in the world around them. It was about teaching them to see the beauty of a flower, to hear the music of the birdsong, to feel the warmth of the sun on their skin, and to taste the goodness of the food that God provides.

The Carmina Gadelica is filled with prayers for the blessing of the senses. There are prayers for waking in the morning, for washing the face, for lighting the fire, and for going to bed at night. These simple, daily prayers helped to cultivate a sacramental imagination, a way of seeing the whole world as being charged with the grandeur of God. We can use these prayers with our own children, or we can create our own simple blessings for the ordinary moments of our day. By doing so, we can help nurture in ourselves and in our children a sense of wonder, gratitude, and the nearness of God.

The spring of life is a time of immense grace and of profound importance. It is the time when the foundations of our spiritual lives are laid. By embracing the Celtic vision of the sacredness of birth, the power of baptism, the wisdom of the Anam Cara, and the blessing of the senses, we can help to ensure that the children in our lives, and the child within our own hearts, are given a firm and beautiful foundation upon which to build a life of faith.

SUMMER: GROWTH, MARRIAGE, AND FRUITFULNESS

If spring is the season of new beginnings, summer is the season of growth, of strength, and of fruitfulness. It is the time of adulthood, when the potential of our youth begins to bear fruit in the world. It is a season of great energy, of great passion, and of great responsibility. The Celtic tradition, with its deep connection to the rhythms of the land, offers us a rich vision for this vibrant and demanding season of our lives.

The Call to Growth

Summer in the natural world is a time of incredible growth. The trees are in full leaf, the fields are green, and the sun is at its height. In the same way, the summer of our lives is a time for us to grow into the fullness of who we are created to be. This is not just a matter of professional advancement or of accumulating possessions. It is a matter of spiritual growth, of deepening our relationship with God, and of cultivating the fruits of the Spirit: love, joy, peace, patience, kindness, goodness, faithfulness, gentleness, and self-control (Galatians 5:22-23).

The Celtic tradition offers us a powerful model for this kind of growth in the figure of the peregrini, the wandering saints. These men and women left the comfort and security of their homes to embark on a journey of faith, trusting in God to provide for them. Their pilgrimage was not merely a physical journey but also a spiritual one. It was a process of stripping away all that was false and inessential, and of discovering their true identity in Christ. In the summer of our lives, we are all called to be peregrini in our own way. We are called to leave behind the childish things, to embrace the challenges and the uncertainties of the journey, and to grow into the spiritual maturity that is our birthright.

The Sacredness of Marriage

For many people, the summer of life is also the season of falling in love and of entering into the covenant of marriage. In the Celtic tradition, marriage is regarded as a sacred and holy vocation. It is not just a social contract, but a sacrament, a visible sign of an invisible grace. It is a path to holiness, a way in which two people can help each other to grow in love for God and for one another.

The Celtic understanding of marriage is beautifully expressed in the concept of the Anam Cara, the soul friend. While the Anam Cara relationship is not limited to marriage, it finds its most profound expression in the lifelong commitment of two people to one another. To be an Anam Cara to your spouse is to be a true spiritual friend, a companion on the journey who knows you, who loves you, and who is committed to your spiritual well-being. It is to create a relationship that is a "thin place," a place where the love of God is made tangible and real.

The traditional Celtic wedding ceremony was filled with rich and beautiful symbolism. The couple would often be married near a holy well or a sacred tree, a sign that their love was rooted in God's life-giving power. The exchange of rings was a symbol of their enduring love and of God's encircling protection. The handfasting ceremony, in which the couple's hands were tied with a ribbon, was a powerful visual representation of their two lives being bound as one.

These ancient traditions can inspire us to see our own marriages in a new and deeper way. They can remind us that marriage is not just about romance, but about a shared spiritual path. They can challenge us to be true Anam

Caras to our spouses and to support and encourage one another in the life of faith.

The Call to Fruitfulness

Summer is the season of fruitfulness. The purpose of all the growth of the spring and the summer is to produce a harvest. In the same way, the summer of our lives is a time when we are called to bear fruit for the kingdom of God. This fruitfulness can take many different forms.

For some, it will mean raising children. In the Celtic tradition, children are seen as a precious gift from God, a sign of his blessing. The role of a parent is a sacred trust, a calling to nurture and to guide a new generation in the ways of faith. The prayers for children in the Carmina Gadelica are characterised by a deep sense of love and responsibility, asking for God's protection and guidance for the child at every stage of their life.

But fruitfulness is not limited to the raising of children. We can also be fruitful in our work, creative pursuits, and service to others. The Celtic tradition has a deep respect for the work of the artisan, the poet, and the scholar. It sees all honest work as a form of co-creation with God, a way of bringing more beauty, more truth, and more goodness into the world. In the summer of our lives, we are called to find the work that is ours to do, the unique contribution that we are called to make to the world. We are called to offer our gifts and our talents in the service of God and of our neighbour, and to find our joy in a life of fruitful service.

The summer of life is a season of great blessing and of great challenge. It is a time of growth, of love, and of service. By embracing the Celtic vision of the wandering pilgrim, the soul friend, and the fruitful life, we can navigate this season with grace and with purpose, and we can produce a harvest that will be a blessing to the world.

AUTUMN: MATURITY, WISDOM, AND LETTING GO

After the vibrant and energetic season of summer, we enter the autumn of our lives. This is the season of maturity, of midlife and beyond. In the natural world, autumn is a time of harvest, of brilliant colour, and of a slow and graceful letting go. It is a season of great beauty, but also of a certain melancholy, as the days grow shorter and the air grows colder. The Celtic tradition, with its keen sensitivity to the cycles of nature, offers us a profound wisdom for navigating this rich and complex season of the soul.

The Harvest of Wisdom

Autumn is the season of the harvest. It is the time when we reap the fruits of all the labour of the spring and the summer. In the autumn of our lives, we also experience a kind of harvest. It is the harvest of wisdom. The experiences of our lives, our joys and our sorrows, our successes and our failures, have all been tilling the soil of our souls. In the autumn of life, we have the opportunity to reap a harvest of wisdom, of a deeper understanding of ourselves, of God, and of the world.

The Celtic tradition has a deep reverence for the elder, the wise person who has journeyed through the seasons of life and reached a place of deep, settled peace. The saints of the Celtic Church were often sought out for their wisdom and for their ability to offer guidance or comfort. They were the "salmon of wisdom," who had swum the long and arduous journey up the river of life and had tasted the hazelnuts of wisdom that fall into the well of Segais.

In our own youth-obsessed culture, we have often lost this reverence for the wisdom of age. We see ageing as a problem to be solved, a decline to be managed. But the Celtic tradition reminds us that the autumn of life is not a time of decline, but a time of ripening. It is a time when we can become who we were always meant to be, when we can finally let go of the false selves that we have constructed and can rest in our true identity as beloved children of God.

The Grace of Letting Go

One of the most beautiful and poignant aspects of autumn is the shedding of the leaves. The trees, in a final, glorious blaze of colour, shed the leaves that have sustained them throughout the summer. This act of letting go is not a sign of death, but of a deep and ancient wisdom. The tree knows that it must let go of the old to make way for the new. It must enter into a period of rest and of dormancy in order to gather its strength for the spring to come.

In the autumn of our lives, we are also called to a process of letting go. We are called to let go of our youthful ambitions, of our need to prove ourselves, of our attachment to our physical strength and beauty. We are called to let go of our children as they leave home to begin their own lives. We are called to relinquish our roles and identities that have defined us for so long. This process of letting go can be painful. It can feel like a series of small deaths. But it is also a path to a new and deeper freedom. It is the path of kenosis, of self-emptying, that is central to the Christian life.

As we let go of all that we have been clinging to, we discover that our hands are now open to receive a new gift. It is the gift of a deeper and more intimate relationship with God. It is the gift of peace that is independent of our circumstances. It is the gift of joy that is found not in doing, but in being.

The Beauty of a Mature Faith

The faith of our youth is often a faith of passion, of certainty, and of clear-cut answers. It is a beautiful and necessary stage of the journey. But as we move into the autumn of our lives, our faith is often called to mature, to become more nuanced, more compassionate, and more comfortable with mystery. The easy answers of our youth may no longer satisfy us. We may find ourselves wrestling with doubt, ambiguity, and the painful questions of suffering and injustice.

This is not a sign that we are losing our faith. It is a sign that our faith is growing. The Celtic tradition offers a model of mature faith in the figure of the "holy hermit," the one who has withdrawn into the wilderness to seek God in solitude. The hermit is not a person who has all the answers. They are a person who has learned to live with the questions. They are a person who has learned to be still and to listen for the still, small voice of God in the silence.

The autumn of life is a time when we are invited to cultivate our own inner hermit. It is a time to create more space for silence, for solitude, and for contemplation. It is a time to read the scriptures not for information, but for transformation. It is a time to be in the presence of God, without any agenda or any need to perform. It is in this place of quiet and of stillness that we discover the beauty of a mature faith, a faith that is less about having all the answers and more about resting in the loving arms of the One who is the Answer.

The autumn of life is a season of profound beauty and of deep spiritual opportunity. It is a time to harvest the wisdom of our lives, to embrace the grace of letting go, and to cultivate the beauty of a mature and contemplative faith. It is a season that prepares us for the final journey into the winter of our lives, and for the eternal spring that lies beyond.

WINTER: AGEING, DEATH, AND THE ARS MORIENDI

We come now to the final season of our earthly pilgrimage: the winter of our lives. It is the season of old age, of diminishment, and of our final journey into death. In contemporary Western culture, which is often obsessed with youth and vitality, winter is a season we fear and deny. We do everything we can to hold it at bay, to pretend that it will not come for us. But the Celtic tradition, with its honest and earthy wisdom, invites us to a different path. It invites us to embrace the winter of our lives as a sacred season, a time of unique spiritual opportunity, and a final preparation for the eternal spring that awaits us.

The Spiritual Gifts of Ageing

In the Celtic world, the elder was not a figure of pity, but of reverence. The elders were seen as the keepers of the stories, the guardians of the tribe's wisdom. Their physical diminishment was not seen as a loss, but as a hollowing out, a creating of space for the Spirit of God to dwell more fully. The winter of life was understood as a time of becoming a "thin place," a person through whom the veil between the worlds was becoming transparent.

This is a radical and beautiful vision of ageing. It suggests that the final years of our lives are not a time of decline, but of a final and glorious ripening. As our physical senses begin to dim, our spiritual senses can become more acute. As our outer world begins to shrink, our inner world can expand. As we are compelled to relinquish our roles and responsibilities, we can discover a new freedom in simply being. The winter of life is a time when we are invited to become contemplatives, to spend our days in prayer, in stillness, and in the quiet and joyful anticipation of meeting our Beloved face to face.

The Journey into Death: The Final Pilgrimage

The Celtic tradition does not shy away from the reality of death. It looks it squarely in the face, not with fear, but with a quiet and a steady faith. Death is not seen as the end, but as a transition, a doorway into a new and greater life. It is the final peregrinatio, the final pilgrimage, the journey home to God.

The prayers and poems of the Celtic saints are filled with a sense of longing for this final journey. They speak of death as a release from the exile of this life, as a return to the true home of the soul. St. Columba, on the day of his death, is said to have blessed the monastery of Iona and then to have gone to the barn to bless the white horse that had been his faithful companion. The horse, sensing his master's departure, began to weep. Columba, with a gentle smile, said, "Let him alone, for he is weeping for me." This beautiful and poignant story captures the Celtic attitude toward death: a gentle sadness at parting, but an underlying sense of peace and acceptance.

The Ars Moriendi: The Art of Dying Well

Because death was regarded as a significant transition, the Celtic tradition developed a rich spirituality around the practice of dying well, the *ars moriendi*. This was not a morbid obsession with death, but a practical and pastoral concern for helping people to navigate their final days with faith and with courage.

The *ars moriendi* included a number of key practices:

• **The Presence of the Anam Cara:** It was considered essential for a dying person to be accompanied by their Anam Cara, their soul friend. The soul friend would sit with the dying person, listen to their fears and regrets, pray with them, and offer them the comfort and assurance of God's love. The presence of a loving and prayerful companion was seen as a powerful defence against the fear and loneliness that can so often accompany the dying process.

• **The Reconciliation of Relationships:** The time of dying was a time for the healing and the reconciliation of broken relationships. The dying person would be encouraged to seek forgiveness from those they had wronged and to offer forgiveness to those who had wronged them. This was seen as essential for dying in a state of peace, both with God and with one's neighbour.

• **The Prayers for the Journey:** Some specific prayers and blessings were said for the dying, prayers that were intended to be a kind of spiritual viaticum, a food for the journey. These prayers would often invoke the protection of the Trinity, of the Virgin Mary, and of the saints. They would ask for a peaceful death, for the forgiveness of sins, and for a safe passage into the arms of God. The famous prayer of St. Patrick, the "Breastplate," is a powerful example of this kind of encircling prayer, a calling upon the power of God to protect and to guide the soul on its final journey.

• **The Wake: A Celebration of Life:** After a person had died, the community would gather for a wake. This was not a sombre and silent affair. It was a celebration of the deceased's life, a time for telling stories, singing songs, and sharing food and drink. It was a way of honouring the memory of the deceased, of comforting the grieving, and of affirming the Christian hope in the resurrection. The wake was a powerful expression of the belief that even in the midst of death, life goes on, and that the bonds of love and of community are stronger than the grave.

The winter of our lives is a season that calls for great courage and for great faith. It is a season that we will all one day face. By embracing the wisdom of the Celtic tradition, by seeing the spiritual gifts of aging, by preparing for our final pilgrimage, and by practicing the art of dying well, we can face this final season not with fear, but with a quiet and a joyful hope, knowing that the God who has been our companion throughout all the seasons of our lives will not abandon us at the last, but will lead us gently through the darkness of death and into the light of an eternal spring.

THE PRACTICE: A RITUAL FOR LIFE TRANSITIONS

My dear friend, our lives are a series of transitions. We are constantly moving from one season to another, from one stage of life to the next. These transitions, whether they are joyful or painful, are sacred moments. They are thresholds, liminal spaces where we are invited to let go of the old and to embrace the new. The Celtic tradition, with its love of ritual and its deep understanding of the human heart, offers us a beautiful and powerful way to mark these moments. This practice is a simple and adaptable ritual that you can use to honour any significant transition in your life, from the birth of a child to the death of a loved one, from starting a new job to moving to a new home.

This ritual is designed to be done with a small group of trusted friends, your sacred circle or your Anam Caras. It can also be adapted for use in a larger church setting. The ritual has four parts: The Naming, The Telling, The Blessing, and The Crossing.

1. The Naming: Honouring the Transition

The first step is to name the transition that you are marking. This may seem obvious, but it is a crucial step. In our fast-paced world, we often rush from one thing to the next without pausing to acknowledge the significance of what is happening. By taking the time to name the transition, you are declaring that this is a sacred moment, a moment worthy of attention and of honour.

Gather your sacred circle together. Light a candle to signify the presence of Christ, the light of the world. The person undergoing the transition (the "pilgrim") should then speak the transition's name aloud.

For example:

• "I am here today to mark my transition from being a single person to being a married person."

• "I am here today to mark my transition from my old home to my new home."

• "I am here today to mark my transition from health to illness."

• "I am here today to mark my transition from the life of my beloved mother to a life without her physical presence."

This simple act of naming is a powerful way to begin the ritual. It creates a space of intention and of focus, and it honours the reality of the pilgrim's experience.

2. The Telling: Sharing the Story

The second step is the telling of the story. The pilgrim is invited to share the story of their transition with the group. This is a time for honesty and for vulnerable sharing. The pilgrim should be encouraged to share not only the facts of the transition but also the feelings, hopes, and fears associated with it.

The role of the sacred circle during this time is to listen. This is not a time for giving advice, for offering platitudes, or for sharing your own stories. It is a time for deep, compassionate listening, the hallmark of the Anam Cara relationship. As the pilgrim speaks, the group should listen with an open and prayerful heart, offering the gift of their loving and non-judgmental presence.

After the pilgrim has finished speaking, the ritual leader may invite a period of silence, allowing the story to settle into the hearts of everyone present.

3. The Blessing: The Encircling Prayer

The third step is the blessing. This is a time for the community to surround the pilgrim with their love and their prayers. The leader may invite group members to offer spontaneous prayers for the pilgrim. These prayers should be sincere and straightforward.

For example:

• "God, we pray for your peace to surround our sister as she begins this new chapter of her life."

• "We pray for your strength for our brother as he faces this time of uncertainty."

• "We thank you for the gift of this new life, and we pray for your wisdom for these new parents."

After the spontaneous prayers, the group should perform the Caim, the encircling prayer. The pilgrim should stand in the centre of the group. The group members should then join hands to form a circle around the pilgrim. If the group is small, they can also place their hands on the pilgrim's shoulders or head.

The leader then says a prayer of blessing, such as this one:

"Circle of God, be around [Name]. Circle of Christ, be around [Name]. Circle of the Spirit, be around [Name]. The three-in-one, our protector, be around [Name] and in [Name]. From this day forth, and forevermore. Amen."

This powerful and ancient prayer is a tangible expression of the community's love and of God's encircling protection. It is a reminder to the pilgrim that they do not undergo this transition alone but are held and supported by a great cloud of witnesses, both in heaven and on earth.

4. The Crossing: Stepping Over the Threshold

The final step of the ritual is the crossing of the threshold. A threshold is a powerful symbol of transition. It is the line between the old and the new. To mark this crossing, you can create a simple physical threshold. You might lay a branch or a scarf on the floor. You might use the room's actual doorway.

The pilgrim stands on one side of the threshold, representing the old life. The leader says a simple prayer of release, such as:

"God of our past, we thank you for all the gifts and the lessons of the season that is now ending. We release it into your loving hands."

The pilgrim then takes a single, intentional step across the threshold, representing their entry into the new life. As they cross, the community can say together:

"Welcome to the new day! Welcome to the new season! Welcome to the new life!"

The leader then says a final prayer of blessing for the journey ahead, such as:

"God of our future, we pray for your blessing upon [Name] as they begin this new season of their life. Go before them to lead them, behind them to protect them, beneath them to support them, and within them to guide them. May they walk in your light and in your love, from this day forth and forevermore. Amen."

The ritual can then be concluded with a shared meal, a song, or a simple exchange of peace.

This ritual is a gift from the Celtic tradition. It is a way of honouring the sacredness of our lives, of supporting one another through the inevitable changes and challenges of the journey, and of rooting our lives in the unchanging love of God. It is a way of turning the transitions of our lives not into crises to be feared, but into sacred thresholds to be crossed with faith, with courage, and with joy.

CONCLUSION: THE ETERNAL SPRING

My dear friend, our journey through the seasons of the soul has brought us to the heart of the Christian mystery. We have seen that our lives, like the great Wheel of the Year, are a dance of death and of resurrection, of letting go and of new beginnings. We have walked through the spring of our youth, the summer of our strength, the autumn of our wisdom, and the winter of our diminishment. And now, we stand at the threshold of the final mystery, the mystery of death. But as Christians, we do not stand at this threshold in fear. We stand here in hope, for we believe that the winter of death is not the end of the story. It is the gateway to an eternal spring.

The Celtic tradition is shot through with this hope. It is a hope rooted not in vague optimism but in the historical reality of Jesus Christ's resurrection. The resurrection is the great turning point of history, the moment when the power of death was broken forever. It is the promise that the love of God is stronger than the grave, and that the winter of our lives will give way to a spring that will never end.

This hope is beautifully captured in the symbolism of the Yew tree, which we explored in Chapter 7. The Yew, with its ability to regenerate itself, to send up new life from the heart of its own decay, was a powerful symbol of resurrection for the Celtic Christians. They would often plant Yew trees in their churchyards, not as a morbid reminder of death, but as a living sermon of the resurrection. The Yew tree was a sign that the grave is not a place of ending, but a place of planting, a place where the seed of our mortal bodies is sown in the hope of a glorious harvest.

This hope in the eternal spring changes everything. It changes how we live our lives, and it changes how we face our deaths. It frees us from the frantic need to cling to our youth, to our possessions, and to our own lives. It allows us to live with a new and radical freedom, the freedom of those who know that their true treasure is not in this world, but in the world to come. It allows us to face the winter of our lives not with fear, but with quiet, joyful anticipation, knowing that the best is yet to be.

As we come to the end of our journey together in this book, I want to leave you with one final image. It is the image of the Tree of Life, which we first encountered in the Garden of Eden, and which we saw fulfilled in the Cross of Christ. In the final chapter of the Bible, in the book of Revelation, we are given a vision of the new creation, the new heaven and the new earth. And at the centre of that new creation, we see the Tree of Life once again. "Then the angel showed me the river of the water of life, as clear as crystal, flowing from the throne of God and of the Lamb down the middle of the great street of the city.

On each side of the river stood the tree of life, bearing twelve crops of fruit, yielding its fruit every month. And the leaves of the tree are for the healing of the nations" (Revelation 22:1-2).

This is the ultimate vision of our hope. It is the vision of a world restored, a world in which there is no more death, mourning, crying, or pain. It is the vision of a world where we will eat from the Tree of Life and live forever in the presence of God. It is the vision of an eternal spring.

My dear friend, my Anam Cara, this is the journey to which you have been called. It is the journey of the soul, the pilgrimage through the seasons of your life, a journey that leads, at the last, to the foot of the Tree of Life in the heart of the new creation.

May you walk this path with courage, with joy, and with a deep and abiding faith.

And may the blessing of the Three-in-One, the God of the seasons, the God of the journey, the God of the eternal spring, be with you, now and forevermore. Amen.

Chapter 16:

The Grove and the Cross: Living the Cruciform Life

THE SHAPE OF THE CROSS

My dear friend, we have journeyed far together. We began with the whisper of the oak, and we have followed that whisper into the heart of the Celtic Christian tradition. We have explored the sacred archetypes of the trees, we have stood in awe before the Cross as the true Tree of Life, and we have learned to cultivate a life of faith that is rooted, communal, and attuned to the rhythms of creation.

We have, in essence, been learning what it means to live in the grove.

But the grove is not a place of escape. It is a place of formation. The purpose of all that we have learned—the prayers, the practices, the perspectives—is not simply to make us feel more peaceful or more connected to nature. The purpose is to shape us, to form us into the image of Christ. And the shape of that image, the shape of a life lived in Christ, is the shape of the Cross.

In Chapter 8, we explored the Cross as the great cosmic tree, the axis of the world, the place where heaven and earth are reconciled. We saw it as the fulfilment of all three archetypes, the ultimate expression of wisdom, of sovereignty, of life, and of love.

In this chapter, we must ask an important question: What does it mean to live a life shaped by the Cross? What does it mean to live a "cruciform" life?

To live a cruciform life is to live a life that is oriented in two directions at once: the vertical and the horizontal. The vertical beam of the Cross points upward to God and downward into the depths of our own souls. It is the axis of our relationship with God, our life of prayer, of contemplation, of worship. It is our love for God with all our heart, with all our soul, and with all our mind. The horizontal beam of the Cross stretches out to embrace the world. It is the axis of our relationship with our neighbour, our life of service, of compassion, of justice. It is our love for our neighbour as ourselves.

A genuinely Christian life must possess both of these dimensions. A faith that is all vertical, all focused on personal piety and private devotion, can become disconnected from the needs of the world. It can become a form of spiritual narcissism. A faith that is all horizontal, all focused on social action and political engagement, can lose its spiritual roots. It can become a form of burnout-inducing activism, indistinguishable from any other secular movement for social change. The cruciform life holds these two dimensions in a creative and life-giving tension. It is a life in which our love for God flows out in love for our neighbour, and our love for our neighbour leads us back to a deeper love for God.

In this chapter, we will explore this vision of the cruciform life in greater detail. We will examine what it means to live a life shaped by the Cross and how the Celtic tradition can help us do so.

Our journey will be structured as follows:

1. Introduction: The Shape of the Cross: We will introduce the concept of the cruciform life, a life that is oriented both vertically to God and horizontally to the world.

2. The Vertical Beam: Loving God with All Your Heart: We will explore the upward and the inward dimensions of the cruciform life, drawing on the Celtic practices of prayer, contemplation, and the sanctification of the senses.

3. The Horizontal Beam: Loving Your Neighbour as Yourself: We will explore the outward dimension of the cruciform life, drawing on the Celtic practices of hospitality, of soul friendship, and of care for creation.

4. The Intersection: Where Heaven Meets Earth: We will look at the centre of the Cross, the place where the vertical and the horizontal meet, and we will see that this is the place of the heart, the place of incarnation, the place where our love for God and our love for our neighbour become one.

5. The Practice: A Daily Examen of the Cruciform Life: We will learn a simple, practical exercise for examining our own lives in the light of the

Cross, asking ourselves each day: how have I loved God, and how have I loved my neighbour?

6. Conclusion: Becoming the Cross: We will conclude by reflecting on the ultimate goal of the Christian life: not just to admire the Cross, but to be conformed to it, to become, in the words of the mystics, a living cross, a place where the love of God is made visible in the world.

This chapter is the culmination of all that we have explored together. It is the place where all the threads of our journey are woven together into a single, coherent vision of the Christian life.

It is an invitation to move from learning about the grove to becoming the grove, from admiring the Cross to living the Cross. It is an invitation to a life of radical love, a life that has the power to transform not only ourselves, but the world.

THE VERTICAL BEAM: LOVING GOD WITH ALL YOUR HEART

The journey into the cruciform life begins with the vertical beam of the Cross. This is the beam that points upward to God and downward into the depths of our own souls. It is the axis of our personal relationship with the Divine, our life of prayer, of contemplation, and of worship. It is the Great Commandment to love the Lord our God with all our heart, with all our soul, and with all our mind (Matthew 22:37). The Celtic tradition, with its rich and earthy spirituality, offers us a beautiful and practical guide for how to live out this vertical dimension of our faith.

The Upward Reach: The Life of Prayer

The upward reach of the vertical beam is our life of prayer. It is the conscious, intentional turning of our hearts and minds to God. In the Celtic tradition, prayer was not a separate activity that was confined to a specific time or place. It was a way of life. It was an ongoing conversation with the God believed to be always present and always listening. The Carmina Gadelica, the great collection of traditional Scottish prayers and hymns, is a testament to this reality. It contains prayers for every conceivable activity: for rising in the morning, for lighting the fire, for milking the cow, and for going to bed at night. For the Celtic Christians, all of life was an opportunity for prayer, a chance to acknowledge the presence of God and to consecrate the ordinary moments of the day to him.

This is a powerful and liberating vision of prayer. It frees us from the idea that prayer is something that can only happen in a church or on our knees. It invites us to find God in the midst of our ordinary lives, to see our daily tasks as a form of worship.

We can begin to cultivate this kind of prayerful life by following the example of the Celtic saints:

• **Begin the day with a morning offering.** Before you do anything else, before you check your phone or your email, take a moment to offer your day to God. You can use a traditional prayer, or say in your own words, "God, I give you this day. May all that I do be for your glory."

• **Practice the presence of God throughout the day.** As you go about your daily tasks, make a conscious effort to remember that God is with you. You can use a simple "breath prayer," a short phrase that you can repeat silently to yourself. For example, as you breathe in, you might say, "Lord Jesus Christ," and as you breathe out, "have mercy on me." This simple practice can help to keep you centred and connected to God in the midst of a busy day.

• **End the day with a prayer of examen.** Before you go to sleep, take a few moments to review your day with God. Give thanks for the moments of grace and of joy. Ask for forgiveness for the moments when you failed to love. And entrust yourself and all your loved ones to God's care for the night. This practice, which we explored in Chapter 9, is a beautiful way to end the day in a spirit of gratitude and of peace.

The Downward Reach: The Journey into the Soul

The vertical beam of the Cross also points downward, into the depths of our own souls. It is the journey of self-knowledge, of introspection, and of the healing of our inner wounds. The Celtic tradition understood that we cannot truly love God if we do not know ourselves, and that we cannot truly know ourselves if we do not see ourselves in the light of God's love. The journey upward to God and the journey downward into the soul are two sides of the same coin.

The key to this downward journey is the practice of solitude. The Celtic saints were not afraid of solitude. They sought it out. They would retreat to lonely islands, to remote forests, and to desolate mountaintops to be alone with God. They knew that it is only in the silence and the stillness that we can begin to hear the voice of God, and that we can begin to confront the truth of our own hearts. In our noisy and distracted world, the practice of solitude is more critical than ever. We need to create regular times and spaces in our lives where we can be alone, unplug from the world's constant stimulation, and be in the presence of God.

This journey into the soul is not always easy. As we become still, we may be confronted with our own brokenness, our own fears, and our own addictions. We may be tempted to run away, to distract ourselves, to fill the silence with noise. But the Celtic tradition reminds us that we do not make this journey alone. We make it with our Anam Cara, our soul friend. The Anam Cara is the one to whom we can confess our sins, our struggles, and our doubts, without fear of judgment. They are the ones who can hold up a mirror to our souls, helping us to see ourselves as we truly are, and as God sees us. The journey into the depths of the soul is best undertaken with a trusted and loving companion.

The Sanctification of the Senses

The vertical beam of the Cross is not just about prayer and introspection. It is also about the sanctification of our senses. The Celtic tradition has a deep and abiding respect for the goodness of the created world, and for the body as a vehicle of spiritual experience. It is a tradition that invites us to encounter God not only in our minds but also with our whole being: with our eyes, ears, nose, mouth, and hands.

To live the vertical dimension of the cruciform life is to learn to see the world with new eyes, to see the beauty of God in the face of a flower, in the flight of a bird, in the smile of a child. It is to learn to hear the voice of God in the sound of the wind, in the rushing of the water, in the silence of the night. It is to learn to taste the goodness of God in the food that we eat, to feel the warmth of God in the sun on our skin, to smell the fragrance of God in the scent of the rain. It is to live in a world that is charged with the grandeur of God, a world in which every created thing is a sacrament, a sign of the presence of the Creator.

The vertical beam of the Cross is the foundation of the cruciform life. It is our connection to the living God, the source of all our life and all our love. It is a journey that takes us upward in prayer, downward into the depths of our own souls, and outward through our senses into the beauty of God's world.

It is a journey that prepares us for the second great movement of the cruciform life: the outward reach of the horizontal beam, the journey into the love of our neighbour.

THE HORIZONTAL BEAM: LOVING YOUR NEIGHBOUR AS YOURSELF

If the vertical beam of the Cross is our love for God, the horizontal beam is our love for our neighbour. It is the outward reach of our faith, the way in which our inner life of prayer and contemplation flows out into a life of service, of compassion, and of justice. The two great commandments are inseparable.

We cannot truly love God if we do not love our neighbour, and we cannot truly love our neighbour if we do not love God. The Celtic tradition, with its strong emphasis on community and the sacredness of all creation, provides a powerful and practical guide for living out the horizontal dimension of the cruciform life.

The Love of the Soul Friend

The horizontal beam of our faith begins with the people closest to us: our family and friends. The Celtic tradition offers us a beautiful model for these intimate relationships in the figure of the Anam Cara, the soul friend. As we explored in Chapter 12, the Anam Cara is a true spiritual companion, a friend to the soul. It is a relationship of deep love, of radical honesty, and of unwavering support. To have an Anam Cara is to have a person in your life with whom you can be completely yourself, with whom you can share your deepest joys and your deepest sorrows, and who will love you unconditionally.

In our modern world, so often characterised by superficiality and loneliness, the practice of soul friendship is a radical and countercultural act. It is a commitment to go deep with a few people, rather than to remain on the surface with many. It is a commitment to a love that is not based on convenience or on shared interests, but on a shared journey towards God. The horizontal beam of the Cross calls us to cultivate these kinds of deep and meaningful relationships in our own lives. It calls us to be an Anam Cara to others, and to have the courage to allow others to be an Anam Cara to us.

The Love of the Stranger: The Practice of Hospitality

The love of the horizontal beam does not stop with our friends and our family. It extends outward to embrace the stranger, the one who is not a part of our tribe. The Celtic tradition had a radical and beautiful practice of hospitality. In ancient Ireland, it was a sacred duty to welcome any stranger who came to your door. To refuse hospitality to a stranger was a grave sin, for it was believed that in welcoming the stranger, you might be welcoming Christ himself. The monasteries of the Celtic church were famous for their hospitality. They were places of refuge for the poor, the sick, and the traveller. They were centres of learning and culture open to all.

This practice of hospitality is a powerful expression of the horizontal love of the Cross. It is a recognition that all people, regardless of their background or their beliefs, are our brothers and our sisters, created in the image of God. It is a commitment to see the face of Christ in the face of the stranger, and to treat them with the love and the respect that is due to him.

In our own time, we can practice this kind of radical hospitality in many ways:

• **By opening our homes.** We can invite our neighbours, our colleagues, or people from different cultural backgrounds to share a meal with us. We can create a space in our homes that is a place of welcome and of safety for those who are lonely or in need.

• **By welcoming the stranger in our communities.** We can engage in ministries that serve the poor, the homeless, the refugees, and the immigrants. We can be a voice for those who are marginalised and forgotten.

• **By practising a hospitality of the heart.** We can cultivate an inner attitude of openness and of welcome to those who are different from us. We can listen to their stories, learn from their perspectives, and refuse to see them as "other."

The Love of the Enemy: The Path of Reconciliation

The most challenging and the most radical dimension of the horizontal love of the Cross is the call to love our enemies. Jesus was unequivocal about this: "You have heard that it was said, 'Love your neighbour and hate your enemy.' But I tell you, love your enemies and pray for those who persecute you" (Matthew 5:43-44). This is the love that is at the very heart of the Cross. It is the love that forgives, that reconciles, and that refuses to return evil for evil.

The history of the Celtic church is filled with stories of this kind of radical, enemy-loving faith. St. Patrick, who was captured by Irish pirates as a young man and was sold into slavery, later returned to Ireland as a missionary to bring the gospel to the very people who had enslaved him. St. Aidan, the great missionary to Northumbria, was known for his gentleness, his humility, and his love for the poor. He often distributed the gifts he received from the king to the poor, and he was not afraid to challenge the king when he acted unjustly.

This call to love our enemies is a lifelong and challenging practice. It runs counter to all our natural instincts. But it is the path to true freedom and to true peace. It is the path that breaks the cycle of violence and of revenge. It is the path that makes us true children of our Father in heaven, who "causes his sun to rise on the evil and the good, and sends rain on the righteous and the unrighteous" (Matthew 5:45).

The Love of Creation: The Care for the Earth

Finally, the horizontal beam of the Cross extends to embrace not only our human neighbours but also all of creation. As we explored in Chapter 13, the Celtic tradition has a deep and abiding reverence for the natural world. It sees creation not as a collection of resources to be exploited, but as a sacred community to which we belong. It sees the mountains, the rivers, the forests, and the animals as our fellow creatures, our brothers and our sisters in the great family of God.

To live the horizontal dimension of the cruciform life, therefore, is to live in a way that honours and that protects the earth. It is to recognise that our love for our neighbour includes our passion for future generations, who will inherit the world that we leave behind. It is to repent of how our greed and our consumption have wounded the earth, and to commit ourselves to a more straightforward and more sustainable way of life. It is to become, in the words of St. Francis, instruments of God's peace, sowing love where there is hatred, and sowing hope where there is despair, not just in our human relationships, but in our relationship with all of creation.

The horizontal beam of the Cross is a call to a love that is wide, that is inclusive, and that is unconditional. It is a love that embraces the friend, the stranger, the enemy, and the whole of creation. It is a love that is not easy, but it is the love that is at the heart of the gospel. It is the love that has the power to heal our broken world.

THE INTERSECTION: WHERE HEAVEN MEETS EARTH

We have explored the vertical beam of the Cross, our love for God, and the horizontal beam, our love for our neighbour. We now arrive at the centre, where the two beams intersect. This is the heart of the Cross, and it is the heart of the cruciform life. It is the place where our love for God and our love for our neighbour become one, where our contemplation flows into action, and our action leads us back to contemplation. It is the place of incarnation, the place where the divine and the human meet.

The Heart of the Matter: The Integration of Love

In the Christian tradition, the heart is not merely the seat of emotion. It is the centre of our being, the place where our intellect, our will, and our feelings come together. It is the place where we are most truly ourselves. To live a cruciform life is to have a heart that is shaped by the Cross, a heart that is open both to God and to the world. It is to have a heart that is undivided, a heart in which our love for God and our love for our neighbour are not two separate things, but one single, integrated love.

This is the great challenge and the great gift of the Christian life. It is so easy for us to compartmentalise our faith, to have a "God" part of our lives and a "world" part of our lives. We can be very devout in our private prayer, yet go out into the world and act with selfishness and greed. Or we can be very passionate about social justice, but have a spiritual life that is shallow and undeveloped. The Cross calls us to a more integrated way of being.

It calls us to a life in which our love for God is the source and the motivation for our love for our neighbour, and our love for our neighbour is the concrete expression of our love for God. As the first letter of John so powerfully reminds us, "If anyone says, 'I love God,' and hates his brother, he is a liar; for he who does not love his brother whom he has seen cannot love God whom he has not seen" (1 John 4:20).

The Place of Incarnation: The Body as a Thin Place

The intersection of the Cross is the place of incarnation. It is the place where the eternal Son of God took on human flesh and dwelt among us. It is the place where the divine and the human are forever united. To live a cruciform life is to become a place of incarnation in the world. It is to allow our own lives, our own bodies, to become a "thin place," a place where the love of God is made visible and tangible to others.

The Celtic tradition had a deep understanding of this incarnational principle. They did not see the body as a prison for the soul, but as a sacrament of the spirit. They believed that our bodies are temples of the Holy Spirit, and that our physical lives are the arena in which our salvation is worked out. This is why they held such a deep respect for the goodness of creation, the sacredness of the senses, and the importance of physical practices such as pilgrimage and prostration.

To live an incarnational life is to take our bodies seriously. It is to care for our physical health, to get enough rest, to eat good food, and to enjoy the simple pleasures of the senses. It is also to use our bodies in the service of love. It is to use our hands to help, our feet to go where there is need, our arms to embrace the lonely, and our voices to speak words of truth and of grace.

It is to become, in the beautiful words of St. Teresa of Avila, the hands and the feet of Christ in the world:

"Christ has no body now but yours. No hands, no feet on earth but yours. Yours are the eyes through which he looks compassion on this world. Yours are the feet with which he walks to do good. Yours are the hands through which he blesses all the world."

The Still Point of the Turning World: Finding God in the Present Moment

The intersection of the Cross is also the still point in the centre of the turning world. It is the place of the present moment, the eternal now. The vertical beam of the Cross connects us to the past (the journey of our souls) and to the future (our hope of heaven). The horizontal beam connects us to others and to the world around us. But the intersection is the place where we are fully present, fully alive, to this moment, to this person, to this place. It is in the present moment that we encounter the living God.

This is the great secret of the contemplative life, a secret that was well known to the Celtic saints. They knew that God is not to be found in our anxious thoughts about the future, or in our regretful thoughts about the past. He is to be found in the sacrament of the present moment. He is to be found in the gentle rhythm of our breathing, in the warmth of the sun on our skin, in the face of the person who is right in front of us. To live a cruciform life is to learn to be present to the present moment, to find the still point in the centre of our often chaotic lives.

This is not an easy practice. Our minds are constantly wandering, constantly being pulled into the past or the future.

But we can begin to cultivate a greater sense of presence through simple practices of mindfulness:

• **Pay attention to your breathing.** Throughout the day, take a few moments to notice the sensation of your breath entering and exiting simply. This simple act can anchor you in the present moment and can calm your anxious mind.

• **Engage your senses.** As you go about your day, take the time to notice the sights, the sounds, the smells, the tastes, and the textures of the world around you. See the world with the eyes of a child, with a sense of wonder and of awe.

• **Listen deeply to others.** When you are in conversation with someone, give them your full attention. Put away your phone, turn off the television, and be present to them. Listen not only to their words but also to the feelings and needs behind them.

The intersection of the Cross is the place where our love for God and our love for our neighbour become one. It is the place of the heart, the place of incarnation, and the place of the present moment.

It is the place where we are most fully alive, and most fully human. It is the place where we discover that the kingdom of God is not a distant reality, but is here and now, in our midst.

THE PRACTICE: A DAILY EXAMEN OF THE CRUCIFORM LIFE

My dear friend, the vision of the cruciform life is both beautiful and challenging. It is a vision that can inspire us, but it can also feel overwhelming. How can we possibly live a life that is so full of love, so open to God and to the world? The key is to remember that the cruciform life is not a destination that we arrive at, but a journey that we are on. It is a path that we walk one day at a time, one moment at a time. As with any journey, it is helpful to have a map, a way to check our progress and ensure that we are still on the right path.

This practice is a simple, daily examen of the cruciform life. It is a way of prayerfully reviewing our day in the light of the Cross, asking ourselves two simple questions: How have I loved God today? And how have I loved my neighbour today? This practice is best done at the end of the day, before you go to sleep.

It should take no more than ten or fifteen minutes. Find a quiet place where you can be alone and undisturbed. Light a candle if you find it helpful. Take a few deep breaths to calm your mind and be present in the moment.

1. Presence: Placing Yourself in the Light of the Cross

Begin by placing yourself in the presence of God. Imagine that you are standing at the foot of the Cross. See the love that flows from the heart of Christ, a love that is both vertical, reaching up to God and down into the depths of your own soul, and horizontal, reaching out to embrace the whole world. Acknowledge that you are standing on holy ground, and that you are held in a love that is wider and deeper than you can imagine. Ask the Holy

Spirit to guide you in this time of prayer, to help you see your day with honesty, with courage, and with compassion.

2. Gratitude: Giving Thanks for the Gifts of the Day

Next, review your day with a spirit of gratitude. Walk back through the hours of your day, from the time you woke up until this present moment. What are the gifts for which you are most grateful? It might be the beauty of the sunrise, a kind word from a friend, a moment of insight in your work, or the taste of a good meal. Savour these moments of grace. Give thanks to God for his abundant and often unnoticed blessings. Gratitude is the soil in which the cruciform life grows. It opens our hearts to see the goodness of God that is all around us.

3. The Vertical Beam: How Have I Loved God Today?

Now, turn your attention to the vertical beam of the Cross. Ask yourself: How have I loved God today?

As you reflect on this question, you might consider some of the following:

• **Prayer:** Was I able to find moments of conscious connection with God today? Did I begin my day with a morning offering? Did I practice the presence of God in my daily tasks? Did I take time for silence and for solitude?

• **The Senses:** Did I notice the beauty of God's creation today? Did I see, hear, smell, taste, or touch something that reminded me of the goodness of God?

• **The Soul:** Did I pay attention to the movements of my own heart today? Did I notice the moments of joy, of sorrow, of fear, of peace? Did I share my inner life with God or with my Anam Cara?

As you reflect on these questions, do not judge yourself. Notice. Notice the moments when you felt close to God, and give thanks. Notice the moments when you felt distant from God, and ask for his grace to draw closer tomorrow.

4. The Horizontal Beam: How Have I Loved My Neighbour Today?

Next, turn your attention to the horizontal beam of the Cross. Ask yourself: How have I loved my neighbour today?

As you reflect on this question, you might consider some of the following:

• **The Friend:** How did I love the people who are closest to me today? My spouse, my children, my friends? Was I present to them? Did I listen to them? Did I speak to them with kindness and respect?

• **The Stranger:** How did I love the stranger today? The person I met on the street, the cashier at the grocery store, the colleague at work? Did I see them as a person, created in the image of God? Did I treat them with dignity and with compassion?

• **The Enemy:** How did I love my enemy today? The person who has hurt me, the person with whom I disagree, the person who gets on my nerves? Did I pray for them? Did I refuse to indulge in thoughts of anger or of revenge? Did I seek, in some small way, to be a peacemaker?

• **Creation:** How did I love creation today? Was I mindful of my consumption? Did I take the time to appreciate the beauty of the natural world? Did I do anything, however small, to care for the earth?

Again, as you reflect on these questions, do not fall into guilt or self-recrimination. The purpose of this exam is not to make you feel bad, but to make you more aware.

Notice the moments when you were able to love well and give thanks. Notice the moments when you failed to love, and ask for God's forgiveness and for his grace to love more fully tomorrow.

5. Hope: Looking to the Day to Come

Finally, turn your heart to the day that is to come. Ask God for the grace that you will need to live a more cruciform life tomorrow. You might choose one specific area in which you want to grow. For example, you might say, "God, tomorrow I want to be more patient with my children." Or, "Tomorrow I want to take a few moments to be still in your presence simply." Offer this intention to God. Trust that he will give you the grace that you need to fulfil it. End your time of prayer by entrusting yourself, your loved ones, and the whole world to God's loving care.

You might pray the Lord's Prayer, or a traditional Celtic prayer of protection, such as this one:

"Be thou a bright flame before me, Be thou a guiding star above me, Be thou a smooth path beneath me, Be thou a kindly shepherd behind me, Today, tonight, and forever."

This daily examination of the cruciform life is a simple but powerful practice.

It is a way of staying awake to our lives, of paying attention to the movements of God's grace.

It is a way of allowing our lives to be slowly and surely shaped by the love of the Cross.

It is a way of becoming, day by day, the person God has created us to be: a living cross, a place where heaven and earth meet, a sign of God's redeeming love in the world.

CONCLUSION: BECOMING THE CROSS

My dear friend, we have come to the end of our exploration of the cruciform life. We have seen that the Christian life is shaped by the Cross, oriented both vertically toward God and horizontally toward the world. We have explored Celtic practices that can help us cultivate this integrated, holistic faith. We are left with a final and profound question: what is the ultimate goal of this journey? What is it that we are striving for?

The answer is simple and radical. The goal of the Christian life is not just to admire the Cross, or to believe in the Cross, or even to follow the Cross. The goal is to become the Cross. It is to be so conformed to the image of Christ that our own lives become a living cross, a place where the love of God is made visible and tangible in the world. It is to be able to say, with the apostle Paul, "I have been crucified with Christ. It is no longer I who live, but Christ who lives in me" (Galatians 2:20).

This is a high and holy calling. It is a calling that can seem impossible. And in our own strength, it is. We cannot, by our own efforts, make ourselves into living crosses. We cannot, by our own willpower, produce the kind of radical, self-giving love that is at the heart of the cruciform life. But the good news of the gospel is that we do not have to. The Christian life is not a project of self-improvement. It is a process of surrender. It is a process of patiently allowing the Holy Spirit to do his work in us, to shape and mould us into the image of Christ.

This is the work of a lifetime. It is a journey that will have its moments of joy and of consolation, and its moments of struggle and of darkness. There will be times when we feel that we are making progress, and times when we think that we are going backwards. But through it all, we are held in the unwavering and unconditional love of God. He is a great artist, and we are his work of art. He is the potter, and we are the clay. Our part is to remain on the wheel, to remain open and receptive to the shaping hand of the Master.

And what will this life look like, this life that the Cross has shaped? It will resemble a tree planted by the water, deeply rooted in the love of God, and bearing fruit for the healing of the world. It will be a life that is marked by a deep and abiding peace, a peace that is not dependent on our circumstances. It will be a life characterised by radical and inclusive love, a love that embraces the friend, the stranger, and the enemy. It will be a life lived with a sense of purpose and meaning, a life that is a gift to the world.

My dear friend, my Anam Cara, this is the life to which you are called. It is the life of the Cross. It is the life of the grove. It is the life that is truly life. Do not be afraid of its demands. Do not be discouraged by your own weakness. For the one who calls you is faithful, and he will surely do it. He who has begun a good work in you will bring it to completion at the day of Jesus Christ (Philippians 1:6).

So let us go forth from this place, from this book, and let us seek to live the cruciform life. Let us seek to love God with all our hearts, and our neighbours as ourselves. Let us seek to become, by the grace of God, living crosses, signs of hope and of healing in a broken world. And let us do so with joy, with courage, and with a deep and abiding faith, knowing that the one who is the Way, the Truth, and the Life is with us, always, to the very end of the age.

Epilogue: Returning to the Grove

My dear friend, my Anam Cara, our journey is at an end, and yet it is just beginning. We have wandered together through the ancient groves of the Celtic Christian tradition. We have listened to the whisper of the oak, we have stood in the shadow of the Cross, and we have sought to discern the shape of a life that is rooted in the love of God and that reaches out to embrace the world. We have come a long way. And now, it is time to return home.

But we do not return unchanged. We return with new eyes, with new ears, and with a new heart. We return with a new way of seeing the world, a new way of being in the world. We return to the ordinary places of our lives—to our homes, to our workplaces, to our cities—but we see them now as thin places, as places where heaven and earth meet. We return to the ordinary rhythms of our lives—to our work, to our relationships, to our daily tasks—but we see them now as opportunities for prayer, as sacraments of God's presence. We return to the ordinary people in our lives—to our families, to our friends, to our neighbours, to the strangers we meet on the street—but we see them now as our brothers and our sisters, as fellow pilgrims on the journey, as the face of Christ in our midst.

This is the great gift of the Celtic tradition. It does not call us to escape the world, but to enter into it more deeply. It does not call us to a life of spiritual heroics, but to a life of simple, humble, and faithful love. It does not call us to become someone else, but to become who we truly are: beloved children of God, created in his image, and called to be co-creators with him in the healing and the restoration of the world.

The journey we have taken together in this book is not meant to be taken only once. It is a journey meant to be lived, revisited, and deepened over a lifetime. The practices that we have explored—the daily examen, the seasonal rituals, the practice of soul friendship, the art of sacred walking—are not a checklist to be completed, but a rhythm to be entered into. They are a dance, a dance between solitude and community, between contemplation and action, between the love of God and the love of our neighbour.

And so, I invite you to return to the beginning. Return to the whisper of the oak. Return to the silence of your own heart. Return to the simple and profound truth that you are loved, that you are held, and that you are called. The journey ahead will not always be easy. There will be times of doubt, of struggle, and of darkness. But you do not walk alone. The God who is the creator of the grove, the God who is the wood of the Cross, the God who is the breath of the Spirit, is with you. The great cloud of witnesses, the saints of the Celtic tradition, are with you. And I, your brother and your soul friend on the journey, am with you in prayer.

May you find your own grove, your own sacred space, and may you tend it with love and with care. May you find your own Cross, your own unique calling to a life of self-giving love. And may you find, in the heart of it all, the joy, the peace, and the love of the Three-in-One, the God who is, who was, and who is to come.

Go now in peace, my friend. Go in the peace of the Father, the peace of the Son, and the peace of the Holy Spirit. Go, and may the whisper of the oak be with you, always.
Sith,

Stuart McGhie

Bibliography

THE WHISPER OF THE OAK: BOOK 2

Primary Sources

Celtic Christian Texts and Prayers

Carmichael, Alexander. Carmina Gadelica: Hymns and Incantations. Edinburgh: Floris Books, 1992.

De Paor, Liam, ed. Saint Patrick's World: The Christian Culture of Ireland's Apostolic Age. Dublin: Four Courts Press, 1993.

Stokes, Whitley, ed. The Martyrology of Oengus the Culdee. London: Henry Bradshaw Society, 1905.

CELTIC CHRISTIANITY: HISTORY AND THEOLOGY

Allchin, A. M. God's Presence Makes the World: The Celtic Vision through the Centuries in Wales. London: Darton, Longman & Todd, 1997.

Bamford, Christopher, and William Parker Marsh. Celtic Christianity: Ecology and Holiness. Great Barrington, MA: Lindisfarne Press, 1987.

Bradley, Ian. Celtic Christianity: Making Myths and Chasing Dreams. Edinburgh: Edinburgh University Press, 1999.

Colonies of Heaven: Celtic Models for Today's Church. London: Darton, Longman & Todd, 2000.

The Celtic Way. London: Darton, Longman & Todd, 1993.

Cahill, Thomas. How the Irish Saved Civilisation: The Untold Story of Ireland's Heroic Role from the Fall of Rome to the Rise of Medieval Europe. New York: Doubleday, 1995.

Davies, Oliver. Celtic Christianity in Early Medieval Wales: The Origins of the Welsh Spiritual Tradition. Cardiff: University of Wales Press, 1996.

De Waal, Esther. The Celtic Way of Prayer: The Recovery of the Religious Imagination. New York: Doubleday, 1997.

Every Earthly Blessing: Rediscovering the Celtic Tradition. Harrisburg, PA: Morehouse Publishing, 1999.

Etchingham, Colmán. Church Organisation in Ireland, A.D. 650 to 1000. Maynooth: Laigin Publications, 1999.

Joyce, Timothy. Celtic Christianity: A Sacred Tradition, A Vision of Hope. Maryknoll, NY: Orbis Books, 1998.
Low, Mary. Celtic Christianity and Nature: Early Irish and Hebridean Traditions. Edinburgh: Edinburgh University Press, 1996.

Mackey, James P., ed. An Introduction to Celtic Christianity. Edinburgh: T&T Clark, 1989.

Newell, J. Philip. Listening for the Heartbeat of God: A Celtic Spirituality. New York: Paulist Press, 1997.

The Book of Creation: An Introduction to Celtic Spirituality. New York: Paulist Press, 1999.
O'Loughlin, Thomas. Celtic Theology: Humanity, World and God in Early Irish Writings. London: Continuum, 2000.

Journeys on the Edges: The Celtic Tradition. Maryknoll, NY: Orbis Books, 2000.

Sellner, Edward C. Wisdom of the Celtic Saints. Notre Dame, IN: Ave Maria Press, 1993.

Simpson, Ray. Exploring Celtic Spirituality: Historic Roots for Our Future. London: Hodder & Stoughton, 1995.

SAINTS AND HAGIOGRAPHY

Clancy, Thomas Owen, and Gilbert Márkus. Iona: The Earliest Poetry of a Celtic Monastery. Edinburgh: Edinburgh University Press, 1995.

Marsden, John. The Illustrated Life of Columba. Edinburgh: Floris Books, 1995.

Sharpe, Richard, trans. Adomnán of Iona: Life of St Columba. London: Penguin Books, 1995.

Stokes, Whitley, ed. Lives of Saints from the Book of Lismore. Oxford: Clarendon Press, 1890.

Woods, Richard. The Spirituality of the Celtic Saints. Maryknoll, NY: Orbis Books, 2000.

TREES AND NATURE IN CELTIC TRADITION

Paterson, Jacqueline Memory. Tree Wisdom: The Definitive Guidebook to the Myth, Folklore and Healing Power of Trees. London: Thorsons, 1996.

Pennick, Nigel. Celtic Sacred Landscapes. London: Thames & Hudson, 1996.

Rees, Alwyn, and Brinley Rees. Celtic Heritage: Ancient Tradition in Ireland and Wales. London: Thames & Hudson, 1961.

MONASTICISM AND COMMUNITY

Burton-Christie, Douglas. The Word in the Desert: Scripture and the Quest for Holiness in Early Christian Monasticism. Oxford: Oxford University Press, 1993.

Chitty, Derwas J. The Desert a City: An Introduction to the Study of Egyptian and Palestinian Monasticism under the Christian Empire. Crestwood, NY: St. Vladimir's Seminary Press, 1966.

Hughes, Kathleen. The Church in Early Irish Society. London: Methuen, 1966.

Lawrence, C. H. Medieval Monasticism: Forms of Religious Life in Western Europe in the Middle Ages. 3rd ed. Harlow: Longman, 2001.

Ryan, John. Irish Monasticism: Origins and Early Development. Dublin: Four Courts Press, 1992.

Pilgrimage and Spiritual Practice

Clift, Jean Dalby, and Wallace B. Clift. The Archetype of Pilgrimage: Outer Action with Inner Meaning. New York: Paulist Press, 1996.

Davies, J. G. Pilgrimage Yesterday and Today: Why? Where? How? London: SCM Press, 1988.

Sheldrake, Philip. Living Between Worlds: Place and Journey in Celtic Spirituality. London: Darton, Longman & Todd, 1995.

Liturgy and Worship

Hardinge, Leslie. The Celtic Church in Britain. London: SPCK, 1972.

McNeill, John T. The Celtic Churches: A History A.D. 200 to 1200. Chicago: University of Chicago Press, 1974.

Warren, F. E. The Liturgy and Ritual of the Celtic Church. 2nd ed. Woodbridge: Boydell Press, 1987.

Theology and Spirituality

Bonhoeffer, Dietrich. Life Together. Translated by John W. Doberstein. New York: Harper & Row, 1954.

Foster, Richard J. Celebration of Discipline: The Path to Spiritual Growth. San Francisco: HarperSanFrancisco, 1998.

Merton, Thomas. Contemplative Prayer. New York: Image Books, 1971.

New Seeds of Contemplation. New York: New Directions, 1961.

Nouwen, Henri J. M. The Way of the Heart: Desert Spirituality and Contemporary Ministry. New York: Seabury Press, 1981.

O'Donohue, John. Anam Cara: A Book of Celtic Wisdom. New York: HarperCollins, 1997.

Eternal Echoes: Celtic Reflections on Our Yearning to Belong. New York: HarperCollins, 1999.

Peterson, Eugene H. The Contemplative Pastor: Returning to the Art of Spiritual Direction. Grand Rapids, MI: Eerdmans, 1989.

Vanier, Jean. Community and Growth. Rev. ed. New York: Paulist Press, 1989.

Willard, Dallas. The Spirit of the Disciplines: Understanding How God Changes Lives. San Francisco: HarperSanFrancisco, 1988.

CREATION SPIRITUALITY AND ECOLOGY

Berry, Thomas. The Dream of the Earth. San Francisco: Sierra Club Books, 1988.

Berry, Wendell. The Art of the Commonplace: The Agrarian Essays of Wendell Berry.

Edited by Norman Wirzba. Washington, DC: Counterpoint, 2002.

The Unsettling of America: Culture and Agriculture. San Francisco: Sierra Club Books, 1977.

Bouma-Prediger, Steven. For the Beauty of the Earth: A Christian Vision for Creation Care. 2nd ed. Grand Rapids, MI: Baker Academic, 2010.

DeWitt, Calvin B. Earth-Wise: A Biblical Response to Environmental Issues. 2nd ed. Grand Rapids, MI: CRC Publications, 2007.

Leopold, Aldo. A Sand County Almanac: And Sketches Here and There. Oxford: Oxford University Press, 1949.

McFague, Sallie. The Body of God: An Ecological Theology. Minneapolis: Fortress Press, 1993.

Moltmann, Jürgen. God in Creation: A New Theology of Creation and the Spirit of God. San Francisco: Harper & Row, 1985.

Northcott, Michael S. The Environment and Christian Ethics. Cambridge: Cambridge University Press, 1996.

White, Lynn, Jr. "The Historical Roots of Our Ecologic Crisis." Science 155, no. 3767 (1967): 1203-1207.

THE CROSS AND ATONEMENT

Aulén, Gustaf. Christus Victor: An Historical Study of the Three Main Types of the Idea of Atonement. Translated by A. G. Hebert. New York: Macmillan, 1969.

Green, Joel B., and Mark D. Baker. Recovering the Scandal of the Cross: Atonement in New Testament and Contemporary Contexts. Downers Grove, IL: InterVarsity Press, 2000.

Stott, John R. W. The Cross of Christ. Downers Grove, IL: InterVarsity Press, 1986.

Weaver, J. Denny. The Nonviolent Atonement. 2nd ed. Grand Rapids, MI: Eerdmans, 2011.

SEASONS AND LITURGICAL YEAR

Adam, David. The Rhythm of Life: Celtic Daily Prayer. London: SPCK, 1996.

Esler, Philip F. God's Court and Courtiers in the Book of the Watchers. Eugene, OR: Cascade Books, 2017.

Guiver, George. Company of Voices: Daily Prayer and the People of God. London: SPCK, 1988.

Zimmerman, Joyce Ann, and Kathleen Harmon. Living Liturgy: Spirituality, Celebration, and Catechesis for Sundays and Solemnities. Collegeville, MN: Liturgical Press, annual.

DEATH, DYING, AND RESURRECTION

Ariès, Philippe. The Hour of Our Death: The Classic History of Western Attitudes Toward Death over the Last One Thousand Years. Translated by Helen Weaver. New York: Vintage Books, 1982.

Byock, Ira. Dying Well: Peace and Possibilities at the End of Life. New York: Riverhead Books, 1997.

Kübler-Ross, Elisabeth. On Death and Dying. New York: Macmillan, 1969.

Taylor, Jeremy. Holy Dying. 1651. Reprint, New York: Arno Press, 1977.

Wright, N. T. The Resurrection of the Son of God. Minneapolis: Fortress Press, 2003.

URBAN SPIRITUALITY

Bakke, Ray. A Theology as Big as the City. Downers Grove, IL: InterVarsity Press, 1997.

Conn, Harvie M., and Manuel Ortiz. Urban Ministry: The Kingdom, the City, and the People of God. Downers Grove, IL: InterVarsity Press, 2001.

Jacobsen, Eric O. Sidewalks in the Kingdom: New Urbanism and the Christian Faith. Grand Rapids, MI: Brazos Press, 2003.

Linthicum, Robert C. City of God, City of Satan: A Biblical Theology of the Urban Church. Grand Rapids, MI: Zondervan, 1991.

SPIRITUAL FORMATION AND DISCIPLESHIP

Calhoun, Adele Ahlberg. Spiritual Disciplines Handbook: Practices That Transform Us. Downers Grove, IL: InterVarsity Press, 2005.

Mulholland, M. Robert, Jr. Invitation to a Journey: A Road Map for Spiritual Formation. Downers Grove, IL: InterVarsity Press, 1993.

Palmer, Parker J. Let Your Life Speak: Listening for the Voice of Vocation. San Francisco: Jossey-Bass, 2000.

Thompson, Marjorie J. Soul Feast: An Invitation to the Christian Spiritual Life. Louisville, KY: Westminster John Knox Press, 1995.

BIBLICAL STUDIES

Brueggemann, Walter. The Land: Place as Gift, Promise, and Challenge in Biblical Faith. 2nd ed. Minneapolis: Fortress Press, 2002.

The Prophetic Imagination. 2nd ed. Minneapolis: Fortress Press, 2001.

Heschel, Abraham Joshua. The Sabbath: Its Meaning for Modern Man. New York: Farrar, Straus and Giroux, 1951.

Wright, Christopher J. H. Old Testament Ethics for the People of God. Downers Grove, IL: InterVarsity Press, 2004.

ADDITIONAL RESOURCES

Barrington, Candice. American Chaucers. New York: Palgrave Macmillan, 2007.

Bede. Ecclesiastical History of the English People. Translated by Leo Sherley-Price. Revised by R. E. Latham. London: Penguin Books, 1990.

Flower, Robin. The Irish Tradition. Oxford: Clarendon Press, 1947.

Jackson, Kenneth Hurlstone. A Celtic Miscellany: Translations from the Celtic Literatures. Rev. ed. London: Penguin Books, 1971.

Kinsella, Thomas, trans. The Táin. Oxford: Oxford University Press, 1970.

Mac Cana, Proinsias. Celtic Mythology. Rev. ed. New York: Peter Bedrick Books, 1985.

Markale, Jean. The Celts: Uncovering the Mythic and Historic Origins of Western Culture. Rochester, VT: Inner Traditions, 1993.

Matthews, Caitlín. The Celtic Tradition. Shaftesbury: Element Books, 1989.

Ó hÓgáin, Dáithí. Myth, Legend and Romance: An Encyclopedia of the Irish Folk Tradition. New York: Prentice Hall Press, 1991.

Raftery, Barry, ed. The Celts. Milan: Bompiani, 1991.

This bibliography represents key sources that inform the theological, historical, and spiritual content of "The Whisper of the Oak: Book 2." Readers are encouraged to explore these works for deeper study of Celtic Christianity, spiritual formation, and the integration of faith with creation care.

www.ingramcontent.com/pod-product-compliance
Lightning Source LLC
Chambersburg PA
CBHW030818090426

42737CB00009B/770